The **Future** of

Assisted Suicide

and **Euthanasia**

NEW FORUM BOOKS ROBERT P. GEORGE, *Series Editor*

A list of titles in the series appears
at the back of the book

The Future of

Assisted Suicide

and Euthanasia

Neil M. Gorsuch

PRINCETON UNIVERSITY PRESS

PRINCETON AND OXFORD

Published by Princeton University Press, 41 William Street, Princeton,
New Jersey 08540
In the United Kingdom: Princeton University Press, 6 Oxford Street,
Woodstock, Oxfordshire OX20 1TW

Second printing, and first paperback printing, 2009
Paperback ISBN: 978-0-691-14097-1

The Library of Congress has cataloged the cloth edition of this book as follows

Gorsuch, Neil M. (Neil McGill), 1967–
The future of assisted suicide and euthanasia / Neil M. Gorsuch.
p. cm.—(New forum books)
Includes bibliographical references and index.
ISBN-13: 978-0-691-12458-2 (cloth : alk. paper)
ISBN-10: 0-691-12458-2 (cloth : alk. paper)
　　1. Assisted suicide—Moral and ethical aspects—United States.　2. Assisted
suicide—Law and legislation—United States.　3. Euthanasia—Moral and ethical
aspects—United States.　4. Euthanasia—Law and legislation—United States.
I. Title.　II. Series.

R726.G65　2006
179.7—dc22　　　2005052194

British Library Cataloging-in-Publication Data is available

This book has been composed in Minion typeface

Printed on acid-free paper. ∞

press.princeton.edu

Printed in the United States of America

10　9　8　7　6　5　4　3　2

In **memory** of

my **father**

and **mother**

Contents

5.

Casey and Cruzan: Do They Intimate a Right to Assisted Suicide
and Euthanasia?   76

6.

Autonomy Theory's Implications for the Debate over Assisted Suicide
and Euthanasia   86

7.

Legalization and the Law of Unintended Consequences:
Utilitarian Arguments for Legalization   102

8.

Two Test Cases: Posner and Epstein   143

9.

An Argument against Legalization   157

Acknowledgments

THERE ARE many people to whom I am indebted. John Finnis provided thoughtful comments on, and kind support through, draft after draft. John Keown, Dan Callahan, and Timothy Endicott offered valuable input in many areas and support in seeing this project through to completion. Richard Posner, Richard Epstein, Daniel Klerman, Christian Mammen, and Todd Zubler also took the time to review and offer insightful suggestions on portions of what eventually came to form this book. Bryan and Prue Burletson provided years of encouragement.

Draft portions of the manuscript previously appeared as articles: *The Legalization of Assisted Suicide and the Law of Unintended Consequences*, 2004 Wisconsin Law Review 1347 (2004), and *The Right to Assisted Suicide and Euthanasia*, 23 Harvard Journal of Law and Public Policy 599 (2000). I am grateful to both journals for their permission to reproduce what was previously published in their pages. Laura Schulteis and Laura Dickman of the Wisconsin Law Review also made substantial contributions to much of the material that forms the basis of chapter 7.

I would like to thank Robert George and Chuck Myers of Princeton University Press for their support and interest in this book, as well as Mark Bellis and Anita O'Brien for her help in editing the manuscript. Michael Pucci and Tom Humphries provided helpful research assistance, and the Marshall Scholarship Commission made much of the research on which this book is based possible through its generous financial assistance. Yet once again, I am deeply indebted to Bernadette Murphy and Jessica Bartlow for their excellent editorial assistance and unflappable good humor through long hours and days. Despite so much help from so many generous friends and colleagues, I alone am responsible for errors that remain and the views expressed here are, of course, mine alone—not those of any other person or entity.

Finally, and borrowing in part from P. G. Wodehouse, I thank my wife, Louise, and my daughters, Emma and Belinda, without whose constant love and attention this book would've been finished in half the time—but without whom life would've been half as fully lived.

The **Future** of

Assisted Suicide

and **Euthanasia**

1

Introduction

WHETHER to permit assistance in suicide and euthanasia is among the most contentious legal and public policy questions in America today. The issue erupted into American public consciousness on June 4, 1990, with the news that Dr. Jack Kevorkian—a slightly built, greying, retired Michigan pathologist—had helped Janet Adkins, a fifty-four-year-old Alzheimer's patient, kill herself.[1] Dr. Kevorkian later revealed that he had not taken the medical history of Ms. Atkins, conducted a physical or mental examination, or consulted Ms. Adkins's primary care physician.[2] Dr. Kevorkian had simply agreed to meet Ms. Adkins in his Volkswagen van, which he had outfitted with a "suicide machine" consisting of three chemical solutions fed into an intravenous line needle. Dr. Kevorkian tried five times to insert the needle before eventually succeeding.[3] Ms. Adkins then pressed a lever releasing death-inducing drugs into her body. Dr. Murray Raskind, one of the physicians who cared for Ms. Adkins in the early stages of her disease, later testified that she was physically fit but probably not mentally competent at the time of her death.[4]

Since Janet Adkins's death first made national headlines, Dr. Kevorkian claims to have assisted more than 130 suicides.[5] Derek Humphry, founder of The Hemlock Society,[6] a group devoted to promoting the legalization of euthanasia, has praised Dr. Kevorkian for "breaking the medical taboo on euthanasia."[7] The American Civil Liberties Union (ACLU) aggressively took up his legal defense.[8]

While perhaps the most notorious contemporary American proponent of assisted suicide and euthanasia, Dr. Kevorkian hardly stands alone. In 1984 the Netherlands became the first country in the world to endorse certain forms of assisted suicide and euthanasia. The Dutch Supreme Court declared that, although euthanasia was punishable as murder under the nation's penal code, physicians could claim an "emergency defence" under certain circumstances.[9] After several failed attempts, in November 2000 the lower house of the Dutch Parliament voted 104–40 in favor of a physician-assisted suicide exception to the nation's homicide laws, codifying—and liberalizing in some key respects—the prior judicial "emergency defence"; the Dutch Senate gave its assent in April 2001.[10] The Northern Territory of Australia passed a law permitting assisted suicide in 1996, but that legislation was criticized by the Australian Medical Association and quickly voided months later by Australia's federal parliament.[11] Belgium has now also followed the Dutch example, adopting a law that took effect in September 2002.[12]

Within the United States, Dr. Timothy Quill, a University of Rochester professor, provoked early debate on the assisted suicide question in 1991, writing an article in the *New England Journal of Medicine* discussing and defending his decision to prescribe barbiturates to a cancer patient, even though she admitted that she might use them at some indefinite time in the future to kill herself.[13] A New York grand jury was convened but ultimately declined to bring an indictment for assisted suicide; the state medical board also considered pressing disciplinary charges but eventually relented, reasoning that Dr. Quill had written a prescription for drugs that had a legitimate medical use for his patient (as a sleeping aid for her insomnia), and that he could not have definitely known that the patient would use them to kill herself. Ruling, in essence, that the evidence was too equivocal to conclude that Dr. Quill *intended* to cause the death of his patient, the board declared the matter closed.[14]

In 1992 a gynecology resident submitted an anonymous article to the *Journal of the American Medical Association* that was the subject of a long-running debate in prominent American medical journals. Entitled "It's Over Debbie," the article described how the author administered a lethal injection to a terminal cancer patient (an act of euthanasia, not assisted suicide), whom he had never previously met, after her plea to "get this over with."[15]

After its publication in the early 1990s, the Hemlock Society's book, *Final Exit*, quickly rocketed to the *New York Times*'s best-seller list. With more than a half million copies sold, it provides step-by-step instructions (in easy-to-read large print) on various methods of "self-deliverance." In February 2006 its sales on Amazon.com still ranked 9,845 among all books on offer (which is very high indeed), and it was priced at $10.20 ("you save $4.80; usually ships within 24 hours").[16] Chapter titles range from "Self-Deliverance by Plastic Bag" (a recommended method) to "Bizarre Ways to Die" (discussing the relative merits of guns, ropes, and firecrackers) and "Going Together" (ideas for double suicides). A *New England Journal of Medicine* study found that instances of asphyxiation by plastic bag increased markedly shortly after the book's publication.[17]

The public discussion sparked in the early 1990s by Kevorkian, Quill, *Final Exit*, and Dutch practices quickly matured into a growing debate in academic circles. By the mid- to late 1990s, thinkers from a variety of moral and philosophical perspectives began publishing books pressing the case for legalizing assisted suicide and euthanasia—including Ronald Dworkin in 1993,[18] Seventh Circuit Judge Richard Posner in 1995,[19] and Richard Epstein in 1999.[20]

The growing academic and public discussion of assisted suicide and euthanasia was accompanied by increasing political and legal activism. In 1988 an early voter referendum campaign in California aimed at toppling the state's law banning the assistance of suicide failed to attract the necessary 450,000 verified signatures to secure a spot on the ballot.[21] Another effort just four years later not only secured a spot on the ballot, but garnered 48 percent of the vote. A similar 1991 effort in Washington State obtained 46.4 percent of the vote.[22] By 1993 the referenda campaign bore its first fruit when Oregon voters narrowly voted to legalize assisted suicide, 51 percent to 49 percent, though subsequent legal challenges delayed implementation until 1997.[23]

Since 1994, over fifty bills have been introduced to legalize assisted suicide or euthanasia in at least nineteen state legislatures, and two voter referenda modeled on Oregon have been attempted. All have failed so far. In fact, several states have moved to reaffirm or strengthen their laws prohibiting assisting suicide, including Michigan, New York, Maryland, Iowa, Oklahoma, and Virginia. In all, the vast majority of states (approximately thirty-eight) have chosen to retain or have recently enacted statutes expressly banning assisted suicide, and most of the remaining states either treat assisted suicide as a common law crime or have health care directive statutes expressly disapproving of the practice.[24] In 1997 Congress entered the fray, too, and adopted a new law denying the use of federal funds in connection with any act of assisted suicide.[25] In the last several years, a number of other countries, including England,[26] Canada,[27] Australia,[28] New Zealand,[29] and Hungary,[30] have likewise considered and rejected proposals to overturn their laws banning assisted suicide.

With relatively little to show for their early voter referenda and legislative efforts, American euthanasia proponents opened a new front in the mid-1990s, filing federal law suits in Washington State and New York seeking to have statutes banning assisted suicide declared unconstitutional.[31] Wildly disparate trial court rulings resulted. One trial court found a constitutional right to assistance in suicide; another held that no such right exists.[32] Appellate courts reviewing these decisions eventually produced opinions supporting a right to assisted suicide but using very different rationales and only over vociferous dissents.[33] In 1997 the cases culminated in argument before the United States Supreme Court in a pair of cases, *Washington v. Glucksberg* and *Quill v. Vacco*. In 9–0 decisions, the Court upheld the Washington and New York laws banning assisted suicide.[34] At the time, the press hailed the Court's rulings as major victories for opponents of euthanasia and assisted suicide.[35] But few noticed that critical concurring justices addressed only the question whether laws banning assisted suicide are *facially* unconstitutional—that is, unconstitutional in all possible applications—and specifically reserved for a later case the question whether those laws are unconstitutional *as applied* to terminally ill adults seeking death. Thus, far from definitively resolving the assisted suicide issue, the Court's decisions seem to assure that the debate over assisted suicide and euthanasia is not yet over—and may have only begun.

A great many people support legalizing assisted suicide and euthanasia. One of the central purposes of this book is to identify and explore the strengths and weaknesses of the legal and moral arguments deployed by those who seek to overthrow existing laws against those practices. Specifically, in chapter 2, I discuss the Washington and New York cases and seek to ascertain their implications for future legal and ethical debate over assisted suicide and euthanasia. I suggest that these cases raise four key questions, or arguments, on which future debate is likely to focus: Is there historical precedent for legalization? Do principles of equal protection or fairness dictate that, if we permit patients to refuse life-sustaining care like food and water, we must also as a matter of logical consistency allow assisted suicide and euthanasia? Does proper respect for principles of personal autonomy and self-determination compel legalization? And would legalization, in a purely utilitarian calculus, represent the legal rule or solution that would provide the greatest good for the greatest number of persons?

On each and every one of these points, various contemporary moral and legal writers have given conflicting views. Some have suggested that history is moving inexorably toward legalization; others contend that there is no meaningful way to distinguish between the right of a patient to refuse care and the right of a patient to seek out euthanasia; a virtual chorus has argued that proper respect for personal autonomy and self-determination demands that we respect the right of individuals to take their lives with willing assistants; and others still submit that legalization would carry with it more benefits than costs and would thus maximize social happiness on a utilitarian scale. In chapters 3 through 8, I analyze each of these various contemporary arguments for legalization in turn. In the end, I submit, the force of some of these arguments is overstated while the power of others is actually understated. Readers interested in particular lines of argument can focus on individual chapters that address those issues. Chapter 3 focuses on the historical record. Chapter 4 addresses the arguments from equal protection or fairness suggesting that recognizing a right to refuse life-sustaining medical care is tantamount to adopting a right to assisted suicide or euthanasia. Chapters 5 and 6 look to the arguments from personal autonomy. Chapter 7 discusses empirical and utilitarian arguments based on the experiments and experience in the Netherlands and Oregon. Chapter 8 takes a closer look at two leading arguments for legalization from autonomy and utility posed by Judge Posner and Richard Epstein.

Having reviewed extant arguments for legalization suggested by the case law and in contemporary moral-legal debate, in the final part of the book, chapters 9 and 10, I pursue the second purpose of this book, outlining an argument for retaining current laws banning assisted suicide and euthanasia that has received relatively little attention in the American debate over assisted suicide and euthanasia. It is an argument premised on the idea that all human beings are intrinsically valuable and the intentional taking of human life by private persons is always wrong. In chapter 9, I examine the roots of this principle in secular moral theory and the common law, consider its application to the assisted suicide and euthanasia debate, and address a number of potential criticisms along the way. In chapter 10, I suggest that the principle that all human life is intrinsically valuable may help illuminate and provide guidance in end-of-life disputes beyond assisted suicide and euthanasia, including in the increasingly frequent cases involving the discontinuation of life-sustaining medical care for incompetent persons.

Finally, in late 2001 the presidential administration of George W. Bush issued an executive order that sought to prevent Oregon doctors from dispensing federally regulated medicines to assisted suicides. The administration argued that Oregon doctors helping patients commit suicide were not engaged in a "legitimate medical practice" under the Controlled Substance Act, the federal law regulating the use of pharmacological substances. The federal government's order precipitated a legal battle with the state of Oregon and its allies that culminated in a Supreme Court hearing in October 2004 and a ruling—rendered as this book was going to print—that perhaps raises as many questions as it answers. The lawsuit, its resolution, and its implications for future debate over assisted suicide and euthanasia in America are discussed briefly in the epilogue.

Distilled to its essence, this book might be said to have two purposes—to introduce and critically examine the primary legal and ethical arguments deployed by those who favor legalization, and to set forth an argument for retaining existing law that few have stopped to consider. It aims to be of interest to all of those curious about the ethical and legal aspects of the assisted suicide debate, whatever views they espouse, and to contribute to a fuller and more fully informed debate.

Before proceeding further, a definitional note is important. While the term "assisted suicide" is often used to describe Dr. Kevorkian's practices, it is really something of a misnomer. There is no crime called "assisted suicide," and, as we shall see in chapter 3, no legal penalty for the patient who seeks help in dying. Instead, the crime at issue is *assisting* suicide, and it is targeted solely at those who help another commit suicide. The legal right sought by proponents is thus, to be precise, a right to receive assistance in killing oneself without the *assistant* suffering adverse legal consequences. Recognizing its imprecision, I will nonetheless defer to pervasive usage and employ the term "assisted suicide" as a short-hand description for the proffered right.

Using the term "assisted suicide" to describe Dr. Kevorkian's practices is, however, a misnomer in yet another respect. Dr. Kevorkian has sought to establish not only a right to receive assistance in suicide (what we shall call assisted suicide), but also a right to be killed by another person, so long as the act is performed with the consent of the decedent and the killer is motivated by compassion or mercy (what is properly labeled euthanasia). In fact, in 1999 Dr.

Kevorkian killed a patient for a nationwide television audience on the program *60 Minutes*, and he did so specifically to provoke a public debate on the distinct practice of euthanasia. (Dr. Kevorkian was later convicted of second-degree murder, after a trial in which he chose to act as his own counsel.)[36]

Though an analytical distinction exists between assisted suicide and euthanasia, there is a great deal they share in common, and those who support legalizing one tend to support legalizing the other for the same or similar reasons—whether it be out of a sense that fairness requires killing those who wish to die but who cannot kill themselves, a desire to promote individual autonomy whether it is expressed in terms of a desire to kill oneself or have another do so, or a sense that the actions serve a similar social utility in allowing patients to avoid needless suffering. That said, some advocates of assisted suicide, especially in the United States in the last several years, have sought to draw a line between the practices, seeking to obtain legal permission only for assisted suicide but not euthanasia.[37] Oregon's law, for example, permits only assisted suicide, not euthanasia.[38] But is there really any meaningful moral distinction that can be drawn between assisted suicide and euthanasia? If not, what is at work here?

Those who attempt to draw a moral line between the practices often emphasize that the patient exercises more control in assisted suicide, remaining the final causal actor in his or her own death, while in euthanasia another person assumes that role, thus creating a greater chance for physician malfeasance.[39] Yet, morally, in cases of assisted suicide and euthanasia alike, the patient forms an intent to die and the physician *intentionally* helps the patient end his or her life. As Dutch bioethicists Gerrit Kimsma and Evert van Leeuwen (supporters of legalization) have explained, in Dutch practice both are legal and they are "considered to be identical because intentionally and effectively they both involve actively assisting death."[40] The physical difference, too, between assisted suicide and euthanasia certainly need not be, and frequently is not, very great. As John Keown has asked, "[w]hat, for example, is the supposed difference between a doctor handing a lethal pill to a patient; placing the pill on the patient's tongue; and dropping it down the patient's throat?"[41] The view among legalization proponents in much of the rest of the world is summarized by Kisma: "[t]hinking that physician-assisted suicide is the entire answer . . . is a fantasy. There will always be patients who cannot drink, or are semiconscious, or prefer that a physician perform this act."[42]

Ultimately, it is hard to avoid asking whether the assisted suicide–euthanasia distinction some seek to draw reflects anything more than a calculated tactical decision by euthanasia proponents to fight political-legal battles piecemeal in order to enhance their chances of ultimate success. The distinction between the practices is made almost exclusively in American debate—the Dutch and most others who have contemplated legalization see little reason to distinguish between the practices. The notion that assisted suicide is different in kind from euthanasia has emerged as a significant point in the American dialogue, moreover, only in recent years. For decades, American advocates openly pushed for legalized euthanasia and dubbed their leading organization the Euthanasia Society of America, shifting ground and adopting a new nomenclature for their advocacy groups only in the 1970s and 1980s. As we shall see in chapter 3, American euthanasia proponents also have a history of carefully choosing to fight discrete and targeted policy battles to avoid total defeat and to build a public consensus along the way toward their ultimate and more ambitious goals. And at least some contemporary assisted suicide advocates candidly suggest that this is exactly what is going on today. Richard Epstein, for one, has charged his fellow assisted suicide advocates who fail to endorse the legalization of euthanasia openly and explicitly with a "certain lack of courage."[43] Margaret Otlowski has put the point even more strongly: to her, assisted suicide alone simply "is not . . . a satisfactory legal response."[44] And in the case that led to *Glucksberg v. Washington* in the United States Supreme Court, the judges of the Ninth Circuit en banc court, while ruling only in favor of an assisted suicide right, all but admitted that it would prove impossible for litigants in any subsequent case to draw a "principled distinction" between the assisted suicide right that court approved and a claimed right to euthanasia.[45]

2

Glucksberg *and* Quill: *The Judiciary's (Non)Resolution of the Assisted Suicide Debate*

2.1 THE WASHINGTON DUE PROCESS LITIGATION

IN 1994 a group of Washington State physicians and patients, along with an assisted suicide advocacy organization, filed suit in federal district court seeking a declaratory judgment that the state statute forbidding the assistance of another person in committing suicide[1] was unconstitutional under substantive due process doctrine. The case was assigned to District Judge Barbara Rothstein, who became the first judge to hold assisted suicide to be a right guaranteed by the U.S. Constitution.

Under the familiar language of the Fourteenth Amendment, no state may "deprive any person of life, liberty, or property, without due process of law."[2] Despite the procedural tone of the amendment's language, and arguments by commentators as diverse as John Hart Ely and Robert Bork,[3] the Supreme Court has for many years held in case after case that due process contains a "substantive" component—one that imposes a nearly absolute bar on certain governmental actions "regardless of the fairness of the procedures used to implement them."[4] Judge Rothstein observed that many of these substantive rights adduced by the courts pertain to "marriage, procreation, contraception, family relationships, childrearing, and education."[5]

For guidance on whether assisted suicide might qualify as a new addition to this list, Judge Rothstein turned to the then most recent major exposition of substantive due process jurisprudence, *Planned Parenthood v. Casey*,[6] in which the Court reaffirmed the right to abortion. Judge Rothstein observed that, while discussing abortion, the three-justice plurality in *Casey* suggested that matters

> involving the most intimate and personal choices a person may make in a lifetime, choices central to personal dignity and autonomy, are central to the liberty protected by the Fourteenth Amendment. At the heart of the liberty is the

right to define one's own concept of existence, of meaning, of the universe, and of the mystery of human life.[7]

Judge Rothstein found this reasoning "highly instructive."[8] "Like the abortion decision," she reasoned, "the decision of a terminally ill person to end his or her life involves the most intimate and personal choices a person may make in a lifetime and constitutes a choice central to personal dignity and autonomy."[9]

Judge Rothstein also found instructive the Supreme Court's decision in *Cruzan v. Director, Missouri Department of Health.*[10] There, the Court assumed without deciding that the liberty component of the Fourteenth Amendment embraces the right of a competent adult to refuse life-sustaining medical treatment.[11] Given this apparent right, Judge Rothstein posed the question whether there is "a difference for purposes of finding a Fourteenth Amendment liberty interest between refusal of unwanted treatment which will result in death and committing physician-assisted suicide in the final stages of life?"[12] Judge Rothstein concluded that there is not, because both are deeply personal and at "the heart of personal liberty."[13]

A divided panel of the Ninth Circuit reversed Judge Rothstein's decision. Circuit Judge John Noonan wrote a stinging rebuke of the district court that stressed three points. Judge Noonan argued, first, that *Casey*'s discussion of autonomy was a mere "gloss" on substantive due process jurisprudence, one that was later "implicitly controverted by *Cruzan*."[14] *Cruzan*, Judge Noonan pointed out, relied upon an examination of history and tradition—not an abstract conception of "personal autonomy"—in determining whether the asserted constitutional right should be recognized.[15] Turning to the historical record, Judge Noonan concluded that

> [i]n the two hundred and five years of our existence no constitutional right to aid in killing oneself has ever been asserted and upheld by a court of final jurisdiction. Unless the federal judiciary is to be a floating constitutional convention, a federal court should not invent a constitutional right unknown to the past.[16]

Judge Noonan further suggested that taking *Casey*'s personal autonomy gloss so seriously leads to "absurd" results. If "personal dignity and autonomy" is the touchstone of constitutional analysis, he reasoned, every man and woman in the country must enjoy it. Accordingly, a right to assisted suicide cannot be limited to the competent, terminally ill, or aged: "[t]he depressed twenty-one year old, the romantically devastated twenty-eight year old, the alcoholic forty-year old who choose suicide are also expressing their views of existence, meaning, the universe, and life."[17]

Finally, Judge Noonan rejected any attempt to analogize seeking assisted suicide to the right to refuse medical care, contending that the latter merely involves an omission or rejection of medical treatment while the former requires an affirmative act to end life: "When you assert a claim that another . . . should help you bring about your death, you ask for more than being left alone. . . . You seek the right to have a second person collaborate in your death."[18]

Two and a half years after the suit was filed, an *en banc* panel of the Ninth Circuit vacated Judge Noonan's decision and reinstated the trial court's judgment by a vote of eight to three. The majority opinion, written by Judge Stephen Reinhardt, loosely tracked and sought to supplement Judge Rothstein's analysis. It rejected Judge Noonan's assertion that history is "our sole guide" in substantive due process inquiries; indeed, the court reasoned, if history were our only guide, the Supreme Court never would have declared antimiscegenation laws unlawful in *Loving v. Virginia*,[19] since such laws were commonplace at the time the Fourteenth Amendment was adopted.[20] Neither would the Supreme Court have recognized a right to an abortion; more than three-quarters of the states restricted abortions when the Fourteenth Amendment was passed.[21] Besides, the *en banc* court argued, the historical record concerning suicide itself is "more checkered" than Judge Noonan had acknowledged.[22] Judge Reinhardt pointed to the fact that Socrates and Plato endorsed suicide under some circumstances, the Stoics glorified it, and Roman law sometimes permitted it.[23] While conceding that assisted suicide was unlawful under English and American common law, Judge Reinhardt stressed that most states have not treated suicide or attempted suicide as criminal matters since at least the beginning of the twentieth century.[24]

Turning to *Casey* and *Cruzan*, Judge Reinhardt contended that Judge Rothstein's autonomy analysis had been right all along: Basic life decisions are constitutionally protected, and "[l]ike the decision of whether or not to have an abortion, the decision how and when to die is one" of them.[25] The *en banc* court also rejected Judge Noonan's proffered act-omission distinction, discerning little difference between the removal of the tubes through which patients receive artificial nutrition and hydration, on the one hand, and the act of a lethal injection, on the other.[26]

To Judge Noonan's assertion that a right to assistance in suicide would have to be extended to the desperate or depressed, the *en banc* court responded that the state has a legitimate interest in preventing anyone from taking his or her own life "in a fit of desperation, depression, or loneliness or as a result of any other problem, physical or psychological, which *can be* significantly ameliorated."[27] By contrast, the court stressed, the state's interest in preserving life, is substantially diminished with respect to terminally ill, competent adults who wish to die.[28] Yet, even while the court formally restricted its ruling recognizing the right to assisted suicide to competent and terminally ill persons, it deliberately left open the possibility that, at a later date, the right might be extended to persons who are depressed or suffering other psychological ailments that *cannot be*, in its phrase, "significantly ameliorated."[29]

In another critical respect the *en banc* court went further than the trial court. Judge Reinhardt virtually admitted that approving a right to assistance in suicide would necessarily and inexorably lead to approval of a right to euthanasia, and perhaps even one open to all competent adults, whatever their reasons for seeking death or physical condition, so long as death is sought voluntarily:

> We agree that it may be difficult to make a principled distinction between physician-assisted suicide and the provision to terminally ill patients of other forms of life-ending medical assistance, such as the administration of drugs by a physician. . . .

> The question whether that type of physician conduct may be constitutionally prohibited must be answered directly in future cases, and not in this one. *We would be less than candid, however, if we did not acknowledge that for present purposes we view the critical line in right-to-die cases as the one between the voluntary and involuntary termination of an individual's life.*[30]

In this passage at least, the court suggested a constitutional right encompassing no requirement that the patient serve as the final death-inducing actor, nor any rule that death may be sought only by the terminally ill or gravely suffering. Recognizing the logical implications of the court's holding, certain otherwise sympathetic commentators have chided Judge Reinhardt for failing to hold openly and squarely that voluntary euthanasia is a matter of constitutional right.[31]

2.2 The New York Equal Protection Litigation

While the Washington litigation progressed through the trial and appellate stages, a mirror-image battle was being waged on the other side of the country, this time in New York. The New York litigation, filed June 20, 1994, was led by Dr. Timothy Quill, author of the *New England Journal of Medicine* article defending his decision to prescribe barbiturates to a terminally ill patient.[32] Like the Washington litigants, Dr. Quill and his fellow physician-plaintiffs challenged New York's law prohibiting the intentional assistance or promotion of suicide,[33] contending that it violated the substantive component of the Fourteenth Amendment's due process clause.

Chief Judge Thomas Griesa of the Southern District of New York would have none of it. Judge Griesa rejected any attempt to rely on *Casey*, dismissing its discussion of personal autonomy as "too broad" to ordain the outcome of this case: "The Supreme Court has been careful to explain that the abortion cases, and other related decisions on procreation and child rearing, are not intended to lead automatically to the recognition of fundamental rights on different subjects."[34] Like Judge Noonan, Judge Griesa treated the due process claim as depending upon an examination of history and concluded (albeit with little explanation) that the plaintiffs had failed to show that assisted suicide has "any historic recognition as a legal right."[35]

As an alternative ground for relief, Dr. Quill and his fellow physician-plaintiffs argued that, even if no due process right exists, the equal protection clause of the Fourteenth Amendment renders statutes against assisted suicide unlawful. Specifically, they noted that under New York statutory law a competent person may refuse medical treatment—even if doing so will certainly result in death.[36] To treat like persons alike, they argued, assistance in suicide must also be permitted.[37] Judge Griesa was unmoved. He held that New York State needed to present only a reasonable and rational basis for the distinction in its law,[38] and he found that such a distinction exists because a patient refusing treatment is merely "allowing nature to take its course," while the act of suicide involves "intentionally using an artificial death-producing device."[39]

Adding to the already somewhat convoluted history of lower court litigation on the assisted suicide question, the Second Circuit reversed Judge Griesa. The court of appeals did not address the due process theory advanced by Dr. Quill below and adopted by the Ninth Circuit *en banc* court. Instead, it adopted the plaintiffs' equal protection theory. Addressing Chief Judge Griesa's natural-artificial distinction between refusing care and assisting suicide, the Second Circuit could not find anything "natural" about causing death by removing feeding tubes or ventilators: "It certainly cannot be said that the death that immediately ensues is the natural result of the progression of the disease or the condition from which the patient suffers."[40]

New York State responded by proffering another distinction between assisting suicide and refusing treatment, claiming (as Judge Noonan had) that one involves an affirmative act while the other is only an omission. But the Second Circuit rejected this explanation too, reasoning that a prescription to hasten death actually involves a less active role for the doctor than "is required in bringing about death through asphyxiation, starvation, and/or dehydration."[41] Quoting Justice Scalia's concurrence in *Cruzan*, the court held that the act-omission distinction is "'irrelevan[t]'" because "'the cause of death in both cases is the suicide's conscious decision to pu[t] an end to his own existence.'"[42]

While the Second Circuit found it impossible to draw a rational distinction between the right to refuse care and assisted suicide, it, unlike the Ninth Circuit, remained entirely mute on the question whether a law permitting assisted suicide but rejecting euthanasia could survive similar scrutiny. Yet, it seems hard not to conclude that the Second Circuit's reasoning would lead to a right to euthanasia as well: After all, if the long-standing social and legal distinction between refusing care and assisted suicide cannot withstand scrutiny, how can anyone be optimistic about the prospects of maintaining an impregnable analytical wall between assisted suicide and euthanasia?

Judge Calabresi separately concurred.[43] In his view, New York's ban on assisted suicide was neither plainly unconstitutional nor plainly constitutional.[44] Drawing upon his earlier writings when he served as a full-time professor of law,[45] Judge Calabresi argued that, in such circumstances, the courts should avail themselves of a novel procedure—what he called a constitutional remand.[46] Under Calebresi's proposed procedure, laws that fall into a constitutional grey area (such as New York's prohibitions on assisted suicide, in his view) should be vacated on the grounds that they *might* be unconstitutional. The legislative branch would, however, be free to reenact those same laws, if it could provide a strong argument for doing so.[47]

Calabresi's remand procedure, if adopted by the federal courts, would represent a nontrivial extension of Chief Justice Marshall's theory of judicial review in *Marbury v. Madison*,[48] claiming as it does that federal courts have the power under Article III of the Constitution to declare statutory laws enacted by elected legislatures null and void simply because they *might* violate the supreme law of the land, without ever making any finding, as in *Marbury*, that they *do* in fact violate the Constitution. But even if Calabresi's constitutional remand procedure is itself a constitutional device—an interesting question indeed—the justification for employing it seems to depend on some degree of confidence that the law in question has fallen into desuetude. As Judge Calabresi put it, laws should not be permitted simply to "remain in force through passivity or inertia"; a constitutional remand allows courts to "tell[ ] the legislatures and executives of the various states, and of the federal government as well, that if they wish to regulate conduct that, if not protected by our Constitution, is very close to being protected, they must do so clearly and openly."[49]

Passivity and inertia, however, are not labels that can be readily applied to the New York assisted suicide statute. As recently as 1985, Mario Cuomo, then governor of New York, convened a task force composed of twenty-four members representing a wide variety of ethical, philosophical, and religious views and expressly asked them to consider whether the state should drop or revise its laws banning assisted suicide; the task force returned with a lengthy report that unanimously favored retaining existing law, explicating their reasons for doing so in voluminous detail.[50] Given this, New York's law does not seem to be an ideal candidate for "remand," even using Judge Calabresi's criteria. Perhaps recognizing this fact, or concerned about the constitutionality of striking down duly enacted laws merely on the ground that they *might be* unconstitutional, neither of the other members of the Second Circuit panel joined Judge Calebresi's concurrence.

2.3 THE FINAL BATTLE? THE SUPREME COURT DOES (AND DOES NOT) DECIDE

By mid-1996 the Ninth and Second Circuit decisions were ripe for review in the U.S. Supreme Court. The Court consolidated the cases and heard argument on January 8, 1997. Six months later, on June 26, 1997, then Chief Justice Rehnquist delivered two opinions for the Court, overruling both the Ninth and Second Circuits and upholding New York's and Washington's bans on assisted suicide. The chief justice was joined by Justices O'Connor, Scalia, Kennedy, and Thomas.

While widely portrayed in the media as a conservative Rehnquist Court victory for enemies of assisted suicide and euthanasia,[51] any such "victory" could very well prove more pyrrhic than real. Several justices wrote separately to stress that plaintiffs in *Glucksberg* and *Quill* had sought a declaratory judgment that state laws outlawing the assistance of suicide are *facially* unconstitutional—that is, unconstitutional in all possible applications. Neither case, they emphasized, presented a situation in which a state was seeking to prosecute specific persons—a situation in which the affected individuals may raise the narrower question whether laws against assisted suicide are unconstitutional *as applied* to them and persons like them.[52] In their various separate opinions, each of these justices variously hinted at, suggested, or at least kept the door open to the possibly that prohibitions against assisting suicide and euthanasia would be unconstitutional if and when applied to competent, terminally ill adults.

Chief Justice Rehnquist began his opinion for the Court on the substantive due process question by expressing skepticism about the Ninth Circuit's *en banc* court's reliance on *Casey* and *Cruzan*'s discussions of personal autonomy as the sole basis for recognizing a new right. Under Rehnquist's formulation, to qualify as a "fundamental liberty interest," the asserted right must be *both* "implicit in the concept of ordered liberty," such that "neither liberty nor justice would exist if [it] were sacrificed," as *Casey* or *Cruzan* might be read to imply, *and also* "deeply rooted in this Nation's history and tradition."[53] Further, the chief justice added, "[w]e begin as we do in all due process cases, by examining our Nation's history, legal traditions, and practices."[54]

Unlike Judge Reinhardt's historical analysis, Chief Justice Rehnquist did not consult ancient philosophers or Roman law. Instead, he began with English common law experience, though, even there, his analysis began and ended with a single paragraph summarily concluding that suicide and its assistance were never permitted at common law.[55] The chief justice devoted somewhat more attention (a few pages) to American legal history. While conceding Judge Reinhardt's point that the penalties associated with *suicide* were eventually repealed by all American jurisdictions, Rehnquist declined the Ninth Circuit's invitation to read much into that fact because "courts continued to condemn it as a grave public wrong."[56] Of even more direct significance, the chief justice held, is the fact that American jurisdictions have always treated *assisting* a suicide as a felony.[57] Having found that "[t]he history of the law's treatment of assisted suicide in this country has been and continues to be one of the rejection of nearly all efforts to permit it," he concluded that a right to receive assistance in suicide "is not a fundamental liberty interest protected by the Due Process Clause."[58]

Turning to *Cruzan* and *Casey*, the chief justice rejected the notion that the due process clause creates a constitutional guarantee of "self-sovereignty" embracing all "basic and intimate exercises of personal autonomy."[59] *Cruzan*, he wrote, "was not simply deduced from abstract concepts of personal autonomy."[60] Rather, Chief Justice Rehnquist saw its result as dictated by a purely historical analysis: "[G]iven the common-law rule that forced medication was a battery, and the long legal tradition protecting the decision to refuse unwanted medical treatment, our assumption was entirely consistent with this Nation's history and constitutional traditions."[61] The chief justice brushed aside, too, reliance on supposedly "prescriptive" passages in *Casey*: "That many of the rights and liberties protected by the Due Process Clause sound in personal autonomy does not warrant the sweeping conclusion that any and all important, intimate, and personal decisions are so protected, and *Casey* did not suggest otherwise."[62]

The chief justice's equal protection analysis was even more succinct than his due process discussion. New York's distinction between refusing life-sustaining medical treatment and assisted suicide, he wrote, survives rational basis review because it "comports with fundamental legal principles of causation."[63] Specifically, when a patient refuses treatment, "he dies from an underlying fatal disease or pathology; but if a patient ingests lethal medication prescribed by a physician, he is killed by that medication."[64] While essentially adopting Judge Griesa's natural-unnatural distinction, Rehnquist nowhere addressed the Second Circuit's criticism that inducing death by withdrawing life-sustaining medical treatment (e.g., respirators and feeding tubes) is no more "natural" than inducing death by active means (e.g., lethal injection).

Instead, Chief Justice Rehnquist moved on, arguing that the distinction between refusing care and assisting suicide is further justified on grounds of intent, noting that "[t]he law has long used actors' intent or purpose to distinguish between two acts that may have the same result."[65] For example, the common law of homicide distinguishes "between a person who knows that another person will be killed as the result of his conduct and a person who acts with the specific purpose of taking another's life."[66] And, in this case, a physician who withdraws care pursuant to an express patient demand "purposefully intends, or may so intend, only to respect his patient's wishes."[67] By contrast, a doctor assisting a suicide "must, necessarily and indubitably, intend primarily that the patient be made dead."[68]

Chief Justice Rehnquist's due process and equal protection opinions spoke for the Court only by virtue of Justice O'Connor's fifth vote. Justice O'Connor, however, filed a separate statement joined by Justices Ginsburg and Breyer that substantially limited the precedential effect of the chief justice's opinions.[69]

Justice O'Connor stressed that the only question presented in the cases before the Court was whether the New York and Washington laws outlawing assisted suicide are facially unconstitutional, or invalid in *all* possible applications.[70] On that question, Justice O'Connor conceded that laws banning assisted suicide have at least *some* constitutional applications. For example, Justice O'Connor wrote, the possibility that a patient might be coerced into accepting an early death, or that a patient might be killed without his or her consent by mistake, justifies at least *some* restrictions on access to assistance in suicide.[71] But Justice O'Connor expressly left open the possibility that laws against assisting suicide also have unconstitutional applications[72]—and she hinted that a dying patient whose request is "truly voluntary" might present just such a case.[73]

Justices Souter and Stevens also filed separate concurrences. Justice Souter particularly disagreed with the chief justice's contention that substantive due process analysis requires an examination of history or tradition. To him, substantive due process analysis is incapable of "any general formula," except to say perhaps that it should be "like any other instance of judgment dependent on common-law method," with arguments "being more or less persuasive according to the usual canons of critical discourse."[74] In the end, however, Justice Souter concluded that, even using his mode of analysis, states have rational reasons for refusing to permit at least some forms of assisted suicide.[75] But he also noted that states are in the process of reconsidering their laws against assisted suicide, added his view that such reconsideration is a good idea, and strongly suggested that legalization of assisted suicide (at least in some circumstances) should be its result.[76] Justice Souter pointedly commented that he did not want to see "legislative foot-dragging" on the assisted suicide question and that, if such foot-dragging occurs, "[s]ometimes a court may be bound to act regardless of the institutional preferability of the political branches as forums for addressing constitutional claims."[77]

Justice Stevens likewise heavily hinted at how he would rule in an as-applied challenge limited to terminally ill adult patients, analogizing to the Court's decades-long battle over capital punishment in case after case with results varying based on each defendant's individualized state of mind and conduct:

> [J]ust as our conclusion that capital punishment is not always unconstitutional did not preclude later decisions holding that it is sometimes impermissibly cruel, so is it equally clear that a decision upholding a general statutory prohibition of assisted suicide does not mean that every possible application of the statute would be valid.[78]

Lest any doubt remain about how he would rule in an as-applied challenge brought by a competent, terminally ill patient, Justice Stevens offered his view that "[t]he liberty interest at stake in a case like this differs from, *and is stronger than*, . . . the common-law right to refuse medical treatment" underlying the *Cruzan* decision.[79]

On the equal protection question, Justice Stevens argued that the Court's distinction between refusing care and assisting suicide based on intent is "illusory" because a doctor discontinuing treatment can do so "with an intent to harm or kill that patient. Conversely, a doctor who prescribes lethal medication does not necessarily intend the patient's death—rather that doctor may seek simply to ease the patient's suffering and to comply with her wishes."[80] The illusory nature of an intent-based distinction is further demonstrated, Justice Stevens suggested, by the fact that the American Medical Association (AMA) endorses administering pain-killing medication to terminally ill patients suffering pain, even when it results in death. "The purpose of terminal sedation is to ease the suffering of the patient and comply with her wishes."[81] This same intent, Justice Stevens argued, "may exist when a doctor complies with a patient's request for lethal medication."[82]

While rejecting a distinction based on intent, Justice Stevens concurred in the Court's equal protection decision overruling the Second Circuit and agreed with the Court's reasoning, insofar as it held that death in assisted suicide cases is caused by unnatural human intervention, while death in refusal of treatment cases is caused by nature taking its course.[83] Like the Court, however, Justice Stevens declined to address the Second Circuit's provocative criticisms of this natural–unnatural or causation-based distinction.

2.4 THE AFTERMATH OF *GLUCKSBERG* AND *QUILL*

The immediate consequence of the Supreme Court's rulings was to return the assisted suicide question to the states and the political process where it remains the subject of active debate.[84] A less immediate and obvious, but perhaps even more important, consequence is the fact that several justices appear to be open to considering a constitutional right to assistance in suicide for competent, terminally ill persons in an appropriate case, and recent changes in the Supreme Court's composition only intensify the uncertainty over how it might rule when presented with such a case. But, whether the assisted suicide and euthanasia question is ultimately resolved in the legislative or judicial arena, *Glucksberg* and *Quill* make clear that only the opening salvo has been fired in what is likely to be a lengthy, case-by-case litigation war similar, as Justice Stevens suggested, to the fight over capital punishment. *Glucksberg* and *Quill* also help expose the sort of moral-legal arguments we have heard and can expect to hear on both sides of the continuing debate over assisted suicide and euthanasia, suggesting four distinct issues and themes over which much future debate can be expected to focus.

First, there is a clear division between those who see no historical precedent for permitting assisted suicide and euthanasia (former Chief Justice Rehnquist and Judge Noonan) and those who question whether the weight of history is so definitively against the practices (Judge Reinhardt).

Second, there is a difference of opinion over whether principles of fairness (equal protection) require us to permit assisted suicide and euthanasia if we allow patients to refuse life-sustaining medical care. The Second Circuit thought principles of fairness so required. Justice Stevens came close to agreeing with the Second Circuit, disputing any distinction based on intent. But the New York trial court disagreed, and so did a majority of the Supreme Court.

Third, there are those who, like Judges Rothstein and Reinhardt and Justice Stevens, are convinced that the themes of self-determination, personal choice, and autonomy underlying *Casey* and *Cruzan* provide grounds for a right to assistance in suicide and euthanasia. Others, such as Chief Justice Rehnquist, have found abstract notions of personal autonomy completely unavailing.

Finally, there are some who are curious whether society as a whole would be improved or worsened by legalization. Justices O'Connor and Souter expressed open interest in what "experimentation" in the states might "prove" about the utility of legalizing assisted suicide and euthanasia. Would legalization lead, for example, to a more compassionate society or one where the elderly and vulnerable are apt to be pressured into early deaths?

While these four issues represent axes around which the debate has so far evolved, definitive answers have yet to emerge. Is euthanasia antithetical to our nation's tradition? Is it only fair to legalize assisting suicide and euthanasia, given that we allow patients to refuse life-sustaining care? Are rights to assistance in suicide and euthanasia essential to personal choice and identity? Would legalizing assisted suicide and euthanasia bring with it consequences that, on the whole, would do more good or harm? The following several chapters seek to evaluate each of these questions.

3

The Debate over History

 HE RELEVANCE of history to the constitutional debate over assisted suicide and euthanasia is the subject of much dispute. Some (like former Chief Justice Rehnquist) see an analysis of historical legal rules and rights as critical to any substantive due process analysis. Others (such as Justice Souter) think it bears little or no relevance. Others still have questioned the practice of relying upon the preferences of past majorities to interpret the Fourteenth Amendment, which was added to the Constitution in the aftermath of the Civil War with special concern for promoting the advancement of minority rights.[1] But the history test has proven powerfully attractive to federal courts faced with substantive due process disputes. In contrast to the competing test focused on the demands of "personal autonomy" and dependent on "reasoned judgment" (which we shall explore in greater detail later), the history test is perceived by its advocates as offering a comparatively objective approach to due process adjudication. As Justice Powell once put it, "an approach grounded in history imposes limits on the judiciary that are more meaningful than any based on the abstract formula . . . suggested as an alternative."[2]

One of the earliest cases to synthesize the history test into a coherent means for deciding substantive due process fundamental liberty questions was *Snyder v. Massachusetts*. There, in 1934, the Court faced an appeal from a murder conviction. The victim was shot to death during the course of an attempted robbery by three men at a gasoline station in Somerville, Massachusetts, and the jury found "abundant evidence" of the defendants' guilt.[3] One defendant claimed, however, that the trial judge's refusal to permit him to be present at a jury view of the gas station constituted a denial of due process. Justice Cardozo rejected the notion that judges should resolve such due process questions by reference to their unbounded "reasoned judgment" and held that government policy "does not run foul of the Fourteenth Amendment because another method may seem to our thinking to be fairer or wiser or to give a surer promise of protection to" the individual right-claimaint.[4] Instead, Justice Cardozo held, states are free to regulate their courts as they wish so long as they do not "offend[] some principle of justice so rooted in the traditions and conscience of our people as to be ranked as fundamental."[5] The right proffered by the defendant in

Snyder did not qualify under this standard, Justice Cardozo continued, because the opportunity to be present at a view had never been considered critical in the common law of England and America.[6]

Snyder's history test—focused on whether a proffered right is deeply rooted in tradition—is now itself deeply rooted in substantive due process jurisprudence. In a 1972 decision, the Supreme Court decided that compulsory school attendance laws violated the First and Fourteenth Amendments and did so, in part, because a "strong tradition" in "the history and culture of Western civilization" suggested that parents have the right to guide the education of their children; indeed, the Court held, this right was "established beyond debate as an enduring American tradition."[7] Similarly, Justice Powell employed the history test in *Moore v. City of East Cleveland* to strike down a local zoning ordinance that had the effect of forbidding a grandmother from living with her grandchildren, holding that such a law interfered with a long-standing tradition of respect for extended families in our legal system.[8] And, of course, Chief Justice Rehnquist placed great weight on the absence of historical support to turn back the facial challenge to laws banning assisted suicide while also relying on history in *Cruzan* to endorse a right to refuse unwanted care.

3.1 WHICH HISTORY?

Even among those who agree that history should govern substantive due process analysis, however, methodological disputes abound. Supreme Court justices have not been able to agree, for example, what "level" of historical abstraction they should operate on.

A 1989 decision, *Michael H. v. Gerald D.*,[9] provides an illustration of the point. There, Justice Scalia, joined by Chief Justice Rehnquist, argued that courts conducting substantive due process inquiries should "refer to the most specific level at which a relevant tradition protecting, or denying protection to, the asserted right can be identified."[10] In *Glucksberg*, the Court appeared to follow this dictum, focusing only on the narrow question whether history supports a right to assistance in suicide, and eschewing more general historical discussions about personal autonomy and self-definition.[11] Justices O'Connor and Kennedy, however, filed a separate opinion in *Michael H.* to register their view that the Court had not always examined—and need not always rely on—the most specific level of tradition available.[12] Sometimes, they argued, the Court has legitimately examined history at a more "general" level. Justice Souter seemed to take exactly this tack in the assisted suicide cases, pointing to the fact that individuals have settled rights to refuse unwanted medical care and procure abortions as evidence of a more general tradition permitting a patient to "determine what shall be done with his own body."[13] Judge Reinhardt similarly

placed greater stress on the legal history of suicide rather than on the more specific history of assisted suicide and euthanasia.[14]

It is unclear, however, whether Justices O'Connor and Kennedy meant
to suggest in *Michael H.* that a court actually may disregard an on-point specific
tradition (e.g., the history of the law about assisting suicide) in favor of a generally analogous, but less directly applicable, one (e.g., the history of the law
about suicide). The primary case they cited for support, *Eisenstadt v. Baird*,[15]
does not obviously afford such license. There, the Court declared that laws prohibiting the sale of contraceptives to unmarried persons violate the Due Process
Clause on the ground that prior cases (albeit dealing with married couples) suggested a general right to "reproductive privacy." In *Michael H.*, Justices O'Connor and Kennedy pointed to the fact that, at the time *Eisenstadt* was decided,
a long-standing and more specific tradition existed in many states outlawing
the sale of contraceptives to unmarried persons. But Justices O'Connor and
Kennedy neglected to mention that the Court in *Eisenstadt* did not consider or
even identify this more specific tradition, and the Court never offered reasons
why it should be rejected in favor of a more general tradition. That *Eisenstadt*
overlooked a "specific" tradition without comment is not exactly the same thing
as a clear holding that courts may reject specific traditions in favor of more general ones in future substantive due process cases. Besides, *Eisenstadt's* result can
be defended fully, without contortions over historical "levels" and even without
reference to due process doctrine, as an equal protection decision simply and
quite straightforwardly requiring the same access to contraceptives for married
and unmarried persons alike.

Just as there exists dispute among history test adherents over what "level" of historical abstraction should be applied, there is also disagreement over *which* history is relevant. In due process cases, the Supreme Court has frequently looked
not only to this nation's history, but also to English common law. But why stop
there? Why not examine Roman or Greek or some other ancient precedent as,
say, Justice Blackmun did in his opinion for the Court in *Roe v. Wade*?[16] And
what about contemporary experience in other Western countries? The majority in *Lawrence v. Texas* relied heavily on recent European legal development,[17]
while the dissent argued vociferously that the only relevant history is America's
history.[18] In *Glucksberg*, the Supreme Court also focused primarily on U.S. history, though it briefly examined English common law, while Judge Reinhardt
devoted pages of the federal reports to recounting ancient suicide practices.

Even if agreement can be reached on what level of abstraction should
be examined and which history is relevant, there remains the question how far
forward to go. When interpreting the Fourteenth Amendment, should we limit
ourselves to preratification history, as originalists like Judge Robert Bork might
suggest,[19] or should we look to more recent history as well? In *Lawrence*[20] the

majority overturned a Texas law proscribing homosexual sodomy, placing great stress on an "emerging recognition" that adult persons should be allowed a larger sphere of privacy in personal sexual relations.[21] The dissent, meanwhile, countered that fundamental rights should depend on "deeply rooted" traditions, not "emerging awareness[es]."[22]

3.2 THE PROJECT

The history test, for all its promise of constraining judicial discretion, carries with it a host of unanswered methodological questions and does not always guarantee the sort of certainty one might perhaps hope for. Just consider the widely divergent conclusions drawn by Judge Reinhardt and Chief Justice Rehnquist in the assisted suicide cases—or by Justices Kennedy and Scalia in the homosexual sodomy case—from the same agreed historical facts. The apparent inability of the history test to provide better, more objective guidance may suggest, to some, the need to refine its operation (answering definitively, for example, the critical methodological questions: what level? whose history? how far back?). As we shall see in chapter 5, others see the shortcomings of the history test as one reason for deciding substantive due process disputes through moral reasoning rather than engage in backward-looking debates over what past majorities had to say about rights designed to advance and protect minority groups and factions; still others see uncertainties generated by either approach as a basis for eschewing the notion that the due process guarantee contains *any* unwritten substantive component that can be adduced through judicial exposition.

For now, however, the question we face is: given the history test as we know it today, methodological warts and all, what can be said about assisted suicide and euthanasia from the historical record? To attempt to answer this question, we must examine as broad a historical record as possible, consulting the ancients as well as more directly relevant English, colonial, and American history, examining both the specific history of assisted suicide and euthanasia and the more generally relevant history of suicide.

3.3 THE ANCIENTS

While Judge Reinhardt is correct that suicide was sometimes tolerated by ancient Greeks and Romans, often it was not, and—even when suicide was tolerated—there is little evidence that such toleration was linked in any way to concern for the terminally ill.

Athenian law treated suicide as a crime, "punishing" the "guilty" by amputating the corpse's right hand and denying traditional burial rituals.[23] Plato similarly condemned suicide on multiple occasions. In *Phaedo*, Plato argued that a philosopher should embrace natural death when it comes because it will free him from the shadowy cave of human existence and bring him into contact with truth.[24] But, Plato added, it is wrong to seek out death, and choosing suicide is akin to a soldier "run[ning] away" from his or her assigned post and duties.[25] In *Laws*, Plato condemned suicide on the grounds that it "imposes [an] unjust judgment [of death] on [oneself] in a spirit of slothful and abject cowardice."[26]

To his general support of Athenian law, Plato did add three exceptions: suicide might be permissible when compelled by (1) judicial order; (2) excruciating misfortune; or (3) moral disgrace.[27] The first category, however, is not properly a category of suicide at all. Here, Plato acknowledged merely that the victim of state execution coerced to be the agent of his own death (e.g., Socrates accepting the hemlock as his sentence after trial) is morally blameless. Likewise, in the second category, Plato did not endorse (or even appear to contemplate) rationally chosen suicide but instead expressed compassion for deaths compelled (*anankastheis*) by misfortune—the result perhaps of what we would today label depression or mental illness. Only in his third category did Plato provide any form of approval for rational, intentional acts of self-killing, but even this was limited to persons killing themselves as the result of intense moral disgrace.

In *The Republic*, Plato also argued that individuals should be permitted to refuse intrusive medical treatments that may lengthen their lives at the expense of making them very unpleasant:

> But with bodies diseased through and through, [Asclepius] made no attempt by regimes . . . to make a lengthy and bad life for a human being and have him produce offspring likely to be such as he; he didn't think he should care for the man who's not able to live in his established round, on the grounds that he's of no profit to himself or the city. . . .

> And, as for those with a naturally sickly and licentious body, they thought that living is of no profit either to themselves or others, that the art shouldn't be applied to them, and that they musn't be treated—not even if they were richer than Midas. . . .

> Will you set down a law in the city providing . . . for an art of medicine . . . which will care for those of your citizens who have good natures in body and soul; while as for those who haven't, they'll let die the ones whose bodies are such.[28]

This, however, is not so much an argument directed at a right to commit (or assist) suicide as it is an argument for what we would today call the right to refuse unwanted medical treatment.[29] Further, Plato's claim was less that a person has a *right* to choose whether to discontinue intrusive medical treatment and more the distinctly illiberal claim that persons dependent on such care are objectively better off dead than alive—and so should not be kept alive.

Aristotle used suicide to raise the larger question whether self-regarding acts that impose no harm on third parties can ever be considered "unjust."[30] Acts of injustice, Aristotle contended, depend in large measure on the degree of the actor's intent: Involuntary acts can be "neither unjust[] nor just";[31] similarly, acts "done in ignorance" or as a result of negligence ("e.g. he threw not with intent to wound but only to prick"), and those done with knowledge but not after deliberation ("e.g. the acts due to anger or other passions"), do not mitigate the consequence of the act but are sometimes "excusable."[32] By contrast, acts done "from choice" are premeditated and conscious and, thus, matters for which we are always morally responsible: "[I]f a man harms another by choice, he acts unjustly; and *these* are the acts of injustice which imply that the doer is an unjust man."[33]

Having thus distinguished intentional acts from merely accidental, negligent, or foreseen ones, Aristotle turned to the suicide question and remarked that:

> there are some just acts enjoined by law as consistent with virtue in general—e.g. the law does not allow a man to kill himself. Again, when a man voluntarily—that is, knowing who the victim and what the instrument is—injures another . . . contrary to the law, he is acting unjustly. But a man who cuts his throat in a fit of anger is voluntarily doing, contrary to the right principle, what the law does not allow; therefore he is acting unjustly. But towards whom? Surely not himself, but the state; because he suffers voluntarily, and nobody is voluntarily treated unjustly. It is for this reason that the state imposes a penalty, and a kind of dishonour is attached to a man has taken his own life, on the ground that he is guilty of an offence against the state.[34]

In this passage, Aristotle concedes that a suicide imposes no injustice on third persons—"because he suffers voluntarily, and nobody is voluntarily treated unjustly." Nonetheless, Aristotle suggests that suicide, though harmless to others in this respect, is nonetheless properly proscribed because "there are some just acts enjoined by law as consistent with virtue in general" in order to ensure "the right principle" of life.[35] Though the passage is highly ambiguous, Aristotle perhaps can be fairly read to give vent here to the view that the state has a legitimate interest in preventing the destruction of all human lives equally, and that this is a basic feature of justice, or what he calls the "right principle" of life.[36]

Other Greek and Roman thinkers were more varied in their thinking. Stoics—often recalled as champions of enduring adversity without complaint—considered suicide an acceptable response to physical adversity. Cicero, for example, argued that "when a man's circumstances contain a preponderance of things in accordance with nature, it is appropriate for him to remain alive; when he possesses or sees in prospect a majority of the contrary things, it is appropriate for him to depart from life."[37] Pythagoras, meanwhile, strongly opposed suicide.[38] Epicurus, often cited as an advocate of comfort in life and death, was less concerned with the liberty to commit suicide than he was skeptical that suicide could ever be the product of rational choice: "he is of little account who finds many good reasons for departing from life."[39]

Under Roman law, criminals committing suicide to avoid punishment (e.g., the death penalty) or their worldly obligations (e.g., deserting soldiers and runaway slaves) were regularly punished.[40] Their corpses were abused and their fortunes were forfeited to the state, sometimes leaving wives and children penniless. Meanwhile, other forms of suicide were generally allowed:

> Where persons who have not yet been accused of crime, lay violent hands on themselves, their property shall not be confiscated by the Treasury; for it is not the wickedness of the deed that renders it punishable, but it is held that the consciousness of guilt entertained by the defendant is considered to take the place of a confession.[41]

Roman law offered no basis for limiting access to suicide to the terminally ill, or even the rational and voluntary; the physically healthy and mentally ill were as free to kill themselves as the sick or competent. Antony, Brutus, Cornelia, and Cleopatra are a few examples of Roman suicides motivated not by illness but in response to a fear of moral disgrace and dishonor (arguably just the sort of practice Plato meant to endorse in *Laws*). Suicide was also treated as a form of circus entertainment. After publicly promising to do so and amid much fanfare, Peregrinus threw himself into a pyre at the Olympic Games to achieve fame. After losing a battle, Sardanapalus, king of Nineveh and Assyria, apparently gathered his wife and concubines, set himself on a luxurious couch, and ordered slaves to set them all on fire.[42] During the Punic Wars, it was also apparently easy to recruit individuals to volunteer for execution in exchange for money paid to their heirs; others could be found, for a higher price, to be slowly beaten and mangled to death for popular entertainment.[43]

3.4 EARLY CHRISTIAN HISTORY

Though the Bible nowhere explicitly forbids suicide, from its earliest days Christianity taught against the practice. Addressing the question in the fifth century, Augustine argued that intentional self-destruction generally constitutes a violation of the Sixth Commandment:

> It is not without significance, that in the holy canonical books, no divine precept or permission can be discovered which allows us to bring about our own death, either to obtain immortality or to avert some evil. On the contrary, we must understand the Law of God as forbidding us to do this, where it says, "Thou shalt not kill."[44]

Augustine, however, emphasized the distinction between intentional and unintentional self-destruction. At the time of his writing, powerful schismatic forces threatened the unity of the Catholic Church, including the Donatists, a sect of particularly rigorous North Africans who had even attempted to murder Augustine. Donatists believed, among other things, that Christians who had succumbed to persecution before Constantine formally legalized Christianity were unfit to serve the Church, as well as that Church teachings suggesting that the Holy Spirit imbued every clerical office were wrong—the presence of the Holy Spirit entirely depending, in their view, on individual priests being in a state of grace. Donatists were regularly persecuted by church and state authorities, and eventually the death penalty was authorized. Though Augustine opposed killing the Donatists, he also opposed the Donatists' tactic of deliberately provoking their own arrests and executions. Augustine accused some Donatists of going

> so far as to offer themselves for slaughter to any travelers whom they met with arms, using violent threats that they would murder them if they failed to meet with death at their hands. Sometimes, too, they extorted with violence from any passing judge that they should be put to death by executioners . . . it was their daily sport to kill themselves by throwing themselves over precipices, or into the water, or into the fire.[45]

While the Donatists claimed that they were martyrs, Augustine argued that true Christian martyrs are willing to *accept* execution rather than forsake God but are never *deliberate volunteers* for death:

> I have heard that you say that the Apostle Paul intimated the lawfulness of suicide when he said, "though I give my body to be burned," [1 Cor. 13:3] supposing that because he was there enumerating all the good things which are of no avail without charity, such as the tongues of men and of angels, and all mysteries, and all knowledge, and all prophecy, and the destruction of one's goods to the poor, he intended to include among these good things the act of bringing death upon oneself. But observe carefully and learn in what sense Scripture says that any man may give his body to be burned. Certainly not that any man may throw himself into the fire when he is harassed by a pursuing enemy, but that, when he is compelled to choose between doing wrong and suffering wrong, he should refuse to do wrong rather than to suffer wrong, and so give his body into the power of the executioner, as those three men did who are being compelled to worship in the golden image, while he who was compelled threatened them with the burning fiery furnace if they did not obey. They refused to worship the image: they did not cast themselves into the fire, and yet of them it is written that they "yielded their bodies, that they might not serve nor worship any god except their God." This is the sense in which the apostle said, "If I give my body to be burned."[46]

Permitting intentional self-destruction would, Augustine feared, lead down a slippery slope. If seeking death to avoid temporal troubles is acceptable, then why not allow suicide to avoid any risk of future sin or other degradation? After all, if there could be any good reason for suicide, the faithful Augustine reasoned, none could be better than this.[47] In fact, during the sacking of Rome, many Christian virgin women committed suicide in order to avoid rape and, they thought, mortal sin, and early Christians revered these women. But Augustine disagreed: "Why, then, should a [person] who has done no harm do harm to [herself], and, in slaying [herself] slay an innocent [person] so as not to suffer the crime of another? Why should [she] perpetrate on [herself] a sin of [her] own so that another's sin might not be perpetrated upon [her]?"[48]

Aquinas echoed and built upon foundations laid by Augustine (and Aristotle), submitting that suicide is

> altogether wrong for three reasons. Firstly, it runs counter to the natural inclinations of nature and charity to love and cherish oneself. Secondly, it does injury to the community to which each man belongs as a part of the whole. And thirdly, it wrongs God whose gift life is and who alone has power over life and death. What gives man mastery over himself is free will. So he may licitly manage his own life in respect of everything that contributes to it; but his passage out of this life to a happier one is not subject to his own free will but to the authority of God.[49]

Aquinas's third argument involves an expressly religious appeal, and he never fully developed his second argument. But his first argument he did develop, and it forms part of his larger moral theory.

According to Aquinas, there are certain irreducible, basic human goods knowable to all persons by practical reasoning; human life is among them.[50] To do damage intentionally to the basic good of human life, whether one's own life or another's, is contrary to "nature and charity." This is, however, not to say that killing can never be justified. Aquinas, like Aristotle and Augustine, asserted that acts performed to carry out deliberate, rational choice are different in kind from those unintended or involuntary. Intentional choices are ones that we embrace, we rationally accept, and are within our control; while not devoid of moral character, unintended and involuntary actions are not always within our control and thus speak less to who we are—a point to which we shall return in chapter 4.

In a passage directly following his discussion of suicide, Aquinas argued that self-defense undertaken with the intent, not to kill the aggressor, but to stop the aggression can be a morally upright action. The victim may *know* that the aggressor will die as the (unintended) result of his gunshot or blow, but he or she commits no categorical wrong in acting solely with the intent of stopping an act of aggression:

> Nothing keeps one act from having two effects, one of which is in the scope of the agent's intention while the other falls outside that scope. Now moral ac-

tions are characterized by what is intended, not by what falls outside the scope of intention, for that is only incidental, as I explained previously.

Thus, from the act of defending himself there can be two effects: self-preservation and the killing of the attacker. Therefore, this kind of act does not have the aspect of "wrong" on the basis that one intends to save his own life, because it is only natural to everything to preserve itself in existence as best as it can. . . .

[I]f he repels the attack with measured force, the defense will not be wrong. The law permits force to be repelled with measured force by one who is attacked without offering provocation. It is not necessary to salvation that a man forgo this act of measured self-defense in order to avoid the killing of another. . . .

[But] it is wrong for a man to *intend* to kill another man in order to defend himself.[51]

So, too, Aquinas seems to suggest in the suicide context: the act is harmful to the basic good of human life insofar as it is undertaken rationally and deliberately. But *unintended* self-homicides, resulting, for example, from mental illness, depression, duress, fear, grief, or anger, might fall into a different moral category, and they are not, to Aquinas, always morally wrongful.

Augustine's (and Aquinas's) teachings on suicide influenced subsequent Christian law and practice. By 562, the Council of Braga denied funeral rites to suicides; in 693, the Council of Toledo held that anyone attempting suicide should be excommunicated. In England, the Council of Hertford in 672 denied suicides normal Christian burials; a canon dating from King Edgar's time (c. 1000) reaffirmed this position. Christianity continues to teach against suicide to this day. In 1980, the Vatican issued a Declaration on Euthanasia; Pope John Paul II taught against suicide, including in his encyclicals, "Veritatis Splendor" and "Evangelium Vitae."[52] The American Lutheran Church, the Episcopal Church, and all branches of Judaism likewise teach that suicide is an ethical wrong.[53]

3.5 ENGLISH COMMON LAW

Early Christian history is of particular relevance to our analysis because of its influence on the common law's initial view of suicide. Writing in the mid-thirteenth century, Bracton, one of the common law's earliest authorities,[54] endorsed the Roman statute that held that a felon intentionally taking his life to escape punishment by the state was subject to having both his movable goods and real property confiscated.[55] In defiance of Roman statutes, however, Bracton added that one who deliberately kills himself "in weariness of life or because he is unwilling to endure further bodily pain" should also suffer confiscation of his movable goods, though not his real property.[56] Only suicides induced by insanity—undertaken by persons incapable of appreciating the significance of their actions (and, thus, incapable of forming an intent to kill)—escaped punishment: "that a madman is not liable is true."[57]

Historians Michael MacDonald of the University of Michigan and Terence Murphy of American University have asserted that Bracton included "sheer weariness with life along with the mental defects that excused self-slaying."[58] But this is a questionable reading of the record. Under Bracton's formulation, "sheer weariness" with life *reduced* the penalty for suicide to the confiscation of movable goods rather than all real and personal property, but, quite unlike suicides induced by mental illness, acts of self-destruction by those tired of life were *not* excused.[59]

Though Bracton stated a lesser penalty for suicides undertaken out of weariness with life or abhorrence of pain, all acts of intentional self-destruction were condemned. This is particularly notable given that Bracton otherwise permitted Roman statutes to guide his views of English suicide law. Whether Bracton abandoned Roman precedent in this single respect out of deference to intervening Christian teaching against suicide, or perhaps simply because forfeiture of goods had become a secular custom by the Middle Ages, is at best a matter for speculation.[60]

What is not a matter for speculation is that in this one instance where he forsook Roman guidance, Bracton set the course for the common law. Five centuries later, the penalty associated with suicide had changed slightly (suicides of any kind forfeited only their movable goods), but the principle remained the same: all intentional acts of suicide were treated as wrongful. Hale so held.[61] So did Coke.[62] Blackstone went so far as to decry "the pretended heroism, but real cowardice of the Stoic philosophers, who destroyed themselves to avoid those ills which they had not the fortitude to endure."[63] Meanwhile, five hundred years after Bracton, unintentional acts of self-killing remained no crime. Suicide compelled by mental illness was often cited as the classic example.[64] But Hale also provided an illustration of an unintentional (and therefore excusable) act of self-homicide by a rational and competent person: if one were to cut off a limb to prevent the spread of gangrene but bled to death as an accidental result, that would not, Coke emphasized, constitute suicide at common law.[65]

3.6 Colonial American Experience

Prerevolutionary American suicide law generally followed contemporary English common law and norms. Forfeiture was known in the American colonies in the seventeenth and eighteenth centuries. So was the ancient pagan practice, never formally endorsed in English common law, of dishonoring the suicide's corpse, often by burying it at a crossroads where some speculated the dead person's spirit would be lost and unable to find its way home to haunt others.[66]

Virginia recorded cases of ignominious burial in 1660 and 1661; in the latter instance, the coroner's jury explicitly held that the suicide was "to be buried at the next cross as the Law Requires with a stake driven through the middle of him in his grave."[67] Forfeiture was practiced in the colony as late as 1706 and 1707, though it appears that the colony's governor sometimes interceded to protect the heirs from disinheritance.[68]

In Massachusetts, forfeiture was abandoned as early as 1641,[69] though maltreating the suicide's body apparently retained its appeal for some time. The 1672 compilation of the "General Laws and Liberties" of the Massachusetts colony, for example, intones that "considering how far Satan doth prevail," it is

> therefore order[ed], that from henceforth if any person . . . shall at any time be found by any Jury to . . . be willfully guilty of their own Death . . . [he] shall be Buried in some Common High-way where . . . a Cart-load of Stones [shall be] laid upon the Grave as a Brand of Infamy and as a warning to others to beware of the like Damnable practices.[70]

In 1647 what was to become Rhode Island also passed a statute condemning all intentional suicide and applying traditional common law penalties using only slightly less gloomy rhetoric:

> Self-murder is by all agreed to be the most unnatural . . . wherein that he doth it, kills himself out of a premeditated hatred against his own life or other humor . . . his goods and chattel are the king's custom, but not his debts nor land; but in case he be an infant, a lunatic, mad or distracted man, he forfeits nothing.[71]

South Carolina also appears to have proscribed suicide as early as 1706, instructing coroner juries to return a felony verdict "against the Peace of our Sovereign Lady the Q[u]een, her Crown and Dignity" in cases of suicide.[72] In 1715 North Carolina adopted English common law ("the Laws of England are the Laws of this Government") and, with it, the traditional suicide proscription.[73]

3.7 THE MODERN CONSENSUS ON SUICIDE
AND ITS ASSISTANCE

By the late 1700s and early 1800s, enforcement of the common law's forfeiture penalty became a rare event in England, though somewhat astonishingly formal abolition of the forfeiture penalty did not occur until as late as 1870.[74] The ancient pagan practice of dishonoring the corpse also faded, though it, too, was not formally outlawed until much later. Indeed, it apparently took until the 1823 burial of a suicide at the crossroads of Eaton Street, Grosvenor Place, and King's Road in central London to galvanize Parliament into action.[75]

Like England, eighteenth-century America witnessed a change in attitude regarding the criminal penalties associated with suicide. Pennsylvania led the way in 1701 when it rejected criminal penalties for suicide in its new "Charter of Privileges to the Province and Counties."[76] By the opening of the nineteenth century, New Hampshire, Maryland, Delaware, New Jersey, North Carolina, and Rhode Island followed suit, passing statutory or constitutional provisions repealing criminal laws against suicide.[77]

In Britain, Lord Hoffmann has suggested that the eventual decriminalization of suicide amounted to recognition of a de facto *right* to commit the act: "[I]ts decriminalisation was a recognition that the principle of self-determination should in that case prevail over the sanctity of life."[78] American ethicist Dan Brock has offered a similar reading of the historical record,[79] and so of course did Judge Reinhardt in *Compassion in Dying*.[80]

This reading of the historical record offered by Hoffmann, Brock, and Reinhardt, however, is open to question. To be sure, dragging the suicide's body around town, driving stakes through it, and leaving grieving families penniless had lost whatever appeal they once held in the human imagination, but it is a large leap from that merciful fact to the conclusion that suicide had become normalized at law, let alone a matter of legal right. Indeed, even after repealing penalties for suicide, many states continued to describe it in their case law and statute books as "unlawful and criminal" and "*malum in se.*"[81]

Rather than the result of some new social approval of suicide, the elimination of criminal penalties was more likely the result of an enlightened realization that they did no good and hurt complete innocents. With the "wrong-doer" dead and gone, seizure of his or her worldly goods often worked terrible hardships on the surviving spouse and orphans. Zephaniah Swift, an early American treatise writer and later chief justice of the Connecticut Supreme Court, explained that "[t]here can be no greater cruelty, than the inflicting a punishment, as the forfeiture of goods, which must fall solely on the innocent offspring of the offender."[82] Thomas Jefferson, drafting a bill to reform Virginia laws, wrote that the law should "not add to the miseries of the party by punishments or forfeiture."[83] Viewing the issue through the prism of his revolutionary agenda, Jefferson argued that, while penalties for suicide had been enforced in "barbarous times," with forfeiture the product of a greedy crown acting out of a "spirit of rapine and hostility . . . toward [its] subjects," such penalties were "inconsistent with the principles of moderation and justice which principally endear a republican government to its citizens."[84] The Massachusetts Supreme Judicial Court similarly, though writing in very different political circumstances from Jefferson, explained the decision of that state's legislature to repeal suicide's criminal penalties as one "which may well have had its origin in consideration for the feeling of innocent surviving relatives."[85]

The change in attitude toward criminal penalties was also the result of a growing consensus that suicide often betokened a medical problem. Jefferson recognized suicide early on "as a [d]isease."[86] Study after study in our own time by physicians and psychiatrists suggests that perhaps as many as 90 percent of all suicides may suffer from a diagnosable medical disorder.[87] In its commentary to the Model Penal Code, the American Law Institute has reflected the contemporary view, explaining that "[t]here is scant reason to believe the threat of punishment will have deterrent impact upon one who sets out to take his own life" because such a person "more properly requires medical or psychiatric attention."[88]

Reinforcing the conclusion that the law had come to recognize suicide not as an accepted human right, but generally as an indication of depression requiring medical or psychiatric attention, an exception to traditional battery doctrine evolved, providing both the state and private individuals with a legal privilege to detain persons attempting suicide, including by force if need be.[89] Most American states have now codified such an exception to common law battery doctrine; New York's statute is typical, allowing the civil detention of one "who appears to be mentally ill and is conducting himself in a manner which poses substantial risk of physical harm to himself as manifested by threats or attempts at suicide."[90] Similarly, in California, "any person [who], as a result of a mental disorder, is a danger . . . to himself or herself" can be committed involuntarily to a mental health facility for a period of time.[91]

The Hoffmann-Brock-Reinhardt hypothesis that elimination of suicide's criminal penalties signaled an endorsement or acceptance of the practice is further called into doubt by specific developments in the law of assisted suicide and euthanasia. Originally, the common law drew a distinction between different sorts of suicide assistants: Assistants present at the suicide's death could be held guilty of murder or manslaughter, but those clever enough to slip out while the suicide drank the poison they supplied or used the gun they provided were held innocent of any crime. Under ancient common law doctrine, assistants before the fact to *any* crime could not be tried until the principal criminal actor was convicted; since the suicide was unavailable for prosecution, courts (syllogistically) reasoned that they could not try any accessory before the fact to that particular "crime."[92]

So went the common law in England and most American jurisdictions until 1861 when statutes were enacted abolishing the practical effect of the distinction between accessories before and after the fact.[93] Although this change in the criminal law doctrine of accessory liability was made without any specific reference to assisted suicide, courts on both sides of the Atlantic soon came to conclude that accessories before the fact to suicide could be held liable for murder or manslaughter.[94] Thus, almost one hundred years after the abolition of penalties for suicide itself, common law courts were in the process of *expanding* criminal liability for its assistance.

Glanville Williams has charged that this new development in liability for accessories before the fact is an example "of the purely mechanical manufacture of criminal law, with no reference to penal policy."[95] But applying the same rule to the canny suicide assistant who exited the room at a propitious moment and the unsophisticated assistant who remained actually brought the common law into harmony—eliminating (rather than creating) a mechanical distinction; indeed, for precisely this reason it was hailed at the time by legal scholars as an equitable and enlightened change in penal policy.[96] Williams's complaint thus seems, at bottom, less an attack on the logic of the law's progression than the direction it took.

As statutes came to supplant the common law as the primary vehicle for regulating many human affairs, assisted suicide was codified as a crime in most American jurisdictions. By the time the Fourteenth Amendment was ratified in 1868, nine of the then thirty-seven states had adopted statutes making assisted suicide a crime.[97] The Field Code, a reformist model code that influenced legislative codification efforts in state after state during the nineteenth century, included a widely adopted prohibition against assisted suicide.[98]

3.8 THE EUTHANASIA MOVEMENT

Where did today's movement to legalize assisted suicide come from? How did we get to where we are today? Who are the sorts of people and organizations that have led the charge in so many referenda and legislative initiatives over the last decade or two? And where do they find their roots in American society and culture?

Social Darwinist Roots: 1900–1940

The first push for assisted suicide and euthanasia in America dates to the latter part of the nineteenth century and arose in the wake of Darwin's *On the Origin of Species* and *Descent of Man*. So many readers, both in America and abroad, took away from Darwin's work a keen sense that human society itself is, and should be, shaped by the laws of evolution. These so-called social Darwinists argued that throughout history successful societies and the successful individuals within them were endowed with superior genetic abilities that enabled their success, while unproductive members of society (and unproductive societies) had inherited traits that led to degeneracy.[99] Many feared that America was itself headed toward degeneracy—that social undesirables were reproducing in America in alarming Malthusian numbers and constituted nothing less than a public health crisis.[100] The remedy often touted for such concerns was the sterilization and killing of unfit members of society—with or without their consent.

Nor were such views outside the mainstream of leading intellectual thought at the time. In *Descent of Man*, Darwin himself lamented that civilization's philanthropic impulses to provide asylums, hospitals, charities, and therapeutic medicine obstructed the power of natural selection to weed out the "reckless, degraded, and often vicious members of society" and instead permitted them to "increase at a quicker rate than the provident and generally more virtuous" members of the human race.[101] In 1883 Darwin's cousin, Francis Galton, coined the term eugenics for the social measures society would have to take to control what he and others feared was a growing disparity in population between what he saw as productive members of society and those he regarded as human defectives. Eugenics was, in Galton's terms,

> [T]he science of improving stock, which is by no means confined to questions to judicious mating, but which, especially in the case of man, takes cognizance of all influences that tend in however remote a degree to give the more suitable races or strains of blood a better chance of prevailing over the less suitable than they otherwise would have had.[102]

Perhaps the eugenics movement's most successful initial inroads into American society involved the forced sterilization of the mentally ill. By the 1930s fully forty-one American states had embraced the eugenic program of Galton and other social Darwinists and enacted laws mandating sterilization for the mentally disabled. No less than the U.S. Supreme Court and Oliver Wendell Holmes jumped on board, holding in *Buck v. Bell*[103] in 1924 that these sterilization laws passed constitutional muster. There, the Court confronted Virginia's Eugenical Sterilization Act, which permitted the sterilization of inmates of state institutions who were found to suffer from hereditary insanity or imbecility. Carrie Buck, a teenager, was selected by the state to be the first person sterilized under the new law. Buck already had given birth to one child, and her mother was institutionalized. Even worse for her, officials at her mother's asylum claimed that mother and daughter shared hereditary traits of feeblemindedness and sexual promiscuity.[104] In upholding Virginia's law, Justice Holmes delivered a proclamation that epitomized the eugenic mood of the day: "[I]t is better for all the world, if instead of waiting to execute degenerate offspring for crime, or to let them starve for their imbecility, society can prevent those who are manifestly unfit from continuing their kind. . . . Three generations of imbeciles are enough."[105]

Sterilization, however, was just one aspect of the eugenics movement's agenda. The same rationale and arguments used to defend forced sterilization were also vocally deployed to support euthanasia. In 1931, the Illinois Homeopathic Medical Association defended euthanasia for "imbeciles and sufferers from incurable diseases."[106] Harvard Professor and social Darwinist Earnest Hooton advocated that euthanasia for "the hopelessly diseased and the congenitally deformed and deficient" was necessary if America was ever going to reverse what he saw as its continuing biological decline.[107] Another Harvard professor, William G. Lennox, likewise endorsed euthanasia for society's "unproductive members."[108]

In 1937 Dr. Inez Celia Philbrick sought to introduce a bill in the Nebraska legislature legalizing euthanasia.[109] Besides allowing voluntary euthanasia for adults of sound mind suffering from a fatal illness, the bill also included provisions for killing, without their consent, mental incompetents and minors suffering from incurable or fatal diseases.[110] Though the state legislature never took up the bill, Philbrick saw it as only a watered-down first step, hoping eventually to extend euthanasia generally to mental patients in institutions and the mentally retarded, regardless of their physical condition or lack of consent.[111] Philbrick believed that euthanasia was not only a merciful act; "[i]n its social application the purpose of euthanasia [was] to remove from society living creatures so monstrous, so deficient, so hopelessly insane that continued existence [has] for them no satisfactions and entails a heavy burden on society."[112] She argued that a comprehensive euthanasia bill ought to be absolutely mandatory "in the case of idiots . . . monstrosities, the insane, suffering from certain types of insanity . . . [and] the criminal insane should always be put to death humanely."[113]

The Euthanasia Society of America (ESA) was founded a year later, in 1938, and included among its founders and leaders an array of eugenics scholars and polemicists like Philbrick. Charles Francis Potter, the moving force behind ESA, advocated "legalized, safeguarded, and [state-]supervised" mercy killing for suffering patients in the final stages of life.[114] But he also expressly saw euthanasia as a social tool for culling disabled infants, the incurably insane, and the mentally retarded.[115] Potter proposed that the mentally disabled be "mercifully executed by [the] lethal chamber" and derided the "social cowardice that keeps [the unfit] alive."[116]

ESA's early board of directors included a number of eugenicists, such as Potter; Clarence Cook Little, president of the University of Michigan and the American Society for the Control of Cancer; Robert Latou Dickinson, gynecologist and birth control advocate; Oscar Riddle, researcher at the Carnegie Station of Experimental Evolution; Frank K. Hankins, sociologist at Clark University and Smith College; and Stephen Visner of Indiana University.[117] So did ESA's members and supporters. Clarence Darrow of Scopes Monkey fame proclaimed, "Chloroform unfit children. Show them the same mercy that is shown beasts that are no longer fit to live."[118] Novelist Sherwood Anderson and physician Abraham Wolbarst, two future members of the Euthanasia Society of America, openly argued that society had a duty to kill those with defects because they unnecessarily drained community resources.[119] Madison Grant, a New York attorney and Yale Law graduate who also served as a trustee of the American Museum of Natural History and cofounded the American Eugenics Society, proclaimed that "[t]he laws of nature require the obliteration of the unfit and [a] human is valuable only when it is of use to the community or race."[120]

And William J. Robinson recognized euthanasia as simply evolution in action. Using language that is, as we shall see, strikingly similar to that used by many in the present-day right-to-die movement, Robinson explained that "life is sacred when it is pleasant, when it is wanted, when it is bearable. But a life of pain, agony, and anguish is not sacred, no more than a life of crime, shame, disgrace, and humiliation."[121] Robinson saw killing as an appropriate response to all of these problems, without differentiation. In 1939 Ann Mitchell, with Potter an ESA cofounder, welcomed the advent of World War II as a "biological house cleaning."[122] She counseled "euthanasia as a war measure, including euthanasia for the insane, feeble-minded monstrosities."[123] Wyllistine Goodsell, Columbia professor and member of ESA, opined, "There are certain children born congenital idiots and of course I don't think we should keep them alive at all."[124]

Despite their eugenic ambitions, Goodsell and others on the ESA board of directors counseled moderation as the ESA board drafted its first model euthanasia bill.[125] The bill, which would have authorized only acts of voluntary euthanasia, was, according to Potter's private statements, quite self-consciously meant to be the thin edge of the wedge to nonvoluntary euthanasia. As Potter put it, "the immediate objective [was to get a [euthanasia] bill passed as an entering wedge," and "later on we want[ed] to include certain types of insanity" in the bill.[126] Curiously, Potter's successor as president of ESA, Foster Kennedy, expressly called for nonvoluntary euthanasia of what he called "nature's mistakes" in 1939 yet declined to support voluntary euthanasia for the terminally ill because he found that the medical community often misdiagnosed illnesses as incurable.[127]

Backlash: World War II–1960

Whatever the strength of the American euthanasia movement was before the Second World War—and many think it was strong indeed, perhaps on the brink of winning major legislative victories[128]—World War II sapped it of much of its strength. As news dribbled in about Nazi euthanasia practices—practices that included the killing of 200,000 disabled and elderly persons—the American public recoiled. Though euthanasia opponents have sometimes misused the Nazi experience in their arguments, Ian Dowbiggin of the University of Prince Edward Island submits that, "some euthanasia supporters have been equally guilty in denying any comparisons between themselves and the Nazis."[129] In fact, Adolph Hitler wrote to American Madison Grant praising Grant's *Passing of the Great Race*, a eugenic tract, as "his Bible."[130] Crediting American eugenic experiments, Hitler acknowledged:

> [now that] we know of the laws of heredity it is possible to a large extent to prevent unhealthy and severely handicapped beings from coming into the world. I have studied with interest the laws of several American states con-

cerning prevention of reproduction by people whose progeny would, in all probability, be of no value or be injurious to the racial stock.[131]

The intellectual climate in Germany in which Hitler offered these views was not altogether different from the atmosphere in which ESA leaders operated in America. As early as 1920, well before Hitler's ascendancy, Alfred Hoche, a professor of psychiatry, and Karl Binding, a professor of law, published *Permitting the Destruction of Unworthy Life*, arguing, like their social Darwinist counterparts in America, not only that individuals have a right to choose assisted suicide or euthanasia freely, but that nonvoluntary euthanasia of the mentally defective is also necessary, justified by the fact that these individuals are "not just absolutely worthless, but [are] even of negative value," and thus, "eliminating those who are completely mentally dead is no crime, no immoral act, no emotional cruelty, but is rather a permissible and useful act."[132] Upon their ascendance to power in 1933, the Nazis enacted a eugenic campaign that assiduously tracked Hoche and Binding's recommendations. Recalling *Buck*, the Nazis effected the sexual sterilization of 400,000 state wards.[133] By 1939, with half of Germany's physicians joining the Nazi Party, German psychiatrists and their staff at these state institutions were expressly instructed to accept the killing of patients as beneficial to the interests of the state,[134] and, in October 1939, Hitler began a deliberate and secret campaign aimed at the eradication of asylum patients.[135] When the covert operation came to light within Germany in 1941, the Nazis were forced to terminate the program formally, though doing so only led to a chaotic and disorganized approach to the continued practice of euthanasia,[136] and the killing did not stop until after the war.[137]

As the sobering truths about Nazi practices emerged, they served to slow the momentum of the pro-euthanasia movement that had been building since the turn of the century in America. Americans increasingly drew connections between medical killing in the Third Reich and the euthanasia movement in the United States, and they judged Germany harshly for how it treated the most vulnerable of its members of society. The Nuremberg trials showcased Nazi euthanasia practices for the American public. Dr. Leo Alexander, chief U.S. medical consultant at the trials, noted in a 1949 article in the *New England Journal of Medicine* that the Nazi euthanasia program "was merely the entering wedge for exterminations [of] far greater scope in the political program for genocide of conquered nations and the racially unwanted."[138] He analogized the Nazi experience to contemporary American debate and warned the American medical community of a creeping trend to marginalize the terminally and chronically ill patient lest the

> killing center [become] the reductio ad absurdum of all health planning based on rational principles and economy. . . . Physicians have become dangerously close to being mere technicians of rehabilitation. This essentially Hegelian rational attitude has led them to make certain distinctions in the handling of

acute and chronic diseases. The patient with the latter carries an obvious stigma as the one less likely to be fully rehabilitable for social usefulness. In an increasingly utilitarian society these patients are being looked down upon with increasing definiteness as unwanted ballast.[139]

Such revelations and warnings seemed to have had an effect on American attitudes toward euthanasia. Prior to World War II, a 1939 poll indicated that perhaps as many as 46 percent of Americans were in favor of some form of legal euthanasia.[140] Approval of legalized euthanasia dropped to 35 percent by 1950.[141] Nevertheless, even as news reached America of Nazi practices, ESA empaneled a committee in 1943 to draft a bill legalizing nonvoluntary euthanasia for so-called idiots, imbeciles, and congenital monstrosities. Possibly in an effort to shield their own agenda, some ESA members sought to downplay the Nazi atrocities.[142] C. Killick Millard, secretary of the British Voluntary Euthanasia Legislation Society, believed that those killed in Poland were not actually murdered by the Nazis but rather chose suicide.[143] While Ann Mitchell publicly deplored the Nazis and Hitler, she agreed with many of their results. Noting that Nazi doctors killed mentally disabled Polish children, Mitchell equivocated, "of course this is a great blessing but it is too bad that it had to come about in just this way."[144] Mitchell privately assured Millard that she hoped the war would usher in a new biological age, revolutionizing thinking so that mass sterilization and euthanasia would become acceptable.[145]

The Contemporary Euthanasia Movement

While the euthanasia movement suffered a profound setback in the realm of public opinion in the aftermath of World War II, the tide was to shift again, albeit slowly, in the 1960s and 1970s. Skepticism of traditional authority, the rise of the legal right to privacy in the form of birth control and abortion rulings, and the feminist movement all led to renewed debate over the appropriate balance between collective and individual rights. Increasingly, the notion that self-regarding acts are "harmless" and that others have no right to impose their moral views in such situations took hold. At the same time, the influence of religion began to decline in much of the Western world. Euthanasia advocates sought to take advantage of this changing cultural climate and began to argue their position less in terms of social or biological progression, as they had done previously, and more in terms of individual autonomy and privacy. This change in ideological and rhetorical terms coincided to some degree with advances in modern medical care that began to allow doctors to delay death in some cases much longer than previously thought possible, though often only through highly intrusive techniques, and often only on terms that many would consider unduly burdensome. Euthanasia movement activists sought to tap into an increasing fear of a new form of death—one associated with prolonged periods of being hooked up to medical machinery in a weakened and virtually comatose state.

The newly reinvigorated euthanasia movement began, as we saw in chapter 1, an ambitious, multistate legislative and litigation campaign. As we saw in chapter 2, moreover, in this campaign activists have expressly sought to tap into the language in *Casey* and other Supreme Court decisions, stressing that the right they seek to establish is central to self-definition and privacy. In order to stress that a self-regarding right is at stake, they have tailored their efforts, at least in the first instance, to physician assisted suicide rather than also (expressly) advocate voluntary or nonvoluntary euthanasia. Yet, even amid the changing cultural climate, strains from the early euthanasia movement have never completely disappeared, and arguments for assisted suicide and euthanasia stressing a fear of rising medical costs, the burden of the elderly on society, and the legitimacy of eliminating unwanted infants continue to be sounded by movement leaders.

Cambridge Law Professor Glanville Williams, a leading intellectual defender of voluntary euthanasia and a member of ESA, openly favored eugenic sterilization and advocated euthanasia not only in cases of "incapacitating but non-painful affliction, such as paralysis," but also in cases of dementia and "hopelessly defective infants."[146] As long as there is parental consent, Williams also argued that no ethical impediments exist to killing deformed infants on eugenic grounds.[147]

Joseph Fletcher, father of situational ethics, an Episcopal priest, and author of *Morals and Medicine* (1979), spent much of the 1960s, 1970s, and 1980s arguing for a return to the movement's "original task as the [ESA] perceived it."[148] Fletcher called upon the euthanasia movement not only to press for assisted suicide and voluntary euthanasia, but also to advocate euthanasia for "helpless newborns or minors still too young to make any input into decisions about when to stop life-prolonging treatment."[149]

Like earlier ESA members, Olive Ruth Russell, psychologist and author of *Freedom to Die: Moral and Legal Aspects of Euthanasia* (1975), sought to extend legal euthanasia to infants with birth defects.[150] Hearkening back to the Malthusian concerns of the social Darwinists, Russell viewed euthanasia as a means of combating the "surging rise in the number of physically and mentally crippled children."[151] Fearing this same population "time bomb," Hugh Moore, who had made millions selling dispensable paper "Dixie Cups," left ESA's nonprofit wing over a million dollars of his estate.[152] ESA advocate and psychiatrist Florence Clothier argued that in the short term activists should advocate only voluntary passive euthanasia. But when that "becomes legal and generally accepted it [would be] time to begin a public educational program" promoting active voluntary and involuntary euthanasia.[153] For infants in a permanent vegetative state, she did not even think it necessary or appropriate to consult with the child's parents, believing that it was much better for the psyche of the parents to believe that the baby was stillborn or died soon after birth.[154] For infants with lesser handicaps, such as Down's syndrome, severe cerebral palsy, and extreme physical deformities, Clothier suggested that parents should be informed only as far as needed to make "a humane and wise decision."[155]

By 1980 ESA had devolved into a number of splinter groups that have themselves variously splintered and merged over the last quarter century. Among the leaders of the movement today, Derek Humphry, who organized the Hemlock Society in Los Angeles in 1980, certainly has to count as one of the most influential figures—and perhaps one of the most controversial even within the euthanasia movement. In 1989 Humphry left his second wife, Ann Wickett, soon after she had undergone surgery for breast cancer. During the divorce, Wickett alleged that, when Humphry purported to help her mother commit suicide, the resulting death was not fully consensual. Later, Wickett herself committed suicide, even though her cancer was in remission. Her suicide note stated to Humphry, "There, You got what you wanted. Ever since I was diagnosed as having cancer, you have done everything conceivable to precipitate my death." She sent a copy of the note to an anti-euthanasia activist, writing, "My final words to Derek: He is a killer. I know." Her note then proceeded to accuse Humphry of suffocating his first wife.[156]

Although he formally resigned from the Hemlock Society in 1992, Derek Humphry remains a leading public advocate of euthanasia. And while careful to present his message in terms of personal autonomy and the right of individuals to choose death, more than occasionally Humphry has suggested not merely a right to die, but something more akin to a duty to do so. In 2000 he candidly acknowledged that money is an "unspoken argument" in favor of his position: "the hastened demise of people with only a short time to [live] would free resources for others," an amount Humphry estimates could run into the "hundreds of billions of dollars."[157] Former Colorado Governor Richard Lamm has likewise argued publicly that the elderly have a duty to die in order to free up social resources for the young.[158]

Even among those who are most associated with arguments from autonomy and choice, the right to die sometimes appears to morph into a duty to do so. While advocating for voluntary euthanasia, Ronald Dworkin discusses a hypothetical illustration involving an elderly woman suffering from Alzheimer's. Earlier, while still competent, the woman in Dworkin's hypothetical expressed a firm desire to be killed when dementia set in. But now, after dementia has set it, she seems to enjoy life and says she wishes to live. Dworkin asks which request we should respect (and enforce): the earlier, rational request, or the woman's present choice affected by dementia? Dworkin's response is that

> [w]e might consider it morally unforgivable not to try to save the life of someone who plainly enjoys her life, no matter how demented she is, and we might think it beyond imagining that we should actually kill her. We might hate living in a community whose officials might make or license [such a] decision[].

> We might have other good reasons for treating [her] as she now wishes, rather than, as, in my imaginary case, she once asked. *But still, that violates rather than respects her autonomy.*[159]

Though he stops short of saying so expressly, respect for autonomy seems, on Dworkin's account, to go so far as to require society to ignore the plea for life of the demented aged person in favor of some previously signed document or comment that he or she would rather die than become demented.

Others closely associated with the theory of moral autonomy and its message of individualism have sounded remarkably similar themes. In assessing the rights of those suffering severely from Alzheimer's, Dan Brock argues that they "approach more closely the condition of animals" and therefore "lack personhood."[160] He suggests "assimilating . . . into the category of voluntary euthanasia" cases where the patient is incapable of consent but there exists convincing evidence supporting the supposition that a patient in his or her shoes would, if able, express a wish to be killed—that is, effectively endorsing a form of nonvoluntary euthanasia.[161] Margaret Battin, who generally supports a right to assisted suicide on mercy and autonomy grounds, also argues that principles of distributive justice require legalization of nonvoluntary euthanasia for those who do not have a "realistic desire" for continued care.[162] To Battin, it is an act of injustice to allow certain persons to live if they fail to enjoy a certain quality of life; nor is it sufficient in such cases to discontinue life-sustaining care: we may and must outright kill these people. This includes, in Battin's formulation, all persons who are "permanently comatose, decerebrate, profoundly brain damaged, and others who lack cognitive function."[163] It remains unclear just *how* brain damaged or mentally handicapped one must be to qualify for nonvoluntary euthanasia under Battin's formulation, or *what* society should and should not consider a "realistic desire" for continued care in such cases. But Battin does make clear that, for the individuals who fall within her formulation, it means killing them *even if* they left advance directives expressing a different preference: "since such patients cannot want it, they are not entitled to life-prolonging care."[164]

Norman Cantor similarly concedes that, once voluntary euthanasia is allowed, as he believes it should be, the impetus toward nonvoluntary euthanasia for incompetent patients "would be overwhelming."[165] Cantor argues that this is a good thing because

> [w]hen a dying, incompetent patient has reached a point of deterioration that would prompt most competent patients to seek PAD [physician-assisted suicide], the impulse to extend similar "relief" to incompetent patients seems irresistible. This is especially true for a formerly competent patient who previously stated that she did not want to live in such a debilitated status, but it is also true for now-suffering patients who have never been competent to express their own preferences. Infants born with multiple deficits who are destined to live a short but painful existence provide one example.[166]

Cantor's examples are, of course, just that, and the ones he picks emphasize more or less sympathetic cases. In the end, however, Cantor appears to endorse a "default presumption" that nonvoluntary euthanasia is acceptable so long as it is indicated by "common preferences about intolerable levels of indignity."[167] It is not clear, however, what "majority sentiment"[168] might be about whether life is or is not undignified in a great many cases. What about the Alzheimer's patient Dworkin and Battin discuss who left an order to kill her but now wishes to live? The mentally ill individual who suffers grave psychological, but not physical, pain? Infants born with highly debilitating mental or physical deficits but who are not in danger of immediate death? The comatose person who is suffering no pain and left behind no living will? Those with Down's syndrome? Spina bifida? Cerebral palsy? Quadriplegics? The victims of severe strokes? All would appear possible candidates for being killed without consent—so long as some poll or other form of evidence about popular opinion indicates that a sufficient number of people (none of whom share the same deficiencies as those they are judging) are of the view that such lives aren't worth living. And would killing merely be a matter of choice for some surrogate decision maker in such cases—or wouldn't it perhaps become a *duty* incumbent on doctors given the consensus that keeping a patient alive in such circumstances would impose an "intolerable level of indignity"?

Peter Singer is the Ira W. DeCamp Professor of Bioethics at Princeton's Center for Human Values. While we will explore Singer's arguments in depth in chapter 9, for now it suffices to mention that in *Practical Ethics* (2d ed. 1993) and *Rethinking Life and Death* (1994), Singer picks up on Brock's and Battin's suggestion that the inability to express a realistic desire to live is something akin to accepting a duty to die, dismissing infants' claims to personhood because they, too, are incapable of forming a preference for living.[169] On Singer's account, because infants are not self-aware, it is a morally neutral or even a morally upright act to kill them, depending on the circumstances and whether the killing would maximize overall social welfare and happiness.[170] In the circumstances of children with birth defects such as Down's syndrome, Singer asserts the case for infanticide is particularly clear because of the "devastating" effects that raising such a child can have on parents;[171] killing Down's syndrome infants provides parents with a "fresh start."[172] And echoing the same Malthusian fears that animated the early euthanasia movement, in contesting what he terms the "Fourth Old Commandment [to] Be Fruitful and Multiply," Singer asserts "it is unethical to encourage more births" due to projected environmental catastrophes.[173] Although he frames the overpopulation issue in terms of abortion and birth control, Singer hints that Western culture should view infanticide in the same light "especially now that we . . . are in a situation where we must limit family size."[174]

As we shall see in chapter 7, many in the United States and the Netherlands tout the Dutch experiment with euthanasia as a premier example of liberal individualism at work, allowing patients to choose their own destinies and forms of death. Yet, nonvoluntary euthanasia for incompetent adults is already pervasive in the Dutch regime (as Cantor admits[175]), and some Dutch scholars seek formal recognition of the practice; Dutch physicians are also currently contemplating legalizing infanticide for certain children.[176]

Though a variety leading euthanasia activists since the 1960s—leaders like Russell, Moore, Williams, Fletcher, Humphry, Dworkin, Battin, Brock, Cantor, and Singer, as well as the Dutch government and its supporters—have presented arguments well adapted to their times, reflecting the increasing impulse for individualism and autonomy in our society and emphasizing the very real burdens associated with modern medical care, it is hard to disagree with Dowbiggen's conclusion that "though they may not know it, today's defenders of the right to die often echo the justifications of euthanasia first uttered" by early movement leaders.[177] Their commitment to individual autonomy and the relief of suffering, born out of the individualistic impulses of the 1960s and 1970s, seems to extend important rights to individuals in a world where medicine has taken on the power to extend life so long but sometimes only on terms that are invasive and burdensome. Yet, many of the policies they proffer would embrace not just a right to die, but a duty of certain persons to do so—and do so in some cases regardless of whether they consent—suggesting that, far from being a simple story of pushing for greater individual liberty, the history of the euthanasia movement in America remains what Dowbiggen calls "a gravely complex social, political, economic, and cultural matter."[178]

3.9 PREVAILING LAW TODAY

Today, it remains unclear whether Oregon's experiment with assisted suicide is a harbinger of the future or even perhaps the thin edge of the wedge that Potter and other euthanasia advocates have so long sought, or whether it represents a novelty unlikely to be widely emulated in many other American jurisdictions.

Current state laws against assisted suicide and euthanasia date back a century or more, in some cases to the Field Code. Yet, in recent years many jurisdictions have reconsidered and expressly reaffirmed them. In 1980 the American Law Institute conducted a thorough review of state laws on assisted suicide, acknowledged the continuing widespread support for criminalization,[179] and endorsed two criminal provisions of its own.[180] In the 1990s both New York and Michigan convened commissions to reconsider assisted suicide and euthanasia. The New York commission issued a report unanimously recommending that existing laws against the practices be retained.[181] While the Michigan panel was unable to achieve unanimity, the state legislature subsequently chose to enact a statute banning the practice, and its courts have confirmed that it violates the state's common law. Maryland has also recently passed a statute for the first time codifying that state's common law teachings against assisted suicide.[182] Iowa, Oklahoma, and Virginia also have strengthened their laws against the practice in recent years.[183]

Beyond that, since 1994, over fifty bills have been introduced to legalize assisted suicide or euthanasia in at least nineteen states. Remarkably, all have failed—so far.[184] During the same period, voters also rejected Oregon-styled assisted suicide initiatives in Maine and Michigan.[185] In all, the vast majority of states (approximately thirty-eight) have expressly chosen to retain or have enacted statutes in recent years banning the practice of assisted suicide.[186]

With regard to those few states without statutes formally prohibiting assisted suicide, most have disapproved of assisted suicide in some other way. As noted above, Michigan enacted a statute banning assisted suicide that may or may not have lapsed,[187] but, in any event, the state recently confirmed that it considers assisted suicide to be a common law crime.[188] Montana treats assisting a failed suicide as an independent statutory crime[189] but appears to classify assisting a successful suicide as a species of homicide and thus subject to the general homicide statute.[190] Of the remaining states, some appear to treat assisted suicide as a common law crime,[191] and several have health care directive statutes expressly disavowing any approval of assisted suicide.[192] In fact, in recent years, virtually every state in the country has passed statutes establishing living wills or durable powers of attorney in health-care situations, and a great many of these laws contain language stating that the statute is not designed and may not be used to encourage or facilitate suicide or its assistance.[193] At the federal level, a Republican Congress and Democratic president adopted a law in 1997 denying the use of federal funds in connection with any act of assisted suicide.[194]

The law of euthanasia runs an even straighter course than the law of assisted suicide. Consensual euthanasia is a form of intentional homicide—albeit motivated by a sense of mercy and sometimes performed with the consent of the deceased. At common law and by statute, it has been treated as murder.[195] Courts have refused to treat the victim's consent or the killer's motive as a defense or a reason to accede to defendants' requests for a jury instruction on assisted suicide as a lesser included offense,[196] though they have sometimes treated both the victim's consent and the killer's motives as reasons to mitigate the defendant's punishment.[197]

While the proscription of assisted suicide and euthanasia has been virtually absolute in America, a notable exception existed for a short time. In 1902 the Texas Court of Criminal Appeals in *Grace v. State* reasoned, much along the same lines as Hoffmann, Brock, and Reinhardt, that, because suicide and its attempt were no longer crimes, assisting a suicide should not be illegal either: "So far as the law is concerned, the suicide is innocent; therefore the party who furnishes the means to the suicide must also be innocent of violating the law."[198]

Grace is logically unsound. The rationales for decriminalizing suicide—fairness to the suicide's innocent family and recognition of the medical causes of suicide—do not apply to assisted suicide: the penalty for assisted suicide falls on the actor himself or herself, not on his or her family, and there is no reason to presume the suicide assistant to be suffering from any form of mental illness. Moreover, if *Grace* were right, euthanasia and consensual homicide would have to be decriminalized as well—if one who hands a gun to the suicide commits no crime, surely one who pulls the trigger at the suicide's request must not either. Texas courts, however, were unwilling to follow *Grace* to that logical conclusion and instead continued to hold euthanasia illegal.[199] The Texas state legislature subsequently removed any question by adopting a statute criminalizing the assistance of suicide, thus effectively overruling *Grace*.[200]

Recent British experience to some extent parallels the American experience. In 1969, and then again in 1988, the British Medical Association studied the euthanasia issue and issued reports expressing the view that euthanasia should remain unlawful.[201] In 1993–1994, the House of Lords commissioned a select committee to review provisions of Britain's 1961 Suicide Act prohibiting assisted suicide;[202] after lengthy hearings where ethicists, physicians, and legal philosophers were heard, that panel, too, opted in favor of retaining existing law.[203] In 1999 the Council of Europe likewise issued a report on the terminally ill and dying and recommended the retention of laws against intentionally taking the life of the terminally ill, concluding "that a terminally ill or dying person's wish to die never constitutes any legal claim to die at the hand of another person."[204]

In November 2001 a panel of the House of Lords, sitting as England's final court of appeal, heard the case of *Regina (Pretty) v. Director of Public Prosecutions*. The Lords there rejected, by a vote of 5–0, the notion that the European Convention for the Protection of Human Rights and Fundamental Freedoms trumps Britain's 1961 statute and ensconces a right to assisted suicide in European law.[205] The petitioner argued, among other things, that the putative right to assisted suicide flows from Article 2 of the Convention, which, perhaps somewhat surprisingly, protects the right to life. While the Lords acknowledged that this provision was enacted in order to preserve not just life itself but also the full dignity of human life, they held that "an article with that effect cannot be interpreted as conferring a right to die or to enlist the aid of another in bringing about one's own death."[206]

Turning to the petitioner's argument under Article 8 of the European Convention, a provision that protects a right to privacy, the Lords agreed that a nontrivial privacy/autonomy interest was at stake in the proffered right to assisted suicide, but they held that it is "for member states" of the European Convention to balance that interest against "the risk and likely incidence of abuse if the prohibition on assisted suicide were relaxed."[207] The Lords noted that a select committee had considered the assisted suicide question in 1993–1994 and concluded that a blanket prohibition against the practice was justified precisely because of the possibility that "vulnerable people—the elderly, lonely, sick or distressed—would feel pressure, real or imagined, to request early death . . . [and] the message which society sends to vulnerable and disadvantaged people should not, however obliquely, encourage them to seek death, but should assure them of our care and support in life."[208] Finally, the Lords considered the argument that it is discriminatory, and thus a violation of Article 14's guarantee of equal treatment under law, to permit the able-bodied the right to commit suicide while denying those stricken with physical maladies the right to seek needed assistance in their self-destruction. The Lords rejected this argument, too, holding, as I have suggested above, that this argument is "based on a misconception": suicide was decriminalized not because it came to be considered a legal right, but "because it cast an unwarranted stigma on innocent members of the suicide's family."[209] The European Court of Human Rights affirmed the Lords' result on April 29, 2002.[210] In the last several years, a number of other countries, including England,[211] Canada,[212] Australia,[213] New Zealand,[214] and Hungary,[215] also have considered and (so far) rejected proposals to overturn their laws banning assisted suicide.

3.10 CONCLUSION

The history test, originally conceived of as a means of providing objective guidance in substantive due process disputes, somewhat ironically relies on the views of legislative majorities (past ones, at that) to interpret a provision adopted to protect and advance minority rights. And, rather than providing a reliably objective means of resolving substantive due process disputes, the history test is itself the subject of considerable methodological disputes. Mindful of such difficulties, but seeking to apply the history test faithfully, we examined the historical record broadly in terms of time and at different levels of abstraction. We found that ancient suicide practices do lend some support for the normalization of assisted suicide and euthanasia, but that such support is both limited and suggestive not so much of a right to seek out death in response to illness or pain as a right far broader than that, one perhaps extending to some arguably bizarre practices.

As we have seen, some have fastened on the eventual abandonment of criminal penalties for suicide in American and English common law as suggestive of a right to assisted suicide and euthanasia. But this reading of the historical record of suicide is questionable: it appears that the abandonment of criminal penalties for suicide betokened less any social or legal endorsement of the practice than a growing consensus that suicide is essentially a medical problem.

This interpretation is confirmed by the advent of a legal privilege to detain those who attempt suicide; by recently enacted living will statutes that disapprove of suicide and its assistance; and by an examination of the more specific practices of assisted suicide and euthanasia, both of which have generally remained unlawful throughout the history of Anglo-American law and recently reconsidered and reendorsed in many jurisdictions.

4

Arguments from Fairness and
Equal Protection: If a Right to Refuse,
Then *a Right to Assisted Suicide?*

OVER the last thirty years, virtually every American jurisdiction has come to recognize a right to refuse medical treatment grounded in common law principles that bar nonconsensual touchings and require informed consent before the administration of medical treatment.[1] Debate persists over many aspects of this new right, however, including, not insignificantly, whether and how to extend the right to incompetent persons. Increasingly, "living wills" and "advance directives" are used to instruct family members and physicians on a patient's wishes in the event he or she becomes incompetent. But what about infants or adults who have never been competent, or persons who become incompetent but leave behind no instructions? Some states have tried to extend the right to refuse treatment to these persons by "substituting the judgment" of a competent, court-designated person for the judgment of the incompetent patient.[2] Others have developed a "best interest test," whereby courts themselves purport to decide what is in the incompetent's best interests.[3] Both of these doctrines seek to give meaning to a right ordinarily dependent on choice to patients incapable of choosing—and to do so through an agent never selected by the patient.

I will return to some of the central questions raised by patient refusals of care later, in chapter 10. For now, the essential point is that, since the first right-to-refuse case was decided by the New Jersey Supreme Court in 1976,[4] virtually every state in the nation has recognized a right, belonging at least to competent adults, to refuse basic, life-sustaining medical care, including tubes supplying food and water. Given the widespread acceptance of such a right, the question naturally follows whether a right to assistance in suicide and euthanasia must also be accepted. If patients have a right to tell their doctors to remove respirators or feeding tubes, in fairness should they also have a right to tell their physicians to administer lethal injections?

The Second Circuit answered this fairness or equal protection question in the affirmative. So did the federal district court in the Washington State litigation. To be sure, the Supreme Court disagreed, but only in the face of serious questions raised by Justice Stevens and only in the context of a facial challenge; there has been no definitive majority ruling on whether a right to euthanasia and assistance in suicide exists *as applied* to rational, terminally ill patients. And Justice O'Connor, who provided the critical fifth vote, left ample room for us to speculate that the Court might find equal protection arguments more availing in such a case. A number of moral philosophers, too, argue that there is simply no coherent way to defend both laws banning active euthanasia and those that permit patients to refuse or withdraw life-sustaining treatment.[5]

In what follows, I identify three potential bases for distinguishing between the right to refuse, on the one hand, and the proffered right to assistance in suicide or euthanasia, on the other. Various courts have found two of these potential distinctions—based on the act/omission distinction and causation—persuasive grounds for distinguishing between the practices and, thus, upholding laws banning assisted suicide and euthanasia. Upon further examination, however, I find that it is easy to overstate the strength of these distinctions.

I then turn to consider the third potential distinction suggested by the U.S. Supreme Court's decision in *Quill*—based on intent. Unlike the causation and act/omission distinctions, I suggest that an intent-based distinction may work sufficiently well to withstand a constitutional equal protection challenge. Assisted suicide and euthanasia differ from the right to refuse in that they necessarily entail an intent to kill and, with it, the judgment that a patient's life is no longer worth living. Such an intention *may* be present in a decision to refuse treatment, but, I suggest, it need not be. Though this distinction is a limited one, I suggest that it cannot be dismissed as irrational or devoid of moral force.

4.1 An Act/Omission Distinction?

The New York trial court in *Quill* distinguished between assisted suicide and the refusal of medical care on the ground that the former involves an affirmative act while the latter amounts only to an omission. The Second Circuit rejected this distinction, reasoning that the writing of an assisted suicide prescription can involve far less "action" than turning off a ventilator or a feeding tube.[6] The Supreme Court never addressed the act/omission distinction, leaving us to speculate on the reason for its silence: Did it agree with the Second Circuit? Or did the Court simply conclude that there was no reason to reach the issue, having drawn causation—and intent-based distinctions between assisted suicide and refusing care?

There is certainly a case to be made for the act/omission distinction. It is deeply entrenched and regularly employed in American law, and, in a world where medicine has the power to delay death for so long, we do not generally think of the decision to omit such care to be a traditional act of assisted suicide or killing. Ordinarily, the removal or omission of care after it has become unduly burdensome and offers little prospect of improvement is an act of letting the patient die, a recognition that death is inevitable, rather than expressive of any wish to see the patient dead. The act/omission distinction, thus, seems to comport generally with our instincts about the difference between assisted suicide and the right to refuse care.

Still, the act/omission distinction is readily manipulable. Refusing to eat can be cast either as omitting food or actively starving oneself. Removing tubes that supply life-sustaining food and water can be painted as actively pulling the plug or omitting the provision of medical care. As Justice Scalia has asked, why would we "say that one may not kill oneself by walking into the sea, but may sit on the beach until submerged by the incoming tide; or that one may not intentionally lock oneself into a cold storage locker, but may refrain from coming indoors when the temperature drops below freezing?"[7]

The case of Tony Bland illustrates some of the problems Justice Scalia hints at. Tony Bland was a British teenager who was crushed while standing in the spectators' pen at an English soccer match. His injuries left him in a so-called vegetative state. That is, he was not dying of his underlying maladies but depended upon tubes to supply him with food and water so that he could live in a comatose condition. Tony's doctors eventually sought to discontinue this care, and the case worked its way to the House of Lords, for the first time raising the right-to-refuse issue in Britain's highest court. The official solicitor charged with representing Tony argued against removing his feeding tubes on the ground that to do so would amount to the intentional taking of human life and therefore constitute an unlawful act of homicide. A majority of the Lords accepted the submission that the doctors intended to kill Bland.[8] Seeking nonetheless to avoid the unwelcome conclusion that Tony's death would be unlawful, the Lords sought to cast the cessation of care as an omission rather than an active step. Declining treatment would, the Lords reasoned, merely be permitting nature to take its course and, thus, not an act of murder. As Lord Goff put it,

> the law draws a crucial distinction between cases in which a doctor decides not to . . . prolong life, and those in which he decides . . . actively to bring his patient's life to an end. . . . As I have already indicated, the former may be lawful. . . . But it is not lawful for a doctor to administer a drug to his patient to bring about his death, even though that course is prompted by a humanitarian desire to end his suffering. . . . So to act is to cross the Rubicon which runs between on the one hand the care of the living and on the other hand euthanasia—actively causing his death to avoid or to end his suffering. Euthanasia is not lawful at common law.[9]

The Lords thus placed enormous weight on the act/omission distinction, seemingly going so far as to suggest that it represents a moral/legal Rubi-

con between legitimate medical treatment and unlawful homicide. Yet, the Lords
failed to offer any convincing reason for choosing to classify the *removal* of
Tony's tubes as an omission of care, rather than an active step. In fact, the Lords
themselves repeatedly questioned their own classification. Lord Browne-
Wilkinson, for example, candidly admitted that "[t]he positive act of removing
the nasogastric tube presents more difficulty. It is undoubtedly a positive act."[10]
Lord Goff conceded that "it may be difficult to describe what the doctor actually does as an omission, for example where he takes some positive step to bring
the life support to an end."[11] And Lord Mustill expressed "acute unease" about
resting the Lords' decision on the "morally and intellectually dubious distinction between acts and omissions," given, as he put it, that "however much the
terminologies may differ[,] the ethical status of the two courses of action is for
all relevant purposes indistinguishable."[12]

Of equal importance, the Lords did little to explain why omissions of
care cannot sometimes, at least where an intention to kill is present (as they expressly acknowledged it was in the case before them), also qualify as acts of murder. While the removal or omission of modern medical treatment *ordinarily*
seems a very different thing from assisting suicide or euthanasia, is this always
the case? What about parents who intentionally withhold or "omit" food and
water from an unwanted infant? Or the doctor or nurse who withholds effica-
cious, life-sustaining medical care because he or she considers the patient to be
effectively a nonperson (like, say, Singer or Battin)? Or the doctor who goes
around pulling respirators for kicks (such as mass murderer Dr. Harold Shipman[13])? Parents and doctors who withhold life-sustaining care that offers the
patient significant benefits and few burdens are ordinarily susceptible to claims
of malpractice and even criminal charges if the patient dies. The notion that an
omission can never be murder thus seems plainly wrong. In at least *some* cases,
we consider omissions of care criminally culpable, and, as we shall see in a moment, our assisted suicide and euthanasia laws have never turned on whether
the life-taking conduct qualifies as an act or omission. Indeed, contemporary
medical directive statutes have recognized that assisted suicide and euthanasia
can be committed by act or by omission, explaining that they may not be read
or used to "authorize . . . mercy killing or physician assisted suicide or to permit
any . . . deliberate act *or omission* to end life."[14]

4.2 A Causation-Based Distinction?

While the U.S. Supreme Court chose not to endorse the act/omission
distinction, it did conclude, like the New York trial court before it, that refusing
life-sustaining care and suicide are distinguishable because the one merely allows "nature" to take its course, while the other involves an "unnatural" act.[15]
This "natural–unnatural" distinction ultimately boils down to an argument
over causation: According to this line of thinking, rejecting treatment allows

"nature" to cause death, but accepting a lethal injection is "unnatural" because it introduces a new, human causal agent into the picture.

The concept of legal causation, however, is itself notoriously slipperly.[16] To illustrate the problem, suppose that a driver operates a car over miles of highway at an excessive speed and arrives at a street corner just as a child darts from the curb. Do we say that the driver's excessive speed "caused" the death?[17] Suppose we change the hypothetical: the driver knows in advance that the child will dash into the street and drives the car at a calculated speed in order to arrive at the precise moment the child enters the street. Doesn't that change or strengthen our view about the "cause" of the child's death? What we perceive as a responsible or causal force is often determined less by a strictly mechanical review of the physical evidence than by an assessment of someone's mental state, our sense of justice, or common sense. Along these lines, consider the case of Shirley Egan. In March 1999 Egan's forty-two-year-old daughter raised the prospect of putting her sixty-eight-year-old mother into a nursing home. Egan responded by shooting her daughter, paralyzing her from the neck down. When Egan's daughter declined life support and died, prosecutors were left to puzzle over whether to charge Egan with murder, as the causal agent of her daughter's death, or with attempted murder, in effect conceding that the daughter's death was caused by her refusal of extraordinary life-sustaining measures.[18]

Quill itself reflects some of the same difficulties associated with causation-based arguments. There, the U.S. Supreme Court argued that "nature" is the "cause" of death when patients refuse or discontinue unwanted treatment. Meanwhile, three judges of the Second Circuit came to just the opposite view in the *same* case, explaining their view that there

> is nothing "natural" about causing death by means other than the original illness or its complications. The withdrawal of nutrition brings on death by starvation, the withdrawal of hydration brings on death by dehydration, and the withdrawal of ventilation brings about respiratory failure. . . . It certainly cannot be said that the death that immediately ensues is the natural result of the progression of the disease or the condition from which the patient suffers.[19]

While causation may be an imperfect basis on which to distinguish between the right to refuse and assisted suicide or euthanasia, it is possible to mount something of a response to the Second Circuit's criticisms. Patients who refuse life-sustaining care *before* its introduction appear to "let nature take its course," even according to the Second Circuit's reasoning; there is no "intervening" artificial care whose withdrawal can be identified as a cause of death. And even for patients who *withdraw* previously accepted life-sustaining care, one might reasonably debate whether it is more accurate to describe that action as merely allowing "nature" to resume its course after a temporary detour rather than to call it an "intervening" causal agent. After all, we all die sooner or later and physicians can only delay death, not prevent it. To say that the cessation of life-sustaining treatment *caused* the patient's death seems to miss this point and the fact that the life-sustaining care *extended* life; but for the introduction of such care, the patient surely would have died sooner from the underlying malady.

Still, it is hard to say that, at least when patients decide to withdraw basic care like food and water, human choice doesn't play *any* causal role in their deaths. To be sure, in earlier times, before the advent of modern medical technology, the patient would simply have succumbed to the underlying illness at any earlier stage. But, in deciding to withdraw the sorts of life-sustaining medical technology now available to us, or in deciding not to employ it, we cannot ignore the fact that we are now making a judgment and a choice. Death remains a fact of life, but we can now *choose* whether or not to interrupt and delay nature's progress.

To illustrate the role human choice plays, consider a doctor who terminates life-sustaining care for purely selfish reasons—because he or she stands to inherit money, has a grudge against the patient, whatever. What is the cause of death in such cases? To be sure, the patient would have died sooner as a result of the "natural" underlying malady but for the intervening life-sustaining medical care. At the same time, the patient would not have died at that moment but for the human choice to kill. Plainly, the *reason* or *intention* behind the decision to discontinue or withhold care is critical to our interpretation about the cause of death. Saying that "nature" is responsible for deaths in many right-to-refuse cases is thus very much like saying that "speed" is responsible for the death of the child crossing the street. We tend to believe that "speed" killed when the driver didn't intend to kill, but we tend to discredit that argument when the driver deliberately set out on a path to end the darting child's life. Likewise, we find it hard to accept the notion that nature is responsible for death when a doctor or nurse discontinues care deliberately seeking to kill the patient. In such cases, nature surely remains *a* causal factor, but perhaps not the only one, or even the most important one. All of this is to suggest that our views about causation do not just turn on a mechanical analysis of biological actions but also depend on an examination of human intention.

4.3 Toward an Intent-Based Distinction: The Insight of the Double Effect Principle

In 1999 Richard Epstein wrote a book in which he argued for a right to assisted suicide in part on the basis of what he called the "autonomy flip-flop."[20] It is, Epstein argued, an inexplicable paradox that, under the rule laid down by *Glucksberg* and *Quill*, patients are allowed to make their own decisions when to cease medical treatment but are not allowed to make the decision when to seek out death: "The distinction between the two cases is, ultimately, not principled but pragmatic."[21]

Oddly, however, in reaching this conclusion, Epstein (like many others who share his views) failed to pay much attention to the Supreme Court's alternative holding that refusing care and assisted suicide rationally differ because of the *intentions* behind them. A physician who withdraws care pursuant to a patient's request, the Court held, "purposefully intends, or may so intend, only to respect his patient's wishes."[22] By contrast, the Court concluded, a doctor assisting a suicide "must, necessarily and indubitably, intend primarily that the patient be made dead."[23] The Court's distinction, to be sure, was quickly drawn and briefly defended, and it is also open to many criticisms. But, before joining Epstein and concluding that assisted suicide and refusing life-sustaining care are really the same thing, we owe the Court's intent-based distinction a closer look. After all, as our discussion of the act/omission and causation distinctions suggests, one's view about the true cause of death in refusal-of-care cases often turns less on an assessment of mechanical or biological facts than on an assessment about the human choice or intention involved. The act/omission and causation distinctions sometimes seem to be used as proxies for this fact, recognizing that refusals of care *usually* (though not always) betoken no intent to kill and thus do not implicate our traditional concept of assisted suicide and euthanasia.

To ascertain whether a meaningful moral line can be drawn between assisted suicide and the right to refuse on the basis of intent, we must first, of course, consider whether a meaningful moral line can *ever* be drawn between intended and unintended consequences. The notion that intended consequences possess some special moral character, tacitly endorsed by the Supreme Court in *Quill*, is often called the principle of "double effect" and is sometimes associated with Thomistic moral philosophy. The principle is commonly interpreted as setting forth certain conditions for assessing whether a person may morally perform an action from which two effects will follow, one bad, and the other good: The agent may not positively will the bad effect but may merely permit it; if the agent can attain the good effect without the bad effect, he or she should do so; and the good effect flowing from the action must be at least as immediate as the bad effect. In other words, the good effect must be produced directly by the action, not by the bad effect. Otherwise, the agent would be intending a bad means to a good end. Finally, the good effect must be at least as important as the bad effect to compensate for allowing the bad effect to occur.[24]

As suggested by these conditions, the principle of double effect categorically rules out any action that is intended to bring about a bad effect. Yet actions that bring about such effects unintentionally, even if fully foreseen, are not categorically prohibited but are instead analyzed to determine whether the intended (good) effect is proportional to the unintended (bad) consequence.

To be sure, the double effect doctrine's association with Christian moral teaching is often cited as reason enough for disregarding it. Timothy Quill has argued, for example, that

> [t]he rule of double effect has many shortcomings as an ethical guide for either clinical practice or public policy. . . . [T]he rule originated in the context of a particular religious tradition. American society incorporates multiple religious, ethical, and professional traditions, so medicine must accommodate various approaches to assessing the morality of end-of-life practices.[25]

While the double effect doctrine's link to Christian moral teaching is undeniable, that connection obscures the doctrine's roots in Aristotelean moral theory, which, as we saw in chapter 3, places strong emphasis on the measure and nature of the actor's intentions in any assessment of the justice or injustice of his or her action.[26] It also obscures the fact that the doctrine has been recognized to one degree or another by an array of secular moral theorists. Even consequentialist Jeremy Bentham took trouble to distinguish between three different kinds of consequences: those that we intend as our ends or goals; those that we intend as means to our further ends; and those that occur, even if foreseen, as unwanted side effects of what we do intentionally.[27]

In fact, the insight of the double effect doctrine is not remotely theologic. As Justice Oliver Wendell Holmes, himself a frequent utilitarian critic of relying on intent, observed, "even a dog distinguishes between being stumbled over and being kicked."[28] Of course, the question remains why should we, as a secular matter, care more about consequences that are intended versus those that are not? What wisdom, if any, lies behind this distinction? Justice Holmes's homespun illustration suggests the beginnings of an explanation. To kick a dog intentionally—to *choose* to hurt an animal—says something about the kicker, his or her way of interacting with animals, and, perhaps, human beings—in short, it tells us at least something about the kicker's character and beliefs, about *who the kicker is.* By contrast, as Holmes seemed to recognize, watching a person trip over the dog tells us far less about who that person is or about the person's character and beliefs.

The self-defining nature of intended actions can be illustrated by the case, developed earlier in this chapter, of the drivers who hit the child in the street. In one instance, we considered the driver who comes upon a child darting into the street. The driver hits and kills the child by *accident.* In doing so, the driver indubitably effects an awful result—the consequences he brings about are terrible and, as a result, we may censure and punish the driver. But we may very well treat him differently from another driver who *intentionally* hunts down the child with her car. For this latter driver, we may say that no punishment is harsh enough. What undergirds the difference in our reaction to the two drivers? It is the difference in their self-definition, volition, choice. The hunting driver *expresses* herself to the world through her actions, defines who she is and what she believes, in a very different way than the accidental driver. Thus, what really illuminates the darting child hypothetical and ones like it are not arguments over causation but an assessment of human intentions.

The morally defining nature of intentions can be further illustrated by any number of choices we make in daily living. Most of us might be said, for example, to "allow" the poor in our cities and towns to go hungry because we fail to do enough to help them—spending our time and our money in other pursuits, such as family and friends. We may even fully *foresee* or *know* that our failure to do more for the poor will mean that some persons will go hungry. While our choices in such cases indubitably say something about who we are, they do not say the same thing about us as would plotting intentionally to starve others. To seek out to starve another person is to endorse that objective, intelligently choose it, and freely will it. By contrast, the occurrence or nonoccurrence of unintended side effects, even ones we foresee as absolutely *inevitable* (as with the hungry person left unfed), necessarily say less about our success or failure in effecting our free will and intelligence in the world.

Simply put, we live as human beings in a world where we *must* make choices and take actions that, even when entirely legitimate and good, necessarily harm or damage or impinge upon other goods. And this happens at both the individual and societal level. In choosing to spend a weekend with family, it may unavoidably mean that some persons at the soup kitchen will go hungry. In choosing to spend additional money on a prescription drug care program that primarily benefits the elderly, we as a society may know with crystalline clarity that we will not be able to increase spending on education for the young. With so many varied and diverse goods to pursue in this life, we cannot help but make choices in pursuit of legitimate and upright aims that also entail inevitable, if unwanted, negative consequences for other instances of human goods.[29]

In contrast to unintended consequences, intended acts are always within our control, subjects of our free will and choice. Because we *can* always choose to refrain from doing intentional harm to others—because our purposeful actions *are* within our control—our intentional choices necessarily reveal more about our character and individuality than any unintended side effect ever can. To disregard whether or not an act is intended would be, thus, in a very real way to disregard the role of free will in the world—leaving, for example, those who fail to assist charities that feed the hungry open to the same censure and penalties as those who would starve such persons.

Precisely to avoid such acts of injustice and in implicit recognition of the commonsense (nontheologic) moral power of the double effect insight, secular American criminal law has long calibrated different levels of responsibility and punishment based on different levels of mens rea. The purposeful killer is considered for lethal injection while the individual who kills in self-defense, foreseeing death as a consequence but intending only to stop the aggression, may receive no punishment at all. The driver who speeds with reckless disregard for the consequences to others but without any intent to harm the darting child may receive jail time but is often treated far differently from the depraved killer who sets out with a purposeful plan to murder the child. The one who disregards the hungry and homeless likewise may not command respect and admiration, but he or she is not subjected to the same penalties as one who deliberately harms such persons.[30]

The U.S. Supreme Court has identified this critical nexus between respect for intention, individualism, and human free will, explaining that the distinction between intended from unintended consequences "is no provincial or transient notion. It is as universal and persistent in mature systems of law as belief in freedom of the human will and a consequent ability duty of the normal individual to choose between good and evil."[31] In the Court's view, focus on the role of intention, and thus free will, is especially "congenial to an intense individualism [that] took deep and early root in American soil."[32] Roscoe Pound has gone so far as to suggest that, "[h]istorically, [American] substantive criminal law is based upon a theory of punishing the vicious will. It postulates a free agent confronted with a choice between doing right and doing wrong and choosing freely to do wrong."[33]

4.4 SOME (INITIAL) ARGUMENTS AGAINST DOUBLE EFFECT: CONFLATING INTENT AND FORESIGHT

Some concede that a conceptual distinction can be drawn between intended and foreseen consequences but still question whether the line is worth respecting in the law. Glanville Williams, for one, discussed what he called the "doctrine of oblique intent," or what we might more precisely call treating knowledge (or foresight) as interchangeable with intent (or purpose). "To reject the doctrine of oblique intent," and thus draw distinctions between intended and merely foreseen consequences, Williams argued, "would involve the law in fine distinctions, and would make it unduly lenient."[34] Williams used, as an example, terrorists who blow up a plane full of passengers to obtain the insurance payment on the aircraft: While they may not have "intended" the deaths of the passengers, they are villains whose reckless indifference to human life deserves no less punishment than intentional killers, and thus their crimes should be said to be practically equivalent.[35]

Addressing Williams's terrorist example, Andrew Ashworth, in *Principles of Criminal Law*, appears to agree:

> [T]o establish a philosophical distinction between [intent and foresight] is not to conclude the case in favour of a legal distinction. . . . Fundamentally, it is a question of social judgment whether [the aircraft hijacker] should be brack-

eted with the purposeful killer or regarded as merely reckless. The draft [English] Criminal Code has it right, surely, in defining intention so as to cover the person who acts "being aware [i.e., knowing] that [the prohibited consequence] will occur in the ordinary course of events."[36]

Similarly, H.L.A. Hart argued that "a foreseen outcome is enough . . . the law does [and should] not require in such cases that the outcome should have been something intended in the sense that the accused set out to achieve it, either as a means or an end."[37] And Justice Holmes, despite his colorful comment about the underfoot dog, would have gone even further: he advocated abandoning most mens rea requirements in favor of external or objective standards of conduct—such as his famous "reasonable person" test.[38]

The "practical" argument for disregarding the intent/foresight distinction as articulated by Williams and endorsed by others tends to prove too much. We can surely concede that some criminals who kill with reckless disregard for human life, like the terrorists Williams posits, engage in gravely heinous acts that merit sentences befitting their crimes. But doing so does not mean that the intent/foresight line is practically meaningless in all cases, as Williams seems to suggest. The recklessly speeding driver who foreseeably hits the darting child is not obviously the moral equivalent of the driver who purposefully hunts down the child. So, too, the doctor who administers pain killers to his or her patients in order to relieve grave suffering, even when death is likely or even inevitable to result, is not clearly the equivalent of, say, a mass murderer like Dr. Harold Shipman who intentionally killed patient after patient. And the president who orders the shooting down of a plane full of civilian passengers to prevent hijackers from crashing it into a skyscraper is not obviously the equivalent of Williams's terrorist hijackers who perform the same act in an effort to obtain the insurance money.[39] Yet, under Williams's view, in each of the above cases the defendant—the driver, the doctor, and the president—would be considered no less culpable for having foreseeably killed than a defendant who *intentionally* killed. The supposition that intended and merely foreseen homicides are practically equivalent thus fails, at least insofar as it purports to be a rule covering all cases.

Other commentators have suggested that any distinction between intent and foresight (knowledge) should be ignored because, at least in the law, the two concepts sometimes "overlap."[40] As Brendan Thompson has put the point:

> In the law, there is considerable overlap between these two notions [intent and foresight]. The rule of double effect is founded upon the traditional definition of intent in which action X is done to bring about consequence Y. Legal authority, however, also recognizes that a jury may infer intent if death or serious injury is a virtually certain or foreseeable consequence of the defendant's actions and the defendant realized this at the time the action was taken.[41]

Thompson's argument, however, simply points out the fact that juries are free, on the same set of facts, to decide whether an action was intentional or merely knowing or reckless or negligent. That observation—that juries *may infer* that a particular effect was intended or perhaps merely foreseen from the same circumstantial evidence—is unremarkable. It concerns only *how* we go about finding different degrees of mens rea (intent or knowledge or recklessness or negligence)—that is, by observing the same physical evidence and testimony. It does not begin to demonstrate that intent and foresight are the same or should be treated as such, and, to the extent Thompson seeks to make an empirical claim about the state of American law, he overlooks much contrary evidence.

As alluded to by the U.S. Supreme Court and Roscoe Pound, many American jurisdictions find the distinction between intent and foresight to be a valuable component of their criminal law. The Model Penal Code, which has been followed in this respect by most states,[42] takes pains to distinguish intended (or what it calls purposeful) consequences from those that are merely foreseen (or what it calls known). To intend an act or result, it must be one's "conscious object to engage in conduct of that nature or to cause such a result."[43] Meanwhile, a person acts with knowledge or foresight of resulting consequences when "he is aware that it is practically certain that his conduct will cause" a certain result.[44] The Model Penal Code explains the distinction between the concepts of intent (purpose) and knowledge (foresight) as follows:

> Knowledge that the requisite external circumstances exist is a common element in both conceptions. But action is not purposive with respect to the nature or result of the actor's conduct unless it was his conscious object to perform an action of that nature or to cause such a result. It is meaningful to think of the actor's attitude as different if he is simply aware that his conduct is of the required nature or that the prohibited result is practically certain to follow from his conduct. . . .
> . . . [T]here are areas where the discrimination is required and is made under traditional law. . . . This is true in treason, for example, insofar as a purpose to aid the enemy is an ingredient of the offense, and in attempts, complicity, and conspiracy, where a true purpose to effect the criminal result is the requisite for liability.[45]

The distinction here is, as the National Commission on Reform of Federal Law explained, "between a man who wills that a particular act or result takes place and another who is merely willing that it should take place."[46]

Wayne LaFave and Austin Scott, leading American treatise writers on criminal law, observe that the meaning of the word *intent* in the criminal law in the United States was for a very long time "rather obscure," and they acknowledge that in some cases it has been "defined to include knowledge, and thus it is usually said that one intends certain consequences when he desires that his acts cause those consequences or knows that those consequences are substantially certain to result from his acts."[47] Still, LaFave and Scott explain, the evolution of the law has been toward greater, not lesser, attention to mens rea distinctions: "[t]he modern view . . . is that it is better to draw a distinction between intent (or purpose) on the one hand and knowledge on the other."[48] While acknowledging, as Glanville Williams and David Orentlicher suggest, that the distinction is "probably of little consequence in many areas of the law [because] often there is good reason for imposing [the same degree of] liability whether the defendant desired or merely knew of the practical certainty of the results," LaFave and Scott argue that it nonetheless does matter in "several areas of the criminal law."[49] And, indeed, though many crimes are defined to include an act undertaken with either intent or mere knowledge, the distinction between intent and knowledge does play a central, dispositive role in many areas of criminal law— just a small sampling of which are noted in the margin.[50]

Of course, the modern understanding of intent followed by many American jurisdictions in their criminal law is not the only one in currency. The distinction between intent and foresight is, for example, sometimes conflated in the law of torts. The American Law Institute (ALI), in the *Restatement (Second) of Torts*, defines intent to "denote that the actor desires to cause [the] consequences of his act, *or that he believes that the consequences are substantially certain to result from it*."[51] This, of course, directly conflicts with the ALI's treatment of the same subject in the Model Penal Code, where consequences foreseen as a matter of "practical certainty" (a formulation that seems not materially different from the *Restatement's* "substantially certain" wording) are considered to be merely "known" and not "intended."[52] Prosser and Keeton, leading treatise writers in the law of torts, have observed the conflict between the two major pronouncements on the subject of intent by the ALI but have themselves offered no analysis or argument regarding which is to be preferred.[53] Nor has the ALI offered any explanation for its use of competing definitions in the law of crime and tort.[54]

Modern American criminal law stands, too, in some contrast with at least the dominant strain of British criminal law.[55] In describing the state of the English law of mens rea in their treatise on criminal law, Sir John Smith and Brian Hogan acknowledge that "[o]ne view is that . . . a result should never be regarded as intended unless it was the actor's purpose," and that "[t]his is often considered to be the ordinary meaning given to the word by people generally," but they proceed to observe that the criminal courts in England "have consistently given the word a wider meaning, sometimes described as 'oblique' as distinct from 'direct' intention."[56] In fact, the issue of "oblique" intent (foresight), especially in the context of murder, has generated substantial debate in England since at least 1961.[57] Most recently, in a 1999 House of Lords decision, *Regina v. Woollin*, the Lords suggested that juries should be instructed that they may "infer the necessary intention" for a murder conviction when they find that a defendant "realises that it is for all practical purposes inevitable that his actions will result in death or serious harm, . . . however little he may have desired or wished it to happen."[58]

Strictly speaking, the Lords' proposed instruction speaks merely of how juries may infer intent, and it is surely true that the fact that a defendant foresaw a consequence as practically inevitable is customarily accepted as probative evidence on the question whether he or she also intended it.[59] To the extent that the Lords' proposed instruction suggests only that, it is perhaps relatively unremarkable. But the Lords' proposed instruction also goes on to say that an inference that a particular result was intended may be "irresistible" even when the defendant did *not* actually "desire[] or wish[]" it to happen. The terms "desire" and "wish," while ambiguous, seem clearly to refer to intention (rather than motivation); as such, the Lords seem to be suggesting to lower courts that they instruct juries that intention should (or must) be inferred (because doing so is "irresistible") whenever a person foresees death as "for all practical purposes inevitable"—thus conflating the conceptions of intention and foresight. Indeed, one can make a strong argument, as Lord Steyn has, that the upshot of *Woollin* is that "a result foreseen as virtually certain *is* an intended result."[60]

Emphasizing the transatlantic disagreement of opinion over the intent/foresight distinction in the criminal law, the U.S. Supreme Court, albeit in a different context, has expressly rejected a not dissimilar effort to thrust so much (artificially) into the definition of intent. In *Tison v. Arizona*,[61] two petitioners, brothers, had planned and effected the escape of their father from a prison where he was serving a life sentence, remarkably, for having killed a guard during a *previous* escape. The brothers entered the prison with a chest full of guns, armed their father and another convicted murderer, later helped to abduct and rob a family of four, and ultimately stood by and watched as their father and the other convicted murderer killed members of that family with shotguns. Under the Court's Eighth Amendment jurisprudence at the time of *Tison*, it was acceptable under the rule announced in *Emmund v. Florida*[62] to execute an individual convicted of felony murder, even though he did not actually commit the killing, so long as he was additionally guilty of the aggravating circumstance of having "intended" the killing. In *Tison*, the Court confronted a ruling by Arizona's Supreme Court ordering the execution of the two petitioning brothers on the ground that they had "intended" the deaths carried out by their father and the other convict. The Arizona court expressly recognized, however, that the brothers "did not specifically intend" the deaths but deemed this of "little significance."[63] In the Arizona court's view, much like the House of Lords' view in *Woollin*, intent to kill "includes the situation in which the defendant . . . contemplated or anticipated [*viz.*, foresaw] that lethal force would or might be used."[64]

The U.S. Supreme Court, however, disagreed and held that this definition of "intent" wrongly conflated intent with "a species of foreseeability":[65]

Participants in violent felonies like armed robberies can frequently "antici-pat[e] that lethal force . . . might be used . . . in accomplishing the underly-ing felony[,]" . . . [but] [t]he Arizona Supreme Court's attempted reformu-lation of intent to kill amounts to little more than a restatement of the felony-murder rule itself. Petitioners do not fall within the "intent to kill" cat-egory of felony murderer for which [the U.S. Supreme Court's prior holding in] *Emmund* explicitly finds the death penalty permissible under the Eighth Amendment.[66]

While ultimately agreeing that petitioners could be candidates for execution, the Court, rather than artificially manipulate the definition of "intent" as the Ari-zona court had sought to do (and *Woollin* did), instead chose a simpler course. The Court simply extended its precedent in *Emmund* to permit the execution of certain felony murder convicts even when they do *not* intend to kill, holding that the Eighth Amendment does not prohibit the death penalty for defendants whose participation in a felony that results in murder is major and whose men-tal state qualifies as at least reckless indifference to the value of human life, though, the Court emphasized, defendants must be given the opportunity in such circumstances to argue to the jury that the absence of intent mitigates their offense and thus makes capital punishment inappropriate.[67]

    Tison illustrates that some American courts, in contrast to their En-glish counterparts, continue to see value in, and are willing to police, the intent/foresight distinction, at least when it comes to setting certain standards of crim-inal liability and punishment. But, as *Tison* also illustrates, this is not to say that merely foreseen crimes may *never* receive comparable punishments, as Glanville Williams seems to worry; foreseen or reckless crimes can sometimes subject a defendant to penalties similar to those for intentional ones, particularly in the presence of certain additional aggravating circumstances strongly suggestive of indifference to the value of human life—including (as in *Tison*) cases where the defendant engaged in multiple counts of the same conduct and unlawfully re-strained victims (kidnapping) or (as in Williams's hypothetical airplane case) sought to promote terrorism.[68]

4.5 Distinguishing Suicide, Assisted Suicide, and Euthanasia from the Right to Refuse: Intending versus Foreseeing Death

    Having sought to establish that there is a rational, secular moral line to be drawn between intended and foreseen consequences, the question arises whether such a distinction applies to our case: by reference to the intent/fore-sight line, can assisted suicide and euthanasia, on the one hand, be distinguished, on the other hand, from conduct putting into effect a choice made pursuant to the right to refuse? I believe the answer is yes. While the principal and assistant must indubitably *intend* to kill in the case of assisted suicide and euthanasia, such an intent is not necessarily present when persons exercise the right to refuse, and those who assist them need not intentionally help kill. We can test this hypothesis by examining the actions at issue with more specificity.

Suicide

As it turns out, the principle of double effect has always been fundamental to our very definition of suicide. Self-destruction without an intent to die—even when death is foreseen—never qualified as suicide at common law, nor does it fit with common sense. Soldiers who fall on a hand grenade in order to save their mates may well *know* their "number is up," but they hardly commit an act of suicide. Augustine's Christian martyrs may have *foreseen* death as a certainty for refusing to renounce their beliefs, but they did not seek it out. Death is, at most, an accepted *side effect* of such decisions (to save one's mates, to remain faithful to one's religious beliefs, etc.).

In fact, Augustine and Aquinas (and arguably Aristotle) condemned suicide precisely because (and to the extent that) it represents an *intentional* rejection of human life. Augustine endorsed the true Christian martyr's *acceptance* of death, but not the Donatists' deliberate *choice* to seek death out. Aquinas endorsed lethal acts by private persons where the intent is to stop aggression (self-defense), but not where the intent is to kill. Aristotle suggested that only intended wrongs are always and by definition unjust, and he intimated that suicide is wrong because it involves an *intentional* act against the "right principle" of life.[69]

The common law, likewise, traditionally took care to limit the definition of suicide to intentional self-destruction, for fear that any lesser mens rea standard would sweep in too much acceptable conduct. Edmund Wingate explained in the seventeenth century that to be "*felo de se* [a person must] destroy himself out of premeditated hatred against his own life."[70] Blackstone said that, to qualify as suicide, the act had be "deliberate[]" or part of an "unlawful malicious act."[71] So did Coke.[72] Hale likewise held that suicide consists of one who "voluntarily kill[s] himself."[73] Indeed, Hale expressly distinguished between intentional acts of suicide, which he thoroughly condemned, and accidental acts of self-killing, such as cutting off a limb to prevent the spread of gangrene and bleeding to death, which Hale excused.[74] As a commentary to the Model Penal Code explains, the crime of suicide traditionally consisted only "of the intentional self-destruction by person of sound mind and sufficient age"[75]—not actions of self-destruction undertaken negligently, recklessly, or by persons of unsound mind, or even actions, like the soldier who jumps on the grenade, consciously undertaken with full knowledge that death is sure to result.

Euthanasia and Assisted Suicide

As with suicide, the double effect insight not only is consistent with, but has actually always inhered in, our most basic understanding of assisted suicide and euthanasia. Consider two examples. When Dr. Kevorkian set up his "Mercitron" death machine in his Volkswagen van, he plainly intended to help take the life of his "patients," and we do not doubt that he committed acts of assisted suicide and euthanasia.[76] By contrast, when General Eisenhower ordered the D-Day invasion, he well *knew* that he was sending many American soldiers to certain death but hardly *intended* to see them dead. Their deaths were an accepted (foreseen) side effect of his intention of liberating France.[77] This very same commonsense distinction runs throughout the law of assisted suicide and euthanasia.

American state statutes banning assisted suicide were passed at different times and use many different formulations.[78] Yet, they almost universally require that the assister actually *intends* to help the principal kill himself or herself. That is, to be liable, it is not enough for the suicide to wish to die; the *assistant* must also have as one of his or her purposes a wish to see the patient dead—that is, must freely will or intend the patient's death. Wisconsin's statute is simple but emblematic of the assisted suicide laws found in a majority of American states, holding that "[w]hoever *with intent that another take his or her own life* assists such person to commit suicide is guilty of a Class D felony."[79] Texas similarly provides that "a person commits an offense if, with *intent* to promote or assist the commission of suicide by another, he aids or attempts to aid the other to commit or attempt to commit suicide."[80] Though it uses the word "deliberately" instead of "intentionally" or "purposefully," California conveys the same meaning: "Every person who deliberately aids, or advises, or encourages another to commit suicide, is guilty of a felony."[81] Virginia, too, holds it unlawful for a person "with the *purpose* of assisting another person to commit or attempt to commit suicide . . . [to] provide[] the physical means by which another person commits or attempts to commit suicide."[82] Many other analogous examples can be found in appendix A.

The focus on the intent of the assister, while fundamental to the very definition of assisted suicide, is hardly unique to the law of assisted suicide. The double effect insight has long permeated much of American aiding and abetting law. Courts and statutes have traditionally required proof that the aider or abetter shared an intent to effect the criminal result, not just mere foresight (knowledge), in order to establish *any* aiding or abetting offense.[83] And the reason for this is simple: any lesser mens rea requirement could pose what the Model Penal Code calls "the serious risk of over inclusiveness."[84] As classically expressed by Judge Learned Hand,

[i]t is not enough that [a defendant] does not forego a normally lawful activity, of the fruits of which he knows that others will make an unlawful use; he must in some sense promote their venture himself, make it his own, have a stake in its outcome. This distinction is . . . important [to prevent prosecutors from] sweep[ing] within the drag-net of conspiracy all those who have been associated in any degree whatever with the main offenders. That there are opportunities of great oppression in such a doctrine is very plain, and it is only by circumscribing the scope of such all comprehensive indictments that they can be avoided.[85]

Simply put, the requirement that the assister *intends* to assist the principal achieve his or her purpose serves as a break against arguably overzealous prosecution and interference in private affairs—a government-limiting and liberty-maximizing function. The intent requirement ensures that there is no aiding and abetting prosecution, for example, when "[a] utility provides telephone or telegraph service, knowing it is used for bookmaking[;] [a]n employee puts through a shipment in the course of his employment though he knows the shipment is illegal[;] [a] farm boy clears the ground for setting up a still, knowing that the venture is illicit."[86] American aiding and abetting law follows, in this respect, a "sturdy individualist approach,"[87] seeking to avoid writing the moral dictum of being our brothers' keepers into the positive law and focusing opprobrium instead on deliberate choices to do (or assist) a wrong.[88] The intent requirement serves precisely this same function in the law of assisted suicide, serving to restrict the scope of state interference over private conduct. Thus, for example, a pharmacist who sells drugs to another person who states that he intends to kill himself will not be held liable for assisted suicide so long as the seller does not actually *intend* to help kill.[89] The gun shop owner who sells a gun is likewise absolved from being his brother's keeper. And so, too, as we saw in chapter 1, Dr. Quill was not prosecuted or professionally disciplined for prescribing barbiturates for his patient, in part, because unresolved questions existed about whether he specifically *intended* (rather than merely foresaw as possible) that his patient would use the drugs to kill herself rather than merely treat her insomnia.[90]

The Right to Refuse

So far, we have seen that there is some basis in moral theory and legal doctrine for distinguishing between intentional conduct and foreseen but unintended side effects. We have also seen that assisted suicide and euthanasia are acts intended to help kill another person. But what about when patients refuse life-sustaining treatments and physicians and nurses help them? Does this involve intentionally helping to kill? I believe the answer is: not always and not necessarily. And this fact forms a critical, rational moral line that can be drawn between assisted suicide and euthanasia, on the one hand, and the right to refuse care, on the other.

Now, to be sure, a patient *can* refuse care with the intention of dying, and those who assist him or her can intentionally assist in the taking of life. To this extent, I do not dispute that a right to refuse care and the proffered right to assisted suicide and euthanasia can overlap, a feature to which I will return to consider at length in chapter 10. For now, though, I wish to explore the morally significant fact that assisted suicide *always* involves, on the part of the principal, an intent to kill and also requires that the assistant intentionally participate in a scheme to end life, while, by contrast, a patient exercising the right to refuse need *not* intend to end life, and those who assist need *not* intentionally participate in a scheme to take life.

We all know that death cannot be cheated forever. Foreseeing and accepting the inevitability of our own deaths is a sign of maturity and not at all the same thing as intentionally seeking death out. In modern medical practice, where life can often be prolonged so long, everyone in the hospital room or hospice frequently wishes that the patient—the father, mother, son, daughter, or other loved one—could live forever. But everyone in the room also knows that life cannot be prolonged forever wholly dependent on medical machinery. At some point, the treatment becomes unfairly burdensome, it brings too little benefit, the machine has to be removed, the loss of life must be accepted, and it may become unfair to expect resources to be dedicated exclusively to a patient when they could do more good elsewhere. The decision to withdraw care in such circumstances will, at some level, "cause" death, and death is the absolutely foreseeable outcome. But that does not mean, and need not at all involve, an intention to kill and thus constitute an act of suicide, assisted suicide, or euthanasia.

Far from it. The decision to discontinue care is ordinarily a deeply painful one, not a vindication of anyone's wish to kill or help kill. Patients and their families may seek to discontinue care because they are tired of the invasive treatments and tubes and the poking and prodding that have come to characterize much of modern medical care. They may wish to avoid the sense of indignity that dependence on medical machinery can bring. They may wish simply to go and die at home, to be away from the hospital with loved ones, to avoid the endless sleepless ward-room nights, to restore their privacy. They merely may wish to end their fight with death and accept the inevitable. None of these reasons—or any of the other countless reasons for refusing life-sustaining care expressed every day by persons confronting the inevitable death we all face—necessarily betokens an *intent* to die. The patient and his or her family and physician may fully foresee and come to peace with death without necessarily having any *intention* to kill or help kill. Accepting death is an inevitable part of life, and a patient's right to refuse care is simply, and ordinarily, employed without any deliberate design to bring about death. It is, in this respect, morally more akin to General Eisenhower's D-Day decision than to Dr. Kevorkian's eagerness to employ his "Mercitron" machine. Recalling our discussion of the speeding driver, the typical right-to-refuse case is analogous to the case of the driver who speeds along without any intention or design to kill but who happens to hit a darting child. Meanwhile, assisted suicide and euthanasia are, at least in this respect, more analogous the case of the driver who hunts down the child because—in both cases—the aim is always to kill. To recall our discussion of causation, many are attracted to the notion that right-to-refuse cases simply allow "nature" to take its course because in such cases doctors and patients typically come to the conclusion that continuing the medical struggle simply will not reap sufficient rewards and may impose undue burdens—and do so without any deliberate aim or intention to kill the patient.

The American Medical Association has recognized the significance of the role of intention in judging professional conduct in this arena, employing double effect and endorsing existing legal distinctions in drawing a line between routine and acceptable acts of withdrawing life-sustaining care and impermissible acts of killing. In the AMA's formulation, the "withdrawing or withholding of life-sustaining treatment is not inherently contrary to the principles of beneficence and nonmalfeasance," while assisting suicide always is, because the latter involves intentionally using the tools of medicine to kill.[91] The AMA uses the same double effect analysis in addressing the appropriate use of painkillers. Physicians may prescribe high doses—even potentially lethal doses—in order to relieve suffering. That is, the fact that the patient may die is never unethical when a doctor "can point to a concomitant pain-relieving *purpose*"; at the same time, consistent with the double effect insight, the AMA cautions, the very same medical act, if undertaken with the *purpose* of killing, is unacceptable, "exceeding the bounds of ethical medical practice."[92] And, of course, since the beginning of time, important medical procedures of all descriptions have entailed a serious risk of death, but none have been outlawed or considered unethical when they are undertaken with the hope of relieving some form of suffering. Indeed, if a grave risk of death were the touchstone for ethical acceptability, all sorts of breakthrough and novel forms of medical care would never have been tried. So, too, when it comes to the use of high doses of morphine or other palliatives at the end of life: the doctor and family do not want to kill the patient; instead, they seek to relieve suffering as the patient confronts the inevitable end we all face—and do so *even if* that means death will be hastened as a result. The legitimate interest in the relief of suffering, even if it means *accepting* an earlier death, is nothing new to medicine but has been part of its practice since its earliest times. Because the refusal of care and the provision of palliative care are capable of being used in ways that do not necessarily involve an intent to kill, and may in fact be used to relieve human suffering, they differ in kind from assisted suicide and euthanasia, which always entail a purpose to kill and thus have not been traditional components of ethical medical practice.

In 1993 the Select Committee of the House of Lords, charged with re-considering England's 1961 Suicide Act, endorsed drawing a firm line between the provision of potentially lethal dosages of painkillers in response to pain and assisted suicide, and it did so with express reference to the principle of double effect:

> The adequate relief of pain and suffering in terminally ill patients depends on doctors being able to do all that is necessary and possible [to relieve pain]. In many cases this will mean the use of opiates or sedative drugs in increasing doses. In some cases patients may in consequence die sooner than they would otherwise have done but this is not in our view a reason for withholding treatment that would give relief, as long as the doctor acts in accordance with responsible medical practice with the objective of relieving pain or distress, and with no intention to kill. . . . Some witnesses suggested that the double effect of some therapeutic drugs when given in large doses was being used as a cloak for what in effect amounted to widespread euthanasia, and suggested that this implied medical hypocrisy. We reject that charge while acknowledging that the doctor's intention, and evaluation of the pain and distress suffered by the patient, are of crucial significance in judging double effect.[93]

One could easily substitute the right to refuse medical treatment in this analysis and the result would be the same. Like painkillers, medical treatment can be refused—and we have every reason to believe it usually is refused—for entirely upright reasons betokening no intent to kill. It thus has a place in responsible medical practice where death is always a risk and often an inevitable by-product of therapies ranging from palliative care to surgery that are *intended* to help relieve suffering. And this is a place morally different in kind from that occupied by practices always employed specifically *to kill.*

So far, we have posited the case in which neither the patient nor the physician/assister intends to use the removal of care to kill. But what if the two have different intentions? What if the patient refuses any further treatment with a manifest *intent* to die (say, to get insurance proceeds now for his or her family), and the doctor *knows* it: can the doctor still discontinue care in the face of a suicidal request? This question takes us back to the individualistic, liberty-maximizing approach of American aiding and abetting law and the double effect insight it embraces. To be liable for assisted suicide, the aider must share the intent to kill with the principal; nothing less will suffice under typical assisted suicide laws or the standard American rule of aiding and abetting. Thus, just as the pharmacist who fills a prescription for a suicide is not liable, if the doctor discontinues care *without* an intent to help kill, but simply, say, to fulfill a professional duty to discontinue services when they are no longer wanted and permit the patient/client to go his or her own way, the act is *not* one of assisted suicide, even though the doctor may *know* the patient intends to die. So long as the doctor acts with the *purpose* of fulfilling his or her professional responsibility and without an *intent* to kill, the requisite mental element for assisted suicide is not satisfied.[94]

Having proceeded this far, I believe we are now in a position to offer at least a tentative answer to the fairness or equal protection question by acknowledging that a morally and legally sound, intent-based distinction can be drawn between, on the one hand, the right to refuse and, on the other hand, the proffered right to assisted suicide and euthanasia: In cases of refusing care, death need not be intended by the principal or assistant, while in cases of euthanasia, death must be intended by the killer, and in cases of assisted suicide, one must intentionally assist the principal in the objective of intentionally ending his or her life.

4.6 Some (Additional) Criticisms of Double Effect as Applied to the Assisted Suicide Debate

While we have already considered several general criticisms of the principle of double effect and the significance of the role of intention in the law,[95] some additional objections have also been leveled more specifically against the application of the principle of double effect to the assisted suicide question, and these, too, merit consideration.

The Intended Means/Side Effect Problem

Some commentators have argued that the principle of double effect fails to take into account "multilayered or partial intentions" in cases of assisted suicide and euthanasia. In an emblematic passage, Brendan Thompson has suggested that,

> [o]ftentimes, clinicians will not act with one exclusive intent in medicating a terminally ill patient, but will rather hold a variety of intentions which may or may not include offering the patient the possibility of death when suffering becomes overwhelming and no other acceptable means of escape are available. Because the rule of double effect views clinical intentions as being simplistic and one-dimensional, it fails to acknowledge the inescapable multiplicity of intentions which are present in most double effect situations where one intention may not rise above the rest to become the true purpose of a practitioner's actions.[96]

The point here seems to be that the intention to kill is not always the only or even the dominant intention at work in cases of assisted suicide and euthanasia; other intentions, most particularly the desire to end suffering, are also present.

No doubt this is true. But such an observation is not at all inconsistent with the principle of double effect, which recognizes that one may not only intend something as an end unto itself—the final object or purpose of one's behavior—but may also intend something as a means to some further purpose or end. For example, I may intend, as an end, to get some rest from work. As a means of accomplishing that object, I may intend to take a holiday abroad. In such a scenario, failing to achieve my intended means would be as much a frustration of my designs and aims as failing to achieve my intended ends or final goal. Both are intended, and any examination of my intentions must include both my intended ends and my intended means. And so it is in the assisted suicide and euthanasia contexts: Dr. Kevorkian may intend, as an end, to relieve suffering, but he also indubitably intends to kill as his means of doing so. Thus, in a case where the potassium chloride drip he fashioned failed to kill one of his patients, Kevorkian ran off to find a canister of carbon monoxide to allow his patient to finish the job of killing herself.[97] State statutes recognize that intentions equally include intended means and ends and make assisting a suicide unlawful so long as killing is any part of the aider's intentions. The AMA's ethical analysis of assisted suicide recognizes this point as well, holding that the use of palliative care (or, presumably, any other kind of medical treatment) is never acceptable when the physician intends death either as an end itself or as a means to some further purpose, such as relieving suffering: intentional killing is out-of-bounds "regardless what other purpose the physician may point to."[98] And this, of course, is exactly what proponents of legalization wish to undo in current legal and medical practice, making room for acts specifically *intended* to kill the patient, at least insofar as such actions serve as a means to the further intention of relieving suffering; indeed, this is the very definition of euthanasia.

John Griffiths, professor of sociology of law at the University of Groningen in the Netherlands, has charged that the difference between what we might label intended means and unintended side effects "is a pure *ipse dixit.* . . . [T]he *way an act is described* determines which are to be considered means and which side effects."[99] And, to be sure, what qualifies as an intended means as opposed to an unintended side effect is not always free from doubt. Consider this example. A party of explorers is trapped in a cave because a fat member of the party is lodged in the only opening. If a member of the party explodes a charge next to the fat man, should we say that he intended the fat man's death as a means, or that the death was a mere side effect of the desire to free the party?[100] The problem also lends itself to more practical illustration. For example, what if a woman with a serious heart condition becomes pregnant and both she and the fetus will die unless the fetus is removed? If the fetus is removed, is the consequential death of the fetus better described as an intended means, or as a mere side effect of saving the pregnant woman?[101]

In both examples, whether we are inclined to label an action as an intended means or as a side effect turns on whether we view the factual sequence more in its granular detail or as a unitary whole. The more we break down the sequence of events into discrete bits, the more the actor's conduct appears intentional. Thus, if we say that the cave explorer pulled dynamite sticks out of his backpack, placed them near the fat man, struck a match, lit a fuse, and then ran for cover, the fat man's death takes on an intentional hue. To the extent we focus on the conduct as a unitary whole aimed at escaping the cave, the fat man's death seems more of a side effect.

Some have argued that intended means versus side-effect problems can be resolved with a counterfactual hypothetical, asking whether, if the questionable result at issue could have been avoided (e.g., the fat man could have lived; the fetus need not have been destroyed), but all the other positive events also occurred (e.g., the party of spelunkers and the pregnant woman lived), would the actor still have chosen to act as he or she did?[102] Because the *death* of the fat man or fetus is not required to achieve the wished-for results, the reasoning goes, they are not intended means but only unintended side effects.

While the counterfactual hypothetical technique may often prove useful in drawing out and isolating an agent's intentions, it is an incomplete answer. It does not, after all, focus directly on the actor's actual intentions and state of mind but replaces the inquiry with a hypothetical construct. And the construct can go awry, for there is always the possibility that the party of spelunkers *did* wish the fat man dead, or that the pregnant woman *did* wish to terminate her pregnancy. Intentions are complex and fact- and individual-specific, and they are not readily analyzable from the outside by what-if hypotheticals.

Ultimately, however, we do not need any artificial construct to know our *own* intentions; they are knowable to us by self-examination. As to the intentions of other persons, Griffiths argues that discerning intentions from side effects is practically impossible or fruitless: While "God sees everything[,] . . . for purposes of secular morality and legal control, making the responsibility of an actor dependent on his motive is unacceptable. . . . It comes as no surprise that the criminal law rejects the idea of liability based on . . . subjective intentions."[103] But this seems confused on at least a couple levels. In the first place, we are concerned here with the moral and legal consequences of *intentions*, not *motives*, and Griffiths mistakenly conflates the two. In the second place, American criminal law deals every day in the question of intention, resting, as we have seen, many and various kinds of legal duties and penalties on the presence or absence of particular intentions. Griffiths' dismissal of any reliance on subjective intent as somehow a confused religious enterprise simply ignores entire chapters of secular law and their connection to individual free will and government restraint.[104] To be sure, determining whether *other* persons did or did not intend particular results may require inference based on an examination of the facts, but the absence of any systematic metatheory for distinguishing between means and side effects cannot obscure the fact that what was and was not within the scope of the actor's intentions is precisely the sort of question of fact that judges and juries are accustomed to and charged with sorting out every day in our legal system.

Within the realm of assisted suicide and euthanasia, moreover, the problem of determining whether death was an intended means or an unintended side effect is not often an acute one. There is little ambiguity about the fact that Dr. Kevorkian, say, *intended* to help kill his patients, or that physicians in Oregon do as well, at least as a means of relieving suffering. Indeed, the very change in the law that assisted suicide and euthanasia proponents wish to see is the repeal of laws against acts *intended* to help kill. Kevorkian's 1994 acquittal on assisted suicide charges (he was found guilty of murder in a 1999 euthanasia case) further amplifies the point. The trial judge in that case correctly held that assisted suicide is a "specific-intent" crime in the state of Michigan and so instructed the jury that was charged to determine his guilt or innocence. Nothing is at all unusual about juries or other judicial fact-finders being tasked with the job of discerning a defendant's intentions.

In Kevorkian's case, however, the judge did adopt a novel interpretation of what proof is required to establish specific intent, one that seems plainly incorrect. Instead of charging the jury that it had to find that Kevorkian shared an intention to help kill his patient consistent with the traditional law of assisted suicide, the court instructed the jury that it could find Kevorkian guilty only if it found he "intended *solely* to cause" death. Thus, the jury was obligated to acquit Kevorkian if it found that he intended to kill and had some other purpose in mind, such as relieving suffering. In the *Quill* case, Chief Justice Rehnquist, unfortunately, used a somewhat similar, if less demanding, formulation in describing assisted suicide when he stated that a doctor assisting a suicide "must, necessarily and indubitably, intend *primarily* that the patient be made dead."[105] In essence, under the instruction given in Kevorkian's 1994 trial, and arguably under the definition suggested by Chief Justice Rehnquist, if the death of a patient is part of (or, in Chief Justice Rehnquist's formulation, primarily the result of) some larger goal of relieving suffering, it may be treated as an unintended side effect rather than an intended means. This is simply an incorrect description of the law. Assisted suicide laws have never distinguished between intended means and intended ends. And the *Kevorkian* court's instruction would make it impossible to obtain a conviction for assisted suicide so long as the assistant intends to cause death only as a means to some other end—whatever that end may be. The instruction, if correct, would mean that the Roman-style entertainer who assists volunteers in taking their lives in order to amuse his audience would go free, since he intends death merely as a means to some other (primary) end.

It would also mean that Jim Jones, of Jonestown Massacre fame, would have to be acquitted on the ground that he intended to kill his followers only as a *means* of making a political point to "protest[] the conditions of an inhumane world."[106] Those who help kill off grandpa as a means to the end of cashing in on his life insurance policy might have an equally good defense. None of this comports with what we commonly understand to be assisted suicide or euthanasia, which, by their definition, include acts where death is intended—whether as an end or as a means.

Criticisms from Other Quarters

Recalling our discussion in chapter 2, Justice John Paul Stevens wrote separately in *Glucksberg*, commenting there that he saw any distinction between suicide and refusing life-saving care based on intent as purely "illusory."[107] Justice Stevens rested this conclusion on the observation that a physician discontinuing care "could be doing so with an intent to harm or kill that patient; conversely, a doctor who prescribes lethal medication does not necessarily intend the patient's death—rather that doctor may seek simply to ease the patient's suffering and to comply with her wishes."[108] What can we say about this?

At bottom, Justice Stevens seems to depend on a flawed premise. As we have seen, while an intention to kill—either as an end or as a means—is necessarily present in the exercise of a right to assisted suicide or euthanasia, it simply is not necessarily present in the exercise of the right to refuse care. Justice Stevens's hypothetical also seems to conflate very different things. Justice Stevens supposes a doctor who prescribes potentially lethal painkillers to relieve suffering or comply with a patient's wishes. But, critically, Justice Stevens doesn't discuss the operative legal questions—the patient's and physician's state of mind. If the doctor and patient intend only to relieve pain, that is no act of suicide or assisted suicide. If, however, the patient *intends* to kill himself or herself and the doctor *intends* to help in that process, that *is* assisted suicide.

Some, such as Dr. Quill, argue that any intent-based distinction between assisted suicide and the right to refuse treatment is, as a practical matter, too

> difficult to validate externally. . . . Clinicians familiar with the requirements of the rule may learn to express their intentions in performing ambiguous acts such as providing terminal sedation or withdrawing life support in terms of foreseen but unintended consequences; at the same time, other clinicians may reasonably interpret these acts as clear violations of the rule.[109]

John Griffiths, similarly, has submitted that focusing on intentions in the context of assisted suicide and refusals of care "would undermine every possibility of effective control by making those responsible for control dependent on information possess[ed] only by those whose behavior is to be controlled."[110]

These objections, however, merely return us to the generic problem of separating intended from unintended consequences that we discussed above. To be sure, inquiries into the intentions of individual patients in individual cases may be difficult and risk divergent results in similar cases. But these same administrative concerns could be raised about virtually every case in which intent is an issue, and they do little to suggest that an intent-based distinction lacks moral force or is inappropriate for use in a legal setting. It also seems somewhat surprising that Quill and Griffiths would complain about administrative hurdles associated with prosecuting assisted suicide: the strict mens rea requirement for that offense is expressly designed to prevent governmental overintervention in private affairs—such as against the drugstore owner who simply sells over-the-counter medications (if perhaps knowingly or negligently) to a client exhibiting suicidal tendencies; or as against the doctor who recklessly prescribes sleeping pills to a patient who is depressed and talking of killing himself or herself. The choice to impose a strict mens rea requirement in aiding and abetting offenses was deliberately made to protect against what Judge Learned Hand called the "drag-net" effect of secondary liability, restricting legal liability to those who "in some sense promote their venture [themselves], make it [their] own, have a stake in its outcome." Indeed, Quill himself avoided prosecution for assisted suicide precisely because the government was not certain it could meet the strict mens rea standard of proof he criticizes.

Quill's arguments about the difficulties associated with the administration of intent-based laws also are themselves indeterminate—that is, they do not inexorably lead to the conclusion that laws against assisted suicide should be repealed. The costs of administering an intent-based law might be just as easily used to argue for lowering the mens rea requirement (say, to knowledge) and expanding the reach of criminal liability as they might be used (as Quill wishes) to argue for dropping laws against assisted suicide altogether.[111] Such costs might also be used to argue for adopting some other bright line legal rule that generally approximates the intent-based distinction but is more easily administerable. This, in turn, may simply take us back to the act/omission or causation distinctions, both of which (also) are routinely administered by U.S. courts, and both of which, while conceptually imperfect, share the insight that the right to refuse generally need not be (and ordinarily is not) practiced in a way that is morally the equivalent of assisting suicide or euthanasia.

As to the administerability of an intent-based distinction, moreover, Griffiths concedes that his own research has found that, far from being impractical, focusing on intent to distinguish between assisted suicide and refusals of care actually fits with the subjective experience of many doctors,[112] and he acknowledges that any alternative legal regime that "treats things [that doctors] consider profoundly different as one undifferentiated whole [i.e., conflating intended and foreseen deaths] will presumably not be capable of commanding their support."[113]

4.7 CONCLUSION

We have seen that the act/omission distinction and the natural/un-natural (causation) distinction may not succeed in differentiating completely between the right to refuse treatment and the proposed right to receive assistance in suicide. We have also seen, however, that a morally significant distinction does exist, insofar as one practice (the right to refuse) need not involve an intent to kill on the part of the patient or the patient's assistant, while the other (assisted suicide) always involves an intent to kill on the part of the principal, and an intent to help kill on the part of the assistant. We have seen that this distinction not only is consistent with, but also has long been embedded in, the common law and medical ethics. At the same time, we have discussed potential problems with this distinction, including the fact that the right to refuse can be used by individuals to effectuate acts of intentional self-destruction. For purposes of doctrinal equal protection review, however, only a "rational" distinction is necessary to sustain state laws against assisted suicide and euthanasia; the fact that the right to refuse, like the provision of palliative care and all sorts of other risky medical treatments, can be exercised without any intention to kill seems to qualify.

While I have suggested that the right to refuse might be rationally distinguished from assisted suicide and euthanasia, it is important to note that I have not tried to do more than that. That is, I have answered the limited procedural fairness question, but not the underlying substantive question whether assisted suicide and euthanasia (or the right to refuse, when an intent to kill is present) are practices that should be encouraged or discouraged. Those questions we take up in forthcoming chapters.

5

Casey *and* Cruzan: *Do They Intimate a Right to Assisted Suicide and Euthanasia?*

IF HISTORY and principles of fairness do not necessarily command a right to receive assistance in suicide or a right to euthanasia, some would invite us to look to principles of moral autonomy and the legal doctrine that has grown up around those principles. Judges Rothstein and Reinhardt found persuasive the argument that all persons have an inherent (substantive due process) right to choose their own destinies. Justices Stevens and Souter appeared sympathetic to this line of argument, and Justice O'Connor seemed to decline to voice any views with respect at least to terminally ill persons. Such voices (and votes) suggest that autonomy-based arguments will be heard again when an as-applied legal challenge to a state law banning assisted suicide makes its way to the U.S. Supreme Court. Neither are autonomy arguments exclusively judicial in nature. Many legislative advocates of assisted suicide and euthanasia argue that proper respect for individual choice compels legalization.

In this chapter, I address the legal question whether *Casey* and *Cruzan* specifically, and substantive due process doctrine more generally, are hardy enough to sustain a constitutionally protected autonomy interest that could, in turn, sustain a right to assistance in suicide and euthanasia. In chapter 6, I consider whether principles of personal autonomy, as developed by contemporary moral theorists independent of legal doctrine, provide a persuasive analytical basis for legalization.

5.1 THE "REASONED JUDGMENT" TEST AND ITS CRITICS

In *Glucksberg*, Chief Justice Rehnquist gave short shrift to arguments based on *Casey* and *Cruzan*, summarily dismissing the notion that they might sustain a constitutional right to receive assistance in committing suicide.[1] While his analysis proved sufficiently persuasive for the three other members of the Court who adopted it as their opinion, it was apparently insufficient for the remaining (majority of) justices. Given that an as-applied challenge seems virtually certain to return to the Supreme Court, the reach of *Casey* and *Cruzan* will remain a focal point of discussion.

But how are the courts to determine what substantive rights due process shelters from legislative or executive encroachment? While the history test has proven to be perhaps the most persistently popular tool with the Supreme Court, much academic literature over at least the past half-century has pressed the alternative and more expansive view that the Court should serve, in Henry Hart's words, as a "voice of reason, charged with the creative function of discerning afresh and of articulating and developing impersonal and durable principles."[2] In Ronald Dworkin's view, the Court's role is to define our "constitutional morality," which in turn requires the Court to elucidate "the political morality presupposed by the law and institutions of the community."[3] Charles Curtis similarly sought to convince members of the Supreme Court that it should "articulate a creed for the era," by becoming the nation's "philosopher."[4]

This vision of substantive due process adjudication is the vision that at least some of the justices and judges in the assisted suicide cases had in mind. Justice Souter wrote of due process adjudication as an exercise incapable "of any general formula," and dependent instead on "the usual canons of critical discourse."[5] Judge Reinhardt rested heavily on *Casey*'s description of substantive due process adjudication as an exercise in applying "reasoned judgment." And, of course, the *Casey* plurality itself spoke of due process as protecting "the most intimate and personal choices a person may make in a lifetime."[6]

That said, the "reasoned judgment" test, like the history test, is not without its critics or difficulties. If the task of recognizing new rights is one of engaging in moral reasoning and critical discourse about what broad moral imperatives such as autonomy entail, one might ask: Are judges any more competent at the task (or deserving of any more deference) than legislators? How does substantive due process doctrine differ from outright judicial choice, or what is sometimes derisively labeled "legislating from the bench"? How many moral philosophers actually agree, after all, about what metaphysical imperatives such as "autonomy" entail?[7] One might even ask whether it is bold enough to hold that the procedurally oriented language of the due process guarantee contains the enumerated substantive rights of the Bill of Rights; does going any further—holding that the clause is also the repository of other substantive rights not expressly enumerated in the text of the Constitution or its amendments, and thus entirely dependent for their legitimacy solely on the "reasoned judgment" of five judges—stretch the clause beyond recognition?

Such questions are both old and new. As initially drafted, the Bill of Rights prevented the *federal* government from infringing certain familiar substantive rights—the right to free speech, the right to be free from unreasonable searches and seizures, the right to free association in religious matters, and the like—but the document did not prevent infringement of these rights by *state* governments. In a battle waged intermittently over the first half of the twentieth century, the Supreme Court concluded that most of the substantive rights afforded as against the federal government in the Bill of Rights are of such fundamental importance that they practically inhere in the notion of "due process." And since the Fourteenth Amendment's due process clause protects the people as against state governments, this meant that the states, too, were bound to respect at least most of the rights enumerated in Bill of Rights, as rights said to be "incorporated" into the reach of the Fourteenth Amendment.

In his early years on the Supreme Court, Justice Hugo Black led a battle to expand due process to "incorporate" the full substance of the Bill of Rights into the Fourteenth Amendment's restrictions on the states. In Justice Black's later years, however, the Court moved past the Bill of Rights incorporation debate and began to declare new, nontextual, substantive due process rights enforceable against the states. When it did so, the Court left behind Justice Black, who continued to argue that incorporation should be both the floor and the ceiling of substantive due process doctrine.[8]

Justice Black's incorporation-but-no-more position toward substantive due process never managed to attract a majority of the Court. Instead, the Court gravitated variously toward the muscular notion that reasoned judgment is a reliable guide in the creation of nontextual rights and the somewhat more modest (yet majoritarian) notion that history can provide an objective way to decide whether to recognize such rights. Interestingly, however, Justice Black's position has found two converts in recent years.

In his first several years as a member of the Supreme Court, Justice Scalia conceded the constitutional legitimacy of nontextual substantive due process rights, seeking only to limit the creation of any new rights to those deeply ingrained in the nation's history—as he did in the *Michael H.* case we examined in chapter 3.[9] Even in the midst of the contentious abortion debate in *Casey*, Justice Scalia did not suggest that the Court should abandon the history test and the recognition of nontextual substantive due process rights, dissenting solely because, in his view, the right to abortion lacked sufficient basis in the historical record.[10] It appears, however, that the experience of *Casey* may have induced Justice Scalia to reconsider his views. Rumors persist of considerable acrimony among Court members during deliberations in *Casey*, arising perhaps in part because Justice Kennedy reportedly switched his vote after the Court's conference on the case, thereby altering the outcome of the case.[11] In any event, just a year after *Casey*'s reaffirmation of the abortion right, Justice Scalia announced that, while he would continue "to accept the proposition that [due process], despite its textual limitation to procedure, incorporates certain guarantees specified in the Bill of Rights," he would no longer "accept the proposition that [due process] is the secret repository of all sorts of other unenumerated, substantive rights."[12] Since he joined the Court, Justice Thomas has concurred in Justice Scalia's statements rejecting all nonincorporation substantive due process doctrine.[13]

These justices have argued, among other things, that the precedential basis for the "reasoned judgment" test itself may have been overstated in certain cases. By way of example, *Palko v. Connecticut* is "much-quoted"[14] as a leading case espousing a reasoned judgment approach to due process, speaking of the constitutional inquiry as one into whether the asserted right is "implicit in the concept of ordered liberty."[15] Yet, Justices Scalia and Thomas might argue, the Court did not actually recognize the proposed right in that case. In *Roe v. Wade*, the Court did of course endorse a new right in the face of substantial contrary history,[16] but those following Justices Scalia and Thomas might note that even there the Court held that an array of doctrines and theories supported its result, with substantive due process only thrown into the mix as just one more element—one, moreover, that received relatively brief attention in the text of the *Roe* opinion.[17] Like *Palko* and *Roe*, *Loving v. Virginia*, where the Court struck down state laws prohibiting interracial marriage, is often cited as a leading authority for the "reasoned judgment" approach. Indeed, the Ninth Circuit *en banc* majority in *Compassion in Dying* insisted that

> [w]ere history our sole guide, the Virginia anti-miscegenation statute that the Court unanimously overturned in *Loving* . . . as violative of substantive due process and the Equal Protection Clause, would still be in force because such anti-miscegenation laws were commonplace both when the United States was founded and when the Fourteenth Amendment was adopted.[18]

But Justice Scalia or Thomas might respond that the Ninth Circuit partially calls into question its own thesis. The Court in *Loving* analyzed the antimiscegenation law at issue not just—or even primarily—under a due process lens. Instead, the *Loving* court rested its decision almost entirely on a traditional equal protection analysis; its appeal to due process came appended only to the very tail of the opinion.[19]

5.2 CASEY-BASED ARGUMENTS

Even Justices Scalia and Thomas cannot dispute, however, that the Court rendered a strong, explicit defense of a purely reason-based approach to substantive due process in *Casey*'s reaffirmation of the right to abortion. Aware of twenty years' worth of criticism leveled at *Roe v. Wade*, the plurality in *Casey* expressly sought to provide a firmer basis for the abortion right and to shore up the reasoning behind *Roe*'s result. In doing so, the *Casey* plurality purposefully eschewed any effort to examine the history of abortion regulation, stressing instead the importance of "reasoned judgment" in assessing whether to continue recognizing the constitutional right to abortion. Applying such judgment in section 2 of its opinion, the plurality examined past Court decisions protecting the right to use contraception, marry interracially, and exercise control in the childrearing process and, in doing so, came to identify an overriding moral/

philosophical principle running throughout these decisions: "At the heart of liberty is the right to define one's own concept of existence, of meaning, of the universe, and of the mystery of human life. Beliefs about these matters could not define the attributes of personhood were they formed under the compulsion of the State."[20]

From this principle the Court concluded that an abortion right necessarily followed. While forcing a woman to carry an unwanted pregnancy may "ennoble[ ] her in the eyes of others," her "suffering is too intimate and personal for the State to insist, without more, upon its own vision of a woman's role, *however dominant that vision has been in the course of our history and our culture. The destiny of the woman must be shaped to a large extent on her own conception* of her spiritual imperatives and her place in society."[21] It is precisely on the basis of this passage that the Ninth Circuit *en banc* panel and Justice Stevens concluded that *Casey* provides an "almost prescriptive" mandate requiring recognition of a fundamental liberty interest in the receipt of assistance in committing suicide, regardless what history might say otherwise.[22] Assisted suicide, like abortion, is central to one's "concept of existence, of meaning, of the universe, and of the mystery of human life."

It remains, however, unclear whether *Casey*'s "mystery of life" passage is properly understood as a persuasive but nonbinding dictum or an exceptionless holding. First, the *Casey* plurality opinion actually cited two reasons for reaffirming the abortion right recognized in *Roe*. In section 2 of its opinion, the plurality argued that abortion is fundamental to principles of individual autonomy, as Justice Stevens and others stress in the assisted suicide debate. But, in section 3, the plurality argued that the doctrine of *stare decisis*, or respect for long-settled law, required continued adherence to *Roe*'s basic teachings.[23] *Casey*'s reliance on *stare decisis* was the narrower of the two grounds for decision offered by the plurality, and it was, standing alone, sufficient to decide the controversy before the Court. Usually though not always, only the narrowest rationale is said to control future courts, and one can thus make a colorable argument that the single-paragraph autonomy discussion upon which the Ninth Circuit and Justice Stevens so heavily relied in the assisted suicide cases is not only the view of a three-judge plurality, but arguably inessential to that plurality's decision.

At this point, one might recall *Loving*, where the Court also employed two rationales in sustaining the creation of a new nontextual right, one of which was a "reasoned judgment" substantive due process analysis, and the other of which was a traditional equal protection holding. While some initially held out hope after *Loving* that the decision would act to liberate all future due process adjudication from dependence on history and custom, a majority of the Supreme Court has never read the decision so broadly; instead, the Court continued consistently to endorse *Loving*'s result but quickly reverting to the history test in subsequent substantive due process cases. Similarly, it may well be the case that, in time, *Casey* may come to be dominantly read as a *stare decisis* decision—a ruling, in essence, that we must respect the abortion right out of tradi-tional deference to settled law—rather than creating any new, open-ended right to "define one's concept of existence." On the other side of the coin, in its 2003 decision overturning *Bowers* and recognizing a constitutional right to private consensual homosexual sodomy, the Supreme Court expressly built on the "rea-soned judgment" foundation set down by *Casey*, noting that, "[p]ersons in a ho-mosexual relationship may seek autonomy for these purposes [i.e., in *Casey*'s language, to 'define one's own concept of existence, of meaning, of the universe, and of the mystery of human life'], just as heterosexual persons do. The deci-sion in *Bowers* would deny them this right."[24] How far *Casey*'s "reasoned judg-ment" analysis might be extended thus very much remains to be seen.

Supporting the competing view that *Casey* is best read essentially as a *stare decisis* decision is the fact that the plurality decision did not mention, let alone register any dissatisfaction with, the Court's substantial body of cases ad-vancing and applying the history test. *Snyder v. Massachusetts* and *Moore v. City of East Cleveland* are nowhere cited in section 2 of the *Casey* plurality opinion and thus can hardly be said to be supplanted or overruled. Nor did *Lawrence*, applying *Casey* in the arena of homosexual sodomy, express any disagreement with earlier history test cases or with *Glucksberg*, itself a very recent application of the history test.

To be sure, the *Casey* plurality did denounce one application of the his-tory test in section 2—footnote 6 of *Michael H.*,[25] which, the *Casey* plurality stated, would have required the Court to ask whether the asserted liberty inter-est before it was "at the most specific level . . . protected against governmental interference when the Fourteenth Amendment was ratified."[26] But even this does not purport to reject the history test generally. As we saw in chapter 3, *Michael H.*'s version of the history test, requiring focus on the "most specific level" of tradition available, is but one way of applying the history test; two members of *Casey*'s plurality themselves supplied an alternative method for ap-plying the history test in *Michael H.*[27] Moreover, the *Casey* plurality arguably criticized a straw man of its own creation, not the version of the history test actually advanced in *Michael H. Michael H.* did not seek to limit fundamental liberty interests *only* to those practices, defined at the most specific level, that were protected when the Fourteenth Amendment was ratified; rather, *Michael H.* merely suggested that courts may not *disregard* a specific, relevant tradition protecting, or denying protection to, the asserted right—a very different thing indeed.[28]

The Ninth Circuit and Justice Stevens's broader reading of *Casey*, fo-cusing exclusively on its autonomy discussion without regard to its core *stare decisis* holding, is also open to question on the ground that may prove too much. If the Constitution protects as fundamental liberty interests *any* "intimate" or "personal" decisions, the Court arguably would have to support future autonomy-based constitutional challenges to laws banning any private consensual act of significance to the participants in defining their "own concept of existence." As Judge O'Scannlain queried in dissent in the Ninth Circuit's proceedings, "If physician-assisted suicide is a protected 'intimate and personal choice,' why aren't polygamy, consensual duels, prostitution, and, indeed, the use of illicit drugs?"[29] That is a very provocative question indeed. Such a broad reading of *Casey* would be not only inconsistent with the *stare decisis* thrust of the opinion, but also inconsistent with Justice O'Connor's deciding concurring opinion in *Casey* in which she stressed her belief that abortion is "unique" in American due process jurisprudence.[30]

Finally, even if *Casey* is best read as recognizing a substantive due process right to participate in all activities that a court might deem central to personal autonomy and self-definition, there is, the Supreme Court has ruled, only one person's autonomy interest at risk in the abortion context: the woman's. Under *Roe*'s express holding, a fetus does not qualify as a person.[31] By contrast, there are strong autonomy interests belonging to persons on both sides of the assisted suicide and euthanasia issue—the interest of those persons who wish to control the timing of their deaths and the interest of those vulnerable individuals whose lives may be taken without their consent due to mistake, abuse, or pressure in a regime where assisted suicide and euthanasia are legal.[32] In *Roe*, the Court explained that, had it found the fetus to be a "person" for purposes of the Fourteenth Amendment, it could not have created a right to abortion because no constitutional basis exists for preferring the mother's liberty interests over the child's life.[33] That reasoning suggests that even a court reading *Casey* to embrace a broadly defined constitutional autonomy interest would have difficulty deciding whether to prefer the autonomy interest of those who seek to die over the autonomy interest of those who fear inadvertent or wrongful death at the hands of an assisted suicide regime.

5.3 Cruzan-Based Arguments

In arguing that *Cruzan* implies a right to assisted suicide, the Ninth Circuit *en banc* court characterized *Cruzan* as "recognizing a liberty interest that includes the refusal of artificial provision of life-sustaining food and water, necessarily recognizes a liberty interest in hastening one's own death."[34] From that premise, the Ninth Circuit concluded that, if an individual has a right, or protected liberty interest, to hasten one's own death, he or she must have a right to assistance in doing so.[35]

The Ninth Circuit's interpretation of *Cruzan* is arguably less an application of the case than a substantial extension of it. Nancy Cruzan suffered severe injuries in an automobile accident and was left in an apparently permanent comatose state. Cruzan's care was being provided at state expense, but her parents sought to have tubes carrying food and water into their daughter removed. A Missouri state trial court authorized the termination, finding that a person in Cruzan's condition has a fundamental constitutional right to refuse care, but the Missouri State Supreme Court reversed. While recognizing a right to refuse treatment embodied in the common law doctrine of battery and informed consent, the State Supreme Court rejected the argument that Cruzan's parents were entitled to assume those rights in the event of her incompetency without a written living will or competent evidence of her wishes.

The majority of the United States Supreme Court began its own analysis of the case by examining the common law and observing that it has traditionally supplied a right to be free from physical intrusion without consent:

> At common law, even the touching of one person by another without consent and without legal justification was a battery. Before the turn of the century, this Court observed that no right is held more sacred, or is more carefully guarded, by the common law, than the right of every individual to the possession and control of his own person. . . . This notion of bodily integrity has been embodied in the requirement that informed consent is generally required for medical purposes. . . . The informed consent doctrine has become firmly entrenched in American tort law.[36]

The Court next noted that a "logical corollary" has arisen to the common law doctrine of informed consent in the form of a "right not to consent, that is, to refuse treatment."[37] Recognizing that the "logic of the[se] cases . . . would embrace" a liberty interest of constitutional dimension, the Court nonetheless stopped short of recognizing a constitutionally based right to refuse life-sustaining care because "the dramatic consequences involved in refusal of such treatment [i.e., death] would inform the inquiry as to whether the deprivation of that interest is constitutionally permissible."[38] And, indeed, as we saw in chapter 3, the right to be free from unwanted intrusions, while well-entrenched, is not absolute; at common law and under a proliferation of state statutes, for example, persons have long been privileged to interfere with suicide attempts, committing what, in other circumstances, would be deemed to be a battery.

Instead, proceeding cautiously, the Court opted, "for purposes of this case," to "assume that the United States Constitution would grant a competent person a constitutionally protected right to refuse lifesaving hydration and nutrition."[39] Assuming such a right, the Court proceeded to hold that Missouri had legitimate reasons for requiring clear evidence of Cruzan's wishes before allowing her care to be discontinued.[40]

The Supreme Court simply did not discuss or endorse any generic constitutional interest in hastening death, as the Ninth Circuit seemed to suppose. Instead, it merely assumed that the Constitution protects a right to refuse life-sustaining care, and it did so on the basis that the administration of unwanted medical treatment is a form of battery—i.e., an unlicensed touching that offends historical common law principles. Assisted suicide and euthanasia, meanwhile, are not encompassed within the common law concern for unlicensed touchings: neither an unwanted touching (i.e., the administration of medicine) nor a lack of consent is involved in cases of assisted suicide and euthanasia. The common law's interest in protecting bodily integrity from unwanted physical invasions—the interest the Court in *Cruzan* sought to protect—simply is not at issue in cases covered by the proffered right to consensual assisted suicide or euthanasia. Further, as we examined in detail in chapter 4, the refusal of care simply is not logically equivalent to a right to hasten death; to equate the two is to conflate two very different things both morally and legally: refusing life-sustaining care does not necessarily implicate an intent to kill or help kill, while seeking out or participating in assisted suicide and euthanasia always does. Finally, the Supreme Court in *Cruzan* took great pains to make clear that its due process analysis was based on a historical analysis of the development of the common law; the Court was willing to consider embedding recognized common law principles in the Constitution, but nothing in its opinion suggested that it was willing to recognize rights (such as those to assisted suicide and euthanasia) that lack such antecedents.

5.4 Conclusion

Leading legal theorists over the last half-century have suggested that members of the Supreme Court should employ "reasoned judgment" in substantive due process disputes, resolving cases, as Justice Souter put it, by employing "the usual canons of critical discourse" and doctrinal decision making. Others respond that such a methodology offers less certainty and guidance than the competing history test, and its application by the plurality in *Casey* may be partially responsible for leading at least two justices to reconsider Justice Black's view that the substantive component of the due process clause should be interpreted to incorporate against the states the textual rights found in the Bill of Rights, and no more. But the vitality of the "reasoned judgment" approach to substantive due process inquiries cannot be dismissed, and we considered arguments for assisted suicide and euthanasia based on *Roe, Palko,* and *Loving,* as well as *Casey* and *Cruzan.* We found ample language in *Casey* to support an assisted suicide right, but we also found that the same language might be employed to support a right to participate in an array of currently unlawful activities. Given *Casey's* alternative and sufficient *stare decisis* holding, and Justice O'Connor's observation about the unique status of American abortion jurisprudence, we considered whether the decision's broader language about the nature and extent of personal autonomy rights might be considered persuasive but nonbinding authority and noted that, in any event and quite unlike the abortion debate, an appeal to autonomy does not easily resolve the question before us because important autonomy interests lie on both sides of the assisted suicide debate. We then considered an argument for assisted suicide based on *Cruzan* and found that the case did not endorse a generic autonomy-based right to hasten death, but instead simply, and much more narrowly, endorsed refusals of care based on traditional common law concepts of battery.

6

Autonomy Theory's Implications for the Debate over Assisted Suicide and Euthanasia

BECAUSE THE question whether the Constitution protects an interest in self-definition and autonomy constrained only by the limits of "reasoned judgment" remains (despite the arguments of some dissenters) very much in play, we must necessarily ask the next question: What exactly would respect for such an autonomy interest mean for the debate over assisted suicide and euthanasia? If broad personal autonomy interests are protected by substantive due process doctrine, what kind of right to assistance in suicide or euthanasia follows? Though in a somewhat different posture—one unconstrained by constitutional doctrine—legislators also have to consider moral-political arguments for legalization based on conceptions of patient autonomy and choice. Indeed, many moral philosophers have suggested that concepts of autonomy and self-determination provide the strongest argument for legalization.[1] In this chapter, I seek to evaluate the strength of such claims. I begin by briefly outlining the contours of three of the most prominent theories of personal autonomy in contemporary moral-political theory; then I consider their potential application to the assisted suicide and euthanasia debate.[2]

6.1 THE AUTONOMY DEBATE

Joseph Raz has identified three fundamental preconditions for the exercise of personal autonomy with which few can disagree. First, Raz notes that, to exercise autonomy, an individual must be capable of understanding his or her options and choosing between them. If a person is to be the true author of his or her own life, then he or she "must have the mental abilities to form intentions of a sufficiently complex kind, and plan their execution. These include minimum rationality, the ability to comprehend the means required to realize his goals, the mental faculties to plan actions, etc."[3]

Second, Raz argues that one must have a sufficient number of options to choose among for choice to be meaningful, and he illustrates two aspects of this point. A woman left on a desert island with a carnivorous animal that constantly hunts her may be capable of making autonomous choices, but she has no time to do so. Her thoughts are concerned only with survival. Conversely, a man fallen into a pit with enough food and water to survive for the rest of his natural life may have the means necessary for survival, but his available choices are so limited that they leave little room for autonomy.[4] Neither of these individuals has a sufficient number of options and tools for creating an autonomous life in which they might become, in a true sense, the primary author in writing the story of their own lives.

The third precondition Raz posits is that, for a decision to be autonomous, it must be free from coercion or manipulation.[5] For an individual's choice to be one's own, it cannot be dictated by another. But this assertion of moral theory, like the question of what constitutes a "sufficient" number of options to choose among, quickly begs another: how much room and how many choices must the individual have free of state interference in order to live an autonomous life? When and to what degree must the state forswear coercion or manipulation in order to assure adequate respect and room for individual autonomy and choice?

Such questions take us from the realm of moral theory into the realm of political theory and are themselves the focus of substantial debate and disagreement. One possible answer to them is to hold that the state must remain neutral between competing conceptions of the good life (the neutrality principle). Another possible tack is to maintain the state need not remain neutral but may legislate coercively only when harm to others is threatened (the harm principle). Yet another view might be to challenge the necessity of either the neutrality or harm principle to the full and appropriate flourishing of personal autonomy (perfectionism).

6.2 The Neutralist View of Autonomy

Neutralists argue that respect for personal autonomy requires government to forswear any interest in promoting particular moral objectives or ends; the state must leave individuals to choose their own values. The state has no role to play in making men and women moral, no role in "perfecting" persons; to the contrary, the state should aspire to an *anti*perfectionist ideal.

One of the most familiar briefs for state neutrality is John Rawls's defense of equal liberty in *A Theory of Justice*. Rawls hypothesizes an original position, a moral vacuum where individuals have not yet established any religious or moral identity or commitments.[6] Rawls argues that, in such an original position, rationally self-interested persons would demand the freedom to define and pursue their own views of what constitutes a good life without state inter-ference. Ignorant of, say, what religion he or she would hold in society, a ratio-nal person would not permit the state authority to prefer one religion over an-other. People in the original position

> cannot take chances with their liberty by permitting the dominant religious or
> moral doctrine to persecute or to suppress others if it wishes. Even granting
> (what may be questioned) that it is more probable than not that one will turn
> out to belong to the majority (if a majority exists), to gamble in this way would
> show that one did not take one's religious or moral convictions seriously, or
> highly value the liberty to examine one's beliefs.[7]

Accordingly, the state is left free to pursue only those policies and norms that evince equal respect for all competing conceptions of the good.

An array of contemporary theorists have sought to supplement and strengthen Rawls's thesis in various and often competing ways,[8] but all agree that state neutrality is an essential ingredient to personal autonomy. Emblem-atically, David Richards argues that state neutrality alone can ensure "respect [for] the moral sovereignty of the people themselves, the ideal of the sovereign ethical dignity of the person against which the legitimacy of the contractarian state must be judged."[9] Should the state pursue nonneutral ends, it would "de-grade [individuals'] just equal liberty to define their ultimate philosophical and moral aims."[10] Ronald Dworkin succinctly puts the point this way: government must "impose no sacrifice or constraint on any citizen in virtue of an argument that the citizen could not accept without abandoning this sense of his equal worth," nor should it "enforce private morality."[11]

Although antiperfectionists like Rawls, Richards, and Dworkin view state neutrality as the critical bulwark of individual autonomy, their premise is hardly without its critics. Raz, for example, readily accepts the notion that for individual autonomy to mean anything, the individual must have a "large number of greatly differing pursuits among which [he or she is] free to choose."[12] Autonomous individuals cannot be left with too few options like the hypothetical Man in the Pit, or with too little time to make meaningful life-defining choices like the Hounded Woman. But to say that a wide range of choices is a precondition to autonomy does not, to Raz, mean that all con-ceivable options must be available to the individual. A nonneutral or perfec-tionist state might rule out certain ways of life as bad, but, Raz argues, there is no reason to suppose it would leave individuals with insufficient options to lead a fully autonomous life. To the contrary, because there are so many ways of life that exemplify different virtues, even in a perfectionist state we cannot help but believe that ample choices will remain for autonomy to flourish.[13]

Raz goes even a step further. Not only can a perfectionist state foreclose evil options without seriously infringing on individuals' opportunities for self-creation, Raz argues it *should* do so. It should because autonomy is valuable only when exercised in pursuit of a morally upright way of life. A person may be autonomous even when choosing bad ways of life, but Raz argues that

> autonomously choosing the bad makes one's life worse than a comparable non-autonomous life is. Since our concern for autonomy is a concern to enable people to have a good life it furnishes us with reason to secure that autonomy which could be valuable. Providing, preserving or protecting bad options does not enable one to enjoy valuable autonomy.[14]

As for the Rawlsian claim that rationally self-interested individuals would never choose a state that could rule out some competing conceptions of the good, Raz simply disagrees. Individuals in the original position might well permit a perfectionist state to act nonneutrally and rule out bad choices and lifestyles, provided that the state does so in accord with a methodology all can see and accept as fair. Rather than demanding a neutralist state, Raz thinks that rationally self-interested persons might just as easily reach "an agreement to establish a constitutional framework most likely to lead to the pursuit of well-founded ideals, given the information available at any given time."[15]

6.3 THE HARM PRINCIPLE'S COMPETING VIEW

Just as the neutrality principle divides some moral theorists over autonomy's meaning and prerequisites, a parallel debate over whether the state must respect the harm principle divides others. As classically expressed by John Stuart Mill, the harm principle holds that each person must be afforded the right to exercise self-control "[o]ver himself, over his own body and mind," and that the "only purpose for which power can rightfully be exercised over any member of a civilized community, against his will, is to prevent harm to others."[16] The harm principle thus differs from the neutrality principle in one significant respect. Where neutrality bars government from promoting any particular version of morality, the harm principle is concerned with the means used to enforce morality. One may accept that government has a role to play in (nonneutrally) encouraging good choices and discouraging evil ones but also take the view that it may use coercive means (e.g., criminal sanctions) only to prevent those choices that result in harm to others. Thus, to take an example, assume for the moment that bigamy is perhaps immoral but imposes no harms on others. A nonneutral harm principle adherent would, in such a case, allow the state to *teach* against bigamy and attempt to *discourage* it by, for example, refusing to recognize bigamous marriages. At the same time, the nonneutral harm principle adherent would also forbid the state from making bigamy a crime.

Introducing the concept of the harm principle, however, naturally begs the question: what constitutes *harm*? Must there be some physical invasion or interference before the state can intercede? Most adherents to the harm principle recognize the possibility of nonphysical harm but also seek to rule out definitions of harm that expand it so far as to permit the state to criminalize conduct that causes only psychic injury.[17] Yet, efforts at walking this fine line— seeking something broader than the merely physical but narrower than the purely psychic—usually devolve quickly into the abstract and opaque, as Raz's own (valiant) effort illustrates: "[O]ne harms another when one's action makes the other person worse off than he was, or is entitled to be, in a way which affects his future well-being."[18]

Many neutralists, including Rawls, Dworkin, and Richards, also adhere to some form of the harm principle.[19] But Raz amply illustrates that one can reject neutralism and yet endorse the harm principle. While Raz rejects neutrality as unnecessary to ensure personal autonomy, he argues that to disregard the harm principle would violate autonomy in two ways:

> First, it [would] violate[] the condition of independence and express[] a relation of domination and an attitude of disrespect for the coerced individual. Second, coercion by criminal penalties [would be] a global and indiscriminate invasion of autonomy. Imprisoning a person prevents him from almost all autonomous pursuits [recall the Man in the Pit]. Other forms of coercion may be less severe, but, they all invade autonomy, and they all, at least in this world, do it in a fairly indiscriminate way. That is, there is no practical way of ensuring that the coercion will restrict the victims' choice of repugnant options but will not interfere with their other choices.[20]

On this account, the harm principle allows individuals all the freedom they want to pursue their own views of the good life—up to the point where an unwilling person could be harmed. As the familiar saw goes, freedom ends where the next person's nose begins. While the state may teach and promote good behavior, allowing the state to punish bad conduct that results in no harm to others would, if Raz is right, unduly constrain individual choice and opportunities for self-creation. Worse still on this account, coercive state power is an indiscriminate and unwieldy tool; using it to preclude bad but purely self-regarding choices may incidentally foreclose other, good choices. Thus, for example, when legislatures or courts step in trying to ban pornography, someone almost always raises the question whether the lines they draw also (perhaps inadvertently and despite good intentions) infringe upon legitimate artistic expression.[21]

6.4 Perfectionism and Autonomy

The harm principle itself is argued by some as inessential, superfluous to a society of flourishing autonomous individuals. Lord Patrick Devlin classically argued that the state should be allowed to pursue any moral ends it wishes in the name of social cohesion, regardless of whether the morality pursued is true. Though coming from a radically different point of view, Robert George has also taken the position that anyone who rejects state neutrality (e.g., Raz) must also, as a matter of logic, reject the harm principle, and that doing so hardly infringes at all on human liberty; ample room remains, George submits, for meaningful individual choice and autonomy without the state adhering to either principle.

Like Raz, George argues that there are many and varied ways of living a morally upright life, and that individuals should be free to choose from these without state interference.[22] But autonomy is only an instrumental value, George contends, not an absolute one as Raz seems to suppose. Individual choice should be respected to the extent (but only to the extent) it is employed toward ends recognized as morally good: "The value of autonomy is . . . conditional upon whether or not one uses one's autonomy for good or ill."[23] Personal choice, on this account, should be permitted only "in so far as [it is an] important means and condition[] to the realization of human goods and the communities they form."[24] To Raz's claim that the state's use of coercion in the absence of harm to others expresses disrespect for the coerced individual, George replies that coercive laws

> do not, except in the most indirect or implausible senses, deprive the morals offender of any sort of valuable *choice*. . . . [I]t is difficult to perceive violations of autonomy in the legal prohibition of victimless wrongs if we join Raz   in a perfectionist understanding of autonomy as valuable only when exercised in the pursuit of what is morally good. And this raises the suspicion that Raz smuggles into this argument a non-perfectionist notion of autonomy.[25]

Thus, George asserts, coercing an individual to avoid bad choices does not really deprive him or her of any meaningful choice at all.

It is, however, not entirely clear that Raz "smuggles" an antiperfectionist notion of autonomy into his defense of the harm principle, as George suggests. George's submission that the value of human choice depends entirely on the worthiness of the ends chosen may overlook the possibility, latent in the harm principle (though not as explicit as it might be in Raz's work), that the act of choice is *itself* a meaningful societal good; that there is some real social benefit in permitting and encouraging people to make choices, even if they are "bad" ones. Certainly most parents and teachers would accept as a truism that there is an inherent value in allowing their children and pupils to make and learn from misguided decisions. And our most basic principle of government, as embodied in the Declaration of Independence, squarely rests on the conviction that there is inherent (not merely instrumental) value in permitting individuals liberty enough to pursue their *own* visions of happiness.[26]

George advances perhaps a more powerful argument against the harm principle when he contends that the use of coercive laws to prevent victimless bad choices does not display disrespect for the coerced *individual*, but only dis-respect for the bad end chosen. On this view, society seeks to condemn, as it were, the sin, not the sinner:

> Conscientious legislators who vote for morals legislation seek to condemn vices—not people. Indeed, one of their primary concerns is to protect the very people who would, in the absence of laws, against, say, pornography or drugs, fall victim to the very temptation to engage in those vices. . . . Immoral con-duct can be banned without thereby expressing contempt for someone who might otherwise fall into it.[27]

Of course, Raz also argues against laws that offend the harm principle on the ground that they are dangerously indiscriminate tools, not only fore-closing what we might agree to be repugnant choices, but also incidentally in-terfering with other, legitimate choices. George concedes this is so but argues that this fact does not demonstrate that the use of coercion is always wrong as a matter of principle. Instead, he submits, it counsels that we should use coer-cion in the realm of self-regarding choices (and otherwise) both sparingly and prudently:

> [Raz worries] that laws restricting, say, pornography may result in the sup-pression of legitimate and valuable forms of art and literature. This worry is legitimate. . . . The danger of interfering with morally acceptable choices is a consideration that counts against anti-pornography legislation in the practi-cal reasoning of prudent legislators. But it may not be a conclusive reason. In the circumstances, the good to be achieved *may* reasonably be judged as wor-thy of the risks.[28]

At bottom, George's argument thus does not seek to unseat Raz's harm principle, at least as a useful rule of thumb. George concedes the need to be wary of the imprecision of coercive penalties, and he acknowledges that they can re-sult in the accidental suppression of upright choices, but he also submits that such practical concerns do not justify the adoption of a rigid rule permitting all consensual or "harmless" conduct. Indeed, George submits that the risk of over-inclusive and indiscriminate legislation is not confined to morals legislation where there is no "harmed" party, but also exists in other areas of the law. And "[p]rudence is required in [these] other areas as well. The controlling moral norms in the face of risks [of indiscriminate coercive legislation] are, I think, norms of fairness," not the adoption of an absolute rule proscribing any legis-lation over morals or other "harmless" arenas of human activity.[29] That is, to George the best guarantee against indiscriminate legislation that unduly coerces human choices and ways of life isn't the harm principle, but the equal protec-tion guarantee that would require everyone to accede to the same misguided rule. Justice Scalia has advanced a similar view, in a passage George would no doubt approve: "[w]hat protects us . . . from being assessed a tax of 100% of our income above the subsistence level, from being forbidden to drive cars, or from being required to send our children to school for 10 hours a day," is not rigid adherence to any abstract moral theory, such as the harm principle, but simply "the Equal Protection Clause, which requires the democratic majority to accept for themselves . . . what they impose on you and me."[30]

6.5 THE IMPLICATIONS OF AUTONOMY THEORY FOR THE ASSISTED SUICIDE AND EUTHANASIA DEBATE

Having outlined the major competing contemporary theories of personal autonomy, we are now in a position to ask: what effect might these theories have applied to the assisted suicide and euthanasia debate? It is immediately apparent that George's view of personal autonomy does not (and cannot) command the recognition of any new legal or moral right. Evaluating whether persons should have the right to receive assistance in suicide or euthanasia collapses into an inquiry into the moral uprightness of the acts themselves. George admits that a right to choose a way of life (or death) arises if, but only if, it is consistent with the realization of human goods and the communities they form.[31] Autonomy, to George, is an entirely instrumental good, devoid of independent content or value, and incapable of commanding the recognition of a right to assisted suicide or any other substantive right. To say that assisted suicide advances personal choice and autonomy simply does not, for George, do anything to answer the question whether the practices are worthy of legal approbation. For George, "[t]he saving of souls is the whole reason for the law,"[32] and the question whether to recognize any new legal or moral right should be answered with that goal fixed in mind.

In contrast to the perfectionist view of autonomy, the harm and neutrality principles both claim some substantive content and hold out the hope of providing definitive answers to questions like those surrounding the legalization of assisted suicide and euthanasia. One can readily imagine, for example, how the argument that assisted suicide or euthanasia are classic self-regarding acts and, therefore, "harmless" activities might go. But is this inevitably so? Though suicide, especially for the terminally ill, may bring with it benefits for family members (e.g., relief in seeing the suffering of a loved one come to an end), even the most rational act of suicide can impose real "harms" on such persons—at least sometimes. Spouses can be left behind bereft of their companions; children may be orphaned and without support. Also, legalizing the practice assisted suicide and euthanasia may also create an incrementally greater risk that a certain number of persons might be killed without their consent due to abuse, mistake, or coercion (a point we shall explore further in the next chapter). Thus, even while endorsing fully the harm principle, the state might well be free to use its coercive powers to suppress at least some acts of suicide, assisted suicide, and euthanasia to protect against harms befalling unconsenting persons.

In this vein, and in a manner somewhat evocative of Robert George's suggestion that the harm principle should be viewed more as a useful rule of thumb than an absolute command, even highly notable harm principle advocates, including John Stuart Mill and Joel Feinberg, have themselves argued *for* laws banning completely certain practices (e.g., dueling and self-enslavement contracts) that appear, at first blush, to be harmless to others. Though such practices can be expressive of autonomous impulses and are consensual and thus apparently "harmless," the argument runs, they cannot be practiced without an undue risk of mistake, abuse, or coercion—and thus harm to third persons.[33] As Feinberg has put it in the context of slavery contracts:

> Since the renunciation of rights is both total and irrevocable in this kind of transaction, the standard for voluntariness must be higher than for any other kind of agreement (except perhaps suicide pacts and voluntary euthanasia requests). The risks are so great that the possibility of mistake must be reduced to a minimum. . . . [T]he grounds for suspicion are so powerful that the testing would have to be thorough, time-consuming, and expensive. The legal machinery for testing voluntariness would be so cumbersome and expensive as to be impracticable. Such procedures would, after all, have to be paid for out of tax revenues, the payment of which is mandatory for taxpayers. (And psychiatric consultant fees, among other things are very high.)[34]

While first focused on the costs and burdens of determining assent, Feinberg then turns to the risks of abuse, coercion, and mistake:

> The more important point is that even expensive legal machinery might be so highly fallible that there could be no sure way of determining voluntariness. . . . The state might be justified simply in presuming nonvoluntariness conclusively in every case as the least risky course. Some rational bargain-makers might be unfairly restrained under this policy, but on the alternative policy, even more people, perhaps, would become unjustly (mistakenly) enslaved.[35]

Feinberg goes even one step further, evoking a familiar common law maxim and suggesting that "[i]t is better (say) that one hundred people be wrongly denied permission to be enslaved than that one be wrongly permitted."[36] Plainly, at least on this account of the harm principle, one must hesitate before legalizing assisted suicide and euthanasia and first ask about the costs of the legal machinery necessary to ensure that decisions to die are voluntarily made and not coerced or the product of depression or incompetency. One must consider, too, the risks of abuse, coercion, and mistake, asking whether, as Feinberg does in the slavery contract context, the killing of some innocent persons without their consent is a price worth paying for the proffered right to receive assistance in dying. Certainly the potential harm associated with a mistaken or wrongful act of assisting suicide—murder—is comparable to the harm associated with the abusive practice of dueling or consensual slavery contracts. If banning these other practices can be reconciled with the harm principle—and Feinberg and Mill suggest it can be—the harm principle advocate must offer some explanation why banning assisted suicide and euthanasia cannot.

Assuming for the moment that the harm principle adherent could somehow resolve all these questions about the administration of, and the incidence of abuse and mistake in, an assisted suicide or euthanasia regime, what would a right to assisted suicide or euthanasia based on the harm principle look like? Similarly, we might ask, what would be the likely contours of a right to assisted suicide based on the neutrality principle?

In the first place, it is difficult to see how the harm or neutrality principle could discriminate between assisted suicide and euthanasia. Both serve to promote self-determination in the dying process and provide choice. There will also always be at least some people for whom assisted suicide is physically impossible and other persons who have scruples against committing suicide but none against euthanasia. If legalization were limited to assisted suicide, such individuals would be denied the right to self expression in the dying process—a result contrary to the autonomy project. Nor is it clear that the burdens of enforcing compliance with an assisted suicide regime differ in any marked degree from those associated with enforcing a euthanasia regime; as we discussed above, the two acts involve exactly the same moral decision (intentional killing), and the physical difference between them can be almost nonexistent (handing the patient medicine or placing it in his or her mouth). Indeed, many commentators and the Ninth Circuit have recognized these points and candidly conceded the difficulty of distinguishing between assisted suicide and euthanasia from the perspective of personal autonomy.[37]

So we might say that strict adherence to the harm and neutrality principles would tend toward a right to euthanasia as well as assisted suicide. What else might we say? Can, for example, the common distinction made by euthanasia proponents between the terminally ill or those suffering intractable pain, on the one hand, and all other competent adults, on the other, survive scrutiny from an autonomy perspective? To be sure, contemporary proponents of assisted suicide and euthanasia typically propose to limit the availability of these practices, at least in the first instance, to the terminally ill or those suffering intolerable pain. The referendum passed by Oregon voters in 1994 (like unsuccessful efforts in California and Washington State) focused only on assistance for the terminally ill. The World Federation of Right-to-Die Societies similarly has lobbied for a right available only to the "incurably ill and/or intolerably suffering person who persistently requests that help."[38]

Still, defining terms such as "terminally ill" or "intolerably suffering" is a difficult task—perhaps as difficult as defining "harm." It is commonplace to hear stories of people erroneously informed that they have just months to live, and efforts to diagnose terminal illnesses often seem to involve more art than science.[39] But even putting aside such definitional problems, a right limited only to terminally ill persons seems incompatible with full respect for the neutrality and harm principles. While a regime confining the right to assisted suicide to the terminally ill or those suffering grave pain would advance the autonomy interests of some persons, it would do nothing to advance the autonomy interests of others. Many rational, autonomous (and purportedly "harmless") decisions to die would continue to be suppressed. Hearkening back to some examples we have considered, Christian virgins seeking to avoid rapacious invaders, Romeos despondent over lost loves, Sardanapolises weary with life, Buddhist monks seeking to protest war through self-immolation, prisoners tired of their confined lives, disabled people overwhelmed by their disabilities—all would be barred from seeking assistance in taking their own lives in the manner they think most fitting if the right to assisted suicide and euthanasia is limited to the terminally ill or those suffering grave physical pain.

Put another way, in the assisted suicide regime typically proposed today, the individual's rational and "harmless" choice is a necessary, but not a sufficient, precondition to the exercise of the proffered right. Individuals seeking death must not only rationally and autonomously choose it, they must also receive the imprimatur of the state that their lives are of a sort that may be taken; the state alone asserts the authority to make the final moral judgment about which lives are worth protecting even against the rational patient's will. Robert Sedler, an American Civil Liberties Union (ACLU) advocate for the right to receive assistance in suicide, made the point plainly when he argued that the ACLU would extend the right only to the "terminally ill or so physically debilitated that it is *objectively reasonable* for them to find that their life has become unendurable."[40]

Such paternalistic judgments foreclosing free autonomous choice appear inconsistent with the aspirations behind the harm and neutrality principles. Perhaps recognizing this point, Ronald Dworkin testified before the British Parliament that "[p]eople disagree about what kind of a death is meaningful for them," and, precisely because of that disagreement, a state neutral between competing conceptions of the good life (and death) must avoid making any judgments or asserting any power in the area: "[It] is not that we collectively think [assisting suicide or euthanasia] is the decent thing to do, but that we collectively want people to act out of their own conviction."[41] David Richards has similarly written that

> it is an open question, consistent with the neutral theory of the good, how persons with freedom and rationality will define the meaning of their lives, and no externally defined teleological script is entitled to any special authority or

weight in such personal self-definition. Once we see the issue in this way, we can see that the fact of one's own death frames the meaning one gives one's life in widely differing ways.[42]

As these passages imply, the harm and neutrality principles, given full respect, seem to tend toward a right to assisted suicide and euthanasia open to *all* competent adults.

At this point, one might seek to interject that paternalistic nonneutral limits on choice *can* sometimes be justified, even under the neutrality principle. David Richards has argued, for example, that neutralism can

> supply a principle of paternalism and explain its proper scope and limits. From the point of view of the original position, the contractors would know that human beings would be subject to certain kinds of irrationalities with severe consequences, including death and the permanent impairment of health, and they would, accordingly, agree on an insurance principle against certain of these more serious irrationalities in the event they might occur to them.

Yet, even here, Richards appears to endorse only enough paternalistic state interference to ensure a fully competent adult decision (i.e., enough to prevent "irrationalities"). Richards does so out of recognition that to allow more paternalistic interference than insisting on a brief "cooling off" period to ensure that the individual has made a fully rational and considered decision would radically interfere with autonomous self-creation regarding one of the most intimate and personal of matters.[43]

One might try yet another way of defending a "limited" assisted suicide or euthanasia right as consistent with neutralism, arguing that a right limited to persons suffering from a terminal illness or terrible physical pain represents a rough approximation of the result that rational individuals in the original position, having yet formed no commitment to competing conceptions of the good, would select. Such an argument, however, runs the risk of confusing neutralism with majoritarianism or utilitarianism. It suggests adopting a policy that many people might select or vote for, or one that might maximize social utility or happiness, but one that not everyone would freely choose if the state remained neutral. Surely there *are* reasons why some—perhaps many—individuals who are not terminally ill or suffering grave pain may wish to die that we would recognize at least as "rational," and thus worthy of respect by a neutralist state. Who is to call deranged, for example, the peasant in Graham Greene's *Tenth Man* who was willing to sell his life for his family's financial security? Or the Japanese kamikaze pilots who gave up their lives out of religious and political fidelity to their emperor? Or the self-immolating Buddhist monks who sought to protest the war in Vietnam? Or the quadriplegic who would prefer death over years or decades bound to a wheelchair? Or the clinically depressed for whom modern medicine has no way of relieving his psychological suffering? We may not *agree* with these decisions, or make them for ourselves, but it is far from clear we can deem such decisions irrational just because they are eccentric or unpopular. To comport fully with the neutrality and harm principles, the state arguably would have to abstain from coercively interfering with *any* rational adult's private decision to die, whatever the motive or reason for the individual's considered decision, so long as we can assure that the decision is a considered one.

If I am correct, to the extent that the neutrality and harm principles support a right to assisted suicide and euthanasia, it is not a right that can be easily confined to certain classes of persons based upon their likelihood to succumb soon to a terminal illness or their endurance of incurable pain. Instead, the neutrality and harm principles appear to tend toward a right to consensual homicide open to all rational adults. Such a result, essentially a right to consensual homicide, has no precedent or analog in modern history and goes beyond even Rome's precedent. The prisoner sick of her sentence, the exhibitionist who sets himself on a pyre, the impecunious seeking a better life for her family by selling her life for disposal as a lethal form of amusement, and the terminally ill are all treated equally. All differing conceptions of the good death have to be respected—if, perhaps, after a "cooling off" period.

Neutrality and harm principle advocates are only beginning to discuss the possibility of a consensual homicide right open to all competent adults. Gerald Dworkin, for example, advocates the creation of a safeguard "Suicide Board" composed of psychologists to consult with individuals proposing to take their lives.[44] But even Dworkin ultimately seems to concede that neutral respect for personal autonomy requires that the approval of such a board would be unnecessary, and that the decision to die (in any fashion) should always rest with the competent adult.[45] David Richards argues for a right to be assisted in suicide with a vivid discussion of the plight of cancer patients, but, in the end, he, too, admits that his argument extends beyond such sympathetic cases to *any* "voluntarily embraced" decision to die.[46] Margaret Otlowski discusses the promotion of mercy and human dignity as independent moral arguments for legalizing euthanasia.[47] Yet, in the end, she admits that such arguments, tethered in no way to patient choice, could lead to allowing involuntary euthanasia based on the perception of doctors or others that the patient's life is no longer worth living and that killing would be the best solution.[48] As a remedy for such problems, Otlowski contends that the only true touchstone for legalization must be "the fundamental principle of self-determination."[49] While Otlowski goes on to argue for limiting the legalization of euthanasia to the terminally ill (regardless whether they are or are not suffering physical pain), she nowhere explains how such a limitation is consistent with the expansive principle of self-determination she espouses.

Even more pointedly, Joel Feinberg discusses a British television drama, *Whose Life Is It Anyway?* In the program, an active young man, paralyzed from the neck down in a car crash, decides that he would rather die than live out his life as a quadriplegic. Feinberg describes the young man's physical plight in great detail. Yet, Feinberg ultimately admits that the patient's physical condition is utterly irrelevant to the question whether he should be permitted to die. If "the choice is voluntary enough by reasonable tests," Feinberg submits, as a society we should be "firmly committed to a policy of non-interference . . . for the life at stake is [the patient's] life not ours. The person in sovereign control over it is precisely he."[50]

Perhaps most candidly of all, Sherry Colb, professor of law at Rutgers University, has openly criticized fellow assisted suicide advocates who would make what she calls "the distinction between the terminally ill and everyone else."[51] As Colb puts it, such a distinction

> does not keep faith with the ethical foundation for the right to die. The moral principle that distinguishes physician-assisted suicide from murder is a respect for the autonomy of the individual. According to this principle . . . *we should honor that wish [to die] regardless of whether she is terminally ill—out of compassion and respect for the individual . . . . It is essential in this context that we do not substitute our own judgment about which lives are and are not worth living for that of the individual whose own life is at stake.*[52]

This frank admission by a morally serious scholar—that an autonomy-based right to assisted suicide belongs to all competent adult patients—could not be clearer or more honest. Nor does it necessarily represent the end point of autonomy-based arguments. As we saw in chapter 3.8, liberals like Ronald Dworkin, Margaret Battin, Dan Brock, and Norman Cantor argue that respect for personal autonomy and individual liberty are consistent with, and even mandate, certain forms of *nonvoluntary* euthanasia.[53]

While no legislative proposal in the United States or England to date has sought to reach nearly as far as the neutrality or harm principles suggest, just as some neutralist and harm principle adherents are now beginning to discuss the full consequences of their philosophical commitments, the practical implications that might follow are also slowly coming into view. Dr. Kevorkian, of course, regularly used a machine in the back of his van to kill patients who were neither terminally ill nor suffering intolerable pain, including one middle-aged woman in the early stages of Alzheimer's disease still capable of beating her son at tennis—just no longer able to keep score. The Dutch recently relaxed their traditional rule requiring that a candidate for assisted suicide show he or she is suffering intolerable physical pain, now suggesting, as we shall see in the next chapter, that those suffering what they subjectively consider to be intolerable psychological pain can also qualify. And respected Dutch commentators are now widely predicting (and encouraging) the abandonment of even this precondition to assistance in suicide.

If a right to consensual homicide is eventually accepted into the law, we might ask what other ripple effects it could have on social and cultural norms. Why not, for example, allow individuals to sell their body parts or their lives? To be sure, costs of administration to ensure consent might be high. But some notable members of the legal and medical community have already asserted that respect for the personal autonomy of a competent donor should lead to the legalization of a market in body parts.[54] We saw in chapter 2, as well, that suicides were used as entertainment in ancient Rome. Why not again? Such thoughts might seem implausibly lurid, and it would certainly seem difficult to presume consent in such cases. Yet, while not necessarily implied by a right to consensual homicide, can we confidently dismiss these possibilities as intellectually inconsistent with such a right? Or socially implausible? Changing the law to permit consensual homicide would effect such a sea change in our culture, and it is difficult to assess what other forms of consensual conduct would or would not come to seem acceptable in such a very different world. But some hints do exist. In 1997, thirty-nine members of the Heaven's Gate cult systematically ingested Phenobarbital and vodka and asphyxiated each other in a belief that they were releasing their souls to meet with a UFO following in the trail of the Hale-Bopp comet.[55] In a videotaped testament filmed shortly before the suicides, one cult member stated, "I am doing this of my own free will," and "it is not something someone brainwashed me into or convinced me of or did a con job on."[56] In 2000, more than three hundred members of the Movement for the Restoration of the Ten Commandments immolated themselves in a gasoline-drenched compound. And few will forget anytime soon the mass suicide of the Branch Davidian cult at Waco, Texas, or the Rev. Jim Jones's cult at Jonestown, Guyana.[57] The notion that such events could proliferate may seem remote, but how can we dismiss the possibility out of hand that we would see more "choices" of this sort—or others like them? Internet chat rooms devoted to consensual forms of sadomasochism already exist. Armin Meiwes, a forty-one-year-old German computer expert, was arrested in 2003 for killing, butchering, and then eating a willing forty-three-year-old volunteer he found through just such a chat room called Cannibalism Cafe. Meiwes apparently had other individuals lined up to give up their lives, as well, one of whom he rejected as "too fatty." After his arrest, Meiwes told reporters that he "is confident of a light sentence," expressly invoking core neutralist harm principle themes: "'I think I will be out after four or five years. *It isn't as if I killed anyone against their will.*'"[58] In the event, Meiwes may be proven more or less correct: the German court originally considering his case declined to find him guilty of murder, imposing instead a manslaughter verdict. With good behavior, Meiwes could be released by 2008, after about four years in prison.[59] Young Japanese men are also using the Internet in droves to find partners for mutual suicide pacts.[60] Perhaps most eerily reminiscent of Roman era tastes and norms, in October 2003, a band called Hell on Earth sought to stage the suicide of a terminally ill patient via a live Internet broadcast from an undisclosed location in St. Petersburg, Florida. The band's front man claimed that the broadcast was intended to raise awareness of right-to-die issues.[61] A judge ultimately enjoined the performance, and members of the state legislature successfully launched an effort to ban the staging of a suicide for entertainment purposes.[62] But the band promised to try again elsewhere, this time with a form of what it calls "consensual cannibalism." A desperate effort at publicity, to be sure, and perhaps just a story of the bizarre. But if some forms of consensual homicide become legally and culturally acceptable, can we dismiss the possibility that we will see more of this sort of thing? Who, after all, would have imagined twenty years ago that a law banning suicide as stage entertainment might be required?

7

Legalization and the Law of Unintended Consequences: Utilitarian Arguments for Legalization

UNLIKE advocates of neutralism and the harm principle, utilitarians cannot be said to be bound by adherence to philosophical principle that might lead to an assisted suicide right open to all rational adults regardless of motive or physical condition. Instead, approaching the question of assisted suicide (like any other) by asking the practical question what legal rule would provide the greatest social benefits with the fewest attendant costs, utilitarianism holds out the promise of defending a more appealingly limited right, one open only to the incurably suffering or terminally ill.

While this approach offers an apparent advantage over arguments from autonomy that tend toward a right to consensual homicide open to all adult persons, focusing exclusively on social utility raises at least the possibility that the practice of euthanasia might be expanded in other troublesome ways. Disconnected from autonomy and choice, euthanasia might be extended on a utilitarian account even to persons who do not consent to it (involuntary euthanasia) if doing so would promote overall social welfare; to a utilitarian, the question whether to permit involuntary euthanasia cannot be easily dismissed.[1] As we saw in chapter 3.8, the American euthanasia movement has long made all sorts of utilitarian arguments for involuntary euthanasia, arguing that the practice is justified by, say, the social benefit of having to care for fewer "defective" persons and the reduction of medical costs associated with expensive end-of-life care; even recent liberal advocates of an autonomy-based right to assisted suicide have sometimes argued for involuntary euthanasia on grounds of social costs and utility. And, as we shall see, the Dutch experience is trending in that direction as well.

Some members of the U.S. Supreme Court gave hints of utilitarian thinking in *Glucksberg* and *Quill.* Before deciding to read any right to assistance in suicide and euthanasia into the due process or equal protection guarantees of the federal Constitution, Justice Souter and Justice O'Connor both said they

wanted to see the results of state legislative experiments.[2] Arguably implicit in
their position was a desire to see whether the practice of assisting suicide and
euthanasia would carry with it more social benefits than harms. In the legislative arena, too, we commonly hear similar utilitarian arguments for all manner
of proposed laws, with partisans arguing that enacting a certain provision will
(or will not) promote the greatest good for the greatest number; the debate over
assisted suicide in state houses across the country has been no different.

It cannot be denied that legalizing assisted suicide and euthanasia for
those suffering great pain or enduring a terminal illness *would* carry with it tangible benefits. Persons in such conditions who wish to die, but who either cannot or do not wish to kill themselves without assistance, would be able to do so,
thereby avoiding unwanted pain and suffering and fulfilling their own autonomously chosen life plans. What may not be obvious, or at least perhaps not immediately so, is whether there are any costs associated with normalizing assisted
suicide and euthanasia if we do so only for competent adults who are, in fact,
suffering from great physical pain or a terminal illness. In the balance of this
chapter, I explore this question and empirical evidence available from the
Netherlands, Oregon, and elsewhere.

Ultimately, I suggest, we cannot rule out the possibility that nontrivial
costs will attend the legalization of assisted suicide and euthanasia, even when
it is limited to such narrow classes of persons; then, having suggested that legalization is not an entirely costless enterprise, I pose the critical question:
how do we weigh the competing benefits and costs in a consequentialist enterprise? How are we to judge that the benefits associated with normalization are
"enough" to outweigh the costs? I see no convincing answer and ultimately suggest that the project of comparing the benefits and costs of assisted suicide rests
on a flawed premise—that is, that there exists a single scale or currency that we
can use to measure fundamentally incommensurate goods.

7.1 THE DUTCH EXPERIENCE: "VIRTUALLY ABUSE-FREE"?

The Netherlands is one of very few countries in the world with a regularly operating assisted suicide and euthanasia regime.[3] As such, it is a natural
focus of attention for those looking to see how such a regime might be applied
elsewhere. And, despite concerns expressed by some,[4] the Dutch experience is
frequently held out by proponents of legalizing assisted suicide as a model for
emulation and described in glowing terms.

Margaret Battin, for example, has argued that the practice of assisted
suicide and euthanasia in the Netherlands is "virtually abuse-free."[5] Jocelyn
Downie has suggested that the Dutch experience shows that euthanasia, even
when legalized, is rarely employed.[6] Epstein has asserted that "Dutch physicians
are not euthanasia enthusiasts and they are slow to practice it in individual

cases,"[7] and Posner has submitted that the "fear of doctors' rushing patients to their death" in the Netherlands "has not been substantiated and does not appear realistic."[8] Margaret Otlowski, too, has claimed that "there is no evidence that [the Dutch] have moded at all in the direction of unacceptable practices."[9] In what follows, I consider such assertions in light of the formal legal-medical rules associated with the practice of assisted suicide and euthanasia in the Netherlands, as well as data reflecting the actual practices and attitudes of Dutch physicians.

An Outline of Dutch Procedures

While voluntary euthanasia societies existed in Britain and the United States as early as the 1930s, no counterpart Dutch movement arose until considerably later.[10] Indeed, the Dutch euthanasia story does not begin in earnest until 1973, when a Dutch physician, who killed her seventy-eight-year-old mother at her request, was tried for homicide and, after a very closely followed trial, received only a conditional one-week jail sentence along with one year of probation.[11] Though a notable event in Dutch law, however, even that case hardly portended an irrevocable break with the past: between 1969 and 1980, at least three other prosecutions for assisted suicide in the Netherlands resulted in jail sentences ranging from six to eighteen months.[12] The pace of change began to accelerate in 1981, however, when a seventy-six-year-old lay person received a conditional sentence of six months subject to one year probation (after the court found that a jail term would have been too burdensome on the aged defendant), and the court went on to advise in dicta that a *physician* might be exempt from any punishment for killing a patient suffering severe physical duress (arguably approving not just assisted suicide but also euthanasia, without drawing any distinction between them).[13]

In 1984 events reached a crescendo in a case involving an unnamed ninety-three-year-old woman who was bedridden due to a hip fracture, no longer able to eat or drink, and slipping in and out of consciousness.[14] At one point, when the patient regained consciousness, she asked to be euthanized and her physician consented.[15] The case was later reported to the police and ultimately reached the country's supreme court.[16] The Dutch Supreme Court used the dispute to announce an exception, or defense, to the country's penal laws expressly banning the practice of assisted suicide.[17] The court defended the doctor's conduct, moreover, not because of a perceived need to vindicate patient autonomy, but rather because of the perceived "necessity" resulting from a conflict of duties or *force majeure* (*overmacht*) confronting the doctor, explaining that the killing was justified by the *doctor's judgment* about the quality of his patient's life (or, more precisely, the doctor's judgment about the lack thereof):

in accordance with [the] norms of medical ethics, and with the expertise which as a professional he must be assumed to possess—[he] balanced the duties and interests which, in the case at hand, were in conflict, and made a choice that— objectively considered, and taking into account the specific circumstances of this case—was justifiable.[18]

The Royal Netherlands Society for the Promotion of Medicine and the Recovery Interest Society for Nurses and Nursing Aids, at about the same time, set forth certain criteria for assisting suicide or performing euthanasia in conformity with the court's newly recognized necessity defense,[19] and the minister of justice made clear that medical professionals following these guidelines would not be prosecuted.[20]

In 1994 the Dutch Supreme Court substantially extended the physician "necessity" defense in the *Chabot* case.[21] There, the court considered the justifiability or excusability of the killing of a fifty-year-old woman (identified in court papers as "Ms. B") by a psychiatrist, Dr. Chabot.[22] Ms. B's son had committed suicide in 1986; in 1988 her father died; in 1990 she was divorced and her second son was injured in a traffic accident.[23] In the course of her son's treatment, cancer was discovered, and he died in 1991.[24] The same year, Ms. B attempted suicide, unsuccessfully, using drugs supplied by a doctor.[25] Later, through the Dutch Association for Voluntary Euthanasia, Ms. B was referred to Dr. Chabot, who examined Ms. B in four series of meetings over a five- week period, for a total of twenty-four actual hours (although apparently amounting to thirty "billable" hours).[26] Dr. Chabot also consulted with four other psychiatrists, a clinical psychologist, a general practitioner, and a professor of ethics,[27] though none of these professionals actually examined Ms. B.[28] Dr. Chabot then concluded that Ms. B was suffering psychologically in a manner that was subjectively "unbearable" to her, and that she was "without prospect of improvement."[29] In Dr. Chabot's judgment, Ms. B's "rejection of therapy was . . . well-considered."[30] Seven weeks after meeting Ms. B, Dr. Chabot supplied lethal medication to her.[31] She consumed the medication and died a half-hour later.[32]

The Dutch Supreme Court held that, for a request for assisted suicide or euthanasia to be justified on "necessity" grounds, the patient's suffering need not be physical, the patient need not be terminally ill, and purely psychological suffering can qualify a patient for an act of euthanasia.[33] The court held that Dr. Chabot erred only by failing to have the colleagues he consulted examine Ms. B before agreeing to help kill her, though the court ultimately declined to impose any penalty for this oversight.[34] Given the *Chabot* decision, John Griffiths, professor of sociology of law at the University of Groningen in the Netherlands and a leading defender of decriminalization in that country, has surmised that the requirement of unbearable suffering in any form, physical or mental, is likely on the way out: "the decision in *Chabot* may later be seen as having opened the way to a legal development that accepts assistance with suicide to persons who are not 'sick' at all."[35]

And, in fact, Griffiths' prediction seems well on its way to being proven correct. Between 1986 and 1993 at least three legislative efforts to codify the judiciary's expanding necessity defense failed.[36] Finally, in 2001 a bill was approved by the Dutch Parliament permitting assisted suicide and euthanasia when the physician:

1. holds the conviction that the request by the patient was voluntary and well-considered,
2. holds the conviction that the patient's suffering was lasting and unbearable,
3. has informed the patient about the situation he was in and about his prospects,
4. and the patient [held] the conviction that there was no other reasonable solution for the situation he was in,
5. has consulted at least one other, independent physician who has seen the patient and has given his written opinion on the requirements of due care, referred to in parts 1–4, and,
6. has terminated a life or assisted in a suicide with due care.[37]

Under these standards, terminal illness plainly is not a prerequisite to euthanasia, and neither is a physical ailment of any kind. While the doctor must consider his or her patient to be "suffering," that suffering need not be physical or even really present at all: the doctor need only show that he or she believed (or "[held] the conviction") that the patient endured some sort of (unspecified) suffering.[38] And, procedurally, there is no specified waiting period after the request for euthanasia before it may be performed and no requirement that the patient place his or her wishes in writing.[39]

Griffiths' prediction about the future of assisted suicide in the Netherlands, in fact, actually fails to capture the speed and scope of developments there insofar that the 2001 Dutch Act also extends assisted suicide and euthanasia to children as young as twelve:

> [i]f the minor patient is aged between twelve and sixteen years and may be deemed to have a reasonable understanding of his interests, the physician may [carry] out the patient's request [for termination of life or assisted suicide], provided always that the parent or the parents exercising parental authority or his guardian agree with the termination of life or the assisted suicide.[40]

By contrast, minors between sixteen and eighteen who "may be deemed to have a reasonable understanding of [their] interests" can obtain assisted suicide or euthanasia *without* parental consent, although the parents must be "involved" in the decision-making process.[41]

Going yet a step further, in late 2004 the Groningen University Hospital issued a press release announcing that it has proposed guidelines for killing unwanted malformed children—that is, infanticide.[42] The hospital's guidelines are, as of this writing, under review by the Dutch government. According to the hospital's press release, it seems that the proposal is primarily aimed at malformed infants but would nonetheless apply to any child under twelve who is "suffering" in a manner that "cannot be relieved by means of other ways."[43] While parental consent is required, consent is of course impossible to obtain from the children who are the targets of this proposal, and patient autonomy cannot be cited as the basis for this extension of the law. Nor is it clear whether the "suffering" need be physical or might also include mental anguish (as the Dutch courts have already held in *Chabot*). And, if the latter comes to qualify, the question will surely arise: might the psychic suffering of the *parents* qualify without respect to whether the child's physical suffering can be addressed by palliative treatments? All of this, at the moment, remains unclear.

The Dutch Practice of Assisted Suicide and Euthanasia

To date, two large-scale studies have been published regarding Dutch assisted suicide and euthanasia practices, one in 1990 ("1990 Survey") and the other in 1995 ("1995 Survey") (collectively the "Surveys").[44] A third survey was published in *The Lancet* in 2003, albeit in abbreviated form and using data from 2001, the year before the passage of the Dutch statute formally legalizing assisted suicide and euthanasia, thus leaving us without definitive data on the impact of that landmark legislation.[45] All three studies were performed under the auspices of Gerrit van der Wal of the Institute for Research in Extramural Medicine at Vrije Universiteit in Amsterdam and Paul J. van der Maas of the Department of Public Health at Erasmus University in Rotterdam.[46]

The Surveys employed two central methods. First, the authors confidentially interviewed a random sample of slightly more than four hundred physicians, reflecting general practitioners and representatives from five different specialties (cardiology, surgery, internal medicine, pulmonology, and neurology).[47] Second, the Surveys examined a random sample of death certificates over the course of a four-month period for each year under review, followed up by a questionnaire directed to the physicians identified in each death certificate in the sample under study.[48]

Some of the central findings of the Surveys' physician interviews are summarized in table 7.1.

As reflected in the table, the 1990[49] Survey found that fully 1.9 percent of all Dutch deaths (2,447) were attributable to the practice of euthanasia. Far from being legal but rare, substantially more people died in the Netherlands as a result of euthanasia than as a result of HIV, leukemia, or homicide.[50] The 1990 Survey found that an additional 0.3 percent of all deaths—or nearly 400 cases—were the product of physician-assisted suicide. By 1995 these figures had grown measurably: 2.3 percent of all deaths nationwide that year were the re-

TABLE 7.1
Central Findings of 1990 and 1995 Surveys

	1995	1990	% change
Total Deaths	135,546	128,786	5
Number of explicit requests for euthanasia or assisted suicide later in disease	34,500	25,100	37
Number of requests for euthanasia or assisted suicide at a particular time	9,700	8,900	9
End-of-life practices performed			
Euthanasia	3,118	2,447	27
As % of all deaths	2.3	1.9	
Assisted suicide	542	386	40
As % of all deaths	0.4	0.3	
Ending life without patient's explicit request	949	1,030	−8
As % of all deaths	0.7	0.8	

Source: Extrapolated from data in van der Maas et al., *Euthanasia 1996*, 335 New Eng. J. Med. at 1700–1701 & 1701 tbl. 1.

sult of euthanasia (a 27 percent increase), and 0.4 percent were due to assisted suicide (a 40 percent increase). The Surveys also reveal that requests for euthanasia increased dramatically between 1990 and 1995 (prospective requests for euthanasia at a later stage of a disease grew 37 percent, and requests for euthanasia at a particular time rose 9 percent). The actual incidence of euthanasia and assisted suicide also jumped substantially, 27 percent and 40 percent, respectively.

Physician interview data from the 2001 Survey suggests that the significant rise in the incidence of euthanasia experienced between 1990 and 1995 was consolidated and persisted: euthanasia continued to account for approximately 2.2 percent of all deaths in the Netherlands in 2001, approximating the results found in the 1995 Survey.[51] The physician interview results for 2001, however, diverge somewhat from the results of the death certificate study.[52] The latter study suggests that euthanasia became even more common—rising from 1.7 percent of all deaths in 1990, to 2.4 percent in 1995, and to 2.6 percent in 2001.[53] And, again, we currently have no data suggesting how, if at all, the 2001 statute may have affected these numbers.

We do know, however, that things do not always go smoothly. Dutch researchers have found that problems with "completion" arise in 16 percent of assisted suicide cases and 6 percent of euthanasia cases, and "complications" arise in 7 percent of assisted suicide cases and 3 percent of euthanasia cases.[54] These complications include nausea and vomiting, and the problems with completion include patients waking from drug-induced comas and living as long as fourteen days after the administration of death-inducing medication.[55]

In 1995, the authors of the Surveys for the first time systematically examined the frequency with which physicians euthanize their patients without consent. As shown in table 1, they found that 0.7 percent of all deaths nationwide that year were the result of nonconsensual killings (approximately 950). Although the 1990 Survey did not seek to study this issue on a systematic basis, the more limited death certificate study conducted suggested that nonconsensual killings represented 0.8 percent of deaths nationwide (approximately 1,000). Data from 2001 suggest little improvement, with nonconsensual killings persisting at a rate of approximately 0.7 percent of all deaths in the country that year.[56] In all, it appears that, for every three or four acts of voluntary euthanasia, the Dutch regime generates one case of a patient being killed without consent.

Downie has sought to downplay the significance of these nonconsensual killings, noting that "in 600 of the 1,000 cases [of nonconsensual euthanasia in 1990], something about the patients' wishes was known although explicit consent according to the [Dutch Medical Association's] guidelines had not been given."[57] This interpretation, however, does not address the 400 cases in which patients' wishes were not known *at all*.[58] And in the 600 remaining cases, the patient was adjudged even by the euthanizing physician to have expressed something less than the explicit consent required under the Dutch guidelines to avoid potential prosecution.[59] These comments ranged—according to the physicians themselves—from a "rather vague earlier expression of a wish for euthanasia, as in comments like, 'If I cannot be saved anymore, you must give me something,' or 'Doctor, please don't let me suffer for too long,' to much more extensive discussions" that were still insufficient, in the doctor's own judgment, to satisfy Dutch law.[60]

In 1995 the New York State Task Force on Life and the Law appointed by Mario Cuomo recommended against legalizing assisted suicide in part on the strength of the then-available 1990 Survey data.[61] Referring to the 2,700 reported deaths by assisted suicide and euthanasia in the Netherlands and the 1,000 cases of nonconsensual terminations, the task force reasoned that:

> If euthanasia were practiced in a comparable percentage of cases in the United States, voluntary euthanasia would account for about 36,000 deaths each year, and euthanasia without the patient's consent would occur in an additional 16,000 deaths. The Task Force members regard this risk as unacceptable. They also believe that the risk of such abuse is neither speculative nor distant, but an inevitable byproduct of the transition from policy to practice in the diverse circumstances in which the practices would be employed.[62]

All of the foregoing statistics and analyses, moreover, arguably understate both the incidence of euthanasia in the Netherlands and the frequency with which patients are killed without consent. The later Dutch Surveys include only *affirmative* acts of euthanasia in their analysis of the incidence of mercy killings with and without consent.[63] They do not count omissions or withdrawals of care performed without patient consent and with the intention of killing the patient[64]—even though these are acts that Dutch medical guidelines expressly recognize as euthanasia.[66] The 1990 Survey sought to count such deaths separately, but the 1995 and 2001 Surveys, surprisingly and without explanation, simply omitted any such discussion—an unhelpful development for anyone trying to comprehend Dutch practice.[66] The 1990 data reveal, however, that 4,000 deaths were caused that year by the withdrawal or withholding of treatment without explicit patient consent and "'[w]ith the explicit purpose'" of shortening life.[67] The 1990 Survey found an additional 4,750 deaths were caused by withdrawing or withholding without explicit consent but "[p]artly with the purpose" of ending life.[68]

Combined, these figures represent 8,750 cases where care was discontinued by a doctor who intended to kill the patient, and who acted without the explicit consent of the patient; such deaths accounted for some 6.78 percent of all deaths in the Netherlands in 1990.[69] It is hard to understand why the Surveys' authors failed to report data regarding nonconsensual killings by omission in the 1995 and 2001 Surveys, and it would certainly be unfortunate if they did so simply to diminish attention to those facts (though it seems clear their decision not to report the data has that effect). In any event, when added to the 1,000 nonconsensual *affirmative* acts of euthanasia, the total number of intentional killings without patient consent in 1990 was 9,750, or 7.56 percent of all deaths.[70] Extrapolating to the U.S. population, this would translate into approximately 173,650 medically accelerated deaths per year without explicit patient consent (based on the approximately 2.3 million deaths that occur in the United States annually).[71]

Nor is it clear that killing has been used only in extremis to prevent suffering. In the 1990 Survey, physicians involved in nonconsensual affirmative killings volunteered that ending pain and suffering motivated them in only 18.8 percent of the cases.[72] Reasons physicians gave more frequently for terminating life without consent included the "absence of any prospect of improvement (60 percent) . . . avoidance of 'needless prolongation' (33 percent); the relatives' inability to cope (32 percent); and [the physician's judgment that the patient enjoyed only a] 'low quality of life' (31 percent)."[73] In fact, a 2003 regression analysis spanning twenty-five years' worth of data found that patient pain had become a "significantly less important" consideration even in cases of *voluntary* acts of euthanasia and assisted suicide. While cited as a major reason for requesting euthanasia and assisted suicide in over 50 percent of cases in 1977,

by 2001 pain was cited as a major reason for requested assisted suicide and euthanasia in less than 25 percent of cases of consensual killings.[74] Meanwhile, a
patient's sense of "deterioration" and "hopelessness" both increased markedly
over time as reasons cited for motivating assisted suicide and euthanasia
requests.[75]

Some studies suggest, too, that some Dutch physicians may be under-
trained in palliative care techniques that might mitigate the perceived need to
resort to assisted suicide and euthanasia. A 1987 Dutch Health Council study
found, for example, that a majority of cancer patients in pain suffered because
of their caregivers' lack of expertise in pain management,[76] and a 1989 study
found that palliative care was "inadequate in slightly more than 50 percent of
evaluated cases."[77] Even among Dutch doctors, most of whom support assisted
suicide and euthanasia, fully 40 percent have signaled their "agreement with the
proposition that '[a]dequate alleviation of pain and/or symptoms and personal
care of the dying patient make euthanasia unnecessary.'"[78]

Ultimately, a government panel charged with reviewing the 1990 Survey results sought to explain and even defend the seemingly large number of
nonconsensual killings, doing so on the ground that:

> The ultimate justification for the intervention is in both cases [that is, where
> there is and is not an explicit request for assistance in dying] the patient's un-
> bearable suffering. So, medically speaking, there is little difference between
> these situations . . . because in both cases patients are involved who suffer ter-
> ribly. The absence of a special . . . request for the termination of life stems
> partly from the circumstance that the party in question is not (any longer) able
> to express his will because he is already in the terminal stage, and partly be-
> cause the demand for an explicit request is not in order when the treatment of
> pain and symptoms is intensified. The degrading condition the patient is in
> confronts the doctor with a case of [*force majeure*]. According to the Com-
> mission, the intervention by the doctor can easily be regarded as an action that
> is justified by necessity, just like euthanasia.[79]

Thus, it appears that it is not patient autonomy or even the alleviation
of pain that, to the Dutch government at least, stands as the ultimate justification for assisted suicide and euthanasia. Instead, it is the *physician's* assessment
of the patient's *quality of life* as "degrading" or "deteriorating" or "hopeless" that
stands as the ultimate justification for killing. Echoing the Dutch Supreme
Court's decision of 1984, the Dutch government panel found that the "necessity" of assisted suicide stems not from the patient's consent (let alone autonomous choice), but from the *physician's quality of life assessment*.[80] And, as
of this writing, the Dutch are in the process of considering the legalization of
infanticide—that is, killing children without consent.

As reflected in table 7.2, it also appears that the incidence of nonvol-

TABLE 7.2
End-of-Life Decisions in 1995 by Age

	0–49	50–64	65–79	>80
Total death certificates studied	661	652	1,792	2,041
% of all deaths in Netherlands (n=135,675)	8	12	36	44
% of all end-of-life decisions (n=2,604)	6	14	34	46
% ending life without explicit request (n=64)	18	16	31	36
% ending life without explicit request vs. % of all end-of-life decisions	300	114	91	78

Source: Extrapolated from van der Maas et al., Euthanasia 1996, 335 New Eng. J. Med. at 1703 tbl. 3.

untary euthanasia is closely related to age. The 1995 Survey's death certificate study found that younger patients (especially those from birth to age forty-nine) are far more likely than older persons to be killed without their consent.[81]

While the young (from birth to age forty-nine) represented 6 percent of all end-of-life cases surveyed in 1995, they accounted for 18 percent of all cases found where life was ended without an express request; the young were, thus, vastly overrepresented (300 percent) among cases where patients were killed without express consent when compared with their population in the pool of all end-of-life cases. Those between fifty and sixty-four years of age were also overrepresented (114 percent), constituting 14 percent of all end-of-life cases, but 16 percent of cases where life was ended without clear consent. And the 2001 Survey suggests that little has changed since 1995;[82] indeed, the 2001 Survey authors confirm that "[e]nding of life without a patient's explicit request occurred most frequently among people dying at [an] age younger than 65 years" and data concerning the incidence of such problems "remained virtually unchanged" between 1995 and 2001.[83]

Remarkably, the Surveys have consistently found that a significant pro-portion of assisted suicides and acts of euthanasia go unreported, even though Dutch professional and legal guidelines allow the practices and expressly require them to be reported to public authorities; state approval of assisted suicide and euthanasia simply has not, it seems, ended the "grey market" for such services. For example, of the 2,700 cases of assisted suicide and euthanasia recorded in 1990, only 486 were reported pursuant to Dutch medical guidelines, meaning, in effect, that doctors illegally certified 82 percent of these cases as death by "natural causes."[84] Of the 147 physicians interviewed in the 1995 Survey who reported participating in cases of assisted suicide or euthanasia, 84—or 57 percent—admitted they had not reported at least one other case, and none identified any adverse legal consequence from his or her behavior.[85] In the 2001 Survey, the proportion of unreported cases declined, but the authors found that, even after years of unfavorable attention to this issue and the repeated commitment of Dutch authorities to improve physician reporting, as many as 46 percent of all cases of assisted suicide and euthanasia still go unreported.[86]

As reflected in table 7.3, physicians have also admitted that they are far less likely to consult with colleagues or family members, or ensure an explicit patient request, in the cases of assisted suicide and euthanasia they choose not to report to state authorities. Doctors likewise admit that they are far less likely to leave a written record in unreported cases—a record that might permit subsequent inquiries into their conduct.

When asked about their unreported cases, 16 of the 84 responding physicians—or 19 percent—stated that their *most recent* unreported case involved killing the patient without an explicit request.[87] Physicians stated that they had complied with guidelines requiring them to consult with colleagues 100 percent of the time in their reported cases but had respected this requirement only 58 percent of the time in their unreported cases; they likewise revealed that they left behind no written record of their conduct in just 3 percent of reported cases but left no such record (again in violation of professional requirements) in 43 percent of their unreported cases. And fully 40 percent of general practitioners simply dismissed the rule requiring them to consult with another colleague before killing a patient as being not very important.[88]

TABLE 7.3

Characteristics of Reported and Unreported Cases of Euthanasia and Assisted Suicide: 1995 (percent)

	Reported Cases (N=68)	Unreported Cases (N=68)
Patient request was:		
Highly explicit	100	92
"Rather" explicit	0	8
Written will present	73	44
Express written report on decision	36	0
Notes in medical record	84	57
No writing	3	43
Discussion with colleagues	100	58
Contact with patient's relatives	99	92

Source: van der Wal et al., *Notification Procedure*, New Eng. J. Med. at 1709 tbl. 2.

Some Questions about the Future of the Dutch Regime

Faced with the data regarding the prevalence of unreported and non-consensual killings, the *Chabot* decision extending euthanasia to those suffering subjective mental anguish, new laws affording a right to lethal assistance to minors, and a proposal now on the table to legalize infanticide, one might ask what else the future might hold for the practice of assisted suicide and euthanasia in the Netherlands.

For example, is the suffering requirement on its way out as a prerequisite to euthanasia? Griffiths suggests that it is, and the evidence seems to support him. And what about the relatively high rate of euthanasia among younger persons? It seems that these cases deserve special attention: are they happening because of terminal illnesses, or is euthanasia sometimes being employed in response to disabilities? What role is depression playing in these and other cases in the Netherlands? This is all largely unexplored territory. Does a regime dependent on self-reporting by physicians who have no interest in recording any case falling outside the guidelines adequately protect against lives taken erroneously, mistakenly, or as a result of abuse or coercion? How would we ever know? Why do Dutch doctors remain so hesitant about reporting their cases of euthanasia even with a guarantee of state support so long as they follow the guidelines? And how can we explain or come to defend the rates of nonvoluntary euthanasia and the recent introduction of infanticide? To the Dutch government, the ultimate justification for assisted suicide and euthanasia does not really seem to be patient autonomy or suffering at the end of the day, but, increasingly, a physician's subjective assessment about the patient's quality of life.

Griffiths has acknowledged that, his support for legalized assisted suicide and euthanasia notwithstanding, "the present control-regime [in the Netherlands] does not offer effective control,"[89] and that it "is a bit of a paper tiger, in the sense that only a minority of cases (and these the least problematic ones) are reported, and that little serious enforcement is undertaken in reported cases that do not meet the legal criteria."[90] In fact, of all the data gathered on Dutch assisted suicide and euthanasia practices, the low reporting rate is the issue that, to Griffiths at least, "most gives rise to concern."[91]

To encourage greater reporting, especially of cases that do not meet current legal criteria, Griffiths does not argue for greater vigilance and enforcement of laws against killing patients without consent. Instead, somewhat surprisingly, he advocates for the elimination of any criminal penalty associated with such nonconsensual killings.[92] If doctors do not fear criminal prosecution even for killing their patients without consent, Griffiths' reasoning goes, they will be more apt to report their conduct.[93] Echoing and building on the sentiments of the Dutch governmental commission reviewing (and seeking to justify) the data on nonconsensual killings, Griffiths gives us a hint where the

Dutch ultimately may find themselves—namely, routinizing "euthanasia and termination of life *without an explicit request* [such that they are] handled in the same way [as voluntary requests for assisted suicide and euthanasia]: deemed 'normal medical practice' and subjected to the controls applicable to other behavior of doctors."[94]

Absent here, once again, is any linkage between assisted suicide and patient autonomy. A physician would be free to kill his patients *without their consent* and have no reason to fear criminal prosecution. Though Griffiths believes that the decriminalization of nonvoluntary euthanasia would lead to better compliance with self-reporting requirements, he (curiously) does not pause to give any significant consideration to the question whether allowing doctors to kill without consent might also lead to additional cases of abusive, coercive, and mistaken killings. In fact, Griffiths' proposal seemingly would preclude the criminal prosecution not just of those acting out of motives of mercy, but even those (like Dr. Harold Shipman) who act out of very different and even cruel motives.[95] In Griffiths' preferred regime, only professional and civil sanctions would be available as remedies when doctors kill without consent—and even these remedies would be available only if and when doctors kill in the absence of what he calls "normal medical practice"—although Griffiths fails to specify when he thinks killing a patient without consent should be considered "normal."[96]

Nor does Griffiths fairly make out the case that his proposal would even guarantee better self-reporting: doctors who fail to meet the guidelines for "normal" nonvoluntary killings (whatever those might be) may very well still choose to avoid reporting their activities for fear of professional and civil penalties which, for doctors, can mean the end of their careers and financial security. Indeed, Griffiths himself acknowledges that *any* regime relying on physician self-reporting is "intrinsic[ally] ineffective[]."[97] Simply put, the absence of *criminal* penalties may not suffice to ensure that physicians report all cases of killing without consent; the continued presence of financial and professional consequences may still serve as strong deterrents to full and accurate reporting. Meanwhile, Griffiths' proposal would abjure patient autonomy as the touchstone for when assisted suicide is appropriate, in favor of physicians' quality of life judgments, and rewrite the boundary of acceptable medical practice from voluntary to nonvoluntary euthanasia. It does not seem at all far-fetched to imagine, however, that Griffiths, once again, has accurately predicted the future of Dutch practice.

7.2 THE OREGON EXPERIENCE:
AN "ALL-TOO-CONSCIENTIOUS" STATUTORY REGIME?

Among American jurisdictions, to date only Oregon has experimented with assisted suicide. Epstein has hailed Oregon's assisted suicide law as "tightly drafted legislation" and an "all-too-conscientious attempt" to avoid cases of abuse, mistake, and pressure.[98] Otlowski concludes that "many fears associated with the legalization of physician-assisted suicide [in Oregon] have simply proven unfounded."[99] And Oregon's statute is certainly more refined than the medical guidelines long in force in the Netherlands or the recent Dutch statute. But Epstein's and Otlowski's enthusiastic endorsements are themselves subject to question in light of certain deficiencies in both the structure of the Oregon law and its practice in the field.

An Outline of Oregon's Procedures

To qualify for assistance in dying under the Oregon Death with Dignity Act, a patient must be "[a]n adult who is capable . . . and has been determined by the attending physician and consulting physician to be suffering from a terminal disease, and who has voluntarily expressed his or her wish to die"; meeting these qualifications allows a patient to make "a written request for medication for the purpose of ending his or her life."[100]

The term "capable" is defined by statute to mean "that in the opinion of a court or in the opinion of the patient's attending physician or consulting physician, psychiatrist or psychologist, a patient has the ability to make and communicate health care decisions to health care providers."[101] A "terminal disease" is defined as "an incurable and irreversible disease that . . . will, within reasonable medical judgment, produce death within six months."[102] Written requests for assisted suicide must be "witnessed by at least two individuals who, in the presence of the patient, attest that to the best of their knowledge and belief the patient is capable, acting voluntarily, and is not being coerced to sign the request."[103]

An attending physician is required, among other things, to "[m]ake the initial determination of whether a patient has a terminal disease, is capable, and has made the request voluntarily," and to refer the patient to a consulting physician for confirmation of all three of these findings.[104] If the attending or consulting physician believes that "a patient may be suffering from a psychiatric or psychological disorder or depression causing impaired judgment, either physician shall refer the patient for counseling," and no medication to end the patient's life may "be prescribed until the person performing the counseling determines that the patient is not suffering from a psychiatric or psychological disorder or depression causing impaired judgment."[105]

Once the medical review process is complete, the attending physician may prescribe life-ending medications.[106] "No less than fifteen . . . days [must] elapse between the patient's initial oral request and the writing of a prescription"; in addition, forty-eight hours must elapse between the patient's written request and the writing of a prescription.[107] Doctors who write death-inducing prescriptions in good-faith compliance with the Act's requirements are thereafter shielded from criminal, civil, and professional sanctions.[108]

Physicians are responsible for maintaining records regarding each act of assisted suicide, including documents reflecting all of the patient's oral and written requests for assistance in dying; the attending and consulting physician's diagnosis, prognosis, and finding that the patient was capable, acting voluntarily, and with full information; and all reports reflecting any counseling that occurred.[109] Oregon's Department of Human Services is charged with reviewing a sample of these records annually.[110]

While perhaps representing a drafting improvement over the Dutch statute in some areas, a great many questions might still be asked about how the Oregon law is written and practiced. It is, for example, unclear from the language of the statute whether "terminal" means that the patient is expected to die within six months assuming she is given medical care or assuming she is not.[111] And, approximately 50 percent of Oregon physicians have acknowledged that they simply are not confident in their own ability to predict whether patients have more or less than six months to live.[112] In point of fact, putatively terminal patients have received lethal prescriptions in Oregon and waited to use them for as long as 466 days—over fifteen months.[113] Although proponents have argued that Oregon's regime helps dying patients avoid unnecessary pain and suffering, Oregon's law (unlike even the Dutch guidelines) nowhere conditions access to assisted suicide on the existence of pain of any kind, let alone pain that cannot be fully treated by readily available medicines.

Because the attending physician under Oregon law is allowed to choose a consulting physician who may be related to the attending doctor or the patient professionally or personally, the consultant is not guaranteed to be free to render a dispassionate judgment (something even Dutch guidelines purport to mandate). Nor does the Oregon statute require that either physician have any special expertise; trainees are free to render judgments on whether an illness is "terminal."[114] Thus, while approximately 86 percent of patients seeking assisted suicide in 2001 suffered from cancer, prescribing physicians were predominately internal medicine and family practitioners (collectively representing 69 percent of prescribers); oncologists prescribed death-inducing medication in just 25 percent of assisted suicide cases.[115] Significantly, there is also no requirement that any of the physicians involved review with the patient potential alternatives (for example, hospice or pain killers), or that those with expertise in such areas (for example, pain management specialists) be brought in to review care options that may alleviate the patient's perceived need for assisted suicide.

While Oregon's statute requires that the attending and consulting physicians make a finding that the patient is mentally capable, it does not require any mental health qualifications or expertise of either doctor, again leaving potentially specialized questions regarding the diagnosis of potential psychological disorders (for example, depression) to individuals without any relevant expertise—this despite a wealth of evidence suggesting that a significant number of suicides are caused in whole, or part, by clinical depression or mental illness.[116] In fact, 28 percent of Oregon physicians polled have admitted that they do not even feel competent to recognize depression.[117] Nor has Oregon examined the prevalence of depression among the terminally ill, though a recent study of depression in cancer patients (one notably not dependant on physicians' self-assessed ability to detect depression) found that oncologists detected the condition in only approximately 13 percent of patients who described themselves as suffering from moderate to severe levels of depression.[118]

Oregon's statute (again, in contrast to Dutch medical guidelines) also does not require the presence of a doctor when the patient commits suicide, and between 1998 and 2002 prescribing physicians were absent 66 percent of the time.[119] Given this fact, there is no guarantee that a doctor will assess the patient's mental condition at the time of death; indeed, "capability" is assessed only once under Oregon's regime, when the prescription is written, on a day that may be weeks, months, or perhaps even years removed from the patient's decision to die. The physician's absence also means that reviewing state authorities do "not all have information about what happened when the patient ingested the medication,"[120] including information about what, if any, complications may arise.[121] It also means that the complications themselves may also go unaddressed. A nationwide survey of U.S. oncologists found that as many as 15 percent of all attempts at physician-assisted suicide are unsuccessful,[122] and data from the Netherlands, noted above, are similar.[123] In Oregon in 2002, thirty-eight patients ingested lethal medications,[124] and the time to death after ingestion varied widely: one patient lived for fourteen hours, another lived for nine hours, and a third lived for twelve hours;[125] in at least four cases since 1998, a patient has vomited or expectorated immediately after taking the prescribed medication,[126] and patients have lived as long as thirty-seven hours after ingestion.[127]

All of the data that Oregon has collected on completed suicides, moreover, come entirely from the very physicians who participate in the assisted suicide process rather than a more disinterested source—and the physicians must report their activities only after the patient is dead.[128] Consequently, Oregon has no way to review individual cases for compliance with its law until after it is too late to prevent any error or abuse. The Oregon Health Division, which is charged with administering the law, has acknowledged that this statutory arrangement raises "the possibility of physician bias" and means that it "cannot detect or collect data on issues of noncompliance with any accuracy."[129] Additionally, quite unlike the Dutch regime, Oregon does not have any mechanism for surveying doctors confidentially; all reporting is done "on the record."

Without a means of privately asking doctors about their practices, one might question whether we will ever obtain a true and complete picture of the events on the ground in Oregon. And even if a doctor were actually to take the extraordinary step of reporting himself or herself as having violated the law,

Oregon's statute imposes no duty on the health division to investigate or pursue such cases, let alone root them out in the absence of any such self-reports. Thus, while Oregon is often touted as a "laboratory" or an "experiment" for whether assisted suicide can be successfully legalized elsewhere in the United States, Oregon's regulations are crafted in ways that make reliable and relevant data and case descriptions difficult to obtain. Given this, it is unclear whether and to what extent Oregon's experiment, at least as currently structured, will ever be able to provide the sort of guidance needed and wanted by other jurisdictions considering whether to follow Oregon's lead.

Separately, it is also rather remarkable that, while physicians in Oregon are held to a standard of professional competence in administering all other treatments they provide, the Oregon assisted suicide statute creates an entirely different regime when it comes to administering this "treatment," specifically and uniquely immunizing doctors from criminal prosecution, civil liability, or even professional discipline for any actions they take in assisting a suicide, as long as they act in "good faith."[130] Thus, while a doctor may be found liable for mere negligence in any other operation or procedure, there is no recourse for family members when a doctor kills a patient even on the basis of gross negligence by misdiagnosing the patient as terminal or by misassessing the patient as competent.[131]

Oregon's Practice of Assisted Suicide

According to the limited, nonconfidential, and self-reported data available from Oregon physicians, in the first five years of implementation (1998 to 2002), a total of 198 lethal prescriptions were written, and the number of prescriptions increased significantly each year: from 1999 to 2002, the overall number of lethal dosages prescribed rose 76 percent.[132] Many of these prescriptions appear to have been written, moreover, by a very small handful of politically active physicians. In its first-year questionnaire, the Oregon Health Division specifically asked physicians whether the patients they helped kill were referred to them by advocacy organizations, such as Compassion in Dying or the Hemlock Society, but the state inexplicably declined to publish the answer.[133] However, it was later revealed by the media that:

> [T]he first fifteen assisted suicide cases reported involved fourteen different doctors. Compassion in Dying, an out-of-state assisted suicide group that moved to Oregon just weeks after the law was implemented, claimed eleven of the fourteen doctors were theirs.... [A]t least one additional case came through the Hemlock Society. So at least twelve of fourteen, or 86 percent, of the assisted suicide cases were handled by groups politically active in promoting legalization of assisted suicide. This unsettling fact was the one held back, suggesting to many that OHD had become selective in its silence....[134]

TABLE 7.4
Oregon Assisted Suicide Demographics: 1998–2002

Year	1998	1999	2000	2001	2002
Total deaths	16	27	27	21	38
% change from prior year	—	0.7	0	−22	0.8
Median age	69	71	69	68	69
Age range	25–94	31–87	51–93	51–87	38–92
% male	53	59	44	38	71
% female	47	41	56	62	29
% married	13	44	67	38	53
% divorced	27	30	11	33	24
% widowed	33	22	22	24	18

Source: Oregon, First Year's Experience at 13 tbl. 1, at 15 tbl. 3; Ctr. for Disease Prevention and Epidemiology, Or. Dep't of Human Servs., Oregon's Death with Dignity Act: The Second Year's Experience tbl. 1 (2000), available at http://www.ohd.hr.state.or.us/pas/year2/99pasrpt.pdf (site visited Oct. 5, 2005) (hereinafter Second Year's Experience); Ctr. for Disease Prevention and Epidemiology, Or. Dep't of Human Servs., Oregon's Death with Dignity Act: Three Years of Legalized Physician-Assisted Suicide at 16 tbl. 1 (2001), available at http://www.ohd.hr.state.or.us/pas/year3/00pasrpt.pdf (hereinafter Three Years of Legalized Physician-Assisted Suide); Fourth Annual Report at 14 tbl. 1; Fifth Annual Report at 18 tbl. 1.

Just as it is inexplicable that Oregon would suppress results from its first-year questionnaire, it is equally troubling that the state has chosen to drop this question from each of its subsequent annual surveys, and to do so without public mention (let alone defense) of its decision—an incident reminiscent of the Dutch Surveys authors' decision to stop reporting on the incidence of euthanasia by omission after 1990.[135]

Of the 198 patients who have received prescriptions for lethal medication, 129 (or 65 percent) have used them to date.[136] Though these figures provide a small sample, the data do reveal certain correlations, reflected in table 7.4.

As shown in the Table, the number of deaths in 1999 appeared to increase greatly over 1998, although a firm comparison cannot be drawn because the law was not in effect for all of 1998. While the number of deaths in 2001 declined 22 percent compared to 2000, this represented a difference of just six persons. Also, the total number of lethal prescriptions increased in 2001,[137] and two of these prescriptions were apparently filled in 2002,[138] when total deaths increased 81 percent over 2001, to 38 persons, by far the largest number of deaths in any year since the Oregon law went into effect, and representing 41 percent more deaths than occurred in 1999, the first full year of legalization.

The median age for assisted suicide seems to be hovering around seventy, although patients have sought assisted suicide at much younger ages—including as young as twenty-five years old in 1998, thirty-one years old in 1999, and thirty-eight years old in 2002. Surprisingly, no special examination has been made into these cases, although it would clearly be useful to have more information about the physical and mental condition of such young persons committing suicide. There also appears to be a persistent correlation between assisted suicide and divorce. As shown in table 7.5, in each year except 2000, divorced persons have represented over 24 percent of all assisted suicides in Oregon, well in excess of their representation in the population of all deaths due to similar underlying illnesses.

As reflected in table 7.5, divorced persons constituted 25 percent of all assisted suicides in 1998 through 2002, but 18 percent of all deaths in Oregon due to similar underlying maladies as those afflicting the assisted suicide patients. Meanwhile, married persons constituted 47 percent of all assisted suicides, but 49 percent of all deaths due to similar illnesses. These data suggest that divorced persons are nearly twice as likely to commit assisted suicide than similarly situated married patients. And this correlation between divorce and assisted suicide serves to underscore the question whether other things besides terminal illness (for example, social isolation or depression) may drive the decision to seek death.

Of potential concern as well is that the data show that Oregon physicians are increasingly unlikely to refer their patients for psychiatric or psychological consultation before declaring them competent to make the decision to die, despite the evidence consistently linking suicidal impulses to depression and psychological illness.[139] Physicians referred patients in just 13 percent of cases in 2002 (5 of 38), compared with 14 percent of cases in 2001 (3 of 21), 19 percent of cases in 2000 (5 of 27), 37 percent of cases in 1999 (10 of 27), and 31 percent of cases in 1998 (5 of 16).[140] Even when evaluations are done, given the fact that many patients are apparently being shepherded to doctors affiliated

TABLE 7.5
Relative Incidence of Assisted Suicide:
Married vs. Divorced Patients: 1998–2002 (percent)

	Married	Divorced
Assisted suicides	47	25
Oregon deaths due to same diseases	49	18
Estimated proportion of assisted suicide deaths per 10,000 Oregon deaths	29.2	54.5
Relative risk	Reference	1.9

Source: Fifth Annual Report at 4.

TABLE 7.6
Duration of Patient-Physician Relationship (weeks)

Year	1998	1999	2000	2001	2002	Total
Median	11	22	8	14	11	13
Range	2–540	2–817	1–851	0–500	0–379	0–851

Source: Second Year's Experience at tbl. 2; Three Years of Legalized Physician-Assisted Suicide at 20 tbl. 3; Fourth Annual Report at 17 tbl. 3; Fifth Annual Report at 21 tbl. 3.

with advocacy groups that favor assisted suicide, the possibility exists that "a bias may be introduced into the competency evaluation. On balance, the psychiatrists' conclusions may reflect personal values and beliefs more than psychiatric expertise."[141]

Further, physicians in the Netherlands often have long-standing relationships with patients; as a result, they arguably have some basis for assessing the "patient's concerns, values, and pressures that may be prompting the . . . request [for assistance in dying]."[142] By contrast, the AMA has opposed the legalization of assisted suicide in part because American physicians, increasingly employees or agents of large corporate health maintenance organizations, lack such long-term relationships with their patients: in the AMA's view, American "physicians rarely have the depth of knowledge about their patients that would be necessary for an appropriate evaluation of the patient's [assisted suicide] request."[143] And there is data from Oregon that speaks to this concern. In 2002, the median length of the relationship between patients seeking assisted suicide and the physicians who agreed to help them was just eleven weeks, and in some cases was not even a matter of weeks, but of days or hours.[144]

While Oregon reports the duration of the patient-physician relationship, it fails to collect any similar data regarding the length, if any, of the relationship between the patient and the psychiatrist or psychologist who may be called in to assess competency. Given that such a consultation is entirely optional under Oregon's law, it seems likely that these relationships are extremely short, often just a single visit—this despite the fact that a survey of Oregon psychiatrists found that only 6 percent of the psychiatrists surveyed said they were very confident that they could determine whether a patient is competent to commit suicide without a long-term doctor-patient relationship.[145]

Finally, while loss of autonomy topped the list of reasons proffered by patients seeking assisted suicide (a concern in 85 percent of cases between 1998 and 2002), many other reasons were also given, as shown in table 7.7.

Again, these data come from after the fact self-reporting performed by the attending physicians, not a more objective source. Even so, the data reveal that 22 percent of cases between 1998 and 2002 were motivated in part by in-

TABLE 7.7
Reasons Given by Oregon Patients Seeking Assisted Suicide (percent)

Year	1998	1999	2000	2001	2002	Total
Financial implications of treatment	0	5	4	6	3	2
Inadequate pain control	7	53	30	6	26	22
Burden on family, friends, and caregivers	13	47	63	24	37	35
Losing control of bodily functions	53	68	78	53	47	58
Decreasing ability to participate in activities that make life enjoyable	67	47	78	76	84	79
Losing autonomy	80	63	93	94	84	85

Source: First Year's Experience at 16 tbl. 3; Second Year's Experience at tbl. 4; Three Years of Legalized Physician-Assisted Suicide at 18 tbl. 3; Fourth Annual Report at 16 tbl. 3; Fifth Annual Report at 20 tbl. 3.

adequate pain control, which, taken together with the evidence that many Oregon doctors lack sufficient training in palliative care,[146] raise the possibility that suicide may have been substituted for adequate care in some cases. In contrast to the official state numbers, moreover, a 1999 survey of Oregon doctors who received requests for assisted suicide revealed that 43 percent of patients requesting assisted suicide cited pain as an important reason motivating their request; the same survey shows that physicians recommended a palliative care consultation in just 13 percent of cases.[147] Also of concern is the role the cost of care may play in the decision to die and the possibility that requesting continued expensive end-of-life care may be seen as selfish or extravagant when assisted suicide is available: 35 percent of cases involved patients who sought to kill themselves because they were worried about becoming a "burden" on their family and friends; even more pointedly, 2 percent of cases were expressly motivated by concerns over the financial implications of continued treatment (this in one of the nation's most affluent states where one would expect financial concerns to be less pressing than in other jurisdictions where assisted suicide might be legalized).

"Helen" and "Ms. Cheney"

Kathleen Foley and Herbert Hendin have investigated in detail the case of "Helen" (last name unknown), the first person to obtain assisted suicide under Oregon's regime,[148] and of Ms. Kate Cheney, a more recent applicant.[149] Foley's and Hendin's findings offer vivid case studies illustrating some of the questions and concerns I have raised regarding Oregon procedures and practices. Helen was a breast cancer patient in her mid-eighties when the Oregon law went into effect.[150] Helen's regular physician refused to assist in her suicide; a second doctor was consulted but also refused, on the stated ground that Helen was depressed.[151] At that point, Helen's husband called Compassion in Dying.[152] The medical director of the group spoke with Helen and later explained that Helen was "frustrated and crying because she felt powerless."[153] Helen was not, however, bedridden or in great pain but enjoyed aerobic exercises until two weeks before contacting Compassion in Dying and, apparently, she was still performing housework.[154] The Compassion in Dying employee recommended a physician to Helen.[155] That physician, in turn, referred Helen to a specialist (whose specialty is unknown), as well as to a psychiatrist who met Helen only once.[156] A lethal prescription was then supplied.[157]

After Helen died, the prescribing physician was quoted as saying that he regrets that he did not contact Helen's regular physician, as well as that he had only a "very cursory" discussion with the second doctor Helen approached: "[h]ad I felt there was a disagreement among the physicians about my patient's eligibility"—and no doubt there was—"I would not have written the prescription."[158] The prescribing physician further explained that the thought of Helen dying by lethal medication was "almost too much to bear," but that he felt compelled to proceed because he feared how Helen's family might view him otherwise: "I found even worse the thought of disappointing this family. If I backed out, they'd feel about me the way they had [felt] about their previous doctor, that I had strung them along, and in a way, insulted them."[159] An *Oregonian* newspaper reporter who interviewed the family was told that Helen was worried that further care would threaten her financial assets.[160]

When Cheney, an eighty-five-year-old widow, more recently sought a lethal prescription from a physician, her daughter Erika, a retired nurse, accompanied her.[161] Erika described the doctor as "dismissive," so she and her mother requested and received a referral to another physician in the same health maintenance organization (HMO) (in this case, Kaiser Permanente).[162] The second doctor arranged for a psychiatric evaluation; the psychiatrist found that Cheney "did 'not seem to be explicitly pushing for assisted suicide,' and lacked 'the very high level of capacity to weigh options about it.'"[163] The psychiatrist noted that Cheney accepted his assessment when he presented it, but that the daughter became angry.[164]

The HMO then, apparently at Erika's (not Cheney's) request, suggested that the family obtain a second psychiatric evaluation and agreed to pay for it.[165] The second psychologist found that Erika might have been "somewhat coercive" but concluded nonetheless that Cheney was competent to make the decision to die.[166] Cheney thereafter received a lethal prescription, and the drugs were placed under her daughter's care.[167] As time went by, Cheney ate poorly, became weaker, and, to afford Erika and her husband a respite, went to a nursing home on a temporary basis to regain her strength.[168] On the day she returned home, Cheney said "that something had to be done given her declining health," that she did not want to go into a nursing home again, and that she would like to use the lethal pills in Erika's custody.[169] After the daughter consented, Cheney took the pills and died.[170]

Some Questions about Oregon's Experience

Helen's and Cheney's cases encapsulate and illustrate some of the difficult questions about Oregon's assisted suicide regime alluded to by the data reviewed above: what role is depression, as opposed to terminal illness, actually playing in patient decisions to die in Oregon? Are alternative options, including treatment for depression, being fully presented (or presented at all)? Are the doctors that prescribe death even knowledgeable about the alternatives that exist? To what extent are family members unduly influencing patient choices and physician evaluations? What would have happened if family members in each case had argued *against* the request to die and offered care? Should patients be allowed to "shop" around for physicians and psychologists who will find them competent? Do psychologists and physicians have an obligation to do more than a cursory examination? Should they consult the patient's primary care providers and other doctors or psychologists who may have refused prior requests for lethal medication by the patient? Would Cheney's HMO have offered to pay for a second opinion if the first psychologist had found Cheney competent? Do HMOs have a conflict of interest—given that assisted suicide is unquestionably cheaper than continuing care—that may provide an incentive for them to encourage patients to seek death?

7.3 LEGALIZATION AND OTHER UNINTENDED CONSEQUENCES

While the data above raise many questions about the unintended costs that might attend legalization, still others remain to be considered.

The Weak and Vulnerable

What might legalization mean, for example, to the confidence and trust patients have in medicine and medical professionals? Concerned about what might happen to them, many elderly Dutch patients have actually taken to insisting on written contracts assuring against nonvoluntary euthanasia before they will check themselves into hospitals.[171] Poll after poll suggests that ethnic minorities in the United States are relatively more concerned about the prospect of legalized euthanasia and its potential impact on them than are their white counterparts. Indeed, it is an unanswered, but interesting, question whether Oregon's highly homogenous population (approximately 90 percent white)[172] contributed in any way to its adoption of the first-ever U.S. law allowing assisted suicide.

The *Detroit Free Press* has found, for example, that while 53 percent of whites sampled in Michigan could envision requesting assistance in suicide, only 22 percent of blacks could.[173] A poll in Ohio revealed that, while roughly half those sampled favored legalization of assisted suicide, those most likely to favor the practice were people with higher income and education levels, and young adults, and those most likely to oppose the practice were black, people 65 and older, and those with low levels of income and education.[174]

Empirical evidence concerning the medical treatment currently provided to minority groups suggests that their relative unease with the legalization of assisted suicide may not be irrational. The *New England Journal of Medicine* has reported that female, African American, elderly, and Hispanic cancer patients are all less likely than similarly situated nonminorities to receive adequate pain-relieving treatment that may obviate a patient's perceived need to resort to assistance in suicide or euthanasia.[175] Indeed, minority cancer patients are fully three times less likely than nonminority patients to receive adequate palliative care.[176] Minorities also receive poorer AIDS treatment: only 48 percent of blacks receive medicines designed to slow the progress of AIDS, compared to 63 percent of whites; while 82 percent of whites receive effective treatments for preventing AIDS-related pneumonia, only 58 percent of black patients receive similar attention.[177] African Americans have higher mortality rates than whites across disease categories, and recent declines in breast cancer mortality rates have been enjoyed among white, but not black, women.[178] African Americans have fewer physician visits and receive different treatment than whites even within the federally funded Medicare and Veteran's Affairs programs.[179] African Americans are also 3.5 times more likely than whites to have one or more of their limbs amputated, even though diabetes, the most common reason for amputation, is only 1.7 times more common among blacks than whites.[180]

In the events leading up to the consideration of the failed California voter referendum on assisted suicide in 1992, advocates of the measure turned to the American Bar Association (ABA) for support. The ABA, however, ultimately recommended against legalization and did so specifically on the ground that the notion that vulnerable patients would be equally treated in such a regime "is illusory and, indeed, dangerous for the thousands of Americans who have no or inadequate access to quality health and long-term care services."[181]

The Canadian Medical Association, the British Medical Association, the World Medical Association, the American Hospital Association, and the American Nurses Association have all argued against legalizing euthanasia on similar grounds.[182]

The state of New York convened a task force in the mid-1990s composed of twenty-four members representing a wide variety of ethical, philosophical, and religious views and asked the task force to consider whether the state should drop or revise its laws banning assisted suicide; the commission returned with a comprehensive report that unanimously favored retaining existing law.[183] The task force recommended against legalization in part because it would, in the commission's words, impose severe risks on the poor, minorities, and those least empowered in our society.[184] "Officially sanctioning [euthanasia] might also provide an excuse for those wanting to spend less money and effort to treat severely and terminally ill patients, such as patients with acquired immunodeficiency syndrome (AIDS)."[185] Even those task force members who thought euthanasia was justified in some instances concluded that, weighing the costs and benefits, continued criminalization would "[curtail[] the autonomy of patients in a very small number of cases when assisted suicide is a compelling and justifiable response, [but would] preserve[] the autonomy and well-being of many others. It [would] also prevent[] the widespread abuses that would be likely to occur if assisted suicide were legalized."[186]

Michigan appointed a similar commission to study the assisted suicide issue after Kevorkian brought attention to the subject there.[187] While the commission was unable to achieve unanimity like the New York task force, those who concluded that euthanasia should not be legalized focused specifically on the dangers of "social biases."[188] Although "[p]roponents of assisted suicide would . . . point out that the criteria for allowing assisted suicide should be blind to the factors of age or disability," commission members argued that "[t]o suggest that legalizing assisted suicide will not continue to reinforce negative stereotypes and prejudices against [the] disabl[ed] . . . is to ignore the practical realities of how, and for whom, assisted suicide would be applied."[189]

The British House of Lords Committee on Medical Ethics, after lengthy hearings, reached much the same conclusion, recommending against legalization out of

> concern[] that vulnerable people—the elderly, lonely, sick or distressed—
> would feel pressure, whether real or imagined, to request early death. . . . [W]e
> believe that the message which society sends to vulnerable and disadvantaged
> people should not, however obliquely, encourage them to seek death, but
> should assure them of our care and support in life.[190]

Even some enthusiastic advocates of legalization acknowledge that the comprehensive regime of health care in the Netherlands helps mitigate the incidence of abuse or coercion in euthanasia and acknowledge that the American health care system, where so many people are uninsured or underinsured, carries with it a far greater risk that patients will be forced into accepting euthanasia as a result of pressure, abuse, coercion, or general economic forces.[191]

Saving Money, Killing without Consent, and Economic Disincentives to Care

Because normalizing assisted suicide and euthanasia would represent such a sea change in our end-of-life laws and ethics, it would undoubtedly carry with it other consequences for medicine, law, and social norms that cannot be easily predicted or foreseen. Still, we might ask, what glimmers can we make out, if only barely, on the horizon?

By way of example, as a cheaper and easier option (killing) becomes available as a legitimate medical response to terminal illness or grave physical suffering, might it create disincentives to the development and dissemination of other, more expensive end-of-life options? A 1988 study strongly suggested that physician incompetence and the lack of adequate palliative medicines in the Netherlands has, in fact, contributed to the number of requests made for assisted suicide and euthanasia in that country: more than 50 percent of Dutch cancer patients surveyed suffered treatable pain unnecessarily, and 56 percent of Dutch physician practitioners were found to be inadequately trained in pain relief techniques.[192] Another study conducted under the auspices of the U.S. Department of Health and Human Services similarly concluded that:

> Patients with cancer often have pain from more than one source, but in up to 90 percent of patients the pain can be controlled by relatively simple means. Nevertheless, undertreatment of cancer pain is common because of clinicians' inadequate knowledge of effective assessment and management practices, negative attitudes of patients and clinicians toward the use of drugs for the relief of pain, and a variety of problems related to reimbursement for effective pain management.[193]

Providing assisted suicide and euthanasia is indeed a cheap means of responding to patients suffering grave pain—cheaper surely than guaranteeing the care, attention, and pain medication required for some patients to die in comfort. It is only reasonable to ask whether the recognition of killing as a valid medical response to patient discomfort might create disincentives not just to the development of new palliative treatments, but also to the full dissemination of nursing and hospice care as well as existing and readily available pain suppressants that can prevent suffering and the perceived need for assistance in dying. Griffiths, while defending the Dutch euthanasia regime and advocating its extension to nonvoluntary killings, has expressly acknowledged that "there are occasional indications" that economic considerations do play a role in the administration of assisted suicide in the Netherlands, noting that "some 12 percent of the doctors and 15 percent of the prosecuting officials interviewed [in 1995] expect[ed] that drastic budget-cutting in the health-care system could lead to increased pressure on doctors to engage in life-shortening practices."[194] And these findings come in a society where, quite unlike America, virtually everyone is guaranteed medical care.[195]

We may see in the case of Cheney what may, in this respect, be a glimpse of the future for American patients—even ones with medical insurance. The HMO in her case was quite willing to pay (at the daughter's urging) for a second opinion after the first psychologist refused to certify Cheney for death; subsequently, it agreed to allow the assisted suicide to proceed despite evidence of coercion and patient incompetence; and at no point did the HMO intervene to offer continued psychiatric counseling or a palliative care consultation.[196] More recently, the very same HMO has even solicited its doctors to participate in assisted suicide.[197] A Kaiser executive e-mailed more than eight hundred Kaiser doctors asking them to "'act as Attending Physician under the [assisted suicide] law for YOUR patients' and [soliciting doctors] 'willing to act as 'Attending Physician under the law for members who ARE NOT your patients' to contact 'Marcia L. Liberson or Robert H. Richardson, MD, KPNW Ethics Services.'"[198] As one observer has noted, "Kaiser is apparently willing to permit its doctors to write lethal prescriptions [even] for patients [within Kaiser's HMO system whom] they have not treated."[199]

Some, such as Otlowski, contend that it is "misguided" to view the legalization of assisted suicide or euthanasia as likely to detract from medical research and the dissemination of palliative care because proponents of legalization only "wish . . . to expand the options available to patients."[200] But arguments of this sort confuse intentions with consequences, failing to address the possibility that legalization would create strong, if unintended, economic disincentives to the provision of, and research into, improved palliative care. While some have chosen to ignore or perhaps wish to leave implicit the money issue, we saw in chapter 3 that others, like Derek Humphry, cofounder of the Hemlock Society, have made the issue remarkably explicit—with Humphry, among others, candidly acknowledging that money is an "unspoken argument" in favor of his position, adding that legalization would save the economy "*hundreds of billions of dollars.*"[201]

A Duty to Kill? And to Die?

Even overlooking the economic forces that come into play if we treat assisted suicide and euthanasia as legitimate forms of medical treatment, we cannot ignore the possibility that we may also wind up establishing a new standard of care—imposing, in essence, a professional *duty* on physicians to offer to "treat" patients with assisted suicide under certain circumstances. We saw that this strain of thinking has run strong and deep in the history of the euthanasia movement in America.[202] And many contemporary advocates of legalization are, in fact, openly discussing putative professional and legal "duties" along just these lines.[203] If killing should become a professional duty under certain circumstances, what would happen to the medical care professionals who fail to act? Might they open themselves up to suits in negligence by families upset that their relatives suffered needlessly because a doctor or nurse did *not* advocate their death? Might we eventually have a "wrongful life" cause of action?

Also, could legalization foster a culture in which patient consent no longer seems to be an absolute prerequisite to killing? Certainly such a result would *harm*, not help, the objective of patient autonomy that many assisted suicide advocates announce as their goal. But it is a possibility that cannot be considered implausible in an environment where some, like Griffiths and the Dutch government itself, have expressly defended, and even advocated, the decriminalization of *nonvoluntary* killings.[204] In the United States, family members are frequently permitted by common law or statute to use their "substituted judgment" to accept or decline medical treatment on behalf of elderly, incompetent relatives.[205] If euthanasia becomes an acceptable form of medical treatment in a society where substituted judgment is already so deeply ensconced, it would be but a small political and logical step to permit family members to decide whether to kill their relatives without indicia of the patient's consent—that is, commit *nonvoluntary* euthanasia. Margaret Otlowski, who argues strongly for legalizing voluntary euthanasia, recognizes the possibility of such a result in America and considers it a distinct problem.[206] Otlowski submits that euthanasia should be legalized only in cases where the patient expressly and voluntarily consents,[207] but she readily acknowledges that strong pressure will be exerted to extend "substituted judgment" doctrine to cases of euthanasia—and that this represents "perhaps the most plausible slippery slope concern."[208] Cantor goes a step further, conceding that the impetus for nonvoluntary euthanasia in America would be "overwhelming" and a result he would fully embrace.[209]

It might even be asked: would recognizing a right to die morph into a duty to do so? Might a culture that embraces the concept that some people are better off dead than alive decide that some persons should be killed, even if they or their loved ones do not consent? As we saw in chapter 3, Margaret Battin argues that we can (and should) kill incompetent patients even when they provide express directives before becoming incompetent asking to be kept alive. Ronald Dworkin hints at much the same thing. Peter Singer submits that society is better off culling unwanted children. And at least one U.S. court has endorsed the notion that physicians may indeed override a patient's autonomous desire for treatment. In April 1995, a Massachusetts court ruled "that a hospital and its doctors need not provide [life-sustaining] care they deem futile," even if the patient expressly requests it.[210] The case involved an elderly woman, Catherine Gilgunn, who became comatose after suffering irreversible brain damage.[211] Gilgunn's daughter instructed the hospital that her mother wished everything medically possible be done for her should she become incompetent.[212] The hospital, however, ignored the daughter's instructions and refused to place Gilgunn on a respirator or provide cardiopulmonary resuscitation.[213] The lawyer defending the hospital provided his forthright assessment of the ruling: the court's "real point," he said, was that, "physicians can't be required to do things that they feel would be inappropriate and harmful to the patient"—regardless of how the patient herself "feels" (that is, instructs her fiduciary caregiver).[214]

Patricia Mann, who, notably, takes no position in the assisted suicide debate, describes in vivid detail some of the cultural consequences that a shift to legalization might entail for the medical profession:

> [M]any doctors will adjust their practices, and gradually their values. . . . Insofar as assisted suicide is a cost-efficient means of death, doctors are . . . likely to be rewarded by healthcare companies for participating in it. As institutional expectations and rewards increasingly favor assisted suicide, expectations and rewards within the medical profession itself will gradually shift to reflect this. Medical students will learn about assisted suicide as an important patient option from the beginning of their training. We may expect that a growing proportion of doctors will find themselves sympathetic to the practice, and will find themselves comfortable with recommending it to their patients.[215]

But, as Mann notes, members of the medical profession would not be the only ones affected:

> Family members may want a loved one to remain alive as long as possible, while also harboring secret desires to be done with this painful process. Many people today are ashamed of such secret desires. . . . But if assisted suicide becomes legal, such desires will cease to be wrongful in such an obvious way. If patients themselves may decide to put an end to this painful process of dying, then it is not blameworthy for relatives of such a patient to inquire whether he or she may be thinking along these lines, and to offer sympathetic support for the idea.
>
> . . . Once assisted suicide ceases to be illegal, its many advantages to busy relatives will become readily apparent. More than merely an acceptable form of ending, relatives and friends may come to see it as a preferred or praiseworthy form of death.[216]

Nor can Mann's predictions be dismissed as the stuff of science fiction. Battin, Brock, Dworkin, and Cantor, if in perhaps slightly nuanced and varying ways, all describe a world much like the one Mann describes, as does the former governor of Colorado, Richard Lamm, who has openly and repeatedly defended the view that the elderly have a duty to die to make room (and save resources for) the young.[217] Besides, we readily understand and accept that economic incentives play a role for HMOs in the care they choose to dispense (and not dispense); why should this arena prove any different? Although doctors and hospitals may have incentives to keep patients alive to generate higher bills for additional care, if assisted suicide comes to be considered a legitimate (or perhaps even a professionally preferred) form of "care" in such cases, wouldn't we *expect* HMOs to cut back on reimbursement for more expensive options? Is it not possible—even likely—that more expensive forms of end-of-life care may come to be seen as luxuries, "elective," and nonreimbursable (or only partially reimbursable) options? Perhaps even extravagant? Or selfish? As Mann notes:

> If dying sooner is more cost efficient, their profit-based concerns will make them prefer patients to choose assisted suicide. . . . Economic interests may still seem crass in relation to dying patients, and yet we are already accustomed to recognizing them in the context of treatment, as well as in all other contexts of daily life. When we legalize assisted suicide, it too becomes a part of daily life.[218]

Indeed, "[i]n our society, where almost everyone is pressed for time, and many are pressed for money, individual notions of agency and the fabric of social agency relations may evolve very quickly to reflect [assisted suicide's] conveniences and cost efficiency."[219] If anyone should doubt how quickly economic forces can change cultural norms and expectations, Mann asks us only to look back to the 1950s and 1960s and compare how rapidly we have changed our views about women working outside the home—with many people today going so far as to "consider it somewhat indulgent and eccentric" for highly educated women to give up professional careers in favor of remaining at home.[220] How can we doubt that our views of dying (and what amounts to self-indulgent behavior in the dying process) would change just as radically if assisted suicide were legalized?[221]

7.4 DECRIMINALIZATION AS A "COSTLESS" ENTERPRISE?

John Griffiths and Helga Kuhse have sought to press the somewhat counterintuitive notion that the decriminalization of assisted suicide is an essentially "costless" enterprise. Just because assisted suicide is routine today in the Netherlands, the reasoning goes, that fact does not necessarily mean that the number of such deaths "increased after legalization" or that the number of such deaths "is higher in the Netherlands than elsewhere."[222] In fact, Griffiths argues, assisted suicide and euthanasia are practiced on a "widespread, if hidden," basis in the United States "at rates roughly comparable [to] those in the Netherlands," a "fact" that leads Griffiths to conclude that the "[l]egalization of euthanasia apparently does not lead to an increase even in the rate of euthanasia itself."[223] This argument sounds deeply appealing, but is it sound?

Griffiths' Argument

To be sure, Griffiths is right to note that the data we have from the Netherlands, like the data from Oregon, only tells us about the incidence of assisted suicide and euthanasia *after* they became legally permissible in those jurisdictions, and that we lack much data regarding the rate of voluntary or nonvoluntary killings in those jurisdictions *before* legalization. But Griffiths does nothing to dispel concerns that Dutch and Oregon procedures and practices raise on their own terms, and he goes far beyond noting the limitations of current data to an argument that is itself unwarranted on the available evidence.

First, Griffiths' hypothesis—that decriminalization of assisted suicide and euthanasia does not result in any additional cases of those practices—runs directly contrary to the intuitive principle of the law of demand. The law of demand holds that, other things being equal, the quantity demanded of a good falls when the price of the good rises.[224] Consistent with the law of demand, one would expect that if certain "costs" associated with assisted suicide and euthanasia (for example, the social stigma and difficulty of finding a willing physician to help when the practices remain illegal) are lowered or eliminated by legalization, *more*, not fewer, people would take advantage of this fact and seek an early death. Advocates of legalization usually champion exactly this point, arguing for the regularization of assisted suicide precisely because doing so would allow *more* people the autonomy to decide to kill themselves. Griffiths gives us no reason to adopt a contrary, and entirely counterintuitive, assumption.

Second, while Griffiths asserts that assisted suicide and euthanasia are secretly practiced in the United States on approximately the same scale as they are openly practiced in the Netherlands, the only authority he provides for this claim is a citation to an amicus brief in *Glucksberg* signed by Ronald Dworkin, among others, and described by its authors as the "Philosophers' Brief"; that legal advocacy piece hardly purported to provide a systematic study of assisted suicide and euthanasia rates in the United States.[225]

Griffiths' empirical assertion is, in fact, contradicted by available data—data that are, not surprisingly, entirely consistent with what one would expect under the law of demand. The 1995 Survey of Dutch physicians found that 63 percent of general practitioners and 37 percent of clinical specialists in the Netherlands (53 percent of all physicians) had performed euthanasia or assisted suicide.[226] By contrast, a survey of physicians in Oregon conducted prior to the legalization of assisted suicide in that state found that only 21 percent had received a request for euthanasia or assisted suicide and just 7 percent had written a lethal prescription at a patient's request.[227] Further, a 1996 nationwide survey of over 1,900 U.S. physicians (conducted by, among others, Timothy Quill, a highly vocal assisted suicide advocate)[228] found that, over the entire course of their careers, 11.1 percent of physicians had received a request for euthanasia, 18.3 percent had received a request for assisted suicide, and approximately 6 percent had acceded to at least one request for either euthanasia or assisted suicide.[229] One of Quill's coauthors remarked that the "most important finding" in this survey was that "[t]his is really not happening very often. . . . It's a rare event."[230] Though a defender of the Dutch regime, van der Maas, too, has conceded that the figures from the United States "are consistently lower than those we found" for the Netherlands,[231] and extant data suggest that "the proportion of deaths in the United States that involve physician-assisted suicide and euthanasia is likely to be small."[232] The American Geriatrics Society has concurred as well, suggesting that the widespread practice of assisted suicide and euthanasia "seems unlikely. Three-quarters of all deaths happen in institutions where a regularized practice would require the collusion of a large number of persons."[233]

Third, even supposing, counterfactually, that the rates of voluntary assisted suicide and euthanasia in the United States (where the practices are generally illegal) and the Netherlands (where the practices are allowed) are at present comparable, it would be an error to leap to the conclusion that legalization in the United States would therefore be a "costless" enterprise. It would be equally consistent with the facts to suppose that different countries have different baseline (prelegalization) rates of assisted suicide and euthanasia because of unrelated cultural phenomena and that, consistent with the law of demand, legalizing voluntary assisted suicide and euthanasia (and thus reducing the "price" associated with the practices) would lead to an *increase* in the frequency of the practices when compared with baseline, prelegalization rates in any given country.

Kuhse's Argument

In a variation of Griffiths' hypothesis, Kuhse rejects any suggestion that "the rate at which doctors intentionally end patients' lives without an explicit request is higher in a country where voluntary euthanasia is [practiced] openly . . . than in a comparable country which prohibits the practice."[234] Simply put, in her view, "laws prohibiting the intentional termination of life . . . do not prevent doctors from intentionally ending the lives of some of their patients" without consent.[235]

As with Griffiths' theory, however, the foundation on which Kuhse seeks to build her argument is not free from question. Kuhse argues that nonvoluntary killings in her home country of Australia, where assisted suicide is now illegal, occur more frequently than in the Netherlands,[236] and, therefore, that legalization is likely to reduce (or at least not increase) the total number of cases of nonvoluntary killings.[237] But, again, the fact that nonvoluntary killings in Australia may already be high when compared with the Netherlands does not mean that the problem of nonconsensual killings will not be exacerbated in Australia if voluntary assisted suicide and euthanasia are legalized there. Kuhse's empirical claim is equally consistent with the supposition that Australia simply starts from a different (higher) baseline of nonconsensual killings and that, as voluntary assisted suicide and euthanasia become more common, so too will nonconsensual killings due to abuse, mistake, or coercion.

Similarly, Kuhse's thesis—like Griffiths'—is in tension with the law of demand. As nonconsensual killings become more acceptable—as they surely have in the Netherlands, where the government has sought to justify them as a "necessity,"[238] and where some, such as Griffiths, have urged their complete decriminalization[239]—one would expect the number of such cases to increase, not remain constant as Kuhse seems to suppose. While an exception to the law of demand is not inconceivable, any theory that depends on such an exception would require considerable proof.

The empirical data Kuhse cites, like her theory itself, are open to question. Kuhse's data come from a postal survey of physicians that she conducted together with Peter Singer.[240] Beyond her academic and survey work, Kuhse is past president of a euthanasia advocacy group, the World Federation of Right-to-Die Societies.[241] Singer, DeCamp Professor at Princeton University's Center for Human Values, is, like Kuhse, a vocal exponent of legalizing assisted suicide.[242] Indeed, Singer even advocates killing unwanted infants—that is, infanticide.[243] Kuhse and Singer's survey was limited to Australian doctors and makes no findings that would permit them to reach any conclusions about the frequency of assisted suicide in the United States.[244] Within Australia, their most fundamental finding was that voluntary euthanasia and assisted suicide collectively represent approximately 1.8 percent of all deaths.[245] By comparison, however, voluntary euthanasia and assisted suicide accounted for 2.2 percent of all deaths in the Netherlands in 1990, and 2.7 percent of all deaths there in 1995.[246] These data, standing alone, are hardly consistent with the thesis that legalization does not result in more killings; rather, they suggest that euthanasia and physician-assisted suicide were 50 percent more common in the Netherlands in 1995 than in Australia in 1996, exactly what one would expect given the law of demand.

Kuhse and Singer, perhaps unsurprisingly, seek to emphasize other findings from their survey. By way of example, Kuhse claims that passive (that is, by omission) nonvoluntary euthanasia is more common in Australia than the Netherlands, despite its greater acceptability in the Netherlands.[247] But at least some of the data on which Kuhse and Singer base this conclusion do not seem to support their assertion. For example, they claim that 22.5 percent of all deaths in Australia were the result of omissions of care without "explicit" patient request, and they seek to contrast this figure with the Dutch experience, noting that *all* decisions to omit treatment, consensual and nonconsensual, accounted for 13.3 percent of deaths in the Netherlands in 1995.[248] After unearthing data buried in a table, however, one finds that included within the critical 22.5 percent figure of supposedly nonconsensual killings is a very large number of cases (21 percent of all omission cases) where patient-physician discussions, if any, are *unknown* because the participating physicians simply declined to provide any information in the write-in postal survey.[249] The analogous nonreport rate in the Netherlands was far lower (5 percent).[250] This large difference could perhaps be attributed to the fact that Kuhse's survey depended on voluntarily mailed-in results, while the van der Maas survey relied on in-person interviews and studies of mandatory death certificates filed with the state; accordingly, it would have been relatively easy (and understandable) for doctors in the Australian survey to bypass questions about what, if any, private (and privileged) doctor-patient discussions they may have had.

In any event, an apples-to-apples comparison of nonvoluntary euthanasia by omission, avoiding nonreport cases, seems to undercut Kuhse and Singer's thesis. According to Kuhse and Singer, 28.6 percent of all deaths in Australia are the result of omissions of care with or without consent.[251] Of that universe, only 27 percent occurred without some indication, explicit or less than explicit, of patient consent;[252] thus, deaths by omission of care without any indication of patient consent amounted to just 7.72 percent of all deaths in Australia. From the 1995 survey, by comparison, we know that omissions of care accounted for about 20.2 percent of all deaths in the Netherlands in 1995.[253] And we know that 51 percent of these cases involved no physician-patient discussion at all—nearly double the same applicable percentage for Australia.[254] Accordingly, approximately 10.3 percent of patients in the Netherlands—or 33 percent more persons than in Australia—appear to have died as a result of omissions of care without any indicia of consent.[255]

Other problems exist in Kuhse and Singer's data. Robert Manne of Australia's LaTrobe University, for example, has questioned the finding that 64.8 percent of all deaths in Australia are the result of some medical decision, formally labeled as a "medical decisions concerning the end of life" (MDELs).[256] By comparison, Dutch data show that MDELs occur in approximately 40 percent of all deaths.[257] This considerable disparity has led Manne to ask:

> As about 30 per cent of deaths in Australia must be, as in Holland, sudden or acute where MDELs could not take place, what [the authors] are effectively claiming is that while in Holland an MDEL takes place in a little over *one-half* of non-acute deaths, in Australia a medical decision concerning the end of life takes place in *almost every case*. . . . To my mind this finding calls into question the scientific rigour of the whole study.[258]

Finally, *even if* Griffiths and Kuhse could convincingly prove their counterintuitive hypotheses that decriminalization does not encourage more cases of voluntary and nonvoluntary assisted suicide and euthanasia, it would not necessarily demonstrate that decriminalization is the appropriate policy response. As the U.S. Department of Justice has observed,

> [b]y parity of reasoning, if it could be shown that physicians violated traditional medical canons of ethics more often than is usually supposed, *e.g.*, by engaging in sexual relations with their patients or disclosing patient confidences, it would follow that the evidence of such deviations overturned the professional standards prohibiting such misconduct.[259]

Simply put, evidence about the pervasiveness of the "clandestine" practice of assisted suicide and euthanasia under current law can be wielded by partisans on both sides of the debate—constituting to some a reason for greater vigilance and enforcement rather than a reason for legalization. Certainly, the contemporary debate over the status of illicit drugs illustrates this point, with politicians and the public on both sides agreeing that drug usage occurs on a large scale but utterly disagreeing on whether to step up enforcement measures or repeal possession laws. And, of course, we have seen how the argument has played out so far in the American debate over assisted suicide: the recent activities of Kevorkian and his followers have induced most state legislatures across the country, along with the U.S. Congress, to take steps aimed at enhancing, not watering down, the enforcement of laws against the practice.[260]

One might, at this point, respond that legalization would at least allow the state to oversee and regulate the practice of assisted suicide and euthanasia, ensuring that safeguards are respected by bringing the practices out of the closet and into the light of day. But the evidence from the Netherlands and Oregon does not seem to offer great comfort that decriminalization would result in zealous regulatory reporting or enforcement. As we have already seen, Oregon officials admit that they have no idea how often state law is violated, and no way to detect cases of abuse and mistake.[261] Meanwhile, as we discussed earlier, nearly half of Dutch doctors admitted in 2001 that, *despite* the acceptability of assisted suicide and euthanasia in the Netherlands, they have refused to comply with reporting requirements—and they have done so disproportionately in cases where they kill the patient without consent and fail to consult professional colleagues.[262] Even Griffiths has acknowledged that the present control regime in the Netherlands "is a bit of a paper tiger,"[263] one apparently so irremediable that the only solution Griffiths offers is the decriminalization of *nonconsensual* homicide—an alternative that may well make enhanced enforcement of existing law look preferable by comparison to many.

7.5 How to "Balance" the Costs and Benefits of Legalization?

To this point, I have sought to suggest that legalization, even if narrowly limited to the terminally ill or gravely suffering, cannot readily be labeled a "costless" enterprise in a sound utilitarian calculus. It is perhaps equally important, however, to emphasize what I have *not* done: I have not proven that the costs we might associate with legalization outweigh the benefit of permitting people who really wish to kill themselves the liberty of doing so. I have not even sought to show that the costs and benefits of normalization are in equilibrium. All I have done or sought to do, to this point, is to question whether the application of a utilitarian analysis inexorably leads to the conclusion that legalization represents the best solution for the greatest number of persons. Having suggested that the utilitarian scales do not obviously or necessarily tip in the direction of legalization, the question remains: how are we to balance the competing costs and benefits? Accepting that legalization may bring with it unintended and unwanted consequences, as well as real benefits, the utilitarian wants somehow to try to sum up these competing costs and benefits and arrive at the most efficient or optimal social policy result. But how?

Utilitarians do not, of course, uniformly line up in favor of legalizing assisted suicide or euthanasia. In the 1950s, Glanville Williams wrote *The Sanctity of Life and the Criminal Law*, the classic utilitarian case for euthanasia.[264] Soon afterward, Yale Kamisar published an article arguing for the opposite conclusion while applying the same utilitarian approach and methods.[265] The most interesting feature of the Williams-Kamisar debate is not that two utilitarians disagree. Nor is it in trying to determine who offered the more complete or accurate utilitarian calculation based on data from long ago. Instead, the interesting question raised by the debate they began (and which, as we have seen, continues with vigor to this day) is whether—even if one could definitively identify *all* of the positive and negative consequences associated with assisted suicide or euthanasia—one could then rationally and objectively weigh those consequences to ascertain the "correct" result. On a purely utilitarian account, how can we compare, for example, the interest the rational adult seeking death has in dying with the danger of mistakenly killing persons without their consent?

Such questions suggest a fundamental problem besetting *both* Williams' and Kamisar's projects: the absence of any agreed scale on which the utilitarian can weigh or compare radically different competing values. Endeavoring to compare or weigh, say, the interest the rational adult tired with life has in choosing death against the interest the incompetent elderly widow has in avoiding being killed by a greedy guardian and heir, without reference to any extrinsic, agreed upon moral rule or code is a seemingly impossible, even senseless, enterprise. It is senseless in the way that it is senseless to compare or commensurate the virtues of apples to those of oranges, or "in the way that it is senseless to try to sum up the quantity of the size of this page, the quantity of the number six, and the quantity of the mass of this book."[266]

Battin appears to identify the incommensurability problem underlying utilitarian arguments against assisted suicide and euthanasia, acknowledging that:

> The wedge argument against euthanasia [that is, the fact that allowing voluntary euthanasia may lead to acceptance of nonvoluntary euthanasia] usually takes the form of an appeal to the welfare or rights of those who would become victims of later, unjustified practices. Usually, however, when the conclusion is offered that euthanasia therefore ought not be permitted, no account is taken of the welfare or rights of those who are to be denied the benefits of this practice. Hence, even if the causal claims advanced in the wedge argument are true . . . they still do not establish the conclusion. *Rather, the argument sets up a conflict.* Either we ignore the welfare and abridge the rights of persons for whom euthanasia would clearly be morally permissible in order to protect those who would be the victims of corrupt euthanasia practices, or we ignore the potential victims in order to extend mercy and respect for autonomy to those who are the current victims of euthanasia prohibitions.[267]

Although she seemingly identifies the incommensurability problem—namely, that utilitarian reasoning merely "sets up a conflict" between competing goods without resolving it—Battin claims to see a way out using utilitarian reasoning:

> To protect those who might wrongly be killed or allowed to die might seem a stronger obligation than to satisfy the wishes of those who desire release from pain, analogous perhaps to the principle in law that "better ten guilty men go free than one be unjustly convicted." However, the situation is not in fact analogous and does not favor protecting those who might wrongly be killed. To let ten guilty men go free in the interests of protecting one innocent man is not to impose harm on the ten guilty men. But to require the person who chooses to die to stay alive in order to protect those who might unwillingly be killed sometime in the future is to impose an extreme harm—intolerable suffering —on that person, which he or she must bear for the sake of others. Furthermore, since, as I have argued, the question of which is worse, suffering or death, is person-relative, we have no independent, objective basis for protecting the class of persons who might be killed at the expense of those who would suffer intolerable pain; perhaps our protecting ought to be done the other way around.[268]

In this latter passage, Battin intimates that the conflict between the competing autonomy interests of those who wish to die and those who wish not to be killed without their consent *can* be resolved, and perhaps resolved in favor of allowing euthanasia—that is, "perhaps our protecting ought to be done the other way around."[269] Battin begins, however, by acknowledging that the "ten guilty men" maxim, frequently cited as an ideal of our justice system, seems to cut against her position.[270] Battin responds to this by suggesting that the maxim is not properly applicable in, or analogous to, the assisted suicide and euthanasia debate.[271] She suggests that society's traditional willingness to protect the one innocent man even at the expense of letting ten guilty men go free is based, at least in part, on the fact that doing so imposes no "harm" on the guilty men; by contrast, Battin observes, preventing persons from seeking assistance in dying does impose real harms on them.[272]

This argument simply does not work. The point of the "ten guilty men" is not that we protect innocent human life against the risk of mistaken or wrongful killings *only* when it imposes no harm on the guilty, as Battin seems to suggest. Rather, it is that society protects the innocent individual life against such risks *even when* it means accepting harms to the guilty men's potential future victims and to the other innocent victims of those emboldened by the state's leniency. Thus, any attempt to apply the maxim in the consensual homicide context would surely result in the conclusion that it is wrong to endorse a regime that allows even one innocent person to be killed as a result of abuse, mistake, or coercion—and it would do so even if it means accepting the fact that other innocent persons may be forced to forgo the opportunity to obtain assisted suicide or euthanasia.

Other utilitarians seeking a way around the incommensurability problem sometimes seem to resort to the principle of double effect we explored in chapter 4, arguing that the undesirable consequences associated with permitting assisted suicide and euthanasia (for example, deaths caused by abuse, mistake, or pressure) may be discounted because they are *unintended*; in legalizing assisted suicide, society *intends* not to do anyone any harm but only to permit freely chosen decisions to die. Joel Feinberg, for one, argues that we should

> consider reasonable mistakes in a legalized voluntary euthanasia scheme to be "the inevitable by-products" of efforts to deliver human beings, at their own requests, from intolerable suffering, or from elaborate and expensive prolongations of a body's functioning in the permanent absence of any person to animate that body.[273]

Williams similarly downplays the fact that legalizing assisted suicide is likely to carry with it (additional) killings due to abuse, mistake, or pressure: "[i]t may be allowed that mistakes are always possible, but this is so in any of the affairs of life."[274] Yet, Williams' apparent reliance on double effect doctrine in this context—distinguishing between "mistakes" or other unintended consequences associated with legalization, and those consequences that are intended—is distinctly at odds with his vociferous attack on the principle elsewhere.[275] It is also, fundamentally, a recognition that utilitarianism cannot, by itself, solve the assisted suicide question. In suggesting that *intended* consequences are more important or weighty than *unintended* ones, Feinberg and Williams step outside a purely utilitarian analysis aimed at enhancing pleasurable or social welfare–maximizing consequences to endorse a *separate, independent moral theory* for ranking or scoring different kinds of consequences, one that is foreign to a strictly utilitarian account.

Even supposing they could somehow rank consequences based on the intent behind them without undermining the promise of their consequentialist-utilitarian enterprise (and it is hard to see how they could), Feinberg's and Williams' argument still does not end the assisted suicide debate. Rather, it only raises the question whether a state that chooses legalization, with the *intent* to permit freely chosen deaths (with the unintended and unwanted "expense" of new cases of killing due to abuse, mistake, and pressure), is preferable, by reference to some moral principle, to a state that chooses to make assisted suicide illegal, with, say, the *intent* of fulfilling the ten guilty men maxim and protecting innocent life against nonconsensual killings due to abuse, mistake, or pressure (though with the unintended and unwanted "expense" of denying some people who wish to die a legal right to obtain help from others). Simply put, merely referencing intent is hardly enough: Feinberg and Williams still owe us some explanation why a regime that *intends* to allow some persons the freedom to engage legally in assisted suicide is to be preferred to one that *intends* to protect innocent life by prohibiting such practices.

7.6 Conclusion

In this chapter, I have sought to show that the utilitarian case for assisted suicide and euthanasia is not altogether free from doubt. To be sure, benefits would flow from legalization, including the possibility that some persons would be able to end painful suffering. I do not seek to discount such benefits or to suggest that they are "outweighed" by attendant costs. Instead, I have sought only to show that legalization may also entail costs and, thus, that the utilitarian interested in selecting the legal rule that serves the greatest-good-for-the-greatest-number is presented with a nontrivial choice.

Such practical concerns about the costs attendant to legalization have, in fact, persuaded many authorities to retain laws against assisted suicide. The Canadian Supreme Court declined to find a right to assisted suicide precisely because, in its judgment, "the concerns about abuse and the great difficulty in creating appropriate safeguards" make it impossible to say that a blanket prohibition on assisted suicide is inappropriate or fails to reflect "fundamental values at play in our society."[276] The British House of Lords also once recommended against legalization, in part because "it would not be possible to frame adequate safeguards against non-voluntary euthanasia if voluntary euthanasia were to be legalised. It would be next to impossible to ensure that all acts of euthanasia were truly voluntary, and that any liberalisation of the law was not abused."[277] In the United States, Justice Souter, concurring in *Glucksberg*, declined to find a constitutional right to assisted suicide because, in his view, "[t]he case for the slippery slope is fairly made out here . . . because there is a plausible case that the right claimed would not be readily containable by reference to facts about the mind that are matters of difficult judgment, or by gatekeepers who are subject to temptation, noble or not."[278] Such judgments, I submit, cannot be ruled out as unreasonable on the available evidence.

In the end, moreover, I submit that the utilitarian focus on competing costs and benefits—such as the interest in allowing patients to exercise their autonomy versus the interest in preventing the nonconsensual killing of innocent persons—may help sharpen our thinking about the policy choice we face, but it provides us with no definitive guidance when it comes to choosing between such radically different, and ultimately incommensurate, interests. A utilitarian approach to the assisted suicide question may help clarify the consequences of legalization or nonlegalization, but it will not—and, more fundamentally, cannot—resolve the debate.

8

Two Test Cases: Posner and Epstein

IN RECENT years, Richard Posner and Richard Epstein have published provocative arguments for the legalization of assisted suicide. Posner introduced *Aging and Old Age* in 1995, and Epstein followed in 1999 with *Mortal Peril*. Posner argued for legalization primarily on practical, or utilitarian, grounds. The benefits associated with legalization, he claimed, outweigh any attendant costs. Legalization would, in this sense, be the "efficient" legal response. Epstein's argument, meanwhile, was equally characteristic of his body of work: in deference to the harm principle and libertarian ideal, he argued that government should leave people unfettered to make their own decisions. These authors exemplify some of the arguments developed in the two preceding chapters and, thus, provide us with test cases: Do the points I have suggested with respect to autonomy- and utilitarian-based theories of assisted suicide and euthanasia withstand these recent thoughtful writings?

Ultimately, I believe they do. The empirical benefits Posner claims will flow from legalization are open to question, and Posner's utilitarian calculus founders on the incommensurability problem. Eventually, as I hinted in the last chapter, Posner himself offers an alternative argument; joining Epstein, he suggests that persons should be left to decide for themselves whether to seek assisted suicide because no harm befalls any third party. Yet faithful adherence to libertarian theory tends not merely toward legalizing assisted suicide for the terminally ill, but also toward legalization of assisted suicide, euthanasia, and consensual homicide for all competent adults, regardless of their physical condition or reasons for action.

8.1 POSNER'S UTILITARIAN CASE FOR ASSISTED SUICIDE

Posner argues for legalization of assisted suicide primarily on the strength of an empirical claim that it would lead to fewer, not more, suicides.[1] Without assisted suicide as a viable legal option, the argument runs, people frightened of disability associated with terminal illness are forced either to kill themselves while they still can or face the prospect of losing self-control.[2] If assisted suicide were legalized, people would not feel compelled to kill themselves early, but would instead rest assured that assistance in dying will be available to them even after they become physically incapacitated:

> If the only choice is suicide now and suffering later, individuals will frequently choose suicide now. If the choice is suicide now or suicide at no greater cost later, they will choose suicide later because there is always a chance that they are mistaken in believing that continued life will impose unbearable suffering or incapacity on them. They would give up that chance by committing suicide now. The possibility of physician-assisted suicide enables them to wait until they have more information before deciding whether to live or die.[3]

Posner's hypothesis—that the primary benefit of legalization accrues to elderly persons faced with the prospect of oncoming disability—is, however, oddly in tension with his simultaneous assertion that "some of the strongest cases of rational suicide" do not involve the elderly at all, but "people who face an indefinite lifetime of paralysis, severe pain, or other terrible disability."[4] In this case, one thinks not of the aged patient facing a terminal illness, but the young quadriplegic with years to live. The primary empirical benefit Posner claims for legalization (fewer and older suicides), thus, seemingly has little to do with what he identifies as the most compelling cases for assisted suicide (young persons who suffer from neither a terminal illness nor unendurable pain). Posner's hypothesis also depends heavily on the supposition that people frequently use suicide as a rationally calculated means of escaping future and oncoming disabilities. But Posner presents no evidence for this supposition; in fact, extant evidence strongly suggests that suicide is more often linked not with such careful rational reflection but with depression and psychological diagnosable ailments.[5] Further, by far the highest rates of suicide in the United States today belong not to younger or middle-aged adults supposedly responding in a reasoned way to the fear of future illness and disability, but to the very elderly (those over seventy-five)—thus suggesting that one of the primary benefits Posner seeks to achieve through legalization (later suicides) may have been accomplished already.[6]

While the foregoing analysis indicates an unresolved tension between Posner's thesis and his stated goal, and while it raises the question whether there really are significant numbers of relatively younger persons who have coolly chosen to kill themselves rather than risk the prospect of future illnesses, none of this directly addresses the specific empirical data that Posner offers in support of his fewer-and-later-suicides hypothesis.

Posner's Argument from U.S. Data

The first piece of evidence Posner presents in support of his fewer-and-later-suicide hypothesis is a regression analysis testing the relationship between suicide rates and the status of state law on assisted suicide:

The question whether allowing physician-assisted suicide in cases of physical incapacity would increase or reduce the suicide rate can be studied empirically. [The table] regresses state suicide rates in the United States on state per capita income, the percentage of the state's population that is black (blacks have much lower suicide rates than whites), and a dummy variable that takes a value of 1 if a state has a law criminalizing physician-assisted suicide and 0 otherwise.

Regression of Suicide Rate on Assisted-Suicide Law and Other Variables
(t-statistics in parentheses)

Per Capita Income	Percentage Black	Assisted-Suicide Law	R^2
−.0005	−.1287	−.7601	.31
(−3.388)	(−2.999)	(−0.951)	

The coefficients of the income and percentage-black variables are negative and highly significant statistically, and these two variables explain a good deal of the variance across states in the suicide rate. The coefficient of the law variable is also negative, implying that states that forbid physician-assisted suicide do have lower suicide rates than states that permit it. But it is not statistically significant, though perhaps only because most suicides are not committed by terminally ill or otherwise desperately ill people and thus do not come within the scope of the hypothesis that I am trying to test. Although these results do not suggest that repealing an assisted-suicide law is a sound method of reducing a state's suicide rate, they cast at least some doubt on the hypothesis, which I have been questioning despite its intuitive appeal, that making suicide easier is likely to lead to more suicides.[7]

Posner here concedes that he finds no statistically significant relationship between assisted suicide laws and the rate of suicide. Yet, somewhat remarkably, Posner proceeds to argue that the data lend support to his hypothesis anyway: "[a]lthough these results do not suggest that repealing an assisted-suicide law is a sound method of reducing a state's suicide rate, they cast at least some doubt on the hypothesis . . . that making suicide easier is likely to lead to more suicides."[8] But Posner's findings simply are not helpful to his own thesis. Before a regression's findings are deemed sufficiently reliable for an economist to offer them in evidence in a federal court, typically they must reflect a 95 percent confidence level (with a t-statistic of 1.96).[9] Posner's t-statistic for assisted suicide laws is less than 1.00 (0.951), suggesting a possibility of sampling error of approximately *40 percent*.

Posner also reveals that his data regarding the status of state assisted suicide laws are drawn from a single footnote in a student-written law review note.[10] That student note, however, merely declared that "most states" ban assisted suicide by statute and proceeded to cite a great many state laws as *exam-*

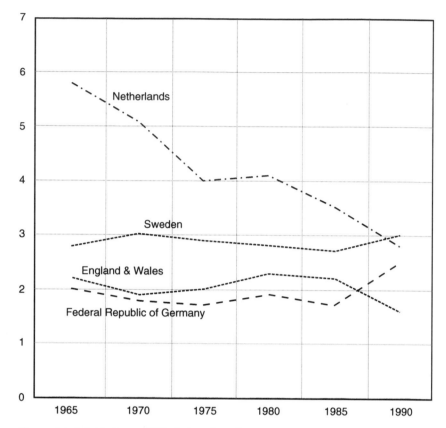

Figure 8.1 Suicide Rate of Elderly Dutch Males as a Multiple of the Total Dutch Male Suicide Rate, 1965–1990

ples to support that claim.[11] When constructing his regression, Posner apparently (mis)inferred that the remaining, unlisted states do not have statutes banning the practice. In fact, at least ten states not identified by the student note have statutes banning assisted suicide.[12] Posner's "dummy variable" column thus actually runs counter to available evidence.

Posner's Argument from Dutch Data

Lacking meaningful support for his thesis based on American data, Posner also seeks to rest his argument on evidence from the Netherlands. He posits that the rate of elderly male suicide was "very high in the Netherlands before euthanasia became common in the early 1970s and has fallen since, both absolutely and relatively" compared to other Western European countries,[13] and he points to data reproduced in Figure 8.1.

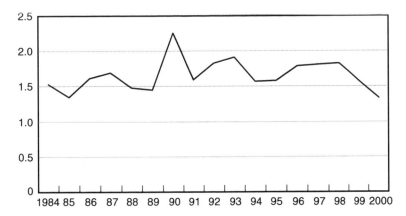

Figure 8.2 Suicide Rate of Elderly Dutch Women as a Multiple of the Total Female Suicide Rate, 1984–1997

Posner asserts that the legalization of assisted suicide caused the drop in the Dutch male suicide rate between 1965 and 1990, yet, somewhat surprisingly, he makes no effort whatsoever to consider —let alone rule out—the statistical significance of other potential causal factors for the phenomenon he observes in the data.[14] There are, moreover, ample reasons to question Posner's untested causal assertion.

First, assisted suicide became legally permissible only with a decision by the Dutch Supreme Court in 1984 recognizing a limited "necessity" defense to homicide charges for physicians who kill the terminally ill.[15] The fact that the male suicide rate, as depicted in Figure 8.1, declined profoundly between 1970 and 1984—before the key judicial decision—suggests that other factors, besides legalization, may have been responsible for reducing the incidence of suicide. Since the Dutch effectively legalized assisted suicide in 1984, moreover, Figure 8.1 reveals that the rate of Dutch male suicides has followed roughly the same trajectory as the rate of male suicides in England and Wales, where assisted suicide remains unlawful, casting doubt on whether one can attribute the decline between 1984 and the present to any factor unique to the Netherlands.

Second, Posner curiously rests his argument on suicide data for *men*. He relegates to a footnote any mention of equally available data for women.[16] And, as reflected in Figure 8.2[17] an examination of the data for Dutch women shows that the rate of elderly Dutch female suicides has not meaningfully declined since de facto legalization in 1984.[18]

Third, World Health Organization data depicted in Figures 8.3 and 8.4 reflect that, after nearly two decades of de facto legalization (and the very large number of deaths now attributable to assisted suicide and euthanasia in the Netherlands), the rate of *unassisted* suicides among older people in the Netherlands remains comparable to the rate of elderly suicides in many other countries where assisted suicide is unlawful.[19] For example, the suicide rate for el-

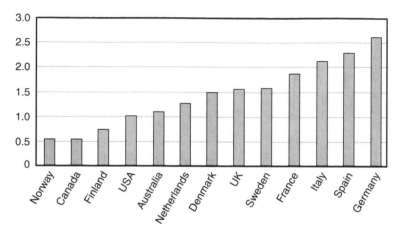

Figure 8.3 Suicide Rate of Elderly Women as a Multiple of the Total Female Suicide Rate

derly women is actually *higher* in the Netherlands than it is in the United States. (Meanwhile the suicide rate for elderly men is only slightly lower in the Netherlands than it is in America, but still higher than the comparable suicide rate for elderly men in Britain, Canada, or Australia.) Arguably, the most one might venture to state with confidence about the Dutch experience is that decades ago the suicide rate among older persons was out of kilter with many other Western countries and in recent years has more or less fallen in line.

Fourth, while Posner focuses on the rate of elderly Dutch suicides as compared to that country's overall suicide rate, such a comparison tells us only the relative percentage of suicides committed by *older persons*. Posner's comparison sheds little or no light on his self-declared hypothesis, namely, that legalization of assisted suicide should result in *younger* and *healthier* persons committing suicide less frequently.

Indeed, if Posner's hypothesis were true—and younger and healthier persons commit fewer suicides when assisted suicide is legally tolerated—one might expect to find that the *overall* number of Dutch suicides, including those committed by younger, healthier persons, declined after 1984 when assisted suicide was effectively legalized. Posner, however, does not squarely address that question, nor would doing so appear to aid his argument. The overall suicide rate in the Netherlands is nearly double what it was fifty years ago—9.4 deaths per 100,000 persons in 2000 versus 5.5 per 100,000 persons in 1950.[20] Since 1980, four years before de facto legalization, the Dutch suicide rate has consistently hovered somewhere in the range of 9.4 and 11.3 deaths per 100,000 persons.[21] Simply put, the Dutch appear to have been unable to effect meaningful decreases in the overall suicide rate despite de facto legalization of assisted suicide in 1984.

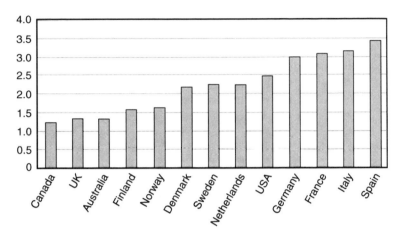

Figure 8.4 Suicide Rate of Elderly Men as a Multiple of the Total Male Suicide Rate

Finally, Posner's thesis—much like the theories offered by Griffiths and Kuhse[22]—appears to be in tension with the law of demand, suggesting that legalizing assisted suicide (that is, reducing the costs and barriers associated with its practice) would result in fewer, rather than more, cases of suicide and assisted suicide overall. Unlike Griffiths or Kuhse, Posner at least recognizes the inconsistency between his argument for assisted suicide and the law of demand and openly argues for a rather extraordinary exception to the rule:

> It may be objected that my entire analysis violates the economist's Law of Demand; that lowering the price of a good or service—here, suicide—must increase rather than reduce the demand for it. This is not the correct way to frame the issue. We have two goods, not one: unassisted suicide, and physician-assisted suicide. They are substitutes, so lowering the price of the second (by legalizing it) will reduce the demand for the first, and nothing in economics teaches that this reduction must be fully offset by the increased demand for the second good. A razor blade that retains its sharpness for ten shaves is a substitute for one that retains it for only one shave, but if the former takes over the market the total number of razor blades produced and sold will decline even if the longer-lasting blade is no more expensive than the other blade.[23]

Essentially, Posner supposes that demand will simply shift from unassisted suicide to assisted suicide, and that no additional demand will be generated from the latter's legalization. But Posner offers no evidence that assisted suicide is a one-for-one substitute for unassisted suicide, and available data do not seem to support this proposition. Contrary to what one would expect to find if Posner's hypothesis were true, the Dutch suicide rate has *not* changed substantially since assisted suicide was effectively legalized in 1984.[24] At the same time, although we do not have pre-1984 data for assisted suicide and euthanasia, we know that assisted suicide and euthanasia have become leading causes of death: more deaths now result from those practices combined than from many other significant causes (for example, HIV, leukemia, or homicide).[25] In 1995 alone, the Dutch recorded 3,118 acts of euthanasia, 542 assisted suicides, and 949 affirmative killings without patient consent, for a total of 4,609 deaths, amounting to 3.4 percent of all deaths in the Netherlands that year.[26]

Posner's exception to the law of demand hypothesis runs not only against the grain of the available empirical data, but his hypothetical analogy lacks explanatory value in the "market" for end-of-life services. In Posner's hypothetical, unassisted suicide is like a disposable, single-use razor blade.[27] With the introduction of a reusable, ten-shave razor (which Posner likens to assisted suicide) the overall output of razor blades declines.[28] But, notably, Posner's analysis omits any discussion about consumer *demand* for the service rendered by both products (that is, the total number of shaves) in his hypothetical market. Nor, in fact, is there reason to suppose that the advent of a new razor would lead consumers to wish to shave less often. If anything, one could imagine reasons why the advent of reusable disposable razors would lead consumers to shave more often.

Likewise, there is no reason to suppose that the introduction of assisted suicide would reduce total consumer demand for end-of-life services. The only reason Posner supposes for a decline in razor sales in his hypothetical market has nothing to do with a reduction in consumer demand for shaves, but rather, involves an innovation (the reusable razor) that permits manufacturers to satisfy a constant (or even growing) consumer demand for shaves with a smaller supply. Translating to the suicide market, Posner's imaginary razor market gives us no reason to think that overall *demand* in the unassisted suicide-assisted suicide market would decline, and quite unlike a ten-shave razor that is capable of satisfying higher demand with a smaller supply, the "new product" he promotes (assisted suicide) is, like the original product (unassisted suicide), good for just one use per customer.

Rather than analogizing to a ten-shave razor, perhaps a more accurate analogy might be between razors with equally long useful lives for the consumer. The disposable single-use razor blade (like unassisted suicide) has been available to consumers for years, but some find it uncomfortable to use. Eventually, the razor merchants devised the "sensitive skin" single-use razor, which sports a "moisturizing strip." Like assisted suicide, this new razor has the same basic use as the original disposable, but it also contains an added feature that some consumers find superior and thus prefer. One would expect the introduction of such a product to lead to an *increase* in overall sales of disposable razors; indeed, this is precisely why manufacturers introduce line extensions of this sort and business scholars develop complex models for evaluating how to use line extensions to maximize consumer demand and profits.[29] Similarly, as progressively easier and less stigmatizing options to suicide become available, first assisted suicide and then euthanasia, the overall use of such "end-of-life services" might be expected to increase. Posner offers little evidence that this particular arena of human activity presents any exception to the law of demand, and his analogy to a hypothetical razor market simply does not prove the point on its own terms.[30]

Posner's Analysis of the Costs Associated with Assisted Suicide

The purpose of a utilitarian project like Posner's is to weigh the competing costs and benefits of alternatives to determine which, on balance, produces the "best" or "most efficient" result. While Posner's own analysis focuses intently on the possible benefits associated with legalization, he readily, and significantly, admits that his argument for legalization can be considered only "tentative" precisely because he does not attempt to enumerate or consider the costs associated with legalization.[31]

That said, through a colorful anecdote about his grandfather, Posner at least implicitly touches on the possibility that legalization would bring with it the unwanted "cost" of some patients being killed erroneously. Physicians told Posner's grandfather, then in his forties, that he had a fatal kidney disease but might manage to live a year or two if he gave up meat.[32] Posner's grandfather refused to give up meat, lived to be eighty-five, and died of an unrelated ailment.[33] "Like other professionals," Posner explains, "doctors sometimes speak with greater confidence than the facts warrant."[34] Although Posner does not directly acknowledge the point, in the very regime he advocates, his grandfather would have been a prime candidate for an early, and mistaken, act of euthanasia.

While Posner gives only scant attention to the potential for mistaken and abusive killings, he does discuss in some detail another possible cost associated with legalization. If, as Posner hypothesizes, fewer people would decide to kill themselves and those who do decide to kill themselves would do so later, Posner worries that medical costs would rise in a regime where assisted suicide is lawful.[35] People who decide not to end their lives early would incur substantial additional costs as they age and become sicker, and in our society Posner expresses concern that many of these costs would be borne by third-party payers, not the individual patient.[36] We cannot, Posner tells us, "disregard [such] tangible costs borne by people who through their taxes, health-insurance premiums or doctors' bills are forced to pay other people's medical expenses."[37] Although he stops short of saying so explicitly, Posner seems to suggest (remarkably) that we might not want to legalize assisted suicide because it is cheaper for society to have more people commit suicide at a younger age (as Posner posits they now do) rather than linger longer, spend more on health care, and raise our taxes and health insurance premiums in the process.

The Incommensurability Problem in Posner's Work

Posner himself hints at the incommensurability problem confronting his utilitarian argument for assisted suicide when he acknowledges that medical costs may be borne by the public if assisted suicide is legalized. Fearful of these costs, Posner backs away from his argument for legalization and submits that it would be "difficult to say whether allowing physician-assisted suicide would be cost-justified."[38] Posner, at least here, sees real costs and benefits on both sides of the ledger and admits that he is not sure how the balance should be struck. But even if we could estimate with accuracy the increased medical costs Posner identifies, how are we as a society to measure the benefit of fewer and later suicides against increased medical costs to be borne by the public through increased taxes or health insurance premiums?

In the end, Posner seems to admit the inability of a purely utilitarian calculus to resolve this dilemma, offering no utilitarian-based answer and instead falling back upon the harm principle—or what he calls "Mill's approach."[39] According to Posner, "Mill's approach" holds that each person must be afforded the right to exercise self-control "[o]ver himself, over his own body and mind," and that the state may coerce an individual to take actions against his or her will only to "prevent harm to others."[40] Assuming that assisted suicide is a purely self-regarding (or, more precisely, harmless-to-others) activity, Posner argues that "Mill's approach" "enables us to exclude (*as a strictly economic or utilitarian analysis would not*) the disutility"[41] associated with legalization, thus vindicating the right to assisted suicide and euthanasia regardless of the real, negative side effects that would attend the regularization of such practices.

8.2 Posner's and Epstein's Libertarian Case for Assisted Suicide

While Posner migrates away from utilitarian arguments for assisted suicide toward a libertarian claim, Richard Epstein makes no such migration. Epstein, like Posner in his final defense of assisted suicide, argues that respect for the harm principle dictates legalization of assisted suicide for the terminally ill, whatever the "costs" and "benefits" may be.

While Posner and Epstein generally confine themselves to discussing a potential right for the terminally ill, much of their reasoning, inspired by Mill's harm principle, tends toward a right open to all competent adults. Posner, for example, argues that "the strongest cases of rational suicide" in his mind do not involve persons with a terminal illness suffering incurable pain, but people who confront "an *indefinite lifetime* of paralysis . . . or other terrible disability."[42] Posner adds, too, that his "conception of the appropriate scope of legal regulation" is based upon the harm principle, and thus rests on the premise that "the only voluntary activities of [any] competent adult[] with which government can properly interfere are those that impose tangible harms."[43] Posner's principle is in no way conditioned upon the physical condition or capabilities of the competent adult.

Followed to the logical end, Posner's libertarian principle would seem to tend toward, if not require, the legalization not only of assisted suicide and euthanasia, but of *any* act of consensual homicide. Sadomasochist killings, mass suicide pacts (e.g., Marshall Applewhite and his thirty-eight followers who killed themselves in San Diego in 1997 to transport themselves to a spaceship that they believed trailed behind the Hale-Bopp comet), duels, and the sale of one's life (not to mention the use of now illicit drugs, prostitution, or the sale of one's organs) are no more foreign to the version of the harm principle he posits than assisted suicide for the terminally ill. Certainly none of these other acts is any less voluntary or self-regarding than assisted suicide or euthanasia.

Posner does not address these potential corollaries of his Millian argument for assisted suicide, and, in fact, he sometimes seems to resist them. Posner insists, for example, that freely agreed upon suicide contracts are "beyond the gravitational field of American morality" and their enforcement is "unthinkable."[44] But what is "unthinkable" about enforcing freely entered contracts to a libertarian? Posner suggests it is unthinkable that suicide contracts "would be enforced and a person dragged to his death against his will because he had signed a contract and was now deemed incompetent to repudiate it, or even that it would be enforced by the forfeiture of a bond or by some other monetary sanction."[45] But contracts of any kind are rarely subject to judicial decree requiring specific performance, so the specter of dragging someone around to enforce an assisted suicide contract is something of a red herring. Posner's apparent willingness to abandon even merely *financial* consequences for repudiating a contract that is voluntarily agreed and harmless to third persons, however, is telling. It suggests that Posner is willing to deny ordinary judicial enforcement to private, consensual, and considered decisions by competent adults simply because they are, in Posner's words, "immoral" and "unthinkable" and violate "immovable intuitions concerning the priority of human beings," not exactly the ordinary stuff of libertarian analysis.[46]

Epstein takes a somewhat different and more nuanced approach in his argument for assisted suicide and euthanasia. He begins by contending that respect for libertarian ideals requires legalization of assisted suicide and eu-

thanasia whenever those actions are "necessary."[47] But this, of course, only begs
the question: when, in Epstein's estimations, is killing a person a "necessary"
response?

Epstein clearly believes that the consenting terminally ill qualify—that
is, they "need" to be killed under certain circumstances. But his formula for determining necessity does not strictly depend on the presence of a terminal physical ailment. Instead, Epstein indicates that he would allow assisted suicide and
euthanasia whenever a "rational agent could prefer death to life."[48]

But this formulation in turn only raises more questions: when, we
might ask, does Epstein think persons could rationally choose death? Are there
any real, objective limitations on assisted suicide requests imposed by this formulation? If so, what are they?

In some places, Epstein suggests that his formulation would limit the
availability of assisted suicide and euthanasia to persons suffering from a terminal illness because such a restriction would comport best with "our" "prior
estimates of rationality":[49]

> In political theory, the rational reconstruction of consent has to do all the
> heavy intellectual work because no observed transactions can be found in
> some state of nature to provide individuated evidence.... The background
> norms of rational behavior ... assume a [very strong] role within the frame-
> work when the question is whether killing another individual is so contrary to
> that person's self-interest that the per se bar should be maintained in the face
> of individuated evidence on consent that cuts the other way. Clearly, this cat-
> egorical approach sets out the correct rule in many cases: if a person of nor-
> mal health and disposition were deliberately killed by another person, the
> background judgments are so strong that individuated evidence would be ex-
> cluded. We do not believe the scenario in which that deal makes sense to the
> deceased individual. ... The background position can no longer be that con-
> sent is impossible to have; rather it is that consent is so unlikely that to intro-
> duce evidence in individual cases produces more error than ignoring that ev-
> idence altogether. This rule seems perfectly sensible given the massive amount
> of feigned or improperly procured evidence that could be presented, especially
> when the decedent is no longer around to explain his side. However, there are
> limits to this approach. The standard prescription should not be made in the
> same fashion for individuals hurt in boxing matches, which are often heavily
> regulated by the state. In these cases, the prospects of fame and fortune could
> explain why someone takes the risk of death. ... When the focus is solely on
> the subset of cases involved with end-of-life conditions, the background con-
> ditions change, and so too our prior estimates of rationality. ... In this con-
> text, taking one's own life begins to make sense, ... [and] the prohibition on
> all killings in the criminal law should not be retained in the context of termi-
> nal illness.[50]

As we explored in chapter 6, such restrictions on purely consensual conduct can be reconciled with the harm principle—indeed, Mill, Feinberg, and other adherents to the principle have regularly argued for absolute bans against other, less lethal forms of private consensual conduct on exactly these bases. Feinberg has even suggested that it is better to prevent one hundred freely consenting persons from entering slavery contracts than it is to allow one person to be wrongly subjected to a contract of servitude. Given all this, one might ask, why can't exactly the same be said of euthanasia, especially where a wrongfully permitted case can mean that an innocent person is murdered? That is, if laws absolutely proscribing slavery contracts and dueling can be defended as consistent with the libertarian ideal, why not also laws banning all forms of assisted suicide and euthanasia? Epstein owes us some explanation, but he supplies none, failing even to pause to consider the question posed by his fellow Millians. Likewise, if a little differently, Raz, himself a defender of a form of the libertarian harm principle, concedes that human autonomy or liberty requires a sufficiency of options be available to individuals to avoid the fate of the Man in the Pit, but emphasizes that this does not mean that every imaginable avenue of self-creation must be permitted. Here, again, Epstein does not engage, offering no reasoned explanation why assisted suicide and euthanasia are essential ingredients to any regime that seeks to protect and assure the full expression and flourishing of human liberty.

Ultimately, after attempting a rather incomplete defense of a right to assisted suicide and euthanasia limited to the terminally ill and suffering, Epstein himself seems to express the view that the practices should always be a matter of unrestrained individual choice. While he says that the background norm should be that assisted suicide should be permitted only when a person is suffering pain, Epstein eventually admits that

> it is one thing to reject a categorical position [against assisted suicide], and quite another to develop an alternative position. Thus the next question on the agenda asks just how much pain and despair are needed to justify active euthanasia in an individual case. That question is one of degree. *Its uniqueness and subjectivity cries out for individual choice and thus precludes collective power* in the absence of independent evidence of physician or family abuse in hastening or securing death.[51]

Thus, on the one hand, Epstein relies on "estimations" of rationality to argue for retaining laws against assisted suicide for "healthy" persons but, on the other hand, he contends that only individuals, according to their own unique and subjective standards, may determine for themselves whether they are "healthy" or not. With this maneuver Epstein effectively creates an exception that seems destined to swallow the rule. That is, if the individual may, without collective supervision, decide how much pain or despair is too much to endure, what is the point of defending a rule against assisted suicide for "healthy" persons in the first place? Nearly every act of assisted suicide could be justified under such a regime: the mentally depressed Ms. B from the *Chabot* case would be as free to obtain assistance in dying as any terminally ill patient suffering from physical pain. Under such a rule, any person could simply decide, "I've had enough," and obtain euthanasia, no matter whether he or she is suffering from a terminal illness or what might instead be a transitory bout of depression. The "uniqueness" and "subjectivity" of suffering, in Epstein's regime, simply and absolutely preclude collective power. And so it seems that we end up in very nearly the same place whether we follow Epstein's comparatively circuitous path or Posner's more-or-less direct line of libertarian analysis: that is, a regime in which assisted suicide and euthanasia are seemingly a matter of absolute and inviolable right to all competent adults without respect to the individual's objective physical or psychological circumstances.

9

An Argument against Legalization

SO FAR, we have considered arguments for assisted suicide and euthanasia based on history, fairness, neutrality, the harm principle, and utilitarianism. I have suggested that, if the harm and neutrality principles support any assisted suicide right, they tend toward (if not require) a right open to all competent adults; that arguments from history and fairness seem not to compel such a right at all; and that arguments from utilitarianism are indecisive.

In this chapter, I seek to lay the groundwork for a different argument, one that has been largely overlooked in contemporary American debate over assisted suicide and euthanasia. It is an argument for retaining existing law on the basis that human life is fundamentally and inherently valuable, and that the intentional taking of human life by private persons is always wrong.[1] My argument, based on secular moral theory, is consistent with the common law and long-standing medical ethics.

To be clear from the outset, I do not seek to address publicly authorized forms of killing like capital punishment and war. Such public acts of killing raise unique questions all their own.[2] In this chapter, I seek only to explain and defend an exceptionless norm against the intentional taking of human life by private persons. I begin by seeking to suggest that there are certain irreducible and non-instrumental human goods (and evils); I then proceed to argue that there is a moral imperative not to do intentional harm to such goods, and that such a rule would prohibit assisted suicide and euthanasia.

9.1 The Inviolability of Human Life

What do I mean by a basic good? And what does it mean to claim human life as a basic good?

In claiming something as a basic good, I have in mind something that is understood and felt as intrinsically worthwhile, an end that is a reason, sufficient in and of itself, for action and choice and decision. I have in mind something that is categorically good, not something that is good only because of its instrumental usefulness in achieving some other end. By definition, a basic good is an end in and of itself, fulfilling in its own right. It is not something whose value must be (or can be) deduced by reference to some prior premises or contingent on other factors or arguments. To claim something as a basic good is, as I see it, to claim something as inherently worthwhile, something in which an indefinite number of persons can participate and do so in any number of ways and do so at any point in human history.[3]

The existence of such basic goods, and the moral imperative to respect them, has been suggested by Aristotle[4] and Aquinas,[5] among others.[6] But our understanding of basic goods ultimately comes not from abstract logical constructs (or religious beliefs); it is, instead, I think simply a product of our practical human experience. Thus, in the *Nicomachean Ethics*, when Aristotle tried to identify particular basic human goods (and evils), he argued not from logical premises or by reference to some unreal world or hypothetical construct or original position. Instead, he argued from life's experiences and observations of human nature. And this is as it must be. I do not purport that I can "prove" the existence of basic goods or moral absolutes by reference to logical syllogism. Rather, I can and seek only to suggest their existence by reference to the practical, pragmatic experience of each of us in the world. And in doing so I must readily admit that much of life is spent on what can only be described as instrumental pursuits—for example, seeking money or clothes or food so that we may use and enjoy them. But is the notion of the noninstrumental, the concept of categorical rights and wrongs, altogether foreign in our lives? I would suggest that the answer is no. Don't we, at least sometimes, honor our family members or friends, or the works of nature or art, or those older and wiser or younger and more vulnerable, not for any instrumental or contingent usefulness they may have, but simply out of respect for their innate value? Don't we sometimes respect persons and things because of what they are, not because of what they can do for us? Indeed, our entire political system is premised on the notion and acceptance of such basic, fundamental rights (and wrongs), as reasoned from human experience. Our Declaration of Independence begins the substance of its work with the bold assertion that certain "truths" about human nature are indeed "self-evident," that these self-evident truths include the impulse for life and the value of liberty, and all that follows in the Declaration, the whole purpose and ideal of government as envisioned by the founding document of our country, is to establish a government that is aimed at securing and protecting what our founders considered to be self-evident human rights and truths.[7]

To claim that human life qualifies as a basic good is to claim that its value is not instrumental, not dependent on any other condition or reason, but something intrinsically good in and of itself. That this is true is suggested in part by the fact that people every day and in countless ways do something to protect human life (one's own or another's) without thinking about any good beyond life itself. We seek to protect and preserve life for life's own sake in everything from our most fundamental laws of homicide to our road traffic regulations to our largest governmental programs for health and social security.[8] We have all witnessed, as well, family, friends, or medical workers who have chosen to provide years of loving care to persons who may suffer from Alzheimer's or other debilitating illnesses precisely because they are human persons, not because doing so instrumentally advances some other hidden objective. This is not to say that *all* persons would always make a similar choice, but the fact that some people have made such a choice is some evidence that life itself is a basic good.

Perhaps the most profound indicium of the innate value of human life, however, lies in our respect for the idea of human equality. The Fourteenth Amendment to the U.S. Constitution guarantees equal protection of the laws to all persons; this guarantee is replicated in Article 14 of the European Convention and in the constitutions and declarations of rights of many other countries. This profound social and political commitment to human equality is grounded on, and an expression of, the belief that all persons *innately* have dignity and are worthy of respect without regard to their perceived value based on some instrumental scale of usefulness or merit. We treat people as worthy of equal respect because of their status as human beings and without regard to their looks, gender, race, creed, or any other incidental trait—because, in the words of the Declaration of Independence, we hold it as "self-evident" that "all men [and women] are created equal" and enjoy "certain unalienable Rights," and "that among these are Life."[9]

If one were to start from a different premise about the value of human life, assuming perhaps that different human lives bear different value depending on their instrumental worth to society or other persons, a critical rationale for equal protection would wither if not drop away altogether. Why treat people as if they are equal if, in fact, we really don't believe that they are equal? As the House of Lords Select Committee on Medical Ethics recognized in its report rejecting the legalization of euthanasia, the belief that human life is inherently valuable and worthy of protection "is the cornerstone of law and of social relationships. It protects each one of us impartially, embodying the belief that all are equal."[10]

An old chestnut British case familiar to all first-year law students, *Regina v. Dudley and Stephens*, illustrates this relationship between the innate value of all human life and the promise of human equality. There, two shipwrecked men faced with impending starvation ate their cabin boy and, when later rescued and charged with murder, pleaded that the killing was "necessary."[11] In essence, they argued that the life of the cabin boy could be treated as violable because of its instrumental value in keeping them alive. The court rejected this plea—and did so precisely because it saw all human lives as worthy of equal dignity and respect and any alternative rule as morally unacceptable; if we reject the notion that all human life is equally and innately valuable and argue instead that it bears only instrumental value, the court asked, "By what measure is the comparative value of lives to be measured? Is it to be strength, or intellect, or what?"[12] If life bears only instrumental value and may be extinguished whenever "necessary" for other ends and purposes, the court reasoned, "It is plain that the principle leaves to him who is to profit by it to determine the necessity which will justify him in deliberately taking another's life to save his own. In this case, the weakest, the youngest, the most unresisting, was chosen."[13] In *United States v. Holmes*, an American court reasoned to the same result, rejecting a claim of necessity by a ship's first mate who had ordered eighteen passengers thrown overboard from a grossly overcrowded lifeboat. The court in *Holmes* explained that, if decisions had to be made about whom to kill intentionally, they can only be made by lot because "[i]n no other than this or some like way are those having equal rights put up on an equal footing, and in no other way is it possible to guard against partiality and oppression, violence and conflict," which might arise if some persons are permitted to sit in judgment on the value of other persons' lives.[14]

The notion of equal and intrinsic human dignity embodied in *Dudley* and *Holmes* is not, of course, universally accepted. Some, even within our society and even among the most liberal and progressive of us, reject the premise that all human beings are intrinsically and equally valuable, asserting instead that human life has value only insofar as, and to the extent that, a person can do projects and activities that have value to them. Judge Posner, for one, candidly expresses this sentiment when he writes that "[r]espect for human life must have *something* to do with perceptions of the value, not wholly metaphysical, of that life. . . . The better the quality of lives, the greater the perceived value of preserving them."[15] A similar distinction is made, if more subtly, by Ronald Dworkin. Dworkin first speaks of human life being intrinsically valuable, even sacred, and rejects the view that nothing is valuable absent instrumental value.[16] But then Dworkin proceeds to suggest that one reasonable (if not exclusive) "interpretation" of the value of human life is the "liberal view" that the importance of human life depends on the level of "human creative investment" in it—namely, that human life is inviolable because (and only to the extent that) it is "created . . . by personal choice, training commitment and decision."[17] In short, the value of human life to Dworkin turns on the ability of persons to express themselves autonomously. Thus, Dworkin takes the view, as we discussed in chapter 3, that the life of the person suffering from Alzheimer's, while once capable of self-expression and self-creation, has lost its value. Such a person is, in Dworkin's idiom, "no longer capable of the acts or attachments that can give [life] value. Value cannot be poured into a life from the outside; it must be generated by the person whose life it is, and this is no longer possible for him."[18] As we have seen, Margaret Battin, Dan Brock, Norman Cantor, Richard Epstein, and Peter Singer all, to one degree or another, appear to embrace a similar instrumental view of human life, as of course do the Dutch.[19]

But if one's valuable humanness (and thus legal inviolability) turns on one's currently exercisable abilities for self-creation and self-expression, what specific traits and qualities must one exhibit? And how developed must they be before one qualifies for equal protection under the law? Dworkin tells us the Alzheimer's patient does not meet his criteria. But what about those with low IQs? The mentally disabled? The autistic? Stroke victims? Infants with Down's syndrome? The variations between persons, even those suffering from the same species of disability, are subtle and nearly endless, and any attempt to draw lines between different sorts of lives based on their current capacity for self-creation seems almost inevitably to become more or less an arbitrary and subjective enterprise. This arbitrariness is itself illustrated by the competing opinions and various views we have seen expressed by Dworkin, Battin, Brock, Posner, Epstein, and Singer, all of whom otherwise agree that life's value is instrumental, not innate.

For example, while Dworkin posits that it would be acceptable to kill Alzheimer's patients to accord with their prior, autonomously expressed wishes, even though they now resist, Posner, after denying that human life is anything more than an instrumental good, declares that infanticide is immoral and "not up for reconsideration,"[20] arguing that it violates "intuitions" that "precede and inform, rather than follow" from philosophical analysis.[21] Epstein, meanwhile, waffles on the infanticide question, asking whether parents have the duty to undertake ordinary surgery to preserve the life of a Down's syndrome child and answering that "after some misgivings perhaps, [the answer should be] an emphatic yes. But, if for some reason, the parents have no duty to keep the child alive, active euthanasia is probably preferable to the slow starvation of a helpless infant."[22] Peter Singer does no such waffling, noting that infants are not currently capable of autonomous self-creation and, thus, as we shall explore in more detail shortly, concluding that there is nothing wrong with infanticide. Yet, while endorsing the murder of young children, Singer suggests that we must extend a right to life to adult animals because, in his view, they have a higher capacity for self-awareness that merits absolute protection. That is, it's ok to kill small children, but not adult animals. And this, somewhat circuitously, takes us back to Dworkin: No doubt the abilities for self-creation of many of the animals Singer wishes to protect from being killed are less developed than those of many human adult Alzheimer's patients Dworkin would have us kill.

Simply put, while Dworkin, Posner, Epstein, and Singer agree that human life is valuable only when accompanied by certain instrumental capacities for self-creation, they differ markedly on *which* human lives possess the relevant capabilities and thus are valuable enough to merit equal and full protection under the law. And their various and competing theories on which humans count as full persons provide only a few examples. As we saw in chapter 3, American history is replete with arguments for applying eugenics theories (such as sterilization) to this or that group on the grounds that such persons lack this or that arbitrary prerequisite for full "personhood." Dworkin, Posner, Epstein, and Singer, while writing in a different context and time, share the same fundamen-

tal premise of the social Darwinists. Like their social Darwinist predeces-
sors, each seeks to replace traditional Anglo-American commitment to human
equality with something they consider more progressive and enlightened. Rejecting the notion that all persons are innately and equally valuable deserving
of the same dignity and respect, each instead endorses a view that the worth and
dignity of individual human beings depends at least in some measure on that
individual's current instrumental capacities for autonomy or self-creation. In
their eyes, like those of their early twentieth century eugenic forebearers, some
persons' lives are simply worth more than others.

To the objection that their theories differ and disagree on who should
be treated as fully human and who should not, they might respond that a certain amount of uncertainty or arbitrariness is hard to avoid and perhaps inevitable in many policy decisions—who can say for certain what the "right"
answer is in deciding how much to spend on guns versus butter this year, or
whether to extend the franchise to eighteen or twenty-one year olds? But even if
a certain degree of arbitrariness or uncertainty is tolerable and perhaps even inherent in many policy decisions, it is simply not acceptable when we are deciding who is and is not treated as fully human. In fulfillment of our civic promise
of equal treatment under law, American courts closely scrutinize and strike
down virtually any legal distinction made between persons on the basis of race,
gender, or age when education or other government services are at stake. Indeed,
it is at the heart of the promise of equal protection that like persons are treated
alike by their government. It would be radically inconsistent with that promise
to permit legislatures and states to employ rationales like those offered by
Dworkin, Posner, Epstein, or Singer in order to discriminate between persons
based on their capacities for "autonomous self-creation." As *Dudley* and *Holmes*
suggest and seek to express, it is incompatible with the promise of equal justice
under law that any of us should feel at liberty to sit in judgment to decide who
is and who is not entitled to the benefits of that promise.[23] Yet, Dworkin et al.
essentially ask us to do just that—to sit in judgment on our fellow human beings and deny the full humanness and value of some persons because they lack
certain instrumental capacities for self-creation. They ask us, too, to enforce a
distinction between persons not with respect to social security or education or
other government services, but with respect to the most fundamental question
of all, namely, whose lives should be treated as inviolable under law and whose
may be subject to intentional destruction by others. In sum, they ask us to enforce in a very real way a form of discrimination that would separate those who
are entitled to the full panoply of protections as a human being and those whose
lives are worth fewer and lesser protections. They ask us to accept, judge, and
decree that certain persons with certain (rather arbitrarily chosen) instrumental capacities are worth our total respect—inviolable under law—while other
persons who lack those capacities do not merit such esteem, respect, and pro-

tection. In the name of progressive policy, they would create a second class of citizens.

9.2 What Does It Mean to Respect Human Life as a Basic Good?

Even accepting the notion that human life qualifies as a basic, noninstrumental good, important questions remain. What does it mean to respect life as a basic good? When, if ever, can we take any action that harms life? Must we always strive to keep persons alive under any and all circumstances?

Such questions lead us back to a key distinction drawn in chapter 4. There I suggested that it is a basic feature of our world that we do not live like the proverbial Man in the Pit without any meaningful choices for crafting our lives. Instead, we live in a world with many and varied options for living good and upright lives. As a result of this fact, I suggested that we simply cannot avoid making worthwhile, meaningful, and good choices about how to live without also unintentionally doing harm to other valuable ends or goods. In choosing one upright path in life we cannot help but exclude others. And choices of this kind—those made in the pursuit and affirmation of one good—do not necessarily imply any disrespect for the value of other goods that are not chosen, even when they are incidentally harmed. Thus, to recall some examples, soldiers who accept an assignment leading to certain death do not *deny* the innate goodness of life—rather, their sacrificial choice *affirms* the existence of other worthwhile ends (such as saving or liberating others). Parents who choose to devote themselves primarily to raising children *affirm* the goodness and importance of family—they in no way imply any *rejection* of the inherent value of other ways of life (such as devoting oneself to the homeless or hungry). To say that something is a basic or innate good thus cannot possibly mean that persons may *never* do harm to it in any fashion, even as an unintended side effect. Our world, with its many varied and different forms of the good life, precludes that possibility.

By contrast, as I suggested in chapter 4, one thing we *can* do is control our *intended* actions. Quite unlike unintended side effects, our freely willed choices are entirely and uniquely within our control. It is a basic feature of the belief in the freedom of the human will, moreover, that our deliberate decisions about how to live life in a world with so many varied options define who we are and what our particular lives are about.[24] Our intended decisions speak about what we value and cherish and who we are and wish to become. Unlike unintended side effects, too, intended decisions to harm someone or something represent a denial that the objects of our actions possess innate value. Thus, for example, to run down deliberately for sport the child darting into the street, or to kill grandpa for the insurance money, or to shoot a hostage to make a political point is to make a willed denial that these objects of our actions hold anything akin to innate value worthy of our respect simply by virtue of their being. Such actions demonstrate a judgment or a decision that the objects of our actions have value to us only as instruments of our pleasure or pique, as means to an end. To harm something intentionally is, thus, simply and necessarily to deny that it contains inherent, rather than instrumental, value.

Recalling these principles from chapter 4, how do they speak here and to the question of what it means to respect life as a basic, innate good? The short answer is that if, as I have argued, human life qualifies as a basic good it follows that we can and should refrain from actions intended to do it harm. Such actions, after all, by their very definition evince a denial of life's innate worth; they bespeak the view that human life is not itself a sufficient reason for action in and of itself but may be deliberately subordinated to other efforts and ends. To act intentionally against life is to suggest that its value rests only on its transient instrumental usefulness for other ends. At the same time, nothing in this answer suggests that we may never take actions that end life—even when death is fully foreseen. To defend human life as a basic good, to declare innately valuable, we need not (and cannot) say that human life must never be harmed under any circumstances, or even that the preservation of human life is the most important object for human action that must always come first in some absolute and vitalistic fashion. Indeed, the inviolability-of-life view I espouse represents something of a mean between two extremes—between the extreme (just explored) of those who would deny equal treatment to some persons' lives and effectively declare them less than fully human and the other extreme of those who would demand that the respirator never be pulled, or the feeding tube never withdrawn out of rigid adherence to a view that life must be categorically preferred to any other end or good.

How so? Recall our discussion of palliative care or the refusal of treatment in chapter 4. The inviolability-of-life principle would, to be sure, rule out cases where the doctor intends to kill his or her patient. And this would mean that current laws against assisted suicide and euthanasia largely should be retained. Indeed, those laws, as we have seen, have focused carefully on the issue of intent, proscribing only those actions where a specific intention to end human life. At the same time, the inviolability-of-life principle would do nothing to rule out categorically actions or omissions where death is foreseen but not intended. The sweep of the principle I suggest, thus, is relatively narrow, paralleling traditional common law proscriptions on secondary liability and limiting state interference with private choices only to cases where the actor's subjective and specific intent to harm a basic good exists and can be proven. In this respect, the inviolability-of-life principle also parallels modern medical ethics, which has placed heavy emphasis on the double-effect principle in dealing with end of life care issues. Indeed, the inviolability-of-life principle affords us what may be the strongest explanation for why society has drawn the lines it has in the law and medical ethics of the end of life, as well as the clearest, most consistent secular explanation and defense for our current regime that proscribes intentional killings but does not seek to enforce any broader rule interfering with patient autonomy and choice.

As we saw in chapter 4, the double-effect doctrine on which the inviolability-of-life principle turns would do nothing to preclude the traditional practice of employing high doses of painkillers, even when such doses are sufficient to cause death, in order (that is, with the intent) to relieve patient suffering. Such actions may result in death, but they are commonly and appropriately undertaken with a design not to murder but to prevent pain. Indeed, alternatives are typically employed exhaustively before the strongest painkillers like morphine are introduced, and, when introduced, their administration is ordinarily reviewed with great care and frequency by attending physicians. Hospice advocates sometimes argue that the regulation of the strongest painkillers is so heavy that physicians often fail to relieve all the pain they can and should; those who oppose them sometimes have cited concerns about potential patient addiction or abuse. But the critical and revealing feature of such debates is the fact that both sides focus on the question of how best to care for patients, not how to kill them.

The inviolability-of-life principle would likewise do nothing to preclude patients from discontinuing even basic life sustaining medical care when death is foreseen. As we discussed in chapter 4, in a world where medical technology has advanced to the point of being able to keep patients alive for so long, but can do so frequently only under circumstances many would wish to avoid, there are plenty of reasons why patients might (and do every day) choose to forgo continued care without intending death. They may choose to reject care and accept death intending only to be left unmolested by further invasive treatments, to be left in peace to die, to avoid imposing further burdens on loved ones, or just to leave the hospital and go home. Such choices and others like them are made not out of any suicidal impulse but out of a recognition of the inevitability of death, an acceptance of it, and an intention only to avoid further burdens, be left in peace, return to family, and so forth. The inviolability of life recognizes and accepts that many other legitimate ends and goods exist besides life itself, and the difficulty of choosing between such goods in a world that is not at all like that faced by the Man in the Pit. To pursue and affirm objects and ends besides life does something to define and express who we are as persons. The selfless soldier who seeks to save a mate while risking his or her own life does much to define his or her life by such a choice; so, too, how each one of us chooses to face and accept death does something to define each of our lives. But none of this need involve an *intent* to die or kill.[25] Death is simply and unavoidably a part of nature's order; every one of us will and must die. At best, patients and their physicians can only delay that process, not avoid it. Learning to accept the inevitable end and to choose to die in a graceful way consistent with our own values and commitments is in no way inconsistent with the inviolability-of-life principle.

Indeed, to suggest that life must always be preferred to any other good would itself cause manifest injustices. It would deny the freedom of the soldier to choose to defend his or her fellow citizens even if it means accepting the soldier's own death; reject as illegitimate the choice of the human rights protestor to remain standing in Tiananmen Square true to his cause rather than back down in the face of the tanks; devalue the choice of martyrs who refused to recant their faith under persecution; and undermine the claim of those who declined to hide or deny their belief in human equality when threatened with lynching by racial supremecists in the American South. While life is certainly one basic human good, it is far from the only one, and it is impossible to say that it should always be preferred to other basic, innate goods that are themselves entirely independent and sufficient reasons for action—like the freedom and equality of one's countrymen, the liberty of others, or one's faith in God. In the end-of-life arena, too, such a principle would work grave injustices, forcing on patients continued care even when it is gravely burdensome. Nothing in the inviolability-of-life principle commands such a result.

Having sketched out the inviolability-of-life principle, one might ask about particular cases and how it might apply to them. Chapter 10 is devoted to doing just this—exploring common end-of-life issues and how the inviolability-of-life principle might come to inform and help decide particularly hard cases. But for purposes of finishing the sketch of the general principle, let us pose one difficult case now. What might the inviolability-of-life principle say when the patient has made manifest his or her intent to die in order to get insurance proceeds to the family straight away? Can a doctor or nurse assist in the discontinuation of treatment in such a case? As I alluded to earlier,[26] I believe they can. Assisting a suicide is a specific intent crime, and the inviolability-of-life principle focuses narrowly on intentional acts against life; both rule out only a relatively narrow scope of human conduct. While a case along these lines may present great moral qualms for the doctor or nurse, and while they may decline to participate for other reasons, the inviolability-of-life principle would not preclude a willing doctor or nurse from discontinuing services on the ground that they are no longer wanted by the patient/client. To be sure, a doctor who participates with the design of killing—like, say, a Dr. Kevorkian or a Dr. Shipman—is in a very different moral category. But nothing in the ordinary case of a physician who feels obliged to cease professional services at the direction of a patient/client betokens an intent to kill and thus implicates the inviolability-of-life principle.

9.3 Some Objections

The inviolability-of-life principle I've described is largely consistent with current law, modern medical ethics as expressed by the AMA, as well as the advice of various panels (in New York and England, among others) that have considered the question of end-of-life care.[27] Still, criticisms are easily imagined from several quarters.

A Neutralist and Libertarian Objection

The neutralist or libertarian might object that the inviolability-of-life principle I have sketched evinces an illegitimate disregard for liberty: consenting adults should be permitted to do as they wish without state interference. Of course, as we saw in chapters 6 and 8, faithful adherence to the neutrality or harm principles tends to lead toward, if not dictate, results—such as the legalization of consensual homicide, prostitution, or the use of illicit drugs—that even some advocates of the harm and neutrality principles have tended to suppress or ignore. But for those who openly defend such conduct, how do we answer their principled objection that treating human life as inviolable infringes unduly on human liberty? After all, the rule I am advocating *would* suppress liberty—if only to the limited extent of taking actions *intentionally* aimed at ending life.

This question takes us back to the issues we discussed in chapter 6. As noted there, Raz posited three essential preconditions for human liberty: sufficient leisure and means to make choices (the Hounded Woman); sufficient options to choose among (the Man in the Pit); and an absence of coercion. Recognizing a rule against intentional assaults on human life does not implicate Raz's first precondition at all. As to the second, a neutralist may argue that, for human autonomy to flourish, the state must remain neutral among all competing conceptions of a good life (and death). To this, however, I would respond that ruling out assisted suicide and euthanasia, while surely nonneutral, does not remotely leave us in a world with insufficient options for individual self-creation. Recognizing a rule against the intentional taking of human life hardly means that we are left like Raz's Man in the Pit with no meaningful choices to make.

While laws against assisted suicide plainly restrict *some* choice, consistent with the inviolability-of-life principle, they restrict only a limited arena of human actions—those *intended* to help kill. Indeed, the strict mens rea limitation inherent in most American laws banning assisted suicide serves, as we discussed in chapter 4, an important liberty-preserving function in the arena of secondary liability, preventing the state from "sweep[ing] within the drag-net of conspiracy all those who have been associated in any degree whatever" with the principal, and restricting judicial attention to those who "in some sense promote[d] [the] venture himself, ma[d]e it his own, ha[d] a stake in its outcome."[28] The inviolability-of-life principle does not suggest that the government should criminalize or regulate every act where life is *foreseeably* taken but rather ensures that prosecutions will be rare and government oversight judicious. Far from a wooden, vitalistic demand that every effort be made to keep all persons alive under all circumstances—a demand that would itself entail serious injustices—the inviolability-of-life principle I have described would permit patients ample room and liberty to accept and reject care of all kinds, even when death is foreseen as an inevitable result. Far from impinging significantly on choice and freedom, the inviolability-of-life principle allows us to chart what is, in a very real sense, a "middle way"[29] between the extremes of treating life as a mere instrumental good and treating it as something that we must preserve at any cost—affording, in the process, significant liberty to patient and doctor alike to discontinue or apply palliative treatment even in circumstances where death is foreseen as a certainty and precluding any reasonable suggestion, I think, that patient or doctor is left in a position remotely akin to Raz's Man in the Pit.

Raz's third and final precondition for the flourishing of human liberty and autonomy involves the absence of coercion. Precluding assaults on human life, one might argue, represents "coercion" in the sense that certain consensual activities are forbidden. As we saw in chapter 6, Raz argues that coercion of any consensual adult human activity undermines liberty and autonomy in two ways—first, it evinces "an attitude of disrespect for the coerced individual"; second, coercion is often "indiscriminate . . . [and offers] no practical way of ensuring that the coercion will restrict the victims' choice of repugnant options but will not interfere with their other choices."[30]

I would respond to Raz's concerns by pointing out that a law ruling out a "bad choice" does not necessarily evince disrespect for the chooser, but for the choice he or she made; by way of example, parents punish children who make bad choices not because they disdain them, but because they love them and do not wish to see them make bad decisions.[31] In addition to this, an absolute rule against intentionally taking human lives cannot, I think, be viewed legitimately as "indiscriminate" coercion disruptive of human liberty because the prohibition against the intentional taking of human life also serves to protect against the coercive, mistaken, and abusive taking of human life and thus serves as a guardian of human liberty and equality. In chapters 6 and 8, we saw that even the most steadfast harm principle advocates deny the premise that every law criminally banning consensual practices constitutes an impermissible encroachment on human liberty; indeed Feinberg and Mill argued for absolute bans against dueling and slavery contracts, contending that such a result is consistent with, and critical to the protection of, human liberty because of the dangers dueling and slavery contracts pose for the liberty of nonconsenting persons as a result of their mistaken, neglectful, or abusive practice. A harm principle or neutralist's right to consensual homicide open to all adults poses risks to human liberty similar to those posed by slavery contracts or dueling.[32] There is thus no reason to assume that a rule against the intentional taking of human life represents an unreasonable restriction on human liberty. Though laws banning assisted suicide surely result in the suppression of some consensual conduct, that simply is not, even for such libertarians as Feinberg and Mill, a conclusive reason against their adoption or retention. Laws protecting against abuse, mistake, or coercion may be appropriate (and perhaps even generally required of a just state) notwithstanding the side effect that a certain amount of liberty of some consenting persons may be suppressed.

Do Our Concepts of Self-defense and Necessity Authorize Intentional Killings?

In a different vein, one can imagine that the practically minded might question whether, whatever the principled concerns a harm or neutrality principle advocate might have, the law already permits the use of deadly force with the intention to kill by private persons in at least some extreme contexts where self-defense or necessity compels it, thereby calling into question the inviolability-of-life principle, at least at a doctrinal or practical level. But is this really so?

The use of deadly force in self-defense is, to be precise, legally permitted in most American jurisdictions only when one "reasonably believes" that such force is necessary to protect against an imminent threat of unlawful force.[33] Thus, if the defendant can show that he or she acted with an actual, honest intention of self-protection, a court will uphold a claim of self-defense; if, however, the defendant did not reasonably believe that he or she needed to use deadly force to stop an aggression, his or her act will be treated as murder or manslaughter.[34] Simply put, it is a requisite element to a claim of self-defense that the defendant acted with the intention of stopping an unwarranted aggression. Not only is an intention of this kind required, there is no need for a person to act in self-defense with any intent to kill. Even when one uses deadly force *foreseeing* the assailant's certain death, one may *intend* only that the aggression stop. Aquinas, for one, justified acts of private self-defense specifically on this basis.[35]

Admittedly, the American law of self-defense does not directly interest itself in the case where someone who "reasonably believes" that she is in imminent danger of death and intends to use force to save herself *also* uses the occasion to satisfy some *further* intention of seeing the assailant dead. But, just as with the right to refuse, the state *is* interested in ensuring that exactly what was done *can* be done uprightly—i.e., without an intent to kill—asking whether a person under the circumstances faced by the defendant would have felt reasonably compelled to use lethal force to save himself or herself from imminent death. As Chief Justice Rehnquist and the Court acknowledged in *Quill*, there is a difference between those acts that *can* be performed without any intent to kill (e.g., the right to refuse treatment, self-defense) and those that can *only* be performed with the unlawful intent to kill (e.g., assisting suicide, euthanasia). And, like the right to refuse, acts in self-defense indubitably *can* be done without any intent to kill. The law has, moreover, developed doctrinal nuances that do much to weed out and protect against the most typical situations where a further intention to kill might arise. A claim of self-defense is not allowed, for example, where one provokes the assailant's use of force or where one could have avoided the use of deadly force simply by retreating. Thus, the battered wife who lies in wait with a gun for her returning husband in order to provoke him into rage, or who refuses to leave the house when she could have easily done so instead of shooting him, may not escape punishment for her husband's death.[36]

Perhaps more so than self-defense doctrine, the law of necessity, if interpreted to belong in the law of *intentional* homicide, could run the risk of providing legal authority for killings inconsistent with the principle that human life is inviolable. Indeed, necessity doctrine is the very legal theory the Dutch government has employed to justify acts of nonconsensual assisted suicide and euthanasia.[37] And, as we saw from *Dudley*, once we open the door to excusing or justifying the intentional taking of life as "necessary," we introduce the real possibility that the lives of some persons (very possibly the weakest and most vulnerable among us) may be deemed less "valuable," and receive less protection from the law, than others.[38]

While common law courts in America and England have traditionally resisted the use of necessity doctrine to justify intentional killings (as *Dudley* and *Holmes* illustrate), some commentators have called for the use of necessity doctrine to justify or excuse acts of intentional homicide. Though we shall explore another example in the next chapter, for our purposes here it suffices to consider a hypothetical offered by the drafters of the Model Penal Code. While "recognizing that the sanctity of life has a supreme place in the hierarchy of values" and much contrary precedent, the Model Penal Code's authors have argued for the introduction of necessity doctrine into the law of intentional homicide,[39] suggesting that the case for necessity doctrine is illustrated by (among other examples) the case of a hypothetical mountaineer, "roped to a companion who has fallen over a precipice, who holds on as long as possible but eventually cuts the rope."[40] Such life-taking acts, the Model Penal Code drafters argue, are justified as necessary reactions to extreme circumstances.[41]

This example, however, seems unpersuasive on its own terms. Morally, the hypothetical mountaineer intends only to save himself and in no way wishes to do any harm (let alone kill) others. The mountaineer may *foresee* that his actions will cause harm, but he does not *intend* any such thing. The mountaineer would (quite unlike Dr. Kevorkian with his clients) prefer that everyone could live. The Model Penal Code's hypothetical defendant simply need not resort to claims of "necessity" to defend his actions. Doctrinally, too, the Model Penal Code's example can be defended at law without resort to a necessity defense. The mountaineer cuts the rope not with the intent of killing anyone, but out of self-defense in response to an imminent threat posed by the person at the end of the rope. In fact, the only significant difference between the case of the mountaineer, on the one hand, and the classic case of self-defense or defense-of-others, on the other hand, involves the nature of the threat. In the usual case of self-defense, a menacing aggressor points a gun and threatens to kill; in the case of the mountaineer, the man at the end of the rope poses the same deadly threat, though he does so blamelessly—that is, the man at the end of the rope is, for lack of a better term, an "innocent aggressor."

The common law of self-defense and defense-of-others, and even the Model Penal Code itself, however, fully anticipate and cover such cases. A successful claim of self-defense or defense-of-others formally requires proof that the threatened force faced by the claimant of the defense is "unlawful,"[42] but that term is really a misnomer because an "unlawful" force includes *any* force that (1) is employed without the consent of the person against whom it is directed, and (2) is not affirmatively privileged at law.[43] Thus, the mountaineer, even though confronted with threats in no way intended by the person at the end of the rope, is free to take actions to defend himself and others, without resort to necessity doctrine, because the force he faces is not one he agreed to and is not privileged at law. As the Model Penal Code puts it:

> It [is] immaterial that other elements of culpability, e.g., intent or negligence, are absent. Whatever may be thought in tort, it cannot be regarded as a crime to safeguard an innocent person, whether the actor or another, against threatened death or injury that is unprivileged, even though the source of the threat is free from fault.[44]

And there are good reasons for this rule: if the law were otherwise, requiring the threat faced to be intentional, it would have been impossible for dangerously threatened persons to defend themselves or others at common law against attacks by, for example, the mentally insane, minors, or other incompetent persons—persons who are, by definition, unable to commit criminal or intentionally tortious acts, though clearly capable of imposing real threats.[45]

In suggesting that the case for necessity in the common law of *intentional* homicide faces contrary common law authority and seems incomplete in the face of the principle of double effect and the availability of other defenses, I do not mean to foreclose the possibility that the doctrine might have a legitimate role in the law of *nonintentional* homicide or other areas within criminal or civil law; certainly such a role would not conflict with the inviolability-of-life principle, which categorically rules out (only) *intentional* acts against the basic good of human life.

Peter Singer's Thesis

While we have discussed potential criticisms of the inviolability-of-life principle from libertarianism and legal doctrine, perhaps the most aggressive and notorious contemporary challenge to this principle comes from Peter Singer in his argument for infanticide. It is worth pausing here to unpack and consider his provocative argument in detail.

Infanticide is, of course, nothing new. In earlier times, nothing could be done for many infants with genetic defects and children were left to die, as with the children left on mountainsides by ancient Spartans. What may be new, or at least new to our society, is the notion that infants who can be helped, and perhaps even perfectly healthy children, may be left to die or affirmatively killed, a position Peter Singer openly advocates. Nor can Singer's views of infanticide be fairly labeled as outside the "mainstream." His books are published by mainline academic publishers, he is a professor of bioethics at Princeton, and the *New England Journal of Medicine* has praised him as having "a larger popular readership than any professional philosopher since Bertrand Russell, and more success in effecting changes in acceptable behavior."[46]

Singer begins by encouraging us to "put aside feelings based on the small, helpless, and—sometimes—cute appearance of human infants."[47] If we shelve such "emotionally moving but strictly irrelevant aspects of the killing of a baby," he argues, "we can see that the grounds for not killing persons do not apply to newborn infants."[48] Having thus disposed of "emotional" claims, Singer proceeds first by endorsing utilitarian reasoning and explaining that, from what he calls the "classic or indirect utilitarian" perspective, the primary reason for a rule against murder is to ensure that our own lives and happiness are protected. Such reasons, he then argues, simply "do not apply" to the murder of infants because

> no one capable of understanding what is happening when a newborn baby is killed could feel threatened by a policy that gave less protection to the newborn than to adults. In this respect, Bentham was right to describe infanticide as "of a nature not to give the slightest inquietude to the most timid imagination." Once we are old enough to comprehend the policy, we are too old to be threatened by it.[49]

Singer also identifies what he calls the "preference utilitarian" perspective, according to which "an action contrary to the preference of any being is, unless this preference is outweighed by contrary preferences, wrong. Killing a person who prefers to continue living is therefore wrong, other things being equal."[50] But, Singer argues, newborn babies "cannot see themselves as beings who might or might not have a future, and so cannot have a desire to continue living."[51] Finally, from the viewpoint of the moral theory of personal autonomy, Singer notes that "a newborn baby is not an autonomous being, capable of making choices, and so to kill a newborn baby cannot violate the principle of respect for autonomy."[52]

In Singer's account, one's existence as a "member of the species Homo sapiens" is "not relevant to the wrongness of killing; it is, rather, characteristics like rationality, autonomy, and self-consciousness that make a difference. Infants lack these characteristics. Killing them, therefore, cannot be equated with killing normal human beings, or any other self-conscious beings."[53] Simply put, on Singer's account, it is wrong to kill those who are aware of the pleasures of living, thereby reducing the overall (utilitarian) balance of societal happiness. But it is not necessarily wrong to kill "conscious beings" (e.g., infants) who do not (yet) possess sufficient self-awareness to value pleasure.

Singer's argument thus unpacked highlights an interesting feature about utilitarianism, one suggested in chapter 7: it is an imperfect guarantor of a right to life—or any other good perceived to be a moral absolute or human right. Like anything else, life is a good worthy of protection if, and only to the extent that, it is perceived to maximize happiness. On a strictly utilitarian account, nothing can lay claim to status as a right or moral or political absolute, a good in and of itself; any "right" is valuable and worthy of respect only if, and to the extent that, it is *instrumentally* helpful in delivering pleasurable consequences and preventing painful ones. And so it comes perhaps as little surprise that the Dutch, who so heavily depend on utilitarian arguments to justify their euthanasia regime, have themselves recently come to view parental decisions to kill infants as morally and legally acceptable.[54]

Singer also offers insight into some of the more extreme potential consequences of autonomy theory discussed in chapter 6. Infants do not enjoy the most basic precondition for autonomy we identified—they do not have the ability to comprehend the means required to realize their goals; they are in no sense the authors of their lives capable of using their faculties to plan and make choices.[55] Accordingly, to the extent that autonomy is considered a precondition for possessing human rights, and Singer certainly sees it that way, a human infant surely must matter very little. Singer's argument, in this respect, is but a modest extension of the argument advanced by Ronald Dworkin or Margaret Battin that we should ignore the (demented) pleas of the contented Alzheimer's patient to live and instead abide by his or her prior (rational/autonomous) request to be killed when dementia sets in. Human life, at both ends of its spectrum where capacity for autonomy may be at its lowest ebb, is of little account in theories where rights depend on an individual's presently exercisable capacity for autonomous self-creation.

While Singer limits his discussion of the acceptability of infanticide to the context of "deformed" children, it ought not go unnoticed that the autonomy rationale he offers does not appear to rest in any way on the physical condition of the infant. A healthy baby is no more capable of Singer's self-awareness than one with Down's syndrome or spina bifida. Singer himself stops short of openly admitting as much, but he does come close: Singer contends that his argument "is [not] meant to suggest that someone who goes around randomly killing babies is morally on a par with a woman who has an abortion" and that "[w]e should certainly put very strict conditions on permissible infanticide," but he then proceeds to concede that "*these restrictions might owe more to the effects of infanticide on others than to the intrinsic wrongness of killing an infant.*"[56] Singer thus seems worried not about the life of the infant, but only the consequential loss of pleasure by *others* "who love and cherish the child."[57] Of course, when parents do *not* want the child, there is no such consequential loss to worry about, and Singer himself admits that, under his view, "infanticide can . . . be equated with abortion when those closest to the child do not want it to live."[58] Infanticide is primarily justified, then, on the basis of lack of parental interest, not on the basis of the child's health or "deformities." A healthy child who is unwanted seems therefore as much a candidate for infanticide as an unhealthy one.

Singer frankly admits, too, that part of the calculation that goes into determining parental interest revolves around "replaceability." A child with a condition like Down's syndrome or hemophilia might give parents less overall pleasure than a child without such conditions and, so, parents should be free to choose to kill such children. While "neither haemophilia nor Down's syndrome is so crippling as to make life not worth living from the inner perspective of the person with the condition," and "their lives, like those of small children, can be joyful,"[59] an infant with no self-awareness appears to have no claim against being replaced: "I cannot see how one could defend the view that fetuses [also non-self-conscious beings] may be "replaced" before birth, but newborn infants may not be."[60] But if this is so, what about parents who might find more pleasure from blond-haired, blue-eyed babies than brunettes with brown eyes, or from boys rather than girls? Singer's reasoning would seem to apply fully to such cases, licensing parents to cull their infant children to achieve any such desired traits (at least before the children become "self-conscious," an age Singer leaves undefined).[61]

Singer dismisses the view I have been defending in this chapter, that human life is intrinsically valuable, on the ground that it is an anachronistic product of "early and mediaeval Christian writers"[62] whose "doctrines are no longer generally accepted."[63] But, while the inviolability-of-life position undoubtedly has religious supporters, Singer nowhere considers the possibility that (as I have sought to suggest) the position is entirely defensible on secular grounds. Even Ronald Dworkin, who appears to agree with Singer's argument in certain other respects, acknowledges that "there is a secular as well as a religious interpretation of the idea that human life is sacred. Atheists, too, may feel instinctively that [assisted] suicide and euthanasia are problematic because human life has intrinsic value."[64] It is also somewhat remarkable that Singer dismisses the inviolability-of-life position on the ground that it is the product of doctrines that assertedly are no longer "generally accepted" when the alternative he offers is not exactly dominant in popular culture. And curiously, Singer himself at points appears to veer away from strict utilitarianism to argue for the absolute rule that there is "special value" or "claim to protection" in the life of certain persons.[65] Singer would, of course, define the term "person" to include *only* autonomous, choosing, rational beings.[66] But, interestingly, Singer actually *endorses* a rule protecting the "special value" of (autonomous) persons absolutely, thus appearing to take issue with the inviolability-of-life principle at the end of the day only insofar as it relies on what Singer calls a "species boundary," protecting all human beings as a class regardless whether particular individuals enjoy self-awareness and consciousness.

Singer explains that, in his view, relying on "species membership" as a basis for rights and privileges is the moral equivalent of racism against animals: "The biological facts upon which the boundary of our species is drawn do not have moral significance. To give preference to the life of a being simply because that being is a member of our species would put us in the same position as racists who give preference to those who are members of their race."[67] The alternative to the human-animal boundary that Singer offers, however, tends only to confirm the defensibility of the "species" boundary he criticizes. While human infants are not worthy of a right to live, Singer submits, adult chimpanzees, dogs, and cats are "rational and self-conscious beings, aware of themselves as distinct entities with a past and a future";[68] even with their comparatively modest inherent capacities for self-fulfillment and autonomy, these animals are, in Singer's special language, "nonhuman persons" deserving of legal protection and a right to live. As Singer puts it, "[s]ome members of other species are persons [and thus enjoy a right to life]: some members of our own species are not."[69] And Singer warns that,

> if dogs and cats qualify as persons, the mammals we use for food cannot be far behind. We think of dogs as being more like people than pigs; but pigs are highly intelligent animals and if we kept pigs as pets and reared dogs for food, we would probably reverse our order of preference. Are we turning persons into bacon?[70]

It is no exaggeration to say that Singer would leave parents free to kill human children capable, with time and nurturing, of autonomous flourishing in ways radically different from any animal, yet at the same time, he would have us acknowledge a right to life for all (adult) pigs.

While it is difficult to discern anything akin to what is ordinarily understood as racism in the traditional human-animal distinction, Singer's alternative—granting the "right" to life only to those beings, human and animal, who manage to run the gauntlet of infancy and achieve the status of "rational and self-conscious beings" in adulthood, all as a result simply of being lucky enough to be the offspring of parents who chose not to kill them—is a prime example of what some would label "agism,"[71] and what I might suggest is further evidence of the arbitrariness of instrumentalist accounts of human value.[72] In fact, under Singer's logic, it would seem to be perfectly acceptable for humans to kill not only their own young, but also young animals—to eat spring lamb but not grown sheep, veal but not steak. Though Singer does not discuss this apparent consequence of his analysis, the reader is left to wonder whether Singer, a well-known animal-rights activist and author, would really want to so limit his defense of animal lives, even if he sees little basis for protecting infant human beings.

Notably, too, like his fellow utilitarian Posner, Singer ultimately seems to endorse, in part, something akin to the inviolability-of-life principle, suggesting that *certain* lives must be protected, regardless of their instrumental worth. But, where Posner appears to find the lives of *young* human beings inviolable, Singer would limit his argument for the inviolability-of-life to *adult* humans and animals (i.e., "rational" and "self-conscious" beings). Yet, Singer—like Posner—never supplies a complete account of why the lives of only *some* arbitrary subset of persons, rather than all, should be held inviolable and fully equal, or why his understanding of "personhood"—embracing only adult persons, but also adult animals—is superior to traditional understandings defined by reference to a "species boundary."[73]

Further, Singer seems to mistake the inviolability-of-life's affirmative assertion that all human life has intrinsic and equal dignity for the negative claim that no other forms of life have intrinsic moral significance worthy of protection. A secular inviolability-of-life principle may not *mandate* the notion that animals have a right to life, but neither does it rule out such a position; and it certainly is consistent with the traditional view that certain ways of treating animals are morally *wrong* (even if the animal has no *right* not to be so treated). To make the argument that human lives are entitled to special and differential protection and respect is not to say that animals may be treated poorly or cruelly, but simply to say that it is not always and categorically wrong to take an animal's life intentionally.

9.4 THE FUTURE OF THE OREGON EXPERIMENT?

I began this chapter by suggesting that there are certain irreducible human goods, and that human life itself is among these. From that premise, I then argued that, while we cannot help but choose between (and incidentally harm) competing goods in a world rich with possibilities, intentional acts by private persons against basic goods, including life, are categorically wrong. After offering this thesis, I proceeded to address certain prominent objections. Having now proceeded this far, we might take a step further and ask how the inviolability-of-life principle might inform future legal debate over Oregon's assisted suicide regime. The Supreme Court has recently heard a narrow administrative dispute over whether Oregon doctors may prescribe lethal medications to their patients, consistent with the federal Controlled Substances Act. The Court's decision, to be rendered after this book goes to print, will be discussed in an epilogue. But beyond the currently pending statutory dispute, a larger constitutional question, one intimately connected to the issues and themes we have discussed in this chapter, remains lurking in the background, unresolved.

When Oregon's law was first enacted, a group of disabled persons, physicians, and other concerned citizens brought a legal challenge seeking a declaration that it violated federal equal protection guarantees. A federal trial court in *Lee v. Oregon*[74] sustained their challenge, holding that Oregon's law did not rationally advance, or, in equal protection parlance, "fit," its stated objectives.[75] The trial court's decision was later reversed by the Ninth Circuit, but only on technical standing and ripeness grounds; the appellate panel expressly declined to reach the merits of the trial court's equal protection holding and did nothing to foreclose the possibility that properly situated plaintiffs may have standing in a future case to challenge Oregon's law on equal protection grounds or that the trial court's analysis might correctly apply in such a case.[76]

In any equal protection analysis, courts typically proceed in a two-step fashion, asking first whether the state's proffered distinction or classification is justified (as either rational or under strict scrutiny, depending on the nature of the distinction or classification), and thereafter asking whether the state's classification "fits," or appropriately advances, its stated policy objectives. The trial court in *Lee* focused intently on the second step of this analysis. But the themes and concepts we have discussed in this chapter suggest that a substantial equal protection argument may exist on both steps.

As we have seen, the inviolability-of-life principle is strongly associated with the concept of human equality; the two are mutually reinforcing ideals. Oregon's law, however, candidly treats the lives of different persons quite differently. For the healthy, life is legally inviolable; no private person may take it. For the terminally ill, life is violable, and those physicians who help take it "in good faith" are exempted from any form of criminal or civil liability. Oregon defends this distinction as rational and appropriate and does so on the stated ground that any other legal rule "may simply mean prolonging suffering for a person who has no hope of a significant natural life ahead [and thus the state has] a valid public policy to allow choice based on principles of autonomy and self-determination."[77] But is Oregon's defense convincing?

In the first place, it is far from clear that Oregon's scheme should be analyzed merely on the basis whether its distinction between persons is "rational." While the so-called rational basis test controls most equal protection disputes, laws that either embody certain suspect classifications (such as those based on race or national origin) or impinge on fundamental rights receive "strict scrutiny" in equal protection challenges.[78] Classifications based on yet other grounds, such as gender, are sometimes reviewed under an intermediate level of scrutiny.[79] Oregon's decision to make a legal discrimination based on physical health (the terminally ill versus everyone else) seems a candidate for heightened review.[80] This is especially so given that Oregon's law expressly implicates a fundamental right—that is, the scope of the right to life.

Even when courts do apply a so-called rational basis review, moreover, if the state law at issue discriminates against a particular group of persons in a manner suggesting that they possess a less valuable form of living (past cases have involved the mentally disabled, unconventional families, homosexuals, individuals having sexual relations out of wedlock), such laws are typically subjected to a particularly searching form of rational basis review. Once again, Oregon's law may qualify, treating as it does the lives of the terminally ill as meriting fewer protections and safeguards against intentional destruction through mistake, abuse, or coercion than the lives of all other persons.[81]

Whatever the doctrinal rubric ultimately employed to review Oregon's discrimination between terminally ill and healthy persons, a nontrivial legal argument can be made that the law fails to pass muster. As we saw in chapter 7, the class of the "terminally ill" is discernible only in hindsight: patients in Oregon have waited a year or more after their "terminal" diagnoses to make use of their prescriptions, and physicians have admitted that they cannot be sure of their own "terminal" diagnoses; definitions of terminal illness are thus "inherently unstable."[82] Why, we might ask, is it reasonable to rest legal distinctions with the effect of life or death on what is admittedly guesswork? Even more fundamentally, we might also ask, what rational basis is there for treating the lives of those who are diagnosed as having less than six months to live any different from any number of other groups of persons—such as the patient suffering irremediable pain, the quadraplegic, Singer's Down's syndrome infant, or Dworkin's incompetent Alzheimer's patient? Can we rationally single out just the "terminally ill"?

Oregon has responded that keeping terminally ill persons alive is singularly inappropriate because doing so "prolong[s] suffering."[83] Yet, as we saw in chapter 7, suffering simply is *not* a prerequisite for permission to commit assisted suicide under Oregon's statutory regime; persons who are not suffering are equally free to receive a doctor's help in killing themselves. And in this respect Oregon notably departs from the Dutch who do purport to require some indicia of suffering before allowing assisted suicide or euthanasia. Oregon also invokes themes of patient "autonomy" in defense of its statute. But Oregon recognizes the goal of patient autonomy as a sufficient reason to permit assisted suicide only for one group of persons and adjudges it an insufficient reason to allow any number of other groups to obtain assistance in dying. Oregon's law thus vindicates the autonomy of only *some* persons, and not others, who wish to die, and the state has offered no convincing explanation for excluding other groups (e.g., the permanently disabled, or those suffering from progressive diseases). Neither, I have suggested, is the inability of Oregon to draw such a rational line a fluke or accident. For reasons discussed earlier in this chapter, any line we might draw among human beings for purposes of determining who must live and who may die ultimately seems to devolve into an arbitrary exercise of picking out which particular instrumental capacities one especially likes.

Not only does Oregon's law draw an arguably irrational distinction between the terminally ill and everyone else, one can raise serious questions about whether the law operates in ways that reasonably advance or "fit" its putative purpose of enabling considered and rational autonomous choices in dying. For example, as the trial court in *Lee* noted, under Oregon's law there is no guarantee that terminally ill patients seeking death will have trained mental health professionals evaluate them for competency and signs of depression. Yet, when the state wishes to confine persons with suicidal impulses for a period not to exceed five days, the patient is first entitled under Oregon law to an examination by a mental health expert.[84] How can one coherently explain and defend a regulatory regime that affords terminally ill patients less protection against the possibility of a mistaken death due to a psychiatric ailment than it affords all patients against the possibility of a mistaken five-day confinement from the same cause? As the trial court in *Lee* asked, "[w]ith death at issue . . . [why] would [it] be rational to not require mental and social evaluations by appropriately trained professionals"?[85]

As we have already seen, too, doctors helping to kill terminal patients are immunized from liability under Oregon's law so long as they act in "good faith." Yet physicians treating nonterminally ill patients are held to a duty of care commensurate with that used by careful physicians in the same or similar circumstances, and Oregon courts have expressly considered and rejected substituting this standard for a "good faith" duty of care.[86] How can a state rationally hold physicians engaged in hangnail operations to a higher standard of care than physicians who engage in acts deliberately aimed at killing their patients? How does it promote autonomous end-of-life decisions to set up a regime where doctors are immunized from liability even when they negligently kill patients who are not competent or who have not consented?[87]

Likewise, under Oregon's law, physicians must assess patients for consent and competency only at the time the lethal prescription is given; the statute does nothing to assure patient rationality and voluntariness at the actual time of death—which can come months (and perhaps even years) after the prescription is issued. Thus, although Oregon's assisted suicide regime seeks to promote autonomous self-determination, its law does nothing to assure that such preconditions actually exist at the time death is sought. As a result, there is little to prevent mistake, abuse, or coercion from playing a role after a prescription is issued, and nothing to ensure that patients are in control of their mental faculties at the time of death.[88] How does it serve the putative goal of autonomous patient decision making to set up a regime that allows people to commit suicide without considering whether they are, in fact, acting freely, competently, and autonomously at the time of the suicide?[89]

10

Toward a Consistent End-of-Life Ethic:
The "Right to Refuse" Care for Competent
and Incompetent Patients

I HAVE SUGGESTED that life is a fundamental good, that it should not be intentionally destroyed, and I have suggested, too, how that principle might apply to the assisted suicide and euthanasia debate. Before closing, however, one might reasonably ask what this inviolability-of-life principle might say about still other, far more common, yet often very difficult, end-of-life scenarios. Along the way, for example, we have discussed the decision to withdraw or reject life-sustaining care by competent patients; how, we might ask, does the inviolability-of-life principle apply in these important and everyday cases? Similarly, as I alluded to previously,[1] courts have sought to give meaning to the right to refuse treatment even for patients who have never been capable of making treatment decisions for themselves (e.g., infants) and for those who have lost their ability to do so (e.g., Alzheimer's patients and victims, like Terry Schiavo, of accidents that have grievously impaired their mental faculties), often permitting a guardian to decide for the patient on a proxy basis. Indeed, most of the reported right to refuse treatment cases in America have arisen in just these circumstances. But the question how far guardians may go in refusing life-sustaining care for incompetent wards who have made no living will and given no oral directives is increasingly a source of litigation in American (and English) courts. When may guardians discontinue basic (e.g., food and water) treatment? On what authority may they act? How should their decisions be reviewed when under legal challenge? The case law, to date, has produced inconsistent and often underreasoned results in these important cases; before closing, I briefly outline some of the leading cases and suggest the beginnings of potential answers to each of these questions.

10.1 THE INVIOLABILITY OF LIFE AND THE "RIGHT TO REFUSE" FOR COMPETENT PERSONS

To begin, we might ask how the inviolability-of-life principle has fared in right to refuse treatment cases where there *is* a competent patient. It is fair to say, I think, that some courts have taken pains to avoid endorsing the intentional taking of life in such cases. Other courts, however, have suggested that patients may have a right to discontinue care even when they have a suicidal intent to die, and doctors not only may intentionally assist such killings, but may have a *duty* to do so. While a complete review of the growing case law in this area is beyond the scope of this work, certain emblematic right-to-refuse cases involving competent patients in America and England and how they have variously treated the question of intent are outlined below, as well as some suggestions for how the inviolability-of-life principle might come to inform the analysis in future disputes. We then turn to examine separately the issues associated with incompetent patients, both infant and adult.

The American Experience

APPLICATIONS OF THE PRESIDENT AND DIRECTORS
OF GEORGETOWN COLLEGE[2]

An early American case frequently cited in subsequent right to refuse treatment decisions involved Jesse Jones, a twenty-five-year-old mother of a seven-month-old child, who was brought to Georgetown University Hospital's emergency room having lost two-thirds of her body's blood as a result of a ruptured ulcer. Without a prompt infusion of blood, doctors estimated that there was a better than 50 percent chance Jones would die. Jones, however, was a Jehovah's Witness, a sect that historically has rejected the appropriateness of blood transfusions on religious grounds. As Jones faded in and out of consciousness, permission for a transfusion was not clearly forthcoming from her, and her husband expressly objected to any transfusion, so the hospital, fearing potential liability for being an accomplice to suicide, sought a declaratory judgment from the court permitting it to administer a blood transfusion. U.S. Circuit Judge Skelly Wright ultimately granted the declaration on the ground that, as yet, there had been no competent direction from the patient herself, and the transfusion would permit her to regain her faculties and direct her medical care. In the process, however, the Court rejected the hospital's purported concerns about assisting suicide, describing Jones's case very much in the terms of double effect doctrine and rejecting any sort of simple vitalism: "[T]he Gordian knot of this suicide question," the court correctly explained, "may be cut by the simple fact that Mrs. Jones did not intend to die. . . . Death, to Mrs. Jones, was not a religiously commanded goal, but an unwanted side-effect of a religious scruple."[3] Under such circumstances—where death is accepted, not sought—the court suggested that treatment plainly may be rejected without raising the issue of suicide.

SATZ V. PERLMUTTER[4]

Seventy-three-year-old Abe Perlmutter was afflicted by Lou Gehrig's disease, completely incapacitated in a hospital bed, and dependent on a respirator to breathe. He filed a petition seeking to allow his physicians to remove the respirator, after failing to do so himself. The Florida court of appeals granted the petition, recognizing a right to refuse life-sustaining treatment emanating from the constitutional right to privacy and the common law doctrine of informed consent, which requires physicians to obtain advance informed permission from a patient before they may undertake medical procedures. At the same time, the court acknowledged the state's interest in preserving life and preventing suicide and, in turn, squarely focused on the question of intent. The court conceded that "the facts here unarguably reveal that Mr. Perlmutter would die, but for the respirator."[5] But, expressly invoking the rule suggested by *Georgetown College*, the court held that suicide was not an issue because of the unequivocal evidence of the patient's intent: While he was

> fully aware of the inevitable result . . . [t]he testimony of Mr. Perlmutter, like the victim in the *Georgetown College* case . . . is that he really wants to live, but do so, God and Mother Nature willing, under his own power. This basic wish to live plus the fact that he did not self-induce his horrible affliction, precludes his further refusal of treatment being classed as attempted suicide.[6]

Though the facts are not further elucidated in the opinion, it appears that the court granted the petition based precisely on the strength of the double effect distinction, again recognizing that the right to refuse can extend even to basic care so long as intent to die (and help kill) is not present.

IN RE KATHLEEN FARRELL[7]

This case involved a thirty-seven-year-old competent, terminally ill patient, Kathleen Farrell, another victim of Lou Gehrig's disease. After an experimental program that her husband described as "their last hope" for some restorative gain failed, Farrell asked to have the respirator that sustained her breathing removed. Farrell's doctor later explained that he was personally opposed to removing the respirator, but he nonetheless arranged for a psychologist to examine Farrell; the psychologist found no signs of clinical depression and no need for psychiatric treatment. Farrell explained that, having failed at her last chance for some restorative gain, she wished to discontinue the respirator because of the futility of continued care and because she was tired of "suffering." Farrell's husband filed a suit seeking a declaratory judgment that neither he nor anyone assisting his wife in disconnecting her respirator would incur liability for their actions.

The Supreme Court of New Jersey ultimately heard the case and granted the petition, holding that competent patients have a right, grounded in both the common law of battery and the constitutional right to privacy, to order a physician to leave them alone.[8] At the same time, the court, like others before it, acknowledged that the right is not an absolute one but must be tempered against the state's interest in preventing suicide and "preserving the sanctity of all life."[9] The court found those concerns were not implicated in this case, however, given a (now-familiar) causation analysis—namely, that Farrell's declination of further treatment "may not properly be viewed as an attempt to commit suicide. Refusing medical intervention merely allows the disease to take its natural course."[10] Having acknowledged the right of patients to refuse life-sustaining treatment, however, the court stopped short of imposing a duty on an unwilling physician to participate in the process, at least to the extent it would violate professional ethical canons:

> Even as patients enjoy control over their medical treatment, health-care professionals remain bound to act in consonance with special ethical criteria. We realize that these criteria may conflict with some concepts of self-determination. In the case of such a conflict, a patient has no right to compel a health-care provider to violate generally accepted professional standards.[11]

BOUVIA V. SUPERIOR COURT (GLENCHUR)[12]

Former Surgeon General C. Everett Koop once labeled *Bouvia*, a leading California right-to-refuse case, as "the most forthright judicial acknowledgment yet of a 'right' to undergo euthanasia by omission."[13] And he is perhaps correct, though even that decision technically, as a matter of legal precedent, offers no support for *intentional* killings (and, thus, assisted suicide or euthanasia). There, a twenty-eight-year-old woman, Elizabeth Bouvia, suffering from cerebral palsy, sought a writ of mandamus requiring her physicians to remove from her body a nasogastric tube inserted and maintained against her will to keep her alive through involuntary forced feedings. The trial court heard evidence from Bouvia that suggested serious emotional trouble: she had suffered a recent miscarriage, her husband had left her, her parents had asked her to leave home, and she had repeatedly expressed her intent to commit suicide.[14] After hearing the evidence, the trial court refused the writ on the grounds that Bouvia had "formed an intent to die," and thus her refusal of care would constitute a suicide which the state (and Bouvia's doctors) had no duty to assist.[15] An intermediate trial court reversed, holding that

> we find no substantial evidence to support the trial court's conclusion [that Bouvia had formed an intent to die]. Even if petitioner had the specific intent to take her life [at one point], she did not carry out the plan. . . . [I]t is clear that she has now merely resigned herself to accept an earlier death, if necessary, rather than live by feedings forced upon her by means of a nasogastric tube.[16]

While it allowed Bouvia's mandamus petition, the court of appeals' decision is remarkable for the narrowness of its reasoning. The court of appeals did not hold that Bouvia's right to refuse encompassed the right to intentional self-killing by omission (i.e., suicide). It did not hold that Bouvia had a right to assistance in suicide or euthanasia from her physicians. Instead, to arrive at its result, the court took the unusual step of reversing the trial court's factual findings and simply disputed that Bouvia at present had an intention to kill herself, even if she did so previously, thus blinking at the prospect of extending the right to refuse into the terrain of intentional killing.[17]

In a separate concurrence that undoubtedly influenced Dr. Koop's opinion of *Bouvia*, Judge Compton accused his colleagues of "danc[ing]" around the issue.[18] In his mind, there was "no doubt that Elizabeth Bouvia wants [i.e., intends] to die."[19] And, as to that, Judge Compton indicated he *would* recognize a right to refuse treatment even when an intent to die is present, invoking neutralist and harm principle themes: "Can anyone blame her if she wants to fold her cards and say 'I am out'? . . . I believe she has an absolute right to effectuate that decision."[20]

MCKAY V. BERGSTEDT[21]

Kenneth Bergstedt was a mentally competent thirty-one-year-old quadriplegic who had lived in that condition since a swimming accident at the age of ten; though he was able to read, orally operate a computer, and use a wheelchair, Bergstedt was dependent on a respirator. After learning that his father had been diagnosed with a terminal illness, Bergstedt "despaired over the prospect of life without the attentive care, companionship and love of his devoted father" and sought to have removed the respirator on which his life depended.[22] Bergstedt's mother had died years earlier and Bergstedt feared that, without his father, he would lack adequate care and "some mishap would occur to his ventilator without anyone being present to correct it, and . . . he would suffer an agonizing death as a result."[23]

Bergstedt petitioned the Nevada courts for a declaration that persons assisting him in the removal of his ventilator would not be subject to criminal or civil prosecution.[24] Confronted with the argument that Bergstedt's death would amount to suicide, the Nevada Supreme Court, much like the appellate panel in *Bouvia*, strained mightily—and somewhat dubiously—to suggest that Bergstedt harbored no intent to kill himself: "as we will attempt to show, [Bergstedt] harbored no intent to take his life, voluntarily or otherwise."[25] The court, like the court in *Farrell*, reached this conclusion primarily by way of the natural/unnatural or causation distinction we discussed (and questioned) in chapter 4, finding "substantial difference between the attitude of a person desiring non-interference with the natural consequences of his or her condition and the individual who desires to terminate his or her life by some deadly means either self-inflicted or through the agency of another."[26]

This analysis, perhaps unsurprisingly, provoked a dissent. Justice Springer argued, as the Second Circuit suggested in *Quill*, that the "[u]se of the term 'natural death' in this case is only a natural and understandable way of averting the excruciating truth. Bergstedt's explicit and express desire and intention was that of putting an immediate end to his own life. . . . There is nothing natural about Mr. Bergstedt's death; he [sought to] kill[] himself."[27] The dissent further suggested that the majority's natural/unnatural or causation distinction made no sense because

> Mr. Bergstedt was not dying, except in the sense that we are all dying, and he was not in the least danger of imminent death. He had been living steadily for over twenty-three years, breathing with the aid of a ventilator, until he reached a time in his life when he decided to die because, like most other suicides, life had become, temporarily at least, intolerable for him.[28]

Like Judge Compton in California, Justice Springer accused his colleagues of "danc[ing] around the issue [of suicide]";[29] plainly, to Justice Springer, this case presented an act of intentional self-destruction. Quite unlike Judge Compton, however, Justice Springer argued that there is no "judicially created or legal 'right' to commit suicide or to have court-ordered assistance in carrying out one's self-destruction."[30] And Justice Springer detected the equal protection overtones inherent in the abandonment of the inviolability-of-life principle: Bergstedt's assisted suicide "was sanctioned and facilitated only because of his disabled condition . . . . What other conditions, physical or mental, I ask myself, will be brought to the courts as grounds for judicially approved and assisted self-destruction?"[31]

The English Experience

IN RE T [32]

Like *Georgetown College*, this case involved a blood transfusion and a Jehovah's Witness. The patient, "T," a twenty-year-old woman thirty-four weeks pregnant and living with her boyfriend, was admitted to a hospital following a traffic accident, with symptoms of pneumonia. T's mother was a devout Jehovah's Witness, while her father rejected the religion, and the parents were divorced. T described herself as a former Jehovah's Witness when she entered the hospital, though she also stated that she still had certain beliefs and practices. Once admitted, T's condition deteriorated and she went into labor; a caesarian section birth was necessary. Twice T expressed her opposition to any blood transfusion, though both conversations came shortly after she had met alone with her mother. T eventually signed a refusal of care form supplied by the hospital, which was neither read nor explained to her. The following morning, T delivered a stillborn child and her condition deteriorated to such an extent that she was sedated and placed on a ventilator; but for her expressed wishes, she would have been given a transfusion. T's father, at this point, supported by T's boyfriend, applied for a declaratory judgment that it would not be unlawful for the hospital to administer a transfusion.

The case worked its way to England's Court of Appeal, which ultimately concluded that the transfusion could be given. The court began its analysis by observing that cases such as this present an apparent conflict between the patient's interest in "self-determination" and society's interest in "upholding the concept that all human life is sacred."[33] While acknowledging that the right of self-determination is of "paramount" importance, the court held that in cases where doubt exists about whether the individual is actually exercising that right, "that doubt falls to be resolved in favour of the preservation of life for if the individual is to override the public interest, [she] must do so in clear terms."[34] This, the court held, presented just such a case because the right to refuse treatment "presupposes a capacity to do so."[35] T, the court explained, was deeply impaired by narcotic medications at the time she signed the refusal forms and made her oral statements. Doctors faced with refusals of care cannot simply defer to statements made by an impaired patient, but have a duty "to give very careful and detailed consideration to the patient's capacity to decide at the time when the decision was made. . . . What matters is that the doctors should consider whether at that time [she] had a capacity which was commensurate with the gravity of the decision which [she] purported to make."[36]

IN RE B[37]

While *In re T* stressed the care with which a finding of competence must be made in English law, it did not have occasion to address whether a fully competent person may insist on an apparently suicidal refusal of care. *In re B* picked up where *In re T* left off, raising just that question.

In re B involved a forty-three-year-old hospital social worker who suffered paralysis from the neck down in February 2001 due to malformation of blood vessels in her spinal cord; she was placed on a ventilator on which she became immediately dependent. In March 2001, B underwent an operation, after which she regained the ability to move her head, but no more; at that point, B asked for the ventilator to be switched off. Psychiatrists were brought in to assess B's competence, but they rendered conflicting and amended reports, with the upshot being that B was found incompetent. B was subsequently prescribed antidepressants and, by April, reported that she was relieved the ventilator had not been turned off; in May, long-term plans were made to move B to home care or, alternatively, to a nursing home. Doctors reassessed B's competency in June but reached no firm conclusion. In July, B suffered a setback when her left lung collapsed and a bronchoscopy had to be undertaken to clear and reopen the passageway. At B's request, on August 8 another reassessment was conducted, at which time she was found competent to make a decision whether to discontinue care. In September, two further bronchoscopies were performed with B's consent, though, at some point thereafter, B sought the removal of the ventilator. Her doctors responded by offering a one-way weaning program, whereby, over a period of time, the number of breaths supplied by the ventilator is gradually reduced and the patient's body is allowed to become used to breathing on its own again. B rejected this suggestion and sought the immediate removal of the ventilator, without any weaning process, though she was informed the chances of her dying were 99 percent.

At approximately the same time, B filed a claim for a declaratory judgment and damages, arguing that any continued treatment would constitute a tort of trespass on the person. The parties fought primarily over the question of B's mental competency, with the hospital trust's lawyers arguing that B's mental competence was affected, among other things, by her grave physical disability, the absence of her experience of rehabilitation, which was thought likely to be a positive experience, and the effect of so many weeks living in an ICU environment. The hospital also pointed to the history of B's ambivalence about ventilation and to her consent to bronchoscopies. Dame Butler-Sloss, however, was unpersuaded and found B sufficiently competent to make her own medical choices: "There is a serious danger, exemplified in this case, of a benevolent paternalism which does not embrace recognition of the personal autonomy of the severely disabled patient. . . . I am . . . entirely satisfied that Ms. B is competent to make all relevant decisions about her medical treatment."[38]

With the issue of competency resolved, one might have expected the parties and the court to turn to and address with some care the question whether the refusal of life-sustaining care should be treated as a matter of right under the circumstances of the case. One might have expected, for example, the parties and the court to have considered whether B's refusal of care amounted to a suicidal intent to die and whether the hospital could be required to assist in a suicide, or whether B bore no intent to die but merely accepted death as a consequence of a rational decision that the proffered weaning program or the prospect of remaining on the ventilator carried with it too many burdens.

The parties, however, apparently did not join issue on B's intent or these related issues, apparently all assuming instead that, if competent, B had the right to make any decision regarding the removal of care—even if suicidal in nature. Nor did the court, seemingly because it was without any aid from the litigants, explore in any meaningful way the question of suicide and its assistance. Instead, the court seemed to assume that a competent patient has a right to refuse care, even if in doing so it might evince an intent to die: "[o]ne must allow for those as severely disabled as Ms. B., for some of whom life in that condition may be worse than death."[39]

The court not only seemed to endorse a right to refuse care that would embrace suicidal decisions, it suggested that doctors who choose not to assist such decisions might be liable for at least nominal damages: the hospital's failure in this case to "have taken steps to deal with the issue . . . has led me to the conclusion that I should mark my finding that the claimant has been treated unlawfully by the NHS Hospital Trust by a small award of damages."[40] In essence, the court here arguably suggested a *duty* to assist in suicide. Perhaps again as a result of being unaided by the parties, the court nowhere sought to explain how such a holding might be squared with the traditional legal rule holding that persons not only may decline to assist a suicide, but may actually interfere with its attempt, privileged from any claim of battery.[41]

The Future of the Law Surrounding the "Right to Refuse" for Competent Patients

Plainly, as we have seen from this sampling, while the courts universally recognize the right of a competent patient to refuse unwanted care, the exact source and, perhaps more importantly, the scope of this right remains opaque and even confused.

Some courts (e.g., *Georgetown College, Satz,* and *In re T*) emphasize that patients are free to refuse life-sustaining treatment, at least when no intent to die is present, and some (especially illustrated by *In re T*) seek strenuously to ensure that any rejection of care is made while the patient is competent in order to guard against potential abuse, mistake, and coercion.

Other courts, however, have claimed to acknowledge that the state has a legitimate interest in preventing the intentional taking of human life but then arguably have "danced" around its fair application to the facts before them (e.g., *Bouvia, McKay*), seeking, somewhat disingenuously, to avoid admitting that the patients before them intend to kill themselves.[42]

Still other courts and judges have not attached much significance at all to the state's interest in preventing the intentional taking of human life (and thus preserving the equality of all lives), suggesting that competent patients may direct the discontinuation of care without regard to whether they intend death (e.g., Judge Compton in *Bouvia*, *In re B*).

What does the inviolability-of-life principle have to contribute to this muddled legal landscape? Several things, I think.

On their facts, *Georgetown College*, *Satz*, and *Farrell* each involved patients who apparently wished to live but were held entitled to execute a competent decision to refuse life-sustaining treatment. Such cases illustrate that a right to refuse treatment limited to refusals where no suicidal intention is present is a far cry from a vitalist's demand that life-sustaining care may never be declined. Patients can refuse even the most "basic" forms of care (e.g., blood transfusions) for a variety of reasons (e.g., to abide one's religious beliefs, to forgo futile care and avoid the strains of continued dependence on medical machinery) without implicating suicide, assisted suicide, or euthanasia. Indeed, as we discussed in greater detail in chapter 4.5, we have every reason to think that the right to refuse is usually exercised in just such circumstances—the patient usually *wishes* to live but sees no point in further futile care or no longer wants to tolerate the burdens of the respirator, the chemotherapy, the radiation treatment. *Georgetown College*, *Satz*, and *Farrell* illustrate how patient and doctor may foresee death, even accept it as the inevitable consequence of the decision to forgo treatment, without seeking out death. They show how an an inviolability-of-life principle hardly equates to a vitalist's demand that society use maximum efforts to keep all patients alive, but instead affords a wide berth of liberty in which patients may refuse even seemingly simple treatment and may do so even where death is foreseen as a complete certainty.

At the same time, virtually every court to recognize the right to refuse has held that the right, whatever its source, is not absolute (e.g., *Satz*, *Farrell*).[43] And, in fact, to deem as a matter of right all patient refusals of care, even in order to commit suicide, could reasonably be said to amount to an implicit endorsement of a right to assisted suicide by omission. *In re B* hints at how the argument would proceed: if a patient has an absolute right to refuse care (including with an intent to commit suicide), why not permit the patient to solicit volunteers to assist him or her? Taking the argument a step further (as *In re B* does, albeit in contradiction with *Farrell*), if a medical practitioner refuses to assist the patient, why shouldn't he or she become liable (including perhaps in damages) for violating the patient's protected right? Further, as Justice Springer noted in *McKay* and we developed more fully in chapter 9, recognizing a right to assisted suicide by omission that is contingent on a patient's physical or mental condition leads to discrimination among persons based on judicial perceptions about the comparative value of different human lives. And while some decisions we have reviewed seek to distinguish between refusals of care where an intent to die is present from assisted suicide on causation grounds (e.g., *Farrell*, *McKay*), much as some judges sought to do in the *Quill* controversy, we have already seen how tenuous the causation distinction may prove.[44]

A right embracing *suicidal* refusals of care would not only run contrary to the inviolability-of-life principle and raise serious questions of equal protection, it would also disregard repeated legislative guidance. As we saw in chapter 3, most American jurisdictions have laws banning the practice of assisted suicide (i.e., assisting someone intentionally seeking self-destruction), and many of these statutes have been expressly reexamined and reaffirmed in recent years. Most American states have also enacted advance medical directive statutes that preclude courts from construing any living will or advance medical directive authorized by state statute to "authorize . . . mercy killing or physician assisted suicide or to permit any . . . deliberate act *or omission* to end life."[45] To be sure, these state medical directive statutes formally pertain only to the construction and interpretation of medical directives left by formerly competent persons, not to refusals of care voiced by currently competent persons, but the policy embodied in these statutes is in no way analytically contingent on the patient's competency.

Finally, though I have suggested that suicidal patients such as Bouvia should not be said to enjoy a *right* to refuse treatment with suicidal intent, it bears recalling that patients who in fact commit such acts commit no crime at law: as with any act of suicide, the patient is performing something that, as we saw in chapter 3, is, under law, considered neither a matter of right nor of crime. Should the suicidal patient find a physician or other person willing to assist them in effecting the termination of treatment, moreover, the appropriate legal analysis is subtle: As I explored in chapters 4 and 9, assisted suicide is a narrowly defined offense dependent on a showing of the assister's purpose, and so, if the assisting doctor harbors no *intent* to make the patient dead but, say, simply discontinues treatment to fulfill his or her professional obligations, that is no crime. Equally, however, a suicidal patient should have no right to compel a doctor to assist in the intentional taking of human life—an act that would run contrary to the inviolability-of-life principle, constitute a crime in jurisdictions proscribing assisted suicide, and (as *Farrell*, but not *In re B*, seemed to notice) amount to a violation of professional medical ethics canons prohibiting (as the AMA has recognized[46]) acts undertaken with the intention of seeing a patient dead.[47]

10.2 THE "RIGHT TO REFUSE" AND INFANT PATIENTS

Turning from competent to incompetent patients, the "right to refuse" has been extended to and applied in many cases involving both infants and disabled adults, and, given the absence of a competent patient able to make his or her own decisions, concerns associated with abuse and mistake at the hand of proxy decision makers naturally increase. In this section, I explore some of the leading cases in the infant-care context, the issues they raise, and the role the inviolability-of-life principle might play in such disputes.

Leading Infant Care Cases

BABY DOE (INDIANA)[48]

"Baby Doe" (an appellation used to protect the family's privacy) was born in Bloomington, Indiana, on April 9, 1982, with two congenital anomalies, Down's syndrome and esophageal atresia with tracheoesophageal fistula. Down's syndrome is a chromosomal disorder that involves both a certain amount of physical deformity and some degree of mental retardation.[49] Esophageal atresia with tracheoesophageal fistula means that the esophageal passage from the mouth to the stomach ends in a pouch, with an abnormal connection between the trachea and the esophagus. As a result, food and drink pass to the lungs instead of the stomach, eventually resulting in suffocation unless surgery is performed to correct the malformation.[50] Surgery to correct esophageal atresia with tracheoesophageal fistula is routinely performed with success, but the parents of Baby Doe refused to consent to the surgery.

Shortly after Baby Doe was born, a hearing was held at Bloomington Hospital to determine whether the parents had the right to refuse the surgery on behalf of their child. An attorney was present at the hearing to represent the parents, though no one was present to represent Baby Doe's potentially adverse interests. Six physicians attended, three of whom had obstetric privileges and three of whom had pediatric privileges at Bloomington Hospital. The obstetricians "recommended that the child remain at Bloomington Hospital with full knowledge that surgery to correct tracheoesophageal fistula was not possible at Bloomington Hospital and that within a short period of time the child would succumb due to inability to receive nutriment and/or pneumonia."[51] The pediatricians, meanwhile, stated that the appropriate treatment was to undertake corrective surgery immediately, and one of the pediatricians testified that the child might enjoy a reasonable quality of life.[52] The dispute wound up in a state court where the trial judge concluded that the parents had the right to refuse corrective surgery even though their child would die.[53] The Indiana Supreme Court refused to hear an appeal, and the child died on the sixth day after he was born while a guardian ad litem was on his way to Washington, D.C., to appeal the case to the United States Supreme Court.[54]

PHILLIP B[55]

In re Phillip B. involved a twelve-year-old California boy with Down's syndrome with a ventricular septal defect in need of surgical correction. The court received evidence from cardiologists that the risk of death from the procedure was normally between 5 and 10 percent, though children with Down's syndrome face a higher than average risk of postoperative complications. Without the operation, Phillip was certain to become severely incapacitated, and his life span would be significantly diminished. The parents refused to grant permission for the operation, and a trial court affirmed the decision as "within the range of debateable action."

On appeal, the state's intermediate court of appeals began by noting that

> parental autonomy . . . is not absolute. The state is the guardian of society's basic values. Under the doctrine of parens patriae, the state has a right, indeed, a duty, to protect children. . . . State officials may interfere in family matters to safeguard the child's health, educational development and emotional well-being. One of the most basic values protected by the state is the sanctity of human life. (U.S. Const., 14th Amend., § 1.) Where parents fail to provide their children with adequate medical care, the state is justified to intervene.[56]

The court, however, held that the state "should usually" defer to the wishes of the parents, and that it has a "serious burden" to carry before parental wishes can be overcome. In deciding whether the state had carried that burden in the case before it, the court explained:

> Several relevant factors must be taken into consideration. . . . The state should examine the seriousness of the harm the child is suffering or the substantial likelihood that he will suffer serious harm; the evaluation for the treatment by the medical profession; the risks involved in medically treating the child; and the expressed preferences of the child. Of course, the underlying consideration is the child's welfare and whether his best interests will be served by the medical treatment.[57]

In applying the foregoing standards to Phillip's case, the court of appeals did not directly endorse the trial court's result, finding instead merely that its decision "attempt[ed] to balance the possible benefits to be gained from the operation against the risks involved."[58] The trial court had before it a child "suffering not only from a ventricular septal defect but also from Down's Syndrome, with its higher than average morbidity, and the presence of pulmonary vascular changes."[59] "In light of these facts," the appellate panel held, "we cannot say as a matter of law that there was no substantial evidence to support the decision of the trial court."[60]

JOHN PEARSON

A third prominent case, involving the British infant John Pearson, pushed the boundaries of infant nontreatment yet further. John was a baby with

Down's syndrome and no other apparent abnormalities. When John's mother was given the news of his disability, she reportedly told her husband, "I don't want it, Duck." Later that day, the baby was examined by Dr. Leonard Arthur who gave the instruction that the child was to be sedated with a pain-killer and given water but no food. By the evening of his first day, John was "going grey"; within sixty-nine hours after birth, he died.

Dr. Arthur was charged with murder. The court, however, permitted only an attempted murder charge to go to the jury after an autopsy established that John also suffered from pneumonia and a heart defect and, thus, may have died of natural causes rather than from physician-directed starvation. At trial, medical professionals testified both for and against Dr. Arthur. One, the president of the Royal College of Physicians, Sir Douglas Black, opined that when "a child [is] suffering from Downs and with a parental wish that it should not survive, it is ethical to terminate life." (Notably, only 15 percent of the *Dutch* public agree with this proposition.[61]) Before submitting the case for decision, the judge summed up and, in doing so, described Dr. Arthur's directions as a mere "holding operation," despite much contrary evidence; expressed open doubt whether an omission of care ("simply allowing the child to die") can be murder; suggested that a life in an orphanage may not be worth living;[62] and directed the jury to "think long and hard before deciding that doctors of the eminence we have heard . . . have evolved standards which amount to committing a crime." The jury acquitted on the remaining attempted murder charge, leading some to speculate about the role and influence of the judge's thinly disguised endorsement of the defendant's conduct.[63]

Applying the Inviolability-of-Life Principle
to the Care of Infant Patients

What would the principle that life is a fundamental and inviolable good mean for Baby Doe, Phillip B., John Pearson, and cases like theirs? Would it mean any and all treatment must be provided to infants born with Down's syndrome, spina bifida, and other serious maladies? If not, when and under what circumstances can treatment be withheld? A few overarching concepts can be discerned from the cases.

First, John Pearson's case demonstrates as surely as any the moral superfluousness of the act-omission distinction. Here was an infant with a full life expectancy whose only defect apparent to anyone at the time was Down's syndrome. (His other maladies became evident only upon autopsy.) All he seemingly required was food, but that was deliberately withheld from him with the specific design of killing him. While the jury may have developed sympathy for the apparently well-regarded physician (perhaps at the judge's very active prodding), Dr. Arthur's conduct was quite apparently an attempt to kill.

Second, these cases highlight the need for a mechanism to permit parents feeling understandably overwhelmed by the prospect of caring for disabled children to give up legal custody. Simply because a parent is unable to cope (as John Pearson's mother put it, "I don't want it, Duck"), and the child may be relegated to an orphanage or foster care, should not mean that the child's right to life may be forfeited. Without such intervention, we run the risk of acquiescing to Peter Singer's "replaceability" ideal, in which an infant's right to live depends on parental satisfaction.

Third, *Phillip B.* highlights the importance of the appropriate standard of judicial review when cases of alleged parental neglect do arise. In *Phillip B.*, the courts permitted but never endorsed the parents' decision to deny treatment to their twelve-year old son, describing it as, at best, a "debatable" decision and declining to overturn that decision primarily because of traditional notions that parents are due a wide berth in making child-rearing decisions. But it does not follow from the settled common law principle that parents get to choose *how* to raise their child (what schools they should attend, etc.) that parents also get to choose *whether* the child lives or dies; the case for a more searching standard of review is bolstered by the fact that anytime a patient's "refusal of care" is more fictional than real, being made not *by* an individual but *for* him or her by others, the possibility of (often hard-to-detect) selfish motives necessarily arises. Had the parents' decision in *Phillip B.* been reviewed under a less deferential standard, the result might very well have been different, and this is an area where, if the courts fail to act, legislatures might productively enter the field.

Fourth, the cases we have examined raise the related question whether judges and jurors (and parents) have made silent judgments about the relative worth or worthwhileness of the infant's life. In each instance the treatment needed to save the child was relatively simple: Baby Doe needed a routine operation; the proposed operation on Phillip B. had a 5–10 percent chance of mortality (death was certain to follow without the operation), and a high likelihood of ensuring a normal life span; John Pearson appeared to require *no* medical attention, just food like any other infant. Had the infants been physically and mentally healthy, can we imagine that the courts would have acceded to parental decisions to starve John Pearson to death, or to forgo treatment of Phillip B. and Baby Doe? If starving a child to death is an abuse of parental discretion for a "normal" child, from an inviolability-of-life perspective it must also be an abuse of discretion if the child is disabled for all persons are equal, with each person enjoying the right to life no less than any other person. So, too, with forgoing treatment that is affordable, available, and safe, and promises to return the child to health: the relevant issue should not be whether the child is disabled or healthy, but the quality and nature of the proposed treatment.[64]

How do the foregoing general principles apply to the Baby Doe cases we have discussed? Taking John Pearson's case first, the "treatment" at issue there would have imposed little burden on anyone and appeared likely (so far as anyone knew at the time) to promise complete health to the child. Baby Doe and Phillip B. required progressively more extensive treatment with progressively higher risks. But there was no evidence that the contemplated treatments would have imposed any undue expense on the parents or threatened worsened health for the children; to the contrary, the proposed operations, according to the evidence submitted, were relatively simple and promised complete restorative gain. Further down the continuum, one can readily imagine cases where the proposed treatment is riskier, more dangerous, and less likely to assist the child; in such circumstances, a parental refusal of treatment would be easiest of all to sustain.

Perhaps seeking to set forth bright-line rules rather than leave the issue to an often subjective case-by-case adjudication, Congress, shortly after the Baby Doe incident, amended the Child Abuse Prevention and Treatment Act with legislation that provides a model of how the inviolability-of-life logic might be applied in end-of-life legislative solutions.[65] In order for states to be eligible for federal funding under the act, the amendment requires state authorities, among other things, to establish procedures to identify and report to child protective service officials potential cases of "medical neglect," which is now expressly defined to include the "withholding of medically indicated treatment."[66]

Not all decisions to withhold treatment, however, are subject to scrutiny. The "withholding of medically indicated treatment" means the "failure to respond to an infant's life-threatening conditions by providing treatment (including appropriate nutrition, hydration, and medication) which, in the treating physician's or physicians' reasonable medical judgment, will be most likely to be effective in ameliorating or correcting all such conditions."[67] To trigger the statutory reporting requirement, the nontreatment must result in a life-threatening condition. Even when the withholding of treatment is life threatening, the statute comes into play only if the treatment withheld would be "most likely" to "ameliorat[e] or correct[]" the life-threatening condition. Thus, medically risky and untested treatment may be withheld and so may tested treatment that is not likely to substantially benefit the infant. This series of statutory steps confines close review of parental decisions to life-or-death situations and tracks precisely the inviolability-of-life's focus on the quality of the proposed treatment rather than on the quality of the infant's life.

While the statute provides general guidelines for when treatment may be withheld, it also enumerates certain specific conduct for which it offers a "safe harbor" from charges of medical neglect. These include decisions to withhold treatment when:

(A) the infant is chronically and irreversibly comatose;

(B) the provision of such treatment would

    (i) merely prolong dying;

    (ii) not be effective in ameliorating or correcting all of the infant's life-threatening conditions; or

    (iii) otherwise be futile in terms of the survival of the infant; or

(C) the provision of such treatment would be virtually futile in terms of the survival of the infant and the treatment itself under such circumstances would be inhumane.[68]

Even in these circumstances, however, the physician is always required to provide nutrition and hydration.[69] Peter Singer charges that "[t]here are quality of life judgments lurking under all of" Congress's safe-harbor statutory provisions; these lurking quality of life judgments are so obvious, Singer asserts, that they "should need no further spelling out."[70] In fact, however, Congress's safe harbor provisions focus on whether treatment will have beneficial or inhumane effect, not on whether the patient's quality of life will meet certain arbitrary criteria. The statute requires a comparison of the infant's after-treatment condition against his or her current life-threatening condition, not against some standard of human functioning that someone has judged to be necessary to merit protection by the state. The law allows nontreatment when the potential for restorative gain is low or the treatment would be inhumanely burdensome on the infant. Under subsection (A), the proposed treatment by definition must be incapable of providing restorative gain: the child must be in an "irreversible" condition. Subsection (B) endorses withholding treatment only when treatment would "merely" (that is, "only") prolong dying (thus not offering the promise of any restorative gain). Subsection (C) expands the safe harbor to "virtually futile" treatment. Though the statute fails to define the modifier "virtually," Congress gave some sense of its intent to restrict this safe harbor provision to narrow circumstances: the treatment, if not strictly useless, must be not only "virtually futile," but also "inhumane."

Singer argues that terms like "'medically beneficial' serve[], like the term 'futile,' to disguise the fact that a quality of life judgment is being made."[71] To be sure, provisions authorizing the discontinuance of treatment where it is "futile" or not "medically beneficial" do not require the use of maximum efforts to preserve life in all cases. But that does not mean they differentiate between cases based on quality of life assessments. To the contrary, under the statutory regime, determining whether nontreatment is a justified option in no way depends on whether the child is disabled or healthy, only whether the proposed treatment is likely to help; all lives are treated equally.

Despite Congress's statute, there remains room for state legislation. All that hinges on compliance with the federal law is the continuation of federal funding for certain child abuse programs. Moreover, federal law requires that health-care providers only report violations; it does not assure intervention. In the American federal system, Congress is, of course, prevented from regulating many internal state affairs. Some states have already passed laws worthy of consideration, including Indiana in the aftermath of the Baby Doe incident there, and Arizona. In Indiana, an investigation by child protection services is triggered when a "handicapped child is deprived of nutrition that is necessary to sustain life," or "is deprived of medical or surgical intervention that is necessary to remedy or ameliorate a life threatening medical condition, if the nutrition or medical or surgical intervention is generally provided to similarly situated handicapped or non handicapped children."[72] In Arizona, consistent with the inviolability-of-life principle and eschewing the act-omission distinction, medical workers and hospitals are prohibited from withholding "nourishment" or "necessary lifesaving medical treatment or surgical care" from disabled infants "with the *intent to cause or allow the death of the infant* for any reason."[73] If a violation is detected by a health-care worker, it must be reported to state authorities, and the individual reporting the violation is legally protected from workplace recriminations.[74]

THE CASE OF MARY AND JODIE

In September 2000, in a case captioned *In re A*,[75] the English Court of Appeal addressed some of the most fundamental end-of-life questions facing family and criminal law in the infant patient context. While the facts in that case involved newly born conjoined twins and were somewhat extraordinary, the legal questions presented go to the very core of how life-and-death decisions are made for young children, and what principles should apply to guide decision makers.

Mary and Jodie were born joined at the pelvis, and the lower ends of their spines were fused. Internally, each twin had her own brain, heart, lungs, liver, and kidneys; the only organ they shared was a bladder. But, critically, Jodie's heart supported both infants. Medical observation showed that Jodie was intelligent and healthy, and doctors believed that, if separated, she could live a relatively normal life. But doctors also found that Jodie's heart was suffering terrible strain from having to support her sister Mary as well as herself.

Mary, meanwhile, was in a much different condition. Her heart was malformed; if Jodie's heart was not also pumping blood and oxygen through Mary's body, Mary would have died almost immediately after birth. Mary's lungs and brain were also seriously malformed. Doctors confirmed that Mary had no prospect of living independently of Jodie, and that Mary's only hope of survival rested on Jodie's heart. Yet, doctors conjectured that the strain on Jodie's heart from having to support both infants would eventually, indeed, soon, lead to heart failure and the death of both twins if they remained conjoined. Doctors estimated that both infants would die within a matter of weeks or months if no action was taken to separate them.

Mary and Jodie's parents were devoutly religious and interpreted their faith as preventing them from seeking the separation of the twins, nor could they contemplate that one of their children might die to enable the other to survive. The hospital filed suit seeking an order allowing it to disregard the parents' wishes and separate the twins. The hospital wanted to save Jodie but did not want to be held criminally liable for Mary's certain death, and it was also unsure whether it could trump the parents' stated wishes for their own children. The case quickly arrived at the Court of Appeal.[76]

On the question *who* is permitted to decide Mary and Jodie's fate, the three-judge panel reached unanimous agreement, and their views were summarized by Lord Justice Ward in a way that is entirely consonant with the inviolability-of-life principle and that should supply a model for future courts. When the patient is incompetent or a minor, the court reaffirmed the traditional Anglo-American principle that the parents normally have the right to step into their children's shoes and make treatment decisions. But, the court emphasized, there is a close link between the right to make treatment decisions and the duty to do so responsibly; a parent's failure to agree to necessary medical treatment can be a culpable omission.[77] As long ago as Blackstone, the court noted, it was accepted that parental power over children "exists to enable the parent more effectively to perform his duty, and partly as recompense for his care and trouble in the faithful discharge of it."[78]

That is not to say parental wishes are readily ignored: in family law, parental decisions are usually reviewed only for whether they fall within a wide "band of reasonable[ness]."[79] But when it comes to the exceptional question of life or death, the court held, the parents' decisions cannot be afforded such latitude; when contested, all life-and-death decisions—even parental decisions— deserve a more searching review:

> An appraisal of parental reasonableness may be appropriate in other areas of family law (in adoption, for example where it is enjoined by statute) but when it comes to an assessment of the demands of the child patient's welfare, the starting point—and the finishing point too—must always be the judge's own independent assessment. . . .[80]

Very much unlike most of the infant cases we have explored, *In re A* correctly observed that, while courts ordinarily defer to parental choices about how children should live and be raised, parents have not historically been afforded such deference over life-and-death decisions, nor should they be granted such wide berth when the consequence of error is homicide.

Turning from procedural question *who* decides to the substantive question *whether* the operation might constitute the murder of Mary under criminal law, the court's reasoning was far less satisfactory. The court certainly heard from counsel the argument that the principle of double effect should be applied—that the death of Mary, while foreseeable, could not be said to be part of the doctors' intentions in carrying out the operation, and, thus, that there would be no basis for calling the doctors murderers for carrying out an operation to save Jodie's life. The appellate judges, however, considered themselves bound by *Woollin*'s expansive understanding of "intent," under which, as we saw in chapter 4, persons may be deemed to have "intended a death," even when they (only) foresee serious bodily harm as virtually certain to result from their conduct.[81] The double-effect principle, as Lord Justice Ward recognized with a degree of understatement, "may be difficult to reconcile with . . . *Woollin*";[82] indeed, as we explored in chapter 4, *Woollin* is fundamentally inconsistent with double effect doctrine, conflating as it does the analytically separate concepts of intent and foreseeability.

Constrained by the House of Lords' decision in *Woollin*, the judges in the Court of Appeal found no question, on the evidence before them, that the death of Mary was virtually certain to follow from the operation: "[u]npalatable though it may be . . . to stigmatize the doctors with 'murderous intent,' that is what in law they will have if they perform the operation and Mary dies as a result."[83] As Lord Justice Brooke put it,

> [t]here are certainly some powerful dicta in support of a proposition that if a surgeon administers proper surgical treatment in the best interests of his or her patient and with the consent (except in an emergency) of the patient or his or her surrogate, there can be no question of a finding that the surgeon has a guilty mind in the eyes of the criminal law,

but, nonetheless, after *Woollin*,

> an English court would inevitably find that the surgeons intended to kill Mary, however little they desired that end, because her death would be the virtually certain consequence of their acts, and they would realise that for all practical purposes her death would invariably follow the clamping of the common aorta.[84]

Feeling unable to distinguish between intent and foresight for purposes of English criminal law after *Woollin*, the judges in the Court of Appeal each struggled more or less unsatisfactorily to find other ways to defend the doctors' conduct as something less than "murder." Lord Justice Ward sought to invoke the concepts of self-defense and defense-of-others to justify Mary's death. The so-called intentional killing of Mary was justified, he argued, because Mary constituted an "unjust aggressor" who was, in effect, attacking her sister:

> The reality here—harsh as it is to state it, and unnatural as it is that it should be happening—is that Mary is killing Jodie. . . . How can it be just that Jodie should be required to tolerate that state of affairs? One does not need to label

Mary with the American terminology which would paint her to be "an unjust aggressor," which I feel is wholly inappropriate language for the sad and helpless position in which Mary finds herself. . . . [But] I can see no difference in essence between th[e] resort to legitimate self-defence and the doctors coming to Jodie's defence and removing the threat of fatal harm to her presented by Mary's draining her life-blood. The availability of such a plea of quasi-self-defence . . . makes the intervention by the doctors lawful.[85]

Lord Justice Ward's colleagues declined to follow this reasoning, recoiling from the suggestion that Mary was in any sense "an unjust aggressor"; to Lord Justice Walker, "[i]t would be absurd to suggest that Mary, a pitiful and innocent baby, is an unjust aggressor."[86] As we saw in chapter 9.3, however, the term "unjust aggressor" is something of a misnomer: Lord Justice Ward is correct that, to invoke the doctrines of self-defense or defense-of-others, it does not formally matter whether the "aggressor" is unjust or innocent, only that the threat faced is (1) employed without the consent of the person against whom it is directed, and (2) not affirmatively privileged at law.

Lord Justice Brooke, largely followed by Lord Justice Walker, relied on the (now-familiar) argument that the intentional killing of Mary was "necessary." In doing so, Lord Justice Brooke offered a lengthy history of the application of necessity doctrine in other common law arenas but ultimately was unable to identify meaningful precedent for applying the doctrine in the realm of intentional homicide and was forced to rely instead on the persuasive force of "modern academic writ[ings],"[87] which, he argued, would protect the doctors because their "conduct was not harmful because on a choice of two evils the choice of avoiding the greater harm was justified."[88] As we saw in chapter 9.3, introducing necessity as a defense, at least to cases involving a true *intentional* taking of human life, raises with it nontrivial risks. If some human lives may be taken intentionally, *which* lives may be so taken? And who is to be the judge? The fundamental guarantee of equal protection for all human lives can be placed at risk if courts may pick and choose which human lives may be extinguished and which may not. Lord Justice Brooke acknowledged such concerns about the implications of necessity doctrine for the inviolability-of-life and equal treatment among all persons but responded by arguing that, in this particular case, Mary had "self-designated" herself as the appropriate one of the twins to be killed because there was no way to "extend her life beyond a very short span."[89] Accordingly, Lord Justice Brooke seemed to suggest that, unlike other cases of where necessity had been rejected as a defense to intentional homicide (e.g., *Dudley* and *Holmes*), here comparative value judgments about the importance of different human lives need not enter the picture. But is this really so?

To be sure, the case of conjoined twins is certainly unusual, but if a conjoined twin can "self-designate" herself for intentional killing without consent *because she lacks any prospect for an extended life span,* how much of an analytical step really remains before courts might say that terminal patients "self-designate" themselves for nonconsensual euthanasia because they lack any prospect of improvement? Arguably, very little, especially when killing the terminal patient might allow a doctor to do good in the process by, say, harvesting organs so that another patient might live.[90] Recall, in this regard, the rationale the Dutch government used to defend the one thousand cases of nonconsensual euthanasia found by the 1990 Survey: "The degrading condition the patient is in confronts the doctor with a case of force majeure. According to the Commission, the intervention by the doctor can easily be regarded as an action that is justified by necessity."[91] The Dutch government might just as easily have said—and virtually did say—that the patients "self-designated" themselves for being killed without their consent by virtue of their terminal condition. Thus a license to kill without consent those who may be judged to lack full humanness or a particular quality of life emerges.

The problem posed by *Woollin* not only led Lord Justice Brooke to endorse a potentially problematic version of necessity doctrine to justify the operation on Mary and Jodie, it opened the door to other, serious problems in run-of-the-mill end-of-life cases. If we say, with *Woollin*, that the doctors here are "inevitably" guilty of murder because they foresaw the death of Mary as a "virtual certainty," what about doctors who administer strong doses of palliative care to patients suffering grave pain? Or medical care workers who help patients unhook life support machines because the patients wish to go home or prefer to avoid the invasiveness of modern medical care? If the Lords meant what they said in *Woollin*, and a murder charge may follow whenever death is foreseen as virtually certain, doctors and nurses in such situations are arguably just as susceptible to a charge for murder as the doctors operating on Mary and Jodie. And to defend such everyday, upright actions, *In re A* gives us little with which to work. Lord Justice Ward's self-defense and defense-of-others theory would not apply: while Mary could be cast, albeit with difficulty, as an "aggressor" against Jodie, that fact seems unique to conjoined twin cases, and the option does not exist to defend the ordinary palliative care or refusal of care case involving a single patient. That leaves us only with Lord Justice Brooke's necessity doctrine and the risks its application may entail for the concept of human equality and inviolability-of-life.

One possibility that the court did not consider is whether "necessity" might be construed much more narrowly than Lord Justice Brooke (and the drafters of the Model Penal Code[92]) have suggested, limited perhaps to cases where medical professionals, with appropriate permission from the patient or guardian, perform their services in consonance with sound clinical judgment and with *no intent* to kill or help kill either as a means or an end—even if death should occur as a foreseeable side effect. This narrower version of necessity—limited to medical treatment where the principle of double effect applies—not only would cover the case of Mary and Jodie but would avoid also any possibility (however practically unlikely it may be) of English doctors being held responsible for homicide under *Woollin* simply for administering potentially lethal doses of palliative care or unhooking patients from futile life-support machines when they "foresee" death as virtually certain to follow. At the same time, such a rule would be less susceptible to the problem of judicially declared inequality among different human lives because the justifying "need" would depend not at all on the patient's condition (or, in Lord Justice Brooke's terminology, "self-designation") and the rule would sanction the *intentional* killing of no person. Such a narrowly drawn rule could also be reconciled with cases such as *Dudley* and *Holmes* because, quite unlike the situation I posit, there an *intent* to do that which the law prohibits (viz., killing the cabin boy for food) indubitably existed. Here, we conceive of using necessity only to justify *nonintentional* homicides.[93]

Notably, when writing on a clean slate rather than bound by prior case law from the Lords, the Court of Appeal in In re A was quick to adopt and deploy the principle of double effect I endorse for end-of-life decision making. Confronted with the argument that the surgery would not only constitute murder under English law but also violate Mary's right to life under the European Convention, the Court of Appeal judges—formally, at least, unconstrained by *Woollin*—emphasized that the Convention provides that "[n]o one shall be deprived of life *intentionally* save in the execution of a sentence of a court following his conviction of a crime for which this penalty is provided by law."[94] This provision, Lord Justice Walker argued, should be given its "natural and ordinary meaning" and therefore should "appl[y] only to cases where the *purpose* of the prohibited act is to cause death."[95] Simply put, the Court rejected the notion that the term "intention" here embraces mere foresight, distinguishing between, rather than conflating, the two concepts. As Lord Justice Brooke put it,

> I do not consider that the . . . *Woollin* . . . extension of the meaning of the word "intention" is appropriate when determining whether a doctor who performed a separation operation on conjoined twins in circumstances like these was intentionally killing the twin whose life was to be sacrificed. The doctor's *purpose* in performing the operation was to save life, even if the extinction of another life was a *virtual certainty*.[96]

The judges of the Court of Appeal thus seemed to recognize that end-of-life care cases such as Mary and Jodie's merit and virtually beg for the application of the doctrine of double effect, going so far as to throw overboard *Woollin*'s contrary teaching as soon as they found themselves in a context where they were not strictly bound by the Lords' holding on English criminal law.

10.3 The "Right to Refuse" and Incompetent Adult Patients

The inviolability-of-life principle appears to be slowly—over objections from some like Peter Singer and despite setbacks in certain cases—gaining ground in the growing body of American law surrounding the nontreatment of young children, especially through legislative initiative. By contrast, the law surrounding the refusal of care for incompetent adults remains murky indeed. Terry Schiavo's case in 2005—with all of the headlines it captured, the hearts and minds it tugged in so many different directions, and the competing views of so many courts and members of Congress—only served to underscore and illustrate the confused state of our law and policy in this arena.

More and more people are completing living wills or preparing other directives that delineate in advance which forms of care may and may not be administered if and when incompetency may strike.[97] Still, a great many people do not leave behind any written instructions, and some persons never become legally competent; for such persons, the question remains: what to do? The Supreme Court in Cruzan recognized that the states have developed a variety of tests seeking to give meaning to the right to refuse treatment for incompetent adult patients. *Cruzan* held, too, that states *may*, without running afoul of the substantive component of the due process clause, require "clear and convincing evidence" that any discontinuation of care comports with the wishes expressed by the patient while competent. The Court did not, however, consider the related question whether or not states *should* demand clear and convincing evidence of the patient's wishes before permitting the discontinuation of life-sustaining care. At present, there are, in fact, two central and competing strands of cases on just this question. One, exemplified by two Massachusetts decisions and another from England, uses an instrumental approach toward the value of human life; another is perhaps best represented by a 2001 California decision that illustrates how the inviolability-of-life approach might inform this area of the law as well.

Brophy v. New England Sinai Hospital, Inc.

Paul Brophy was afflicted with an aneurysm in his brain in March 1983. Despite the efforts of physicians, surgery was not successful and Brophy never regained consciousness, remaining in what the Massachusetts Supreme Judicial Court called a "persistent vegetative state."[98] In December 1983, with the consent of his wife (who was also his legal guardian), Brophy received a gastrostomy tube ("G-tube") to make it easier to provide him food and water. Fifteen months later, in February 1985, Mrs. Brophy announced her wish that the G-tube should be removed; when Brophy's attending physician objected that removing the tube would be tantamount to causing Brophy's death willfully, Mrs. Brophy sought a declaratory judgment granting her legal authority to override Brophy's physician and secure its removal.

The trial court disallowed the wife's request. The court found that Brophy was not terminally ill, and that, while the use of a G-tube can have certain adverse side effects, Brophy had experienced none of them in a period that, by then, had already lasted approximately eighteen months. The court also found that Brophy showed no signs or symptoms of discomfort, while removing the G-tube would cause death by dehydration, a form of death, the court found, that typically is "extremely painful and uncomfortable," and, while Brophy was unconscious, evidence from his attending physician suggested to the court that it could not "rule[] out" the possibility that Brophy would experience such pain. The court noted evidence from Brophy's wife that her husband had previously stated that he did not want to be placed on life support. But the court also found that Brophy's statements suggested that he would have refused life support not because of a lack of confidence in the procedure or because it would have been painful or burdensome (reasons entirely consistent with the inviolability-of-life principle), but because he would have wished to commit suicide.[99]

The Massachusetts Supreme Judicial Court, by a vote of 4 to 3, reversed. The court held that the right to refuse treatment is a "fundamental principle[] of individual autonomy"[100] but also acknowledged that the right to refuse is "not absolute"; the right to refuse treatment must, the court explained, be "balanced" against the state's dual interests in the "preservation of life" and the "prevention of suicide."[101] Having set forth this balancing test, however, the court did not elucidate *how* such competing and incommensurable interests—individual autonomy versus the state's interest in preserving life (especially against killings due to mistake, abuse, and pressure)—can be weighed, compared, or "balanced" to arrive at a single correct legal resolution.[102]

Instead, the majority simply proceeded to devalue the state's interest in preserving life by characterizing the patient's condition in this case as "helpless" and offering a low quality of life. Meanwhile, on the other end of its scale, the court took the (unusual) step of reversing the trial judge's factual finding that the G-tube was not an "intrusive" treatment on the ground that it was Brophy's subjectively expressed view prior to his illness that he would consider such a tube to be "degrading."[103] Having thus tipped the balancing scales of competing interests, the court took the now-smaller step to conclude that the right to have the G-tube removed—as an exercise of autonomy—was of more significant weight than the state's interest in preserving life.

The court's analysis raises as many questions as it answers. Somewhat surprisingly, the court never paused to consider the possibility that *all* human life is worthwhile, simply disregarding the argument that all lives are worthy of equal protection in the eyes of the state (an argument vocally pressed by all three dissenters). Rather, the court took an entirely instrumental/utilitarian view of human life, tacitly assuming that life's value rests on its capacity to provide pleasure and then making its *own assessment* that Brophy's life was worth little given his "helpless" condition. But if a court's evaluation of the instrumental value of individual lives is a relevant (or apparently decisive) factor, isn't that a sure sign that the judiciary will become enmeshed in the business of subjectively determining on a case-by-case basis whether the quality of life available to each given patient that comes before it is sufficiently "bad," in the eyes of the particular judges at hand, to justify ending it intentionally? Also, the court suggested (much as Epstein has[104]) that the patient's subjective assessment (albeit via his guardian) that his life is "degrading" determines whether death is an acceptable option. But if that is so, doesn't it then follow that the young and healthy as well as the old and sick have a right to suicide whenever they wish? The Massachusetts court addressed neither of these questions pointedly raised by its reasoning.

Instead, the court proceeded to distinguish away the state's interest in preventing suicide on causation grounds, arguing that removing the G-tube would only allow "natural causes" to kill the patient. But its analysis falls squarely into the causation trap we have discussed.[105] Brophy's wife frankly testified that she *intended to cause her husband's death* by removing the G-tube, the trial court made an express finding on this score, and the Supreme Judicial Court did not challenge this testimony or finding. Brophy's underlying illness surely contributed to his inability to swallow water and, thus, his death. But how one could characterize the act of removing the feeding tube as playing no causal role in Brophy's death—when the tube had been in place for eighteen months without incident and the guardian admitted her intention to kill—goes unexplained and undefended in the court's analysis.

The Massachusetts Supreme Judicial Court also misunderstood two critical aspects of the "right to refuse." Like the respondents in *Glucksberg* who argued that *Cruzan* compels a right to assisted suicide, the court read the right to refuse treatment as embracing a fundamental right to "autonomy" and "self-determination" "root[ed]" in the teachings of "John Stuart Mill."[106] Such a reading of *Cruzan* not only would suggest a right to suicide and assisted suicide on demand, it would, as we have seen, militate in favor of legalizing a broad range of currently prohibited conduct from prostitution to drug use that might be considered "harmless" to unconsenting third parties. The Massachusetts court nowhere considered a more modest reading of right-to-refuse case law (one subsequently endorsed by *Glucksberg*, as we saw in chapter 5)—namely, that it is a right developed from battery doctrine and designed to prevent patients from suffering certain unconsented-to touchings.

Perhaps even more fundamentally still, the Massachusetts court rested its decision on an entirely fictional right. Brophy "refused" nothing and was capable of refusing nothing. He left no living will, no written instructions, no spe-

cific oral health-care instructions; the notion that Brophy was exercising anything remotely akin to a right to refuse treatment or a right to control his self-
destiny borders on the incoherent. There may be sound reasons for courts to
allow the treatment of nonterminal incompetent patients to be discontinued,
but such decisions cannot be cogently defended as an exercise of autonomy or
a "right to refuse" care.

Superintendent of Belchertown State School v. Saikewicz[107]

Joseph Saikewicz was a sixty-seven-year-old man with an I.Q. of 10, a
"mental age" estimated to be approximately two years and eight months, and,
as a result of his condition, Saikewicz had lived in a state mental institution for
over fifty years. In April 1976, Saikewicz was diagnosed with a form of leukemia
considered "invariably fatal."[108] A guardian ad litem was appointed and charged
with reporting to the court regarding whether and what treatment should be
administered. The guardian subsequently issued a report indicating that, although chemotherapy was the medically indicated course of treatment, it would
cause Saikewicz significant adverse side effects and discomfort, including ane-
mia, bone marrow depression, increased chance of infection, and bladder irri-
tation, among other things. The guardian ad litem concluded that these facts, as
well as the inability of his ward to understand the treatment to which he would
be subjected and the fear and pain he would suffer as a result, outweighed the
prospect of some "uncertain but limited extension of life," estimated to be between two and thirteen additional months.[109]

The trial court adopted the report, and the Massachusetts Supreme Judicial Court affirmed. The latter court acknowledged that "most people" would
likely choose to accept chemotherapy in Saikewicz's condition, and it acknowledged that the treatment would likely extend Saikewicz's life. But, unlike "most
people," the court emphasized, chemotherapy would plunge Saikewicz into a
state of painful suffering that he would not appreciate or understand. Under
these circumstances, the court held, the guardian ad litem had made a reasonable assessment of the benefits and burdens of the proposed course of treatment
to Saikewicz.

In reaching this conclusion, the court acknowledged the state's interest in the "preservation of life" but held that "[t]he interest of the State in prolonging a life must be reconciled with the interest of an individual to reject the
traumatic cost of that prolongation."[110] In seeking to reconcile these interests,
the court suggested that "[t]here is a substantial distinction in the State's insis-
tence that human life be saved where the affliction is curable, as opposed to the
State interest where, as here the issue is not whether, but when, for how long,
and at what cost to the individual that life may be briefly extended."[111] Rather
than introducing its own assessment of Saikewicz's quality of life, and suggest-

ing that some persons' lives are more valuable than others, the court could have resolved concerns about the state's interest in the preservation of human life simply by pointing out the proposed treatment could be (and was) rejected by Saikewicz's legally appointed guardian without any violation of the guardian's legal duty of care—i.e., it was not intended to kill Saikewicz or otherwise undertaken carelessly.[112] Proceeding in this fashion, rather than focusing on the *quality* of life at issue, would have solved this case readily and without suggesting that some persons' lives are more valuable than others. The point however, was, never considered by the court—likely because it was never presented by the litigants, a not-uncommon problem, as we shall see.

Airedale N.H.S. Trust v. Bland[113]

The *Bland* case, discussed briefly in chapter 4, bears further mention here, sharing many facts and issues in common particularly with *Brophy* and, as we shall see, *Wendland*. The case involved a seventeen-year-old young man, Tony Bland, on the cusp of his majority, who was left in a comatose state after being crushed in a spectator's pen at a soccer match. Bland's doctors and parents eventually sought to remove nasogastric tubes supplying him with food and water, and to discontinue the provision of antibiotics that were being used to treat infections.

Three of the five members of the House of Lords hearing the case expressly admitted or asserted that the cessation of treatment under the circumstances before them involved the intention to kill Tony, yet all five permitted the doctors to proceed. Given that an intent to kill was admittedly present, John Keown has asked, "why, then, would this not be murder?"[114] Several of the Lords seemed to assume that merely classifying the doctors' conduct as omissions of care "solved" the murder question. Lord Goff, we might recall, suggested that the act-omission distinction is something of a moral/legal "Rubicon which runs between on the one hand the care of the living and on the other hand euthanasia—actively causing his death to avoid or end his suffering."[115] But this is simply wrong. Euthanasia and assisted suicide (like suicide itself) can, as we have seen, be accomplished as much through omissions as through action. Indeed, medical practitioners in the Netherlands, where euthanasia is tolerated, readily accept that euthanasia be undertaken either through active means *or by deliberate omissions of care*.[116]

Some of the Lords hearing Bland's case recognized that calling something an omission does not end the inquiry into whether the doctors' conduct constitutes murder, but instead merely raises the question whether the physicians had a duty to supply the (omitted) care, at least in the absence of a living will or other such competent evidence suggesting that Bland would have declined treatment. These Lords, however, proceeded to analyze the duty question in ways that added not clarity but only further confusion. They began with the premise that there is an important distinction between "medical treatment," on the one hand, and "ordinary" care, on the other. On this reasoning, the latter is care that decent persons and communities seek to provide, while the former is an intervention typically performed by doctors and, because of its distinctively "medical" nature, may be withheld when a respectable body of professional medical opinion would so permit.[117] The Lords then proceeded to classify the nasogastric tube and antibiotics on which Bland depended as "medical treatment," and to find that medical opinion would permit its removal: "There is overwhelming evidence that, in the medical profession, artificial feeding is regarded as a form of medical treatment; and even if it is not strictly medical treatment, it must form part of the medical care of the patient."[118] And because the "patient is unconscious and there is no prospect of any improvement in his condition," the court reasoned, Bland's doctors *had* to withdraw the treatment to accord with the "body of reasonable medical opinion" and, thus, meet their professional obligations.[119]

The Lords' attempt to resolve this dispute by semantically classifying certain forms of care as "medical" versus "ordinary" seems as slippery a business as trying to determine whether conduct is an "act" or an "omission," and equally unhelpful. Indeed, a similar classification effort was attempted by some courts in America—there seeking to distinguish "ordinary" from "extraordinary" treatment—but was widely criticized and has been largely abandoned precisely because physicians themselves do not always agree on what is medical or ordinary care, and standards of care change over time; what is considered extraordinary or "medical" treatment today may tomorrow be seen as just ordinary care.[120] Indeed, by way of example, some commentators have sought to suggest that the very nasogastric tubes at issue in *Bland* might today be better classified as "ordinary" care rather than "medical" treatment because they can often be routinely inserted and maintained without any distinctively medical skills.[121]

Distinctions like those between medical/nonmedical or extraordinary/ordinary treatment also run the risk of becoming conclusory pigeonholes, with people simply employing the appropriate label to suit the result they seek. As the Supreme Court of New Jersey has observed, "[t]he claim, then, that the treatment is extraordinary [or "medical"] is more of an expression of the conclusion than a justification for it. . . . To draw a line on this basis . . . leads to a semantical milieu that does not advance the analysis."[122] Such rote categorizations may often do little more than disguise a court's assessment of the patient's quality of life and its endorsement of euthanasia (i.e., intentionally killing), if only by "omission," for persons whose lives the court perceives as inferior.

Indeed, one is left with the sense that the classification of the nasogastric tube in *Bland* as "medical" treatment that should be discontinued was driven as much (if not more) by an assessment of Bland's quality of life than by any formal and rigidly defensible classification of the tube's nature and function. What seemed objectionable to the Lords in *Bland* was not so much the application of supposedly distinctively medical care in violation of some newly announced professional standard of care as the maintenance of a person who, after three years in a comatose state, they considered to be perhaps less than fully human. Lord Justice Hoffmann, for one, frankly described Bland as "grotesquely alive,"[123] and Sir Stephen Brown called him a "shell of [a] body."[124] Simply put, *Bland* may well have already crossed Lord Goff's moral Rubicon, allowing a certain form of euthanasia (i.e., those accomplished by omission) for certain classes of persons (i.e., those whom judges, in candid moments at least, would decree only "grotesquely alive").

Why didn't the Lords adopt, or even stop to consider in any extended way, the intent-based alternative we have outlined above? John Keown has suggested that "[o]ne plausible explanation is that the principle does not appear to have been accurately set out before them by any of the counsel who appeared in the case."[125] The counsel for the official solicitor, for example, appeared to confuse the notion that one may not intentionally take life with the idea that one must take steps to preserve and prolong human life at all costs, regardless of the attendant burdens and costs (vitalism), arguing in the Court of Appeal that if Bland showed any signs of dangerous problems with his heart, lungs, liver, kidneys, spleen, or pancreas, doctors would be under a duty to perform surgery to rectify the issue under any circumstances. This suggestion led the presiding judge in that court to observe that "[s]uch a suggestion is in my view so repugnant to one's sense of how one individual should behave towards another that I would reject it as possibly representing the law."[126] The fundamental problem with *Bland*, therefore, may be, as Keown has put it, that the courts simply were "presented with only two alternatives: vitalism or Quality of life. . . . and . . . the judges (unsurprisingly) opted for Quality of life."[127]

Wendland v. Wendland[128]

In 2001 the California Supreme Court faced a case similar in many respects to those confronted by its sister court in Massachusetts and the Lords in *Bland*, but it reached a different result by very different reasoning.

On September 29, 1993, Robert Wendland rolled his truck at high speed in a solo accident while driving under the influence of alcohol. Following the accident, Wendland remained in a coma, totally unresponsive, for several months. His wife Rose visited him daily and authorized treatment as necessary to maintain his health. Eventually, Wendland regained consciousness, but he remained severely disabled, both mentally and physically, and entirely dependent on artificial nutrition and hydration through a G-tube. At his highest level of functioning, Wendland could throw and catch a ball, operate an electric wheel-chair with assistance, turn pages, draw circles, and perform commands. But when therapy was discontinued, Wendland lost his ability to perform some of these tasks, remained unable to swallow, and suffered from spasticity, severe paralysis, incontinence, and other maladies.

Wendland's wife Rose authorized surgery three times to replace dis-lodged feeding tubes, but when physicians sought her permission a fourth time, she refused. Wendland's mother and sister opposed this decision and sought a restraining order to bar the removal of the feeding tube. In turn, Rose petitioned the court to be appointed her husband's conservator; the court granted the mo-tion but reserved judgment on Rose's request for authority to remove the feed-ing tube.

At the trial, the judge held that Mrs. Wendland, as wife/conservator, would be allowed to withhold artificial nutrition and hydration only if doing so would be in Wendland's "best interests," taking into account the wishes he ex-pressed before becoming incompetent.[129] The court also decided (in conso-nance with In re A but in contrast to the court in Phillip B.) that the conserva-tor would bear the burden of proving facts to justify her decision by clear and convincing evidence. The court rejected Mrs. Wendland's entreaties to impose a more modest preponderance of the evidence standard of proof, holding that the decision to withhold life-sustaining treatment "should be premised on no lesser showing."[130]

During trial, Mrs. Wendland (like Mrs. Brophy) pointed to a handful of preaccident statements made by her husband to the effect that he would not have wanted to "live like a vegetable" or be left alive in a "comatose state." But Wendland had left no written instructions and had not designated anyone to act as proxy to make medical decisions for him. The trial court found that Mrs. Wendland was acting "in good faith" but had failed to show by clear and con-vincing evidence that her husband would have wanted to refuse care when, though severely incapacitated, he was not in a "persistent vegetative state" and was not suffering a terminal illness. The court likewise found insufficient evi-dence that removing treatment would be in the husband's best interests.

On appeal, Mrs. Wendland challenged the burden of proof applied by the trial court, arguing that, so long as a conservator is acting in good faith when "substituting its own judgment" concerning a conservatee's best interests, a court should not interfere. The intermediate appellate court, much like the Mas-sachusetts Supreme Judicial Court in Brophy, sided with Mrs. Wendlend, but the California Supreme Court unanimously reversed and reinstated the trial court's judgment. The Supreme Court began by conceding the right of a competent adult to refuse medical treatment and to leave advance directives in the event of incapacity, noting that the California legislature (like virtually every other American state legislature) has provided for competent persons to execute living wills and medical care proxies authorizing the agent to act "in accordance with the principal's health care instructions . . . and other wishes to the extent known to the agent."[131]

While the right to refuse is guaranteed to competent persons and promotes individual autonomy, the court recognized that the notion that it survives incompetency (assuming no living will or medical care proxy) is a "legal fiction at best."[132] Instead, the court held that

> [i]t would be more accurate to say that incompetent patients retain the right to have appropriate medical decisions made on their behalf. An appropriate medical decision is one that is made in the patient's best interests, as opposed to the interests of the hospital, the physicians, the legal system, or someone else. We do not question the . . . conclusion that incompetent persons have a right, based in the California Constitution, to appropriate medical decisions that reflect their *own* interests and values. But the right to an appropriate decision by a court-appointed conservator does not necessarily equate with a conservatee's right to refuse treatment, or obviously take precedence over the conservatee's right to life and the state's interest in preserving life.[133]

What is the difference between a right to refuse treatment and a right to have decisions made in one's best interest? This difference may, at first, appear merely semantic, but, in fact, it is a substantial one for those who would rely on autonomy theory and the notion of self-governance to justify the discontinuation of care for incompetent patients. Unlike so many other courts, the California Supreme Court recognized that incompetent patients who have left behind no instructions or proxy do not—and cannot—make "autonomous choices." Decisions by conservators derive their authority not from an incompetent patient's fictional exercise of autonomy, the court held, but from the long-recognized common law doctrine concerning the "*parens patriae* power of the state to protect incompetent persons."[134]

Having formulated the legal question at issue in this radically different fashion, the court turned to the question of what burden of proof the conservator, exercising her *parens patriae* power, must satisfy before discontinuing life-sustaining care. The court rejected Mrs. Wendland's argument for a lower preponderance of the evidence standard and accepted the clear and convincing evidence standard employed by the trial court, stressing a point made in chapter 7 and illustrated by *In re A*: that a right to refuse, like a right to assisted suicide or euthanasia, can *interfere* as well as advance individual rights, especially when left in the hands of a proxy. The court explained that the possibility of a conservator deciding to withdraw life-sustaining treatment brought with it not just potential benefits, but also grave risks, thus warranting close judicial review. The risk of an erroneous discontinuation of care, due to mistake or abuse or coercion by the conservator, the court explained, "represent[s] the gravest possible affront to the conservatee's state constitutional right to privacy, in the sense of freedom from unwanted bodily intrusions, and to life."[135]

Two aspects of this holding are remarkable. First, unlike *Brophy* or *Saikewicz* or *Bland*, the California court did not hinge the existence of a patient's rights to privacy and life on his or her physical condition or quality of life; rather it proceeded on the view that all lives equally enjoy the full panoply of constitutional protections. Second, because the risk of error is "manifest" when a decision is made *for* rather than *by* the patient, and the danger posed to his or her interests in life and privacy and equal treatment by an erroneous decision is so profound (death), the California court reasoned that the "degree of confidence required in the necessary findings of fact" should be correspondingly high.[136]

The California court then proceeded to examine the evidence and the question whether Mrs. Wendland had come forward with clear and convincing proof either that Wendland would have wished to discontinue treatment or that doing so would be in his best interests. The court concluded that Mrs. Wendland had offered only "her own subjective judgment that the conservatee did not enjoy a satisfactory quality of life and legally insufficient evidence to the effect that he would have wished to die."[137] On this record, the Court concluded that the trial court's decision was "correct."[138]

The Future for Comatose Adult Patients

I think the reasoning in *Wendland* provides other courts with a model to follow in the especially difficult cases of incompetent adult patients. Throughout its opinion, the Court recognized that incompetent persons are fully equal persons with full entitlement to all the same rights and privileges as any other citizens. It recognized that decisions by conservators are not choices by the patient but properly seen as, and best analyzed under, traditional parens patriae principles. And it reasonably required a significant amount of proof about a ward's best interests or wishes before life-sustaining care may be discontinued.

Throughout its opinion, however, the California Supreme Court stressed that Wendland was, at least to some degree and at some times, conscious, stating variously that he is "a conscious conservatee who is not terminally ill, comatose, or in a persistent vegetative state;"[139] "the [trial] court found no 'clear cut guidance' on how to evaluate a conservator's proposal to end the life of a conscious conservatee who was neither terminally ill nor in a persistent vegetative state;"[140] "the decision to withdraw life-sustaining treatment, because of its effect on a conscious conservatee's fundamental rights, justified imposing [a] high standard of proof."[141] The court never directly stated that a patient in a "permanently vegetative state" should be treated differently, but its emphasis on the fact that Wendland was minimally conscious raises the question whether, to maintain unanimity, that possibility had to be kept open.

I would suggest, however, that the California court's mode of analysis and those courts that choose to follow it should not change depending on whether the patient is comatose or semicomatose. The same fundamental liberty interests are at stake: the right to life, the right to privacy, and the right to be treated as equal to all other human beings. The same standard of review (clear and convincing evidence) is necessary to ensure that a conservator does not, by virtue of abuse or mistake, extinguish these fundamental constitutional rights. Indeed, the only way to defend a laxer standard of review for comatose patients than for minimally conscious patients is to suggest that the quality of one's life makes a categorical difference to the content of one's rights—and this cannot be squared with the inviolability-of-life principle, equal protection requirements, or the California court's stated reasons for rejecting Mrs. Wendland's request.

Having said all this, it is important to recall our earlier discussions of vitalism from chapter 9. Consistent application of the *Wendland* decision and the inviolability-of-life principle should not be confused with, or lead to, the conclusion that all comatose and semicomatose patients must be kept alive regardless of the invasiveness or futility or expense of the care necessary to sustain them. Far from it. To adopt *Wendland*'s reasoning does not necessarily mean that treatment would have been required for each of the patients in *Brophy, Bland,* or *Saikewicz.* It would be, for example, entirely consistent with *Wendland* and the inviolability-of-life principle for a wife to reject further care for a husband on the ground that the husband expressed his wish, prior to incapacity, to be cared for at home or in a hospice in the event of disability in order to be free from unwanted medical intrusions. Neither does *Wendland*'s reasoning preclude a guardian from refusing care of any kind (whether pigeonholed in *Bland*-type language as "ordinary" or "extraordinary," "medical" or "nonmedical") on the ground that it would prove futile or impose inhumane burdens on the ward (e.g., cause continued infections by the insertion of a new feeding tube, or force food into the ward that he or she cannot digest, or cause painful suffering). Nothing in such decisions necessarily betokens an intent to kill. The inviolability-of-life principle recognizes and fully accepts that there are many competing and incompatible goods that persons can legitimately pursue; that life, while one good is hardly the only one; and, thus, that many upright reasons exist why guardians might refuse life-sustaining care for their loved ones having nothing to do with a desire to end life (as the facts, if not all of the reasoning, in *Saikewicz* amply illustrate). The inviolability-of-life principle offers a middle path between the extreme of destroying people because we deem their instrumental capacities for self-creation defective and their quality of life lacking and the equal extreme of insisting that life is the premier or most important good that must always be maintained.

At the same time, to follow where the reasoning of *Bland* would seemingly take us, and permit guardians to refuse care with the intent to end life, would indeed be to cross the Rubicon into the realm of euthanasia. Consistent application of the *Wendland* decision and its rationale would augur in favor of reconsidering the sort of reasoning employed (if not necessarily the results achieved) in cases like *Brophy* and *Bland* and *Saikewicz*, and suggest that third-party decisions to terminate the care of incompetent adult patients should receive the same scrutiny, and be decided with the same appreciation for the inviolability of all human life, that Congress has suggested for incompetent minors. *Brophy* itself was decided only by a 4–3 vote, with all three dissenters stressing *Wendland*-like arguments for the inviolability of life, the inappropriateness of judicial assessments about the relative quality of different human lives, and the need for careful review of any guardian's decision affecting a ward's constitutional rights to life and privacy.

Future courts should consider, too, that states have recently reviewed and reaffirmed their laws banning assisted suicide and have enacted provisions precluding courts from reading advance medical directives or living wills in such a way as to authorize any "deliberate act or omission to end life."[142] If one cannot deliberately kill competent patients (assisted suicide/euthanasia), or construe living wills as permitting the deliberate killing of incompetent patients who have left behind written directives, it would be incongruous indeed for only one class of persons—the incompetent who has not left behind any written instruction—to be subject to intentional destruction by others. Ultimately, however, there may be a need for legislative solutions if the courts fail to act. In such an event, good models already exist: Congress and state legislatures can look to their work in the arenas of infant nontreatment and living wills to fashion similar regulations governing the discontinuation of care for incompetent adults who have left behind no written directives—regulations that are focused not on quality of life, but on the quality of the proposed care, bearing in mind the intrinsic value of all human life.

10.4 Conclusions

In concluding this book, we might return briefly to the basic questions that have framed this analysis and summarize some of the answers suggested here. I hesitate to do so because it has taken so many pages to unpack and explore these issues, but it may be useful, nonetheless, to bring at least some of the highlights of the argument together.

1. Whether to legalize assisted suicide and euthanasia is among the most hotly debated contemporary legal and public policy questions. Dr. Kevorkian's very public killings brought attention to the issue in the early 1990s and were rapidly followed by a cascade of voter initiative referenda and legislative

proposals throughout the United States. With the exception of Oregon's experiment, none of these initiatives and proposals has yet borne fruit, though each has reinforced the deep social and political division over the question of legalization.

2. In the mid-1990s, assisted suicide and euthanasia proponents turned from legislatures to the judiciary and encountered some initial success in the lower courts. In 1997, the Supreme Court rebuffed their efforts, however, holding 9–0 that laws against assisted suicide are not facially invalid. But the Supreme Court's decision was far less definitive than it appears at first blush. Indeed, a majority of the Court reserved judgment on the constitutionality of laws banning the practices as applied to terminally ill adults who choose death. The Court's decision, taken with its language encouraging state legislatures to experiment in this area, raises a number of questions for future courts and lawmakers.

3. The Court's decision, for example, raises the question whether historical precedent exists to support either a constitutional right to, or legalization of, assistance in suicide and euthanasia. As we saw, ancient Rome does offer some precedent for legalization, but few today would be eager to emulate the practices the Romans sometimes tolerated (and even applauded). Looking to English and American common law history, there is no meaningful historical antecedent for a right to assistance in suicide or euthanasia, despite contrary arguments by Judge Reinhardt, ethicist Dan Brock, and Lord Hoffmann, all of whom have erroneously suggested that the "decriminalization" of suicide in the eighteenth, nineteenth, and twentieth centuries betokened approval of that practice.

4. The Court's decision and Justice Stevens's concurring opinion in *Quill* also raise the question whether principles of equal treatment and fairness require that, because we recognize a right to refuse life-sustaining medical care, we must also recognize a right to assisted suicide and euthanasia. I argued that attempts to distinguish between the right to refuse and assisted suicide on causation and act-omission grounds lack persuasive force. But I also suggested that a meaningful moral distinction based on intent does exist: the right to refuse need not imply any intention to die or to help kill on the part of anyone involved; meanwhile, assisted suicide requires someone to assist in the intentional taking of human life. Euthanasia, too, by definition, involves an intent to kill, if sometimes only as a means toward the end of relieving suffering. I tested my conclusions against a number of prominent objections, including those lodged by Timothy Quill, David Orentlicher, and John Griffiths, among others.

5. We explored whether *Casey* and *Cruzan*'s language about the importance of choice and personal self-creation provide a sufficient basis to support the creation of a new right to assisted suicide or euthanasia as a matter of legal doctrine. After considering competing arguments, I suggested that *Casey* may be read as a *stare decisis* decision and how it fails to resolve fully cases where both sides can cite legally cognizable—and diametrically opposing—autonomy-

based arguments; I also suggested that *Cruzan*'s reasoning rests on common law concepts of battery and the prevention of nonconsensual touchings, rationales that do not embrace or suggest a right to assisted suicide.

6. We next considered three competing theories of autonomy found in moral and political theory and whether they might sustain a right to assisted suicide, even if existing judicial doctrine concerning personal autonomy does not. We found that one of them (what we called "perfectionism") does not command a right to assisted suicide or euthanasia (or any other substantive right). I suggested that the two remaining theories, based on the harm and neutrality principles, offer two possible outcomes consistent with their teachings. First, it is possible that persons might reasonably assess the risks associated with legalization of assisted suicide and euthanasia (e.g., unwanted killings due to abuse, mistake, and pressure) to be sufficiently grave that they opt to make the practices unlawful—much as Mill and Feinberg have argued for the absolute prohibition of dueling and slavery contracts. Second, if assisted suicide and euthanasia are legalized, I argued that consistent application of the neutrality and harm principles would tend toward a rule making the practices available to all competent adults without respect to their physical condition or reason for seeking death.

7. We also considered whether utilitarianism provides a basis for legalization. Though legalization would clearly entail certain benefits, it would also, I submitted, likely bring with it nontrivial costs and burdens. I considered the arguments of John Griffiths and Helga Kuhse, who suggest that legalization would not result in any additional cases of voluntary or nonvoluntary assisted suicide and euthanasia. I acknowledged that the costs and burdens associated with legalization do not obviously preclude legalization on utilitarian grounds, but I submitted that they do preclude the easy assumption (voiced by many) that a utilitarian calculus obviously weighs in favor of legalization. In addition, given the existence of legitimate and competing interests on both sides of the legalization debate, we explored whether the utilitarian project of attempting to compare incommensurate goods—the liberty to kill oneself versus the lives of persons who would be killed as a result of abuse, mistake, and pressure—might be analytically unsound.

8. I tested several of the foregoing conclusions against recent works by Judge Richard Posner and Richard Epstein. I concluded that Posner's utilitarian arguments are beset by faulty data and unwarranted causation assumptions, as well as by an incommensurability problem. By contrast, the libertarian arguments proffered by Posner and Epstein illustrate and reinforce my conclusion that the harm principle does not necessarily dictate legalization of assisted suicide but that, to be fully faithful to the harm principle, any scheme of legalization attempted would likely have to be extended not merely to the terminally ill, but to all rational adults.

9. After considering arguments from history, fairness, autonomy doctrine and theory, and utilitarianism, I suggested that courts and legislators may

wish to consider a less frequently voiced perspective on the assisted suicide and euthanasia question, one grounded in the recognition of human life as a fundamental good. Under this view, private intentional acts of homicide are always wrong. Recognizing human life as intrinsically, not instrumentally, valuable, I submitted, would rule out assisted suicide and euthanasia, though it would not lead to, and should not be confused with, a vitalist's view that measures must always be taken to keep human beings alive; to the contrary, it would leave significant room for individual autonomy, restricting state interference only to cases where an intent to help kill is present. After sketching out what we called the inviolability-of-life principle, I considered a number of potential objections, including those suggested by the writings of Peter Singer.

10. In closing, I sought to explore how the inviolability-of-life principle might apply to cases involving competent persons who refuse life-sustaining medical care, as well as to the increasingly common and difficult cases involving nontreatment decisions made on behalf of incompetent persons, both infant and adult. I analyzed several of the leading cases, suggested how the inviolability-of-life principle might be applied to such disputes in the future, defended recent legislative initiatives as consistent with that principle, and offered suggestions for additional action by legislatures and courts.

Epilogue

AS THIS book wends its way through the editorial process, the contours of the assisted suicide debate continue to evolve. While it is impossible to elaborate on every significant new fact or issue in such an active international debate, some of the more salient recent developments are worth noting before the opportunity slips away.

Perhaps foremost among these, at least in the short term, is the Supreme Court's recent decision in *Gonzales v. Oregon*.[1] By a 6-3 vote, the Court affirmed two lower court decisions and rejected an interpretative regulation issued by former Attorney General John Ashcroft under the Controlled Substances Act (CSA). The so-called Ashcroft Directive sought to preclude doctors from using controlled substances to aid suicides intentionally, reasoning that assisted suicide does not qualify as a "legitimate medical practice," as that term is used in regulations enacted shortly after the CSA's enactment many years ago. Significantly, the Supreme Court's opinion rejecting the Ashcroft Directive offered no endorsement of assisted suicide or euthanasia but instead focused on a different (and perhaps comparatively arcane) set of questions about the balance of authority between the states and federal government in the arena of medical regulation, as well as on whether and to what extent the Attorney General is due heightened deference in his interpretation of the CSA and CSA-related regulations under federal administrative law principles.

Lurking just beneath the surface of the Court's federalism and administrative law analysis, however, is a clearly discernible message for the future of the assisted suicide debate. At the outset of its opinion, the Court recalled its recognition in *Glucksberg* that "Americans are engaged in an earnest and profound debate" about assisted suicide, a phrase that suggests a judicial hesitance to tamper with or pretermit that debate. On each subsequent page of the Court's opinion that same hesitance seemed to reappear. Time after time, the Court cast doubt on the Attorney General's suggestion that the CSA somehow affords a "single Executive officer" the authority to issue an interpretive regulation that would, in the Court's words, "substantially disrupt" the Oregon experiment and the debate it has provoked.[2] To be sure, the Court held that the Attorney General's view—that assisted suicide doesn't qualify as a "legitimate medical practice" under the governing CSA regulations—is "at least reasonable."[3] And the Court readily conceded that much evidence supported the Attorney General's conclusion on this score. But infused throughout the Court's opinion was one essential concern: the Attorney General's interpretation, reasonable though it may have been, simply would have effected too "radical [a] shift of authority"[4] over the assisted suicide debate—moving it from the states, where the debate has been so actively and earnestly engaged, to the exclusive control of a single Executive official.[5]

The Court's preference for state legislative experimentation in *Gonzales* seems, at the end of the day, to leave the state of the assisted suicide debate more or less where the Court found it, with the states free to resolve the question for themselves. Even so, it raises interesting questions for at least two future sorts of cases one might expect to emerge in the not-too-distant future. The first sort of cases are "as applied" challenges asserting a constitutional right to assisted suicide or euthanasia limited to some particular group, such as the terminally ill or perhaps those suffering grave physical (or maybe even psychological) pain. *Glucksberg*, as we saw in chapter 2, held only that laws banning assisted suicide are not facially unconstitutional, that is unconstitutional in all possible applications, leaving room for the possibility that such laws might still be deemed problematic as applied to particular groups. In *Gonzales*, the Court reinforced its preference for state legislative experimentation. But it remains to be seen whether in an as applied challenge the Court would stand by its preference for state legislative experimentation or whether it might instead recognize a constitutional right that trumps at least some state legislation against assisted suicide. Putting the point most basically, the Court in *Gonzales* reaffirmed that the Constitution vests authority over the assisted suicide debate in state legislatures rather the federal Executive, but that doesn't definitively tell us how the Court might address a suit seeking to devolve at least some assisted suicide decisions even further, to the individual as opposed to state level.

The second sort of cases involve those like *Lee v. Oregon* (discussed in chapter 9), asserting that laws allowing assisted suicide violate the equal protection guarantee. On the one hand, the gestalt if not the holding of *Gonzales* suggests a the assisted suicide debate should be resolved through state legislative processes. On the other hand, *Gonzales* didn't purport to address the authority of the courts, through the Constitution and its amendments, in the assisted suicide debate. Nor did the design and manner of the Oregon scheme itself come into play in *Gonzales*—the Court simply had no occasion to delve into questions about the rational basis of the regime or the "fit" between its purposes and provisions.[6]

Turning from the judicial to the legislative arena, an Oregon-style bill (AB 654) was introduced in the California Assembly in 2005 and quickly passed through committee. The bill, however, stalled on the floor; when proponents saw their chances waning, they sought to move the fight to the state Senate. Employing a procedure known as "gutting and amending," the sponsors stripped language from another bill (AB 651) that had already passed the Assembly and moved to the Senate. That bill had sought to enhance health care for the poor until it was "gutted" and replaced with language taken from AB654 seeking to legalize assisted suicide. In the event, however, the new assisted suicide version of AB 651 failed to attract sufficient support in the Senate and the sponsors eventually had to suspend their efforts, though they vowed to return to the issue after they had a chance, as they put it, to educate the voters and their fellow legislators.

Half a world away, the British have also faced new legislative initiatives. About a decade after a select committee chaired by Lord Walton conducted a comprehensive review that culminated with a call for the retention of existing laws, Lord Joffe sought to revisit the issue, introducing legislation seeking to authorize assisted suicide and voluntary euthanasia. The House of Lords convened a new select committee under the leadership of Lord Mackay of Clashfern to study Joffe's proposal. That committee returned a report in 2005 but, quite unlike its predecessor, was unable to reach any consensus on the legalization question and instead suggested only that the full House of Lords take up a debate on Joffe's bill in 2006. In the course of the Mackay proceedings, moreover, the British Medical Association decided to stay on the sidelines, forswearing its longstanding opposition to legalization and declaring neutrality on the issue. In the fall of 2005, Joffe sought to mollify criticisms from some quarters by deleting provisions that would have allowed euthanasia, focusing his efforts (for the moment) on the legalization of assisted suicide. Both the Mackay report and Joffe legislation were actively scrutinized and debated in the spring of 2006.[7] In the end, the Lords voted 148–100 to postpone debate for six months, effectively killing the bill as the current session of Parliament is likely to end by then.

The fight over assisted suicide and euthanasia now extends as well into the world of words. Groups have changed their names, with the Hemlock Society, itself an intellectual heir of the Euthanasia Society of America, first becoming End of Life Choices before merging with Compassion in Dying to emerge recently as Compassion & Choices. Meanwhile, the Voluntary Euthanasia Society in England has revamped its image, too, now answering to the name Dignity in Dying. Citing the results of national polls they commissioned on various terms and phrases, leaders of Compassion & Choices recently sought in a national press conference to discourage the media from using the term assisted suicide, asking reporters instead to employ euphemisms like "death with dignity" and "end of life choices" to describe the act of assisting a person to kill himself or herself.[8] According to the co-president of Compassion & Choices, "'[s]uicide,' or 'assisted suicide,' or 'physician-assisted suicide' are loaded, pejorative terms that paint terminally-ill patients in the same negative light as terrorist bombers."[9] Along the same lines, Lord Joffe titled his bill seeking to legalize assisted suicide the "Assisted Dying for the Terminally Ill" Bill—a title that suggests that everyone doesn't need assistance in dying and brings to mind something arguably not at all the same thing as assisted suicide or euthanasia.

Bearing perhaps more concretely on the assisted suicide debate, significant new data continue to emerge. Oregon has now issued its eighth annual report on the operation of its assisted suicide regime.[10] The findings in this latest report tend to reflect, sometimes in even starker terms, the trends identified in the first five annual reports analyzed in chapter 7. Some 64 assisted suicide prescriptions were written in 2005, about double the number of prescriptions written in 1999, the first full year of the law's implementation.[11] The average duration of the patient-doctor relationship before an act of assisted suicide occurs has now declined to approximately 8 weeks from an average of 13 weeks during the first five years of legalization.[12]

Relevant to the potential role of depression and social isolation, the correlation between assisted suicide requests and those who are divorced or who have never been married continues to persist. Those divorced were nearly twice as likely in 2005 to seek out assisted suicide as their married counterparts; the never married were 1.7 times more likely. Despite this, referrals to mental health experts for psychiatric evaluation continue to decline—down to just 5% of cases in 2005 from 37% in 1999. Meanwhile, the fear of being a burden on family and friends was reported to be a motivating factor in 42% of patient requests for assisted suicide in 2005, up from 35% during the first five years of legalization, raising ever more pointedly questions about the tacit role of guilt and a sense of coerciveness in requests for early deaths.

At the same time, the desire to end physical pain—often cited as a primary reason for legalization—was a motivating factor in fewer than a quarter of all cases of assisted suicide, though even this number still may be higher than necessary given continuing concerns about the training in and dissemination of palliative care techniques in Oregon discussed in chapter 7. Those seeking assisted suicide in Oregon also continue to be nearly all white (as of December 31, 2005, not a single African American had sought to take advantage of Oregon's law in the 7-plus years since it went into effect) and highly educated, highlighting the question whether assisted suicide is a matter of necessity or more of a lifestyle choice for persons who have always tended to control their lives and now wish to control their death.[13] Though physicians are present in only a subset of cases to witness whether complications arise with the lethal medication they prescribe, the reported rate of complications continues to hover at about 5%, including one case in 2005 where the patient awoke 65 hours after taking the prescribed medication and died 14 days later of the underlying illness. Two other cases in 2005 involved patients who vomited some of the medication and died 15 and 90 minutes later, respectively.

While data like these tell part of the story, Oregon health department officials continue to operate without the legal authority or resources to investigate cases of potential abuse or mistake or coercion, relying entirely on after the fact reports by physicians when compiling their annual reports. As the health department has admitted on multiple occasions, this makes it impossible to obtain a true picture of what is actually happening on the ground and the data the state health department is able to collect perhaps raise more questions than they answer, including for example: What is the role of untreated depression or social isolation in Oregon assisted suicides? Of mental illnesses? (These are questions Oregon doesn't even *ask* of self-reporting physicians though some of the data collected provocatively point to the issue). What is the role of advocacy groups? Of physical pain versus lifestyle choices? In how many cases where pain is cited as a motivating factor can it be fully treated (short of killing the patient)? Are all cases being reported or is there a Dutch-like grey market in unlawful and unreported cases of assisted suicide? If so, how large is that market and how has it changed over time since legalization in 1998? To the extent physicians are reporting cases, how accurately are they doing so? Given that doctors frequently are not present at the time of their patients' deaths, how often do complications really arise and how severe are they? There's little chance any of these questions and others like them raised in chapter 7—questions essential to a full understanding of the law's effect and a thoughtful assessment of its worthiness for emulation elsewhere—will be answered any time soon given the many limitations Oregon has imposed on its oversight agency.

From the journal *Palliative Medicine* comes a new study by Clive Seale, a Brunel University social scientist, regarding the frequency of assisted suicide and euthanasia in Britain.[14] Modeled on the Australian Singer-Kuhse study discussed in chapter 7, the Seale study sought to estimate, through a voluntary physician survey, the frequency of assisted suicide and other "end of life decisions" by doctors in the U.K. The survey found *no* cases of assisted suicide and estimated the incidence of voluntary euthanasia at 0.17% of all deaths in Britain. (By comparison, recall that the rate of voluntary euthanasia in the Netherlands is 2.3% and assisted suicide accounts for another 0.4% of all deaths.) These data, like similar data from the United States discussed in chapter 7, do much to call into question the claim by some legalization proponents that assisted suicide and voluntary euthanasia are practiced on a widespread, if clandestine, basis in countries where the practices remain illegal. Instead and consistent with the law of demand, it seems from results like these that the existence of laws discouraging assisted suicide and euthanasia really may have an effect on how frequently such actions are carried out.[15] Responding doctors were also afforded room to offer comments at the end of the survey; a number (51) chose to offer views on the legalization debate and of those 82% argued for the retention of current law while 14% expressed dissatisfaction with the status quo.[16]

The Seale study further found that nonvoluntary euthanasia, or killing without explicit consent, accounts for approximately 0.36% of deaths in the U.K. while the incidence of nonvoluntary killing is nearly three times higher in the Netherlands using even statistics most favorable to the Dutch (0.90%).[17] Such data again seem to undercut the claim by some legalization proponents that nonvoluntary euthanasia is prevalent everywhere and that the problem will not be exacerbated by legalizing assisted suicide and voluntary euthanasia.[18] As the survey author noted: "[c]ampaigners for liberalization of the laws covering the intentional hastening of patients' death [argue] . . . that the unregulated practice of euthanasia without consent in countries where criminalization breeds fear of bringing the issues out into the open. Because the rate of [killing without consent] is relatively low in the UK this argument cannot be made."[19] Instead, Seale has suggested, his findings may be the result of the fact that the UK developed palliative care approaches earlier than many other countries and accordingly has developed a "culture of medical decision making informed by a palliative care philosophy."[20]

Finally, significant new data continue to emerge from the Netherlands. News reports suggest that the Dutch government is now considering whether to issue regulations governing infanticide—regulations that would, in essence, codify the Groningen Protocol discussed in chapter 7.[21] That Protocol, developed by lawyers and doctors at a Groningen hospital, sought to establish internal guidelines for the hospital's ongoing infant euthanasia program and to provoke a national discussion about the formal legalization of the practice. Under the Protocol, infanticide is acceptable not just for children born without any chance of survival but also for those who are not dependent on intensive medical treatment; indeed, 13 of 22 cases of infanticide reported in the Netherlands between 1997 and 2002 involved children who had a "long life expectancy."[22] Infanticide in such cases is fully justified, according to the authors of the Protocol, when the infant is perceived to have "a very poor quality of life" and "sustained suffering" in the eyes of the parents and treating physicians.[23] The Protocol authors note that following the terms of their document will not guarantee that prosecutors will look the other way; but, they report, no one in their group following the Protocol's terms has experienced any trouble. Given these developments, one might ask: How much further do the Dutch really have to travel before they reach Peter Singer's "replaceability" theory of human rights (discussed in chapter 9) where parents' subjective pleasure or displeasure with their infant children effectively determines the right of those children to exist or be subjected to "replacement"?

Meanwhile, a group of Dutch researchers recently published in the *Journal of Clinical Oncology* the results of a study into the relationship between euthanasia requests in the Netherlands and clinical depression.[24] The authors candidly admitted that they began their investigation expecting to find that the data would support their anecdotal impression that patients seeking out euthanasia are generally more accepting of their impending deaths and thinking more coolly and rationally than other patients.[25] The survey authors were very surprised to find virtually the opposite to be true.[26] Specifically, their survey of 138 terminally ill cancer patients found that depressed patients are more than four times more likely to request euthanasia than patients who are not suffering from depression. Indeed, fully 44% of depressed patients surveyed requested euthanasia.

The study authors then proceeded to test a different hypothesis, namely that depression is itself a rational response to poor prognoses. The authors were yet again surprised by the data which this time showed that there is *no* statistically significant association between depression and prognosis. That is, depressed patients—not the sickest patients—seem to be the ones seeking out euthanasia.[27]

Much public debate over assisted suicide and euthanasia both in the U.S. and abroad has rested on the implicit premise that requests for assistance in dying are closely linked to pain. But a great many facts have now amassed running counter to this supposition—the Dutch euthanasia regime has moved away from any requirement of physical *or* psychological suffering; Oregon has never required a showing of pain of any kind; clinical studies continue to suggest that modern palliative techniques, if disseminated and practiced by knowledgeable doctors, are able to address pain in most, if not all, circumstances; Oregon's annual reports and repeated Dutch surveys suggest that pain simply is not a leading reason motivating patient demands for euthanasia or assisted suicide; there has now long persisted a suggestive correlation between divorce and requests for assisted suicide. And now comes the *Journal of Clinical Oncology* study suggesting that the major motivation behind assisted suicide and euthanasia requests is not a poor prognosis but depression. Of course, the movement for legalizing assisted suicide and euthanasia is at least in part the result of a culture increasingly influenced by strict neutralist conceptions of autonomy, itself perhaps the byproduct of the baby boomer generation heading into old age, themes we explored in chapters 3 and 6. But when it comes not to defending an abstract "right to die" but to making the very concrete and personal decision whether to die, it seems that something more basic may be in play. We have known since Jefferson's time (chapter 3) that old-fashioned suicide is often motivated by mental ailments, depression foremost among these. Yet contemporary assisted suicide and euthanasia advocates have long denied that depression plays any meaningful role in assisted suicide and euthanasia requests. The findings in the *Journal of Clinical Oncology* now point to a contrary conclusion, suggesting that the desire to seek out any early death at the hands of a doctor is itself not so much the result of a dispassionate and cool response to a poor prognosis as it is the product of diagnosable and treatable depression.[28]

Of course, this question would benefit from further research. So far, Oregon and Dutch officials, for all their reports, have done virtually nothing to explore the role that depression plays in their regimes, instead seeming to take for granted that long-standing evidence about the link between depression and old-fashioned suicide has no bearing on the assisted suicide debate. Nor is merely adding a question to the self-reporting forms in Oregon or the Netherlands likely to do much good; we saw in chapter 7 that physicians are not always good at identifying depression in their patients and they are apt not to comply with reporting requirements in cases where they feel laws insisting on fully rational consent have not been met. Instead, independent and serious work is needed in both Oregon and the Netherlands along the lines of the *Journal of Clinical Oncology* study. And in the interim we might ask: ought doctors handing out suicide prescriptions at least pause to consider their own latent assumptions about the motivating forces behind patient requests? Should they question any preconceived notion they might share with the study's authors that a patient's request for assisted suicide is itself evidence of a cool and reasoned analysis in the face of a poor prognosis? Should they prod a bit more carefully to see whether depression is at play, or perhaps refer patients to doctors with some expertise in the area? Is it possible that the *Journal of Clinical Oncology* study is right and the impulse for assistance in suicide, like the impulse for old-fashioned suicide, might more often than not be the result of an often readily treatable condition?

Appendix A

CERTAIN AMERICAN STATUTORY LAWS BANNING

OR DISAPPROVING OF ASSISTED SUICIDE

42 U.S.C. §§ 14401-14408 (2000) (denying the use of federal funds in connection with acts of assisted suicide).

Ala. Code Ann. § 22-8A-10 (Michie 1997) (stating that Alabama's medical directive statute shall not be construed to condone assisted suicide).

Alaska Stat. Ann. § 11.41.120(a)(2) (Lexis 2002).

Ariz. Rev. Stat. Ann. § 13-1103(A)(3) (West 2001).

Ark. Code Ann. § 5-10-104(a)(2) (Michie 1997).

Cal. Penal Code § 401 (West 1999).

Colo. Rev. Stat. Ann. § 18-3-104(1)(b) (West 2004).

Conn. Gen. Stat. Ann. § 53a-56(a)(2) (West 2001).

Del. Code Ann. tit. 11, § 645 (Michie 2001).

Fla. Stat. Ann. § 782.08 (West 2000).

Ga. Code Ann. § 16-5-5 (2003).

Haw. Rev. Stat. Ann. § 707-702(1)(b) (Michie 2003).

Idaho Code § 56-1022 (Michie 2002) (stating that Idaho's medical directive statute shall not be construed to make legal or condone mercy killing, assisted suicide or euthanasia).

720 Ill. Comp. Stat. Ann. 5/12-31 (West 2002).

Ind. Code Ann. § 35-42-1-2, -2.5(b) (Lexis 2004).

Iowa Code Ann. § 707A.2 (West 2003).

Kan. Stat. Ann. § 21-3406 (Supp. 2003).

Ky. Rev. Stat. Ann. § 216.302 (Michie 1998).

La. Rev. Stat. Ann. § 14:32.12 (Michie 1998).

Me. Rev. Stat. Ann. tit. 17-A, § 204 (West 1983).

Md. Code Ann., Crim. Law § 3-102 (Michie 2002).

Mass. Ann. Laws ch. 201D, § 12 (Law. Co-op. 1994) (stating that Massachusetts's medical directive statute shall not be construed to condone assisted suicide).

Mich. Comp. Laws Ann. § 752.1027 (West 2004) (Annotator's note: "Regarding the recommendations referred to in subsection (5), at the time of publication [2002] recommendations had been submitted to both houses but it was not certain whether the recommendations were those of the full commission or whether both houses 'accepted' the recommendations were presented.").

Minn. Stat. Ann. § 609.215 (West 2003).

Miss. Code Ann. § 97-3-49 (West 1999).

Mo. Ann. Stat. § 565.023.1(2) (West 2003).

Mont. Code Ann. § 45-5-105 (West 2003). An annotator noted: "[u]nder the new sections on Causal Relationship Between Conduct and Result, MCA, 45-2-201, and Accountability, MCA, 45-2-302, a person may be convicted of Criminal Homicide, MCA, 45-5-101 (repealed—now deliberate or mitigated homicide, 45-5-102 and 45-5-103, respectively), for causing another to commit suicide—notwithstanding the consent of the victim."

Annotations to the Montana Code Annotated § 45-5-105 note (2004).

Neb. Rev. Stat. Ann. § 28-307 (Lexis 2003).

Nev. Rev. Stat. Ann. § 449.670(2) (Michie 2000) (stating that Nevada's medical directive statute shall not be construed to condone assisted suicide or euthanasia).

N.H. Rev. Stat. Ann. § 630:4 (Michie 1996).

N.J. Stat. Ann. § 2C:11-6 (West 1995).

N.M. Stat. Ann. § 30-2-4 (Michie 2004).

N.Y. Penal Law § 120.30 (McKinney 2004).

N.D. Cent. Code § 12.1-16.04 (1997).

Ohio Rev. Code Ann. § 2133.12(D) (Anderson 2002) (stating that Ohio's medical directive statute shall not be construed to condone assisted suicide).

Okla. Stat. Ann. tit. 21, § 813 (West 2002).

18 Pa. Cons. Stat. Ann. § 2505 (West 1998).

R.I. Gen. Laws Ann. § 11-60 (Lexis 2002).

S.C. Code Ann. § 16-3-1090 (West 2003).

S.D. Codified Laws § 22-16-37 (Michie 1998).

Tenn. Code Ann. § 39-13-216 (Lexis 2003).

Tex. Penal Code Ann. § 22.08 (Vernon 2003).

Utah Code Ann. § 75-2-1118 (Michie 1993) (stating that Utah's medical directive statute shall not be construed to condone assisted suicide).

Va. Code Ann. § 8.01-622.1 (Lexis 2000) (enacting a civil statute providing that a person may be enjoined from assisting suicide or may be liable for monetary damages by assisting or attempting to assist suicide).

Wash. Rev. Code Ann. § 9A.36.060 (West 2000).

W. Va. Code Ann. § 16-30-2(a) (Michie 2001) (presenting the legislative finding that West Virginia's medical directive statute does not legalize, condone, authorize or approve of assisted suicide).

Wis. Stat. § 940.12 (2003–2004).

Appendix B

STATISTICAL CALCULATIONS

Below are calculations used in preparing certain graphs in the text. All calculations are based on mortality statistics from the World Health Organization.

TABLE B.1
Suicide Rate of Dutch Elderly (75 years +) Women
as a Multiple of the Total Female Suicide Rate, 1984–2000

Year	Elderly (75+) Female Suicide Rate per 100,000	Total Population Suicide Rate per 100,000	Suicide Rate of Elderly Women as a Multiple of Total Female Suicide Rate
1984	14.6	9.6	1.5208333
1985	10.8	8.0	1.35
1986	13	8.1	1.6049382
1987	13.8	8.2	1.6829268
1988	10.7	7.3	1.4657534
1989	10.7	7.4	1.4459459
1990	15.3	6.8	2.25
1991	11.3	7.1	1.5915492
1992	12.2	6.7	1.8208955
1993	12.2	6.4	1.90625
1994	9.5	6.1	1.557377
1995	9.6	6.1	1.5737704
1996	11.2	6.3	1.777777
1997	11.7	6.2	1.8070967
1998	10.9	6.0	1.81066666
1999	9.3	5.9	1.5762711
2000	7.7	5.8	1.3275862

Source: Reg'l Office of Eur., World Health Org., Mortality Indicators by 67 Cause of Death, Age and Sex, at http://www.euro.who.int/InformationSources/Data/20011017_1 (site visited Dec. 22, 2004).

TABLE B.2

Suicide Rate of Elderly Persons (75 years+) as a Multiple
of the Total Suicide Rate

Country (year)	Elderly (75+) Suicide Rate per 100,000	Total Suicide Rate per 100,000 Population	Suicide Rate of Elderly as Multiple of Total Suicide Rate
Finland (2002)			
Men	50.3	32.3	1.56
Women	7.5	10.2	0.74
Norway (2001)			
Men	30.0	18.4	1.63
Women	3.2	6.0	0.53
United States (2000)			
Men	42.4	17.1	2.48
Women	4.0	4.0	1.00
U.K. (1999)			
Men	15.5	11.8	1.31
Women	5.1	3.3	1.55
Sweden (2001)			
Men	42.2	18.9	2.23
Women	12.7	8.1	1.57
France (1999)			
Men	80.5	26.1	3.08
Women	17.5	9.4	1.86
Netherlands (2000)			
Men	28.3	12.7	2.23
Women	7.8	6.2	1.26
Italy (2000)			
Men	34.2	10.9	3.14
Women	7.4	3.5	2.11
Denmark (1999)			
Men	46.6	21.4	2.18
Women	10.9	7.4	1.47
Germany (2001)			
Men	60.9	20.4	2.99
Women	18.2	7.0	2.6
Spain (2000)			
Men	44.9	13.1	3.43
Women	9.1	4.0	2.28

Note: All data are for the most recent year for which the World Health Organization has published online statistics for the country in question.

Notes

Chapter 1: Introduction

1. *See People v. Kevorkian*, 210 Mich. App. 601, 534 N.W.2d 172 (1995).

2. *See id.* at 604–605.

3. *See* Pamela Warrick, *Suicide's Partner*, L.A. Times, Dec. 6, 1992, part E, at 1, col. 2.

4. *See* Isabel Wilkerson, *Prosecutors Seek to Ban Doctor's Suicide Device*, N.Y. Times, Jan. 5, 1991, sec. 1, at 6, col. 5.

5. *See* Brian Murphy, *Kevorkian, Silent, Starts Prison Term*, Detroit Free Press, Apr. 14, 1999, *available at* http://www.freep.com/ news/extra2/qkevo14.htm (hereinafter Murphy, *Kevorkian Silent*).

6. In 2004, the Hemlock Society changed its name to "End of Life Choices." It then merged with Compassion in Dying (CID) to form what is now known as Compassion and Choice. *See* Wesley J. Smith, *Weekly Standard, available at* http://www.theweekly standard.com/content/public/articles/000/000/0004/471lzceh.asp (Aug. 16, 2004). CID was itself originally spun off of the Hemlock Society to focus on assisting suicides, as distinct from the Hemlock Society's legal and political advocacy work. *See id.*

7. Derek Humphry, *Law Reform*, 20 Ohio N.U. L. Rev. 729, 731 (1994).

8. *See* Charlie Cain (comp.), *Key Events in the History of Michigan's Debate over Abortion and Assisted Suicide*, The Detroit News, Mar. 2, 1997, at A8.

9. As developed by Dutch courts, the emergency defense applied when (a) a patient requested assistance freely and voluntarily; (b) the request was well considered, durable, and persistent; (c) the patient was experiencing intolerable suffering with no prospect of improvement; (d) other alternatives to alleviate the patient's suffering had been considered and found wanting; (e) any act of euthanasia was performed (only) by a physician; and (f) the physician had consulted an independent colleague. *See Report of the Select Committee on Medical Ethics, House of Lords*, HL Paper, 21-I, 1993–1994 (hereinafter *House of Lords Report* HL Paper 21-I of 1993–1994 Session), appendix 3, *infra.* These criteria paralleled professional guidelines established by the Royal Dutch Medical Association. *See* Walter Lagerway (trans.), *Guidelines for Euthanasia*, 3 issues, L. & Med. 429 (1988).

10. *See Netherlands Parliament Legalizes Euthanasia, available at* http://www. euthanasia.com/netherlands2000.html; CNN.com/WORLD, *Dutch Law Stokes Death Debate, available at* http://archives.cnn .com/2001/WORLD/europe/04/11/euthanasia. debate.index.html (site visited Oct. 5, 2005). *See also* ch. 7.1, *infra* (discussing legislative changes).

11. For a thorough account of how the Australian law came about, its procedures, and

the seven deaths that took place pursuant to its provisions, *see* David Kissane, *Deadly Days in Darwin*, in *The Case against Assisted Suicide: For the Right to End-of-Life Care* 192 (Kathleen Foley and Herbert Hendin eds., 2002). Switzerland, too, tolerates assisted suicide, even when committed by nondoctors; though "no verified statistics" regarding the practice of assisted suicide in Switzerland are available at present, its regime has received attention recently as the number of "death tourists," primarily from Britain, spiked from three in 2000 to fifty-five in 2001. *See Death in a Consumer Society (Editor's Choice)*, 326 Brit. Med. J. (Feb. 1, 2003); Wesley J. Smith, *Continent Death: Euthanasia in Europe*, National Review Online, Dec. 23, 2003, *available at* http://www.nationalreview.com/comment/smith200312230101.asp; Jo Revilland and Alison Langley, *Suicide Clinic Investigated over Deaths*, The Observer, Nov. 23, 2003, *available at* http://observer.guardian.co.uk/international /story/0,,1091320,00.html (site visited Oct. 5, 2005).

12. *See* Euthanasia.com, *available at* http://www.euthanasia.com/ belgiumlaw.html (site visited July 4, 2003).

13. *See* Timothy Quill, *Death with Dignity*, 324 New Eng. J. Med. 691 (1991). *See also* Timothy Quill, *The Ambiguity of Clinical Intentions*, 329 New Eng. J. Med. 1039 (1993).

14. *See* New York State Task Force on Life and the Law, *When Death Is Sought: Assisted Suicide and Euthanasia in the Medical Context* 5 (1994) (hereinafter *New York Task Force on Life and the Law*).

15. Anonymous, *It's Over Debbie*, 259 Journ. of the Amer. Med. Ass'n 272 (1988).

16. *See* Amazon, http://www.amazon.com/gp/product/0385336535/qid=1140129925/sr=2-1/ref=pd_bbs_b_2_1/002-8179975-3195227?s=books&u=glance&n=283155 (site visited Feb. 16, 2006).

17. *See* P. M. Marzuk *et al.*, *Increase in Suicide by Asphyxiation in New York City after the Publication of Final Exit*, 329 New Eng. J. Med. 1508–10 (1993). Though the book was billed as providing "self-deliverance" information for the terminally ill, the New England Journal of Medicine study found that, of the fifteen suicides who used the book during the study period, six suffered from no illness whatsoever. *Id.*

18. *See* Ronald Dworkin, *Life's Dominion: An Argument about Abortion and Euthanasia* (1993).

19. *See* Richard A. Posner, *Aging and Old Age* (1995).

20. *See* Richard Epstein, *Mortal Peril: Our Inalienable Right to Health Care?* (1999).

21. *See* Allan Parachini, *Bringing Euthanasia to the Ballot Box*, L.A. Times, Apr. 10, 1987, sec. 5, at 1.

22. *See* Sandi Dolbee, *Right to Die Measure Rejected by State Voters*, San Diego Union-Tribune, Nov. 4, 1992, at A3; Jay Mathews, *Term Limits, Assisted Suicide, Abortion Rights Losing in Washington*, Washington Post, Nov. 6, 1992, sec. 1, at A28.

23. *See* Spencer Heinz, *Assisted Suicide: Advocates Weigh In*, Oregonian, Dec. 9, 1994, at A1; Oregon Health Department, *Oregon's Death with Dignity Act: The First Year's Experience* (1998) (hereinafter Oregon, *First Year's Experience*).

24. *See* ch. 3.10, *infra*.

25. *See* Assisted Suicide Funding Restriction Act of 1997, Pub. L. No. 105-12, 111 Stat. 23 (codified at 42 U.S.C. §§ 14401–14408 (2000)).

26. *See House of Lords Report* HL Paper, 21-I of 1993–1994 Session.

27. *See Rodriguez v. British Columbia (Attorney General)*, [1993] 3 S.C.R. 519.

28. *See* note 11, *supra*. Since the Northern Territory's law permitting assisted suicide was struck down by Australia's federal parliament, at least two other Australian States—

Tasmania and South Australia—have formed panels to study the possibility of legalizing assisted suicide. In both cases, the respective committees have strongly recommended against legalization. *See* Community Development Commitee Report on the Need for Legalisation of Voluntary Euthanasia (1998), Report No. 6 of the Community Development Committee, House of Assembly (Tasmania); Parliament of South Australia, *Inquiry into the Voluntary Euthanasia Bill 1996*, 1999 (S. Austl. Acts).

29. See nzoom.com http://onenews.nzoom.com/onenews_detail/ 0,1227,173412-1-7,00.html (site visited July 4, 2003) (noting that 1995 effort at legalization was defeated in parliament 61–29); http://www.lifenews.com/intl14.html (a renewed effort in 2003 was also defeated).

30. *See* Euthanasia.com, *available at* http://www.euthanasia.com/ hung.html (site visited July 4, 2003) (discussing the rejection of a challenge to laws banning assisted suicide by Hungary's highest court).

31. Kevorkian also filed a losing state court challenge to the Michigan law banning assisted suicide. *See* note 1, *supra*.

32. *See Compassion in Dying v. Washington*, 850 F. Supp. 1454 (W.D. Wash. 1994)(finding constitutional right); *Quill v. Koppell*, 870 F. Supp. 78 (S.D.N.Y. 1994) (rejecting constitutional right).

33. *See Compassion in Dying v. Washington*, 49 F.3d 586 (9th Cir. 1995), *vacated en banc*, 79 F.3d 790 (9th Cir. 1995), *rev'd and remanded sub nom. Glucksberg*, 521 U.S. 702; *Quill v. Vacco*, 80 F.3d 716 (2d Cir. 1996).

34. *See Washington v. Glucksberg*, 521 U.S. 702 (1997); *Vacco v. Quill*, 521 U.S. 793 (1997).

35. *See, e.g.*, Joan Biskupic, *Unanimous Decision Points to Tradition of Valuing Life*, Washington Post, June 27, 1997, at A1 (hereinafter Biskupic, *Unanimous Decision*).

36. *See* Murphy, *Kevorkian Silent*.

37. *See, e.g.*, John Deigh, *Physician-Assisted Suicide and Voluntary Euthanasia: Some Relevant Differences*, 88 J. Crim. L. & Criminology 1155, 1157–59 (1998); Timothy E. Quill *et al.*, *Care of the Hopelessly Ill: Proposed Clinical Criteria for Physician Assisted Suicide*, 327 New Eng. J. Med. 1380, 1381 (1992).

38. *See* Or. Rev. Stat. § 127.800–.995.

39. *See* note 37, *supra*.

40. Gerrit Kimsma and Evert van Leeuwen, *Euthanasia and Assisted Suicide in the Netherlands and the USA: Comparing Practices, Justifications and Key Concepts in Bioethics and Law*, in *Asking to Die: Inside the Dutch Debate about Euthanasia* 51 (David C. Thomasma ed., 1998) (hereinafter Kimsma and van Leeuwen, *Euthanasia and Assisted Suicide*).

41. John Keown, *Euthanasia, Ethics and Public Policy: An Argument Against Legalisation* 33 (2002) (hereinafter Keown, *EEPP*); *see also* Rights of the Terminally Ill Act, §§ 3–4, 1995, pt. 1 (N. Terr. Austl. Laws) (defining "assist[ance]" in suicide to embrace euthanasia—namely, to include "the administration of a substance to the patient"), *available at* http://www.notes.nt.gov.au/dcm/legislat/legislat.nsf/d989974724db65b1482561cf0017cbd2/4d6231fd5c4f4e396925657000094754/$FILE/Repr030.pdf (site visited October 1, 2005); Kimsma and van Leeuwen, *Euthanasia and Assisted Suicide* (arguing that there is no "difference . . . perceived if a physician hands over a cup to drink or gives an injection by needle").

42. Kimsma and van Leeuwen, *Euthanasia and Assisted Suicide* 135, 142–43.

43. Epstein, *Mortal Peril* 340 (1999).

44. Margaret Otlowski, *Voluntary Euthanasia and the Common Law* 466 (2000) (hereinafter Otlowski, *Voluntary Euthanasia*).

45. *See Compassion in Dying*, 79 F.3d at 831.

CHAPTER 2: THE *GLUCKSBERG* AND *QUILL* CONTROVERSIES

1. Wash. Rev. Code § 9A.36.060(1) (1994).

2. U.S. Const. amend. XIV.

3. *See, e.g.*, John Hart Ely, *Democracy and Distrust* 18 (1981) ("[T]here is simply no avoiding the fact that the word that follows 'due' is 'process.' . . . Familiarity breeds inattention, and we apparently need periodic reminding that 'substantive due process' is a contradiction in terms—sort of like 'green pastel redness.'"); Robert H. Bork, *The Tempting of America: The Political Seduction of the Law* 238 (1989) ("[Since the recognition of substantive due process] involved transforming the clause from one about due process to due substance, without any guide in constitutional text, history, or structure as to what substance might be due, there was then no limitation on its meaning, natural or otherwise. The clause now 'means' anything that can attract five votes on the Court.").

4. *Daniels v. Williams*, 474 U.S. 327 (1986).

5. *Compassion in Dying*, 850 F. Supp. at 1459.

6. 505 U.S. 833 (1992).

7. *Id.* at 851.

8. *Compassion in Dying*, 850 F. Supp. at 1459.

9. *Id.* at 1459–60 (internal quotation marks and brackets omitted).

10. 497 U.S. 261 (1990).

11. *Id.* at 278 (this right "may be inferred from our prior decisions"); *id.* at 279 ("the logic of the cases . . . would embrace such a liberty interest").

12. *Compassion in Dying*, 850 F. Supp. at 1461.

13. *Id.*

14. *Compassion in Dying*, 49 F.3d at 591.

15. *Id.*

16. *Id.*

17. *Id.* at 590–91.

18. *Id.* at 594.

19. 388 U.S. 1 (1967).

20. 79 F.3d at 805.

21. *Id.* at 806.

22. *Id.*

23. *Id.* at 807–8.

24. *Id.* at 808–9.

25. *Id.* at 813.

26. *Id.* at 816.

27. *Id.* at 820 (emphasis added).

28. *Id.*

29. *Id.*

30. *Id.* at 831–32.

31. Epstein, *Mortal Peril* 340.

32. *See* ch. 1, *supra*.

33. Section 125.15(3) of the New York penal code provides in pertinent part that "a person is guilty of manslaughter in the second degree when: * * * 3. He intentionally . . . aids another person to commit suicide." Section 120.30 provides that "[a] person is guilty of promoting a suicide attempt when he intentionally . . . aids another person to attempt suicide."

34. *Quill*, 870 F. Supp. at 83.

35. *Id.*

36. *See* N.Y. Pub. Health Law §§ 2960–2979 (McKinney 1994 & Supp. 1997); *id.* §§ 2980–2994 (McKinney 1994 & Supp. 1997).

37. *Quill*, 870 F. Supp. at 84.

38. *Id.* The court declined to apply strict scrutiny because, it held, New York's distinction between persons refusing care and those seeking assistance in suicide or euthanasia did not infringe upon any fundamental right and was not based on any suspect classification, such as race. *See id.* at 84, 85.

39. *Id.* at 84.

40. *Quill*, 80 F.3d at 729.

41. *Id.*

42. *Id.* (quoting *Cruzan*, 497 U.S. at 296–97 [Scalia, J., concurring]).

43. *Id.* at 731.

44. *Id.* at 738.

45. Guido Calabresi, *A Common Law for the Age of Statutes* (1982), *cited in Quill*, 80 F.3d at 735.

46. *Quill*, 80 F.3d at 738.

47. *Id.* at 743.

48. 5 U.S. 137 (1803).

49. *Quill*, 80 F.3d at 742.

50. *New York Task Force on Life and the Law* at vii.

51. *See, e.g.*, Biskupic, *Unanimous Decision*.

52. *See, e.g. Quill*, 521 U.S. at 809 (O'Connor, J., concurring); *id.* at 809–10 (Souter, J., concurring in the judgments), *id.* at 809 (Ginsburg, J., concurring in the judgments). *But see Glucksberg*, 521 U.S. at 740 (Stevens, J., concurring) (arguing that cases posed as-applied, not facial, challenges). A facial challenge to a legislative act is "the most difficult challenge to mount successfully since the challenger must establish that no set of circumstances exists under which the Act would be valid." *United States v. Salerno*, 481 U.S. 739, 745 (1987). By contrast, an as-applied challenge requires the challenger to establish only that the Act is unconstitutional as applied to his or her particular set of facts. *Glucksberg*, 521 U.S. at 745 n.3.

53. *Glucksberg*, 521 U.S. at 721.

54. *Id.* at 709.

55. *Id.* at 710–11.

56. *Id.* at 714.

57. *Id.* at 713–16.

58. *Id.* at 728 (discussing Thomas Marzen, *et al.*, *Suicide: A Constitutional Right?*, 24 Duquesne L. Rev. 1 [1985]).

59. *Id.* at 724.

60. *Id.* at 725.

61. *Id.*

62. *Id.* at 727–28 (citations omitted).

63. *Quill,* 521 U.S. at 801.

64. *Id.*

65. *Id.* at 802.

66. *Id.* (quotation marks omitted).

67. *Id.* at 801.

68. *Id.* at 802 (internal quotation marks omitted).

69. *Glucksburg,* 521 U.S. at 736 (O'Connor, J., concurring). Justice Ginsburg added separately, and somewhat cryptically, that she "concurr[ed] in the Court's judgment in these cases substantially for the reasons stated [in]" Justice O'Connor's separate opinion, yet nowhere explained where exactly she differed (or agreed) with Justice O'Connor's (or the Court's) reasoning. *Id.* at 789 (Ginsburg, J., concurring). Justice Breyer joined Justice O'Connor's opinion "except insofar as it joins the opinion of the Court." *Id.* (Breyer, J., concurring).

70. *Id.* at 736.

71. *Id.* at 736–37.

72. *Id.* at 737–38.

73. *Id.* at 738.

74. *Id.* at 769.

75. *Id.* at 787–88.

76. *Id.* at 788.

77. *Id.*

78. *Id.* at 741.

79. *Id.* (emphasis added).

80. *Id.* at 751.

81. *Id.*

82. *Id.*

83. *Id.* at 750.

84. As Chief Justice Rehnquist put it: "Americans are engaged in an earnest and profound debate about the morality, legality, and practicality of physician-assisted suicide. Our holding permits this debate to continue, as it should in a democratic society." *Glucksberg,* 521 U.S. at 735.

Chapter 3: The Debate over History

1. Perhaps most notably, *see* Ely, *Democracy and Distrust* 62. *See also* Oliver Wendell Holmes, *The Path of the Law,* 10 Harv. L. Rev. 457, 469 (1897) ("It is revolting to have no better reason for a rule of law than that so it was laid down in the time of Henry IV. It is still more revolting if the grounds upon which it was laid down have vanished long since, and the rule simply persists from blind imitation of the past.").

2. *Moore v. City of East Cleveland,* 431 U.S. 494, 503 n.12 (1977).

3. 291 U.S. 97, 102 (1934).

4. *Id.* at 105.

5. *Id.*

6. *Id.* at 114–16. Earlier cases that Justice Cardozo cited as antecedents for his history test did use history to guide their analysis, but they did not seem to afford it an especially favored role in resolving due process disputes. *See, e.g., Twining v. New Jersey*, 211 U.S. 78, 106–7 (1908) (noting absence of historical support for the proposed right, but proceeding to consider whether it should be recognized anyway because reason alone suggests that it is "a fundamental principle of liberty and justice which inheres in the very idea of a free government and is the inalienable right of a citizen of such a government").

7. *Wisconsin v. Yoder*, 406 U.S. 205, 232 (1972).

8. 431 U.S. 494, 504 (1977) (plurality opinion).

9. 491 U.S. 110 (1989).

10. *Id.* at 127 n.6.

11. *Glucksberg*, 521 U.S. at 710–19.

12. *See Michael H.*, 491 U.S. at 132.

13. *Glucksberg*, 521 U.S. at 777 (internal quotation marks omitted).

14. *See Compassion in Dying*, 79 F.3d at 806–10.

15. 405 U.S. 438 (1972).

16. 410 U.S. 113, 130 (1973).

17. 539 U.S. 558, 573 (2003).

18. *Id.* at 598.

19. *See, e.g.*, Bork, *The Tempting of America*.

20. 539 U.S. at 572–73.

21. *Id.*

22. *Id.* at 588, 590 (Scalia, J., dissent).

23. A. W. Mair, *Suicide*, 12 *Encylopedia of Religion and Ethics* 26–30 (J. Hastings ed., 1992).

24. Plato, *Phaedo* § 61c (Benjamin Jowett ed., 2000).

25. *Id.* § 62b–6.

26. Plato, *Laws* § 873c7 (David Gallup ed., 1999).

27. *Id.* § 854c4–5.

28. Plato, *The Republic* §§ 407(d), 408(a), 409e–410a (Allan Bloom, ed., 1991).

29. Of course, whether these practices can be distinguished rationally is another matter, one we will take up in chapter 4.

30. Aristotle, *Nicomachean Ethics* § 1138(a)–(b) (J.A.K. Thomson, trans., 1953) (hereinafter Aristotle, *Ethics*).

31. *Id.* § 1135(a).

32. *Id.*

33. *Id.*

34. *Id.* § 1138.

35. *Id.*

36. *Id.*

37. *See, e.g.*, Cicero, *De Finibus III* 60 (Rackham trans., 1914).

38. *See* Cicero, *De Senectute* xx (J. W. Allebn & J. Greenough, trans. & ed., 1866) (stating Pythagoras's view that people should not "depart from their guard or station in life without the order of their commander, that is, of God").

39. *Letters, Principal Doctrines, and Vatican Sayings* 68, Vatican Saying 38 (Russell Geer trans., 1997).

40. 11 *The Civil Law* 129 (S. Scott trans., 1932) (Justinian Digest, bk. 48, tit. 21, para. 3).

41. *Id.*

42. E. Cobham Brewer, *The Dictionary of Phrase and Fable* (1894).

43. Robert Barry, *The Development of the Roman Catholic Teachings on Suicide*, 9 Notre Dame J.L. Ethics & Pub. Pol'y 449, 464 (1995).

44. Augustine, *The City of God* Bk. 1, ch. 20 (R. W. Dyson, ed., 1998).

45. *Select Library of Nicene and Post-Nicene Fathers of the Christian Church* § 185.3.12 (various dates and translators, Eerdmans, rpt. 1976–79).

46. *Id.* § 173.5.

47. Augustine, *The City of God*, bk. I, ch. 27.

48. *Id.*, ch. 17.

49. Thomas Aquinas, *Summa Theologiae* (hereinafter "Aquinas, *ST*"), part 2 of the Second Part, Q.64, a.3.

50. *Id.* part 1 of the Second Part, Q.94, a.1–2; part 1 of the Second Part, Q.10, a.1.

51. *Id.* part 2 of the Second Part, Q.64, a.7.

52. Paragraph 65 of the latter condemns euthanasia as "a grave violation of the law of God, since it is the deliberate and morally unacceptable killing of a human person." Euthanasia is defined in sections 64 and 65 in terms that apply to assisted suicide as well. *See also* National Conference of Catholic Bishops Committee for Pro-Life Activities, *Nutrition and Hydration: Moral and Pastoral Reflections*, 15 J. Contemp. H.L. 2 Pol'y 455 (1999).

53. *See New York Task Force on Life and the Law* 91 (reporting views of American Lutheran Church, the Episcopal Church, and branches of Judaism). *Cf.* Damien Keown, *Buddhism and Bioethics* 44–45 (1995) (discussing respect for human life in Eastern thought).

54. "The crown and flower of English medieval jurisprudence." 1 Frederick Pollock and Frederic Maitland, *The History of English Law before the Time of Edward I* 206 (2d ed. 1952).

55. Bracton, *On the Laws and Customs of England* 424 (Samuel E. Thorne ed., 1968) (hereinafter Bracton).

56. *Id.*

57. *Id.*

58. Michael MacDonald & Terence Murphy, *Sleepless Souls: Suicide in Early Modern England* 22 (1990) (hereinafter MacDonald & Murphy, *Sleepless Souls*).

59. *See* Bracton 424.

60. William Meskill, *Is Suicide Murder?* 3 Colum. L. Rev. 379, 380 (1903).

61. 1 Matthew Hale, *Pleas of the Crown* 411 (1847) (hereinafter Hale, *Pleas*).

62. Edward Coke, *Third Institute* 54 (1644).

63. 4 William Blackstone, *Commentaries on the Laws of England* 189 (1769) (hereinafter Blackstone, *Commentaries*).

64. *E.g.*, 1 Hale, *Pleas* 411; Coke, *Third Institute* 54.

65. Coke, *Third Institute* 54.

66. Glanville Williams hypothesized about the origin of this ancient practice: "An obvious explanation of the choice of the crossroads is that they also helped to lay the ghost by making the sign of the cross; but though this may have contributed to the survival of the custom into the Christian era, it has a much earlier ancestry. In early times and among primitive peoples even honorable burial was frequently performed at cross-roads, but this spot was specifically chosen for murderers and suicides. Among the reasons that have

been suggested for the practice are that the constant traffic over the grave would help to keep the ghost down; or that the number of roads would confuse it and so prevent it from finding its way home." Glanville Williams, *The Sanctity of Life and the Criminal Law* 233 (1958) (hereinafter Williams, *Sanctity of Life*).

67. W. and M. Quart., 16, 181 (Aug. 26, 1661).

68. Arthur P. Scott, *Criminal Law in Colonial Virginia* 108 n.193 (1930).

69. *See Commonwealth v. Mink*, 123 Mass. 422, 425–26 (1877), *modified by Commonwealth v. Catalina*, 556 N.E.2d 973, 975–80 (Mass. 1990).

70. *The Colonial Laws of Massachusetts of 1672* (William H. Whitmore ed., 1887).

71. *The Earliest Acts and Laws of the Colony of Rhode Island and the Providence Plantations*, 1647–1719 19 (J. Cushing ed., 1977).

72. *1 The Earliest Printed Laws of South Carolina, 1692–1734*, 192 (J. Cushing ed., 1978).

73. *Id.* at 322.

74. MacDonald & Murphy, *Sleepless Souls* 346–47.

75. *Id.* at 138–39.

76. *The Earliest Printed Laws of Pennsylvania, 1681–1713* 209 (J. Cushing ed., 1978) ("If any person, through Temptation or melancholly, shall Destroy himself, his Estate, Real & Personal, shall, notwithstanding, Descend to his wife and Children or Relations as if he had Died a natural death").

77. *See* N.H. Const. pt. 2, art. 89 (1783); Md. Const. of 1776, decl. of rts. § 24; Del. Const. of 1792, art. 1, § 15; N.J. Const. of 1776, art. 17; N.C. Const. of 1778; R.I. Pub. Laws § 53, at 604 (1798).

78. *Airedale N.H.S. Trust v. Bland*,[1993] A.C. 789, 827.

79. Dan Brock, *Voluntary Active Euthanasia*, Hastings Center Report 22, no. 2 at 19 (1992).

80. 850 F. Supp. at 1465.

81. *See e.g.*, *Mink*, 123 Mass. at 429. *See also* Wayne LaFave & Austin Scott, *Criminal Law* § 7.8, at 649 (1986); *New York Task Force on Life and the Law* 55.

82. 2 Zephaniah Swift, *A System of the Laws of the State of Connecticut* 304 (1796).

83. 2 Thomas Jefferson, *The Papers of Thomas Jefferson* 496, 496n. (J. P. Boyd ed., 1952) (hereinafter Boyd, *Jefferson Papers*).

84. 6 Boyd, *Jefferson Papers* 152–53.

85. *Mink*, 123 Mass. at 429.

86. 2 Boyd, *Jefferson Papers* 325.

87. *See* Yeates Conwell & Eric Caine, *Rational Suicide and the Right to Die: Reality and Myth*, 325 New Eng. J. Med. 1100, 1101 (1991) ("90 to 100 percent of [suicides] die while they have a diagnosable psychiatric illness"); Edwin S. Schneidman, *Rational Suicide and Psychiatric Disorders*, 326 New Eng. J. Med. 889 (1992); Herbert Hendin and Gerald Klerman, *Physician-Assisted Suicide: The Dangers of Legalization*, 150 Am. J. of Psychiatry 143 (1993); Erwin Stengel, *Suicide and Attempted Suicide* 52 (1964) (arguing one-third of people committing suicide suffer from "a neurosis or psychosis or severe personality disorder"); Eli Robins, *The Final Months* 10, 12 (1981) (94 percent of suicides studied had a mental disorder); Brian Barraclough *et al.*, *A Hundred Cases of Suicide: Clinical Aspects*, 125 Brit. J. Psychiatry 355, 356 (1974) (93 percent of suicides studied suffered from a mental disorder).

88. Model Penal Code § 210.5, cmt. 2.

89. *See, e.g.,* 2 G. C. Addison, *Law of Torts* § 819, at 708 (3d ed. 1870) ("[A] person disordered in his mind who seems disposed to do mischief to himself or another person, the restraint being both necessary for the safety of the lunatic and the preservation of the public peace.").

90. N.Y. Mental Hyg. Law § 9.41 (McKinney Supp. 1983–84).

91. Cal. Welf. & Inst. Code § 5250 (West 1984). *See also* Kate E. Bloch, *The Role of Law in Suicide Prevention: Beyond Civil Commitment—A Bystander Duty to Report Suicide Threats,* 39 Stan. L. Rev. 929, 934 n.36 (1987) (compiling citations to similar statutes in most states).

92. 96.*See, e.g., Rex v. Russell,* [1832] 1 Moody C.C. 356; *Regina v. Ledington,* [1839] 9 Car. & P. 79; 2 Francis Wharton, *Criminal Law* 31–32 (1874). There is a curious tension between this rule and the common law's decision to punish suicide. On the one hand, the common law deemed the deceased beyond the reach of legal process for the purposes of inquiring whether he was a principal in his own murder so that his accessory might be tried. On the other hand, the common law considered the deceased within legal process for the purpose of investing a coroner's jury to inquire into whether the deceased was competent and an adult when he took his own life (and to determine that he did, in fact, kill himself), as well as for the purposes of "punishing" him by forfeiture of his assets to the crown or state.

93. *See* 24 & 25 Vict. ch. 23, § 94; Wharton, *Criminal Law* 33 (noting that by 1874 the "old technical rule" that an accessory before the fact could not be convicted before the principal had been "corrected by statute" in many American states).

94. *See, e.g., Rex v. Croft,* [1944] K.B. 296 (C.C.A.) (upholding conviction of the survivor of a suicide pact); *Commonwealth v. Hicks,* 82 S.W. 265, 267 (Ky. App. 1904) ("In this case, it would be impossible to punish the principal; but it is not believed that under any sound reasoning the accessory [before the fact] would thereby go scot free."); *Burnett v. People,* 68 N.E. 505, 511 (Ill. 1903) ("it becomes immaterial what was the character of the crime committed by the principal or whether there was any crime"); *Regina v. Gaylor,* [1857] D. & B. 228, 169 Eng. Rep. 1011 (C.C.R.) (upholding conviction).

95. Williams, *The Sanctity of Life* 265.

96. *See, e.g.,* Richard Wolfrom, *The Criminal Aspect of Suicide,* 39 Dick. L. Rev. 47 (1934–35).

97. *Kevorkian,* 527 N.W.2d at 731.

98. *The Field Code* § 231 ("Aiding Suicide. Every person, who willfully, in any manner, advises, encourages, abets or assists another person in taking his own life, is guilty of aiding suicide."). The influence of the Field Code can be readily seen by comparing its language to current assisted suicide laws in several states. *See* appendix A, *infra.*

99. Herbert Spencer, *A System of Synthetic Philosophy* (1860).

100. *See, e.g.,* Charles Darwin, 1 *Descent of Man and Selection in Relation to Sex* 138 (2d ed. 1882).

101. *Id.*

102. Francis Galton, *Inquiries into Human Faculty and Its Development* 24 (1883), *quoted in* Diane Paul, *Controlling Human Heredity: 1865 to the Present* 3 (1996).

103. 274 U.S. 200 (1927).

104. *Id.* at 205.

105. *Id.* at 207. The sentiment in *Buck* is all the more remarkable for the fact that it

postdates and stands in such stark contrast to the more enlightened recognition in *Meyer v. Nebraska*, 262 U.S. 390 (1923), that "'putting away . . . the offspring of the inferior, or of the better when they chance to be deformed' [would] do . . . violence to both the letter and spirit of the Constitution." *Id*. at 402.

106. *Death for Insane and Incurable Urged by Illinois Homeopaths*, New York Times, May 9, 1931, at 4.

107. Earnest Hooton, *The Future Quality of the American People*, 154 The Churchman 11–12 (1940).

108. William G. Lennox, *Should They Live? Certain Economic Aspects of Medicine*, 7 The American Scholar, 454–66 (1938).

109. Nebraska Legislature, 52nd Session, Legislative Bill No. 135.

110. *Id*.

111. Ian Dowbiggin, *A Merciful End: The Euthanasia Movement in America*, 48–49 (2003) (hereinafter Dowbiggin, *A Merciful End*).

112. *Id*. at 47.

113. *Id*. at 48.

114. *Dr. Potter Backs "Mercy Killings"*, New York Times, Feb. 3, 1936, at 13.

115. Martin A. Elks, "*The Lethal Chamber": Further Evidence for the Euthanasia Option*, 31 Mental Retardation 201–7 (1993) (hereinafter Elks, *The Lethal Chamber*).

116. *Id*.

117. Dowbiggin, *A Merciful End* 54–55.

118. Philadelphia Inquirer, Nov. 18, 1915, at 7.

119. Sherwood Anderson, *Dinner in Thessaly*, 95 The Forum 40–41 (1936); Abraham Wolbarst, *The Right to Die*, 94 The Forum 330–32 (1935).

120. Madison Grant, *The Passing of the Great Race* 45, 47 (1916).

121. Stephen Louis Kuepper, *Euthanasia in America, 1890–1960: The Controversy, the Movement, and the Law* 38–39, Ph.D. diss., Rutgers University, 1981 (citing William J. Robinson, *Euthanasia, Medico-Pharmaceutical*, 16 Critic and Guide 85–90 [1913]).

122. *Id*.

123. Dowbiggin, *A Merciful End* 55.

124. *Id*. at 57.

125. *Id*.

126. Minutes of the March 30, 1938, meeting of the board of directors of the National Society for the Legalization of Euthanasia. Potter notes euthanasia for "incurable idiots" was the ESA's "ultimate aim." Dowbiggin, *A Merciful End* at 57 n.71.

127. *See e.g.*, Dowbiggin, *A Merciful End* 59–60; Foster Kennedy, *The Problem of Social Control of the Congenital Defective*, 99 Am. J. of Psychiatry 13–16 (1942). *See also The Right to Kill*, Time, Nov. 18, 1935, at 53–54 (Nobel Prize winner at the Rockefeller Institute urging that "sentimental prejudice . . . not obstruct the quiet and painless disposition of incurable . . . and hopeless lunatics"); D. McKim, *Heredity and Human Progress* 189, 193 (1900)(New York physician advocating the elimination of severely handicapped children, including "idiots," most "imbeciles," and the greater number of epileptics, for society's protection, via a "gentle, painless death" by the inhalation of carbonic gas).

128. *See, e.g.*, Dowbiggin, *A Merciful End* 61–64.

129. *Id*. at 65.

130. *Hitler's Debt to America*, The Guardian (Feb. 6, 2004), *available at* http://www.

guardian.co.uk/g2/story /0,3604,1142027,00.html (site visited Feb. 16, 2005) (reviewing Edwin Black, *The War against the Weak: Eugenics and Americas Campaign to Create a Master Race*, Four Walls Eight Windows [2003]).

131. *Id.*

132. Dowbiggin, *A Merciful End* 68.

133. *Id.* at 69.

134. *Id. See also* Leo Alexander, *Medical Science under Dictatorship*, 241 New Eng. J. Med. 39–47 (1949), *available at* http://www.catholicculture.org/docs /doc_view.cfm?recnum=492 (site visited Feb. 16, 2005) (hereinafter Alexander, *Science under Dictatorship*).

135. Dowbiggin, *A Merciful End* 69.

136. *Id.* at 70.

137. *Id.*

138. Alexander, *Science under Dictatorship*.

139. *Id.*

140. Williams, *The Sanctity of Life* 296.

141. David K. Gittleman, *Euthanasia and Assisted Suicide*, 92 Southern Med. J. 370 (Apr. 1999).

142. Dowbiggin, *A Merciful End* 71–72.

143. *Id.* at 71.

144. *Id.*

145. *Id.*

146. Williams, *The Sanctity of Life* 309–10; *see also* Glanville Williams, *Euthanasia and Abortion*, 38 Colo. L. Rev. 178–201 (1966).

147. Williams, *The Sanctity of Life* 311.

148. Dowbiggin, *A Merciful End* 159.

149. *Id.*

150. *Id.* at 126 (citing Olive Ruth Russell, *Freedom to Choose Death: A Discussion of Euthanasia*, lecture given at the Chevy Chase Presbyterian Church [May 20, 1973], NAC, MG31-K13 vol. 2, file 21).

151. Dowbiggin, *A Merciful End* 130.

152. *Id.*

153. *Id.* at 141.

154. *Id.*

155. Dowbiggin, *Merciful End* 159.

156. Rita Marker, *Deadly Compassion: The Death of Ann Humphry and the Case against Euthanasia* 230 (1993); Sue Woodman, *Last Rights: The Struggle over the Right to Die* 122–26 (1998).

157. Derek Humphry and Mary Clement, *Freedom to Die: People Politics and the Right to Die Movement* 339–40, 342, 347, 348 (2000).

158. Dowbiggin, *A Merciful End* 159; *see also, e.g.,* John Griffiths *et al.*, *Euthanasia and Law in the Netherlands* 285–92 (1998); Frances M. Kamm, *Physician-Assisted Suicide, Euthanasia, and Intending Death*, in *Physician Assisted Suicide: Expanding the Debate* 28, 35–36 (Margaret P. Battin *et al.* eds., 1998) (hereinafter Kamm, *Physician-Assisted Suicide*) (stating that a doctor has a "duty to relieve physical suffering" and provide a requested lethal dose as well as personally kill patients); Patricia S. Mann, *Meanings of*

Death, in *Expanding the Debate* 11, 21–22 (Margaret P. Battin *et al.* eds., 1998) (here inafter Mann, *Meanings of Death*).

159. Dworkin, *Life's Dominion* 228–29 (emphasis added).

160. Dan Brock, *Life and Death: Philosophical Essays in Biomedical Ethics* 372, 373 (1993).

161. *Id.* at 109.

162. Margaret Pabst Battin, *Euthanasia: The Fundamental Issues*, in *The Least Worth Death: Essays in Bioethics on the End of Life* 120 (1994).

163. *Id.* at 121.

164. *Id.*

165. Norman Cantor, *On Kamisar, Killing, and the Future of Physician-Assisted Death*, 102 Mich. L. Rev. 1793, 1825 (2004) (hereinafter Cantor, *On Kamisar*).

166. *Id.* (internal citations omitted).

167. *Id.* at 1829–30.

168. *Id.* at 1830.

169. Peter Singer, *Rethinking Life and Death* 210–12 (1994).

170. *Id.* at 210–17.

171. *Id.* at 213.

172. *Id.*

173. *Id.* at 198–99.

174. *Id.* at 215. Nor is the sort of thing Singer advocates unthinkable in modern America. *See, e.g.*, R. H. Gross *et al.*, *Early Management and Decision-Making for the Treatment of Myelomeningocele*, 72 Pediatrics 450, 456 (1983) (reporting on the results of selection of handicapped newborns for treatment between 1977 and 1982 at Oklahoma University Health Sciences Center that babies were provided—or denied—treatment based on such factors as their ambulatory potential, according to a formula that also factored in the "contribution anticipated from his home and family and society").

175. Cantor, *On Kamisar* at 1826. Cantor argues that Dutch nonvoluntary euthanasia practices are sound and desirable, *id.* at 1828, an issue we will explore in chapter 7.

176. *See* ch. 7.1, *infra*.

177. Dowbiggin, *A Merciful End* 176.

178. *Id.* at 177.

179. Model Penal Code § 210.5, cmt. 5, at 101 n.23 (discussing state statutes).

180. *Id.* § 210.5(1) and (2): "(1) *Causing Suicide as Criminal Homicide.* A person may be convicted of criminal homicide for causing another to commit suicide only if he purposely causes such suicide by force, duress, or deception. (2) *Aiding or Soliciting Suicide as an Independent Offense.* A person who purposely aids or solicits another to commit suicide is guilty of a felony of the second degree if his conduct causes such suicide or an attempted suicide, and otherwise of a misdemeanor."

181. *See New York Task Force on Life and the Law.*

182. *See* appendix A, *infra*.

183. *See* appendix A, *infra*; Valerie J. Vollmar, *Physician Assisted Suicide Website at* http://www.willamette.edu/wucl/pas/ (site visited Mar. 1, 2005); *History of Euthanasia*, http://www.euthanasia. com/history.html (site visited Mar. 1, 2005).

184. *See Glucksberg*, 521 U.S. at 717 n.15 (listing failed state legislative proposals from 1994 to 1997); Alaska, H.B. 371 (1996) (died in the House State Affairs Committee); Ari-

zona H.B. 2454 (2003) (died in committee); California A.B. 1592 (1999) (passed on an 8–7 vote in the Assembly Appropriations Committee, but was not introduced in the Senate), A.B. 1080 (1995) (withdrawn by sponsor), A.B. 1310 (1995) (died without hearing); Colorado H.B. 1185 (1996) (defeated 7–4 in the House Committee on Health, Environment, Welfare and Institutions), H.B. 1308 (1995) (tabled in committee); Hawaii S.B. 391 (2003) (referred to committee), H.B. 2487, H.B. 2491 (2001) (passed in the House and the Senate by votes of 30–20 and 13–12, respectively, but was ultimately rejected 11–14 in the Senate upon a second reading), H.B. 709 (2001), H.B. 418, H.B. 347, H.B. 1155, S.B. 981, S.B. 692, S.B. 1037 (1999), H.B. 1669, S.B. 2095, S.B. 2372, (1997); Illinois H.B. 691 (1997) (died in committee); Louisiana S.B. 128 (1999) (withdrawn from further consideration); Maine L.D. 916 (1998) (rejected in the House by a vote of 90-42), H.B. 663 (1997), L.D. 916, 748 (1996); Maryland H.B. 474 (1996) (rejected by House Environmental Affairs Committee 15-4), H.B. 933 (1995) (rejected by House Environmental Affairs Committee 16-5 in 1996); Massachusetts H. 1543 (1997) (died in the 1997–98 legislative session), H. 3173 (1995); Michigan H.B. 5754 (1998), S.B. 653 (1997), S.B. 640, H.B. 4134 (1995) (died in committee); Mississippi H.B. 1023 (1996) (stalled in House Judiciary Committee); Nebraska L.B. 70 (1999), L.B. 406 (1997), L.B. 1259 (1996) (died in Judiciary Committee); New Hampshire S.B. 44 (1999) (died in Senate), H.B. 1433-FN (1998) (died in Committee on Judiciary and Family Law), H.B. 339 (1996) (rejected by House of Representatives 256- 90); New Mexico S.B. 446 (1995) (tabled 6–1 in the Senate Judiciary Committee); New York S.B. 677 (2001) (referred to the Committee on Investigations, Taxation, and Government Operations), S.B. 4834 (1999), S. 1683, S. 5024-A, A. 6333 (1995) (died without a hearing); Rhode Island S.B. 2763 (2001), S.B. 2869 (1998), S.B. 2985 (1995) (died in Judiciary Committee); Vermont H.B. 318 (2003) (tabled for 2004 in the House and Senate), H.B. 493 (1999), H.B. 109 (1997), H.B. 355 (1995); Washington H.B. 6576 (1998), S.B. 5596 (1995); Wisconsin A.B. 348, S.B. 169 (2003), A.B. 417, S.B. 184 (2001), A.B. 297, S.B. 124 (1999), A.B. 32, S.B. 27 (1997), S.B. 90 (1995); Wyoming S.B. 7 (2004). *See* Brief of Amici Curiae United States Catholic Conference *et al.* at 8 n.1, *Washington v. Glucksberg*, 521 U.S. 702 (1997) (No. 96–110) (describing unsuccessful proposals between 1994 and 1997); Death with Dignity National Center, http://www.deathwithdignity.org/law/statutes.asp (site visited Jan. 11, 2005) (same); Rita L. Marker, *Assisted Suicide: The Continuing Debate,* International Task Force on Euthanasia and Assisted Suicide, http://www.internationaltaskforce.org/cd.htm (site visited Dec. 28, 2004) (chronicling state efforts to pass physician-assisted suicide initiatives); Vollmar, *Recent Developments in Physician-Assisted Suicide,* http://www.willamette.edu/wucl/pas (site visited Jan. 24, 2005) (tracking legislative efforts and ballot initiatives to date). In 1995, legislators in Connecticut also attempted to enact an affirmative defense to a second-degree manslaughter for doctors assisting in the suicide of those in a "terminal condition." H.B. 6982 (1995).

185. Michigan voters overwhelmingly rejected Proposal B, an Oregon-styled law, 2,090,357 to 853,957 in 1998. Vollmar, *Recent Developments in Physician-Assisted Suicide,* http://www.willamette.edu/wucl/pas/1999_reports/031999.html (site visited Jan. 24, 2005). Maine voters narrowly defeated a Death with Dignity Initiative 330,671 to 313,303 in 2000. Vollmar, *Recent Developments in Physician-Assisted Suicide,* http://www.willamette.edu/wucl/pas/2000_reports/102000.html#legislation (site visited Jan. 24, 2005).

186. *See* appendix A, *infra.*

187. *See* Mich. Comp. Laws Ann. § 752.1027 (West 2004).

188. *See Kevorkian*, 527 N.W.2d at 716.

189. *See* Mont. Code Ann. § 45-5-105 (West 2003) (defining the crime of assisted suicide as occurring only when "[a] person who purposely aids or solicits another to commit suicide, but such suicide does not occur"); *see also* Annotations to the Montana Code Annotated § 4-5-105 note (2004) ("This section makes it a felony to aid or solicit a suicide attempt which does not result in the death of the victim.").

190. As explained by an annotator's note, those who assist a *successful* suicide may be found guilty of other offenses: "[u]nder the new sections on Causal Relationship Between Conduct and Result, MCA, 45-2-201, and Accountability, MCA, 45-2-302, a person may be convicted of Criminal Homicide, MCA, 45-5-101 (repealed—now deliberate or mitigated homicide, 45-5-102 and 45-5-103, respectively), for causing another to commit suicide—notwithstanding the consent of the victim." Annotations to the Montana Code Annotated § 45-5-105 note.

191. See, e.g., *McMahan v. State*, 53 So. 89, 90–91 (Ala. 1910) (stating that suicide is a common law crime and anyone who is present when someone commits suicide, or advises or counsels someone to commit suicide, is guilty of murder); *Commonwealth v. Mink*, 123 Mass. at 428–29 (discussing involuntary manslaughter); *Kevorkian*, 527 N.W.2d at 716; *State v. Mays*, 307 S.E.2d 655, 656 (W. Va. 1983) (discussing the facts of a case in which a man was convicted of murder for helping another man commit suicide).

192. *See, e.g.*, Ala. Code Ann. § 22-8A-10 (2001); Mass. Ann. Laws ch. 201D, § 12 (2005); Nev. Rev. Stat. Ann. § 449.670(2) (Michie 2000); Ohio Rev. Code Ann. § 2133.12(D) (Anderson 2002); Utah Code Ann. § 75-2-1118 (1993); W. Va. Code Ann. § 16-30-2(a) (Michie 2001).

193. *See* Ala. Code §22-8A-10 (2001); Alaska Stat. Ann. §§ 18.12.080(a), (f) (2004); Ariz. Rev. Stat. Ann. § 36-3210 (West 2005); Ark. Code Ann. §§ 20-13-905(a), (f), 20-17-210(a), (g) (Michie 2004), Cal. Health & Safety Code §§ 7191.5(a), (g) (2004); Cal. Prob. Code Ann. § 4653 (West Supp. 1997); Colo. Rev. Stat. §§ 15-14-504(4), 15-18-112(1), 15-18.5-101(3), 15-18.6-108 (2004); Conn. Gen. Stat. § 19a-575 (2004); Del. Code Ann., tit. 16, § 2512 (2004); D.C. Code § 21-2212 (2004); Fla. Stat. §§ 765.309(1), (2) (2004); Ga. Code Ann. §§ 31-32-11(b), 31-36-2(b) (2004); Idaho Code § 56-1022 (2004); Ill. Comp. Stat., ch. 755, §§ 35/9(f), 40/5, 40/50, 45/2-1 (2004), Ind. Code §§ 16-36-1-13, 16-36-4-19,30-5-5-17 (2004); Iowa Code §§ 144A.11.1-144A.11.6, 144B.12.2 (2005); Kan. Stat. Ann. § 6-28, 109 (2003); Ky. Rev. Stat. § 311.659 (Banks-Baldwin 2004); La. Rev. Stat. 40: §§ 1299.58.10 (A),(B) (2004); Me. Rev. Stat. tit. 18-A, §§ 5-813(b), (c) (2004); Mass. Gen. Laws 201D, § 12 (2005); Md. Health Code Ann. § 5-611(c) (Michie 2004); Mich. Comp. Laws Ann. § 333.5660 (2004); Minn. Stat. §§ 145B.14, 145C.14, (2004); Miss. Code §§ 41-41-227, 41-41-119(1) (Michie 2004); Mo. Rev. Stat. §§ 459.015.3, 459.055(5) (2004); Mont. Code Ann. §§ 50-9-205(1), (7), 50-10-104(1), (6) (2002); Neb. Rev. Stat. §§ 20-412(1), (7), 30-3401(3) (2004); Nev. Rev. Stat. § 449.670(2) (2003); N.H. Rev. Stat. Ann. §§ 137-H:10, 137-H:13, 137-J:1 (2004); N.J. Stat. §§ 26:2H-54(d) (e), 26:2H-77 (2004); N.M. Stat. §§ 24-7A-13(B)(1), (C) (2004); N.Y. Pub. Health Law § 2989(3) (2004); N.C. Gen. Stat. §§ 90-320(b), 90-321(f) (2004) N.D. Cent. Code §§ 23-06.4-01, 23-06.5-01 (2003); Ohio Rev. Code § 2133.12(A), (D) (Anderson 2004); Okla. Stat. Ann. tit. 63, §§ 3101.2 (C), 3101.12(A), (G) (1999); R.I. Gen. Laws §§ 23-4.10-9(a), (f), 23-4.11-10(a), (f) (2004); S.C. Code Ann. §§ 44-77-130, 44-78-50(A), (C), 62-504(O) (Law. Co-op. 2004); S.D. Codified Laws §§ 34-12D-14, 34-12D-20 (Michie

2004); Tenn. Code §§ 32-11-110(a), 39-13-216 (Michie 2004); Tex. Health & Safety Code Ann. §§ 166.047, 099 (Vernon 2004); Utah Code Ann. §§ 75-2-1116, 75-2-1118 (2004); Va. Code § 54.1-2990 (2004); Vt. Stat. Tit. 18 § 5260 (Michie 2005); V.I. Code Ann., tit. 19, §§ 198(a), (g) (2003); Wash. Rev. Code §§ 70,122.070 (1), 70.122.100 (Supp. 1997); W. Va. Code §§ 16-30-10, 16-30C-14 (2003); Wis. Stat. §§ 154.11 (1) (6) 154.25(7), 155.70(7) (2004); Wyo. Stat. Ann. §§ 3-5-211, 35-22-109, 35-22-208 (Michie 2004). *See also* 42 U.S.C. § 14402(b)(1)(2), (4) ("Assisted Suicide Funding Restriction Act of 1997").

194. *See* Assisted Suicide Funding Restriction Act of 1997, Pub. L. No. 105–12, 111 Stat. 23 (1997) (codified at 42 U.S.C. §§ 14401–14408 [2000]).

195. *See, e.g., State v. Fuller*, 278 N.W.2d 756, 761 (Neb. 1979) ("Murder is no less murder because the homicide is committed at the desire of the victim.") (citation omitted); *Turner v. State*, 108 S.W. 1139, 1141 (Tenn. 1908); *Martin v. Commonwealth*, 37 S.E.2d 43 (Va. 1946); N.Y. Penal Law § 125.25 (McKinney 1987) (euthanasia falls under definition of second degree murder).

196. *See, e.g., State v. Cobb*, 625 P.2d 1133, 1136 (Kan. 1981) (rejecting defendant's claim that the court should have instructed the jury on assisted suicide rather than homicide where the defendant "was an active participant in the overt act of shooting [the victim], which caused his death").

197. *See; Model Penal Code*, § 210.5, cmt. at 106; N.Y. Penal Law §§ 125.20(2), 125.25(1)(a) (McKinney 1987).

198. 69 S.W. 529, 530 (Tex. Crim. App. 1902).

199. *Aven v. State*, 277 S.W. 1080 (Tex. Crim. App. 1925).

200. *See* Tex. Penal Code § 22.08 (1999). The statute has been in place for at least three decades in its current formulation. *See id.*

201. Luke Gormally, *Note: Regina v. Arthur*, in *Euthanasia, Clinical Practice and the Law* 177-92 (1994).

202. In 1961 the British Parliament enacted a statute holding that "[a] person who aids, abets, counsels or procures the suicide of another, or an attempt by another to commit suicide, shall be liable on conviction on indictment to imprisonment for a term not exceeding fourteen years." Suicide Act, 1961, ch. 60.

203. *See House of Lords Report* HL Paper, 21-I of 1993–1994 Session. As this manuscript goes to print, the British Parliament is once again reexamining the law of assisted suicide and the possibility of legalization. Notably, the British Medical Association this time has chosen to remain neutral—in contrast to its unequivocal opposition to legalization in earlier iterations of this debate.

204. *Council of Europe's Recommendation 1418* 2–4 (1999).

205. *See* [2001] UKHL 61, 1 A.C. 800.

206. *Id.* Judgment of Lord Bingham of Cornhill § 5.

207. *Id.* § 29.

208. *Id.* (internal quotation marks omitted).

209. *Id.* § 35. Petitioner also raised arguments under other articles of the Human Rights Convention, including those forbidding inhuman torture (Article 3) and guaranteeing freedom of thought (Article 9). These arguments were also rejected.

210. *Pretty v. United Kingdom*, [2002] 2 FCR 97 (Eur. Ct. H.R.). The European Court's handling of the Article 8 issue was notably softer than the Lords'. The European Court began by explaining that, "[w]ithout in any way negating the principle of sanctity of life protected under the Convention, the [C]ourt considers that it is under Article 8 that no-

tions of the quality of life take on significance. . . . The Court is not prepared to exclude that [precluding Ms. Pretty from obtaining assistance in dying] constitutes an interference with her right to respect for private life." *Id.* ¶¶ 65, 67. While suggesting that respect for the sanctity of life and permitting assisted suicide based on quality of life considerations might be reconcilable, the Court did no more to explore or explain that supposition. Instead, the Court proceeded to hold that, even though Ms. Pretty had a valid claim to privacy, states may interfere with such claims to the extent necessary to address "pressing social need" with rules "proportionate to the legitimate aim pursued." *Id.* ¶ 70. Here, the European Court held, the British government had done enough to establish that a blanket ban on assisted suicide is a proportionate (though, the Court heavily hinted, not the only possible) response to the concern that vulnerable persons might be induced or coerced to accept assisted suicide under any other regime. *Id.* ¶ 74.

211. *See* n. 203, *supra.*

212. *See Rodriguez v. British Columbia (Attorney General),* [1993] 3 S.C.R. 519.

213. *See* note chap. 1, note 11, *supra.* Since the Northern Territory's law permitting assisted suicide was struck down by Australia's federal parliament, at least two other Australian states—Tasmania and South Australia—formed panels to study the possibility of legalizing assisted suicide. In both cases, the respective committees have strongly recommended against legalization. *See* Community Development Commitee Report on the Need for Legalisation of Voluntary Euthanasia (1998) Report No. 6 of the Community Development Committee, House of Assembly (Tasmania); Parliament of South Australia, *Inquiry into the Voluntary Euthanasia Bill 1996,* Oct. 20, 1999, *available at* http://www.parliment.tas.gov.au/ctee/old-ctees/euth.htm.

214. *See* nzoom.com, http://onenews. nzoom.com/onenews_detail/ 0,1227,173412-1-7,00.html (site visited July 4, 2003) (noting 1995 effort at legalization was defeated in parliament 61–29); http://www.lifenews.com/intl14.html (a renewed effort in 2003 was also defeated).

215. *See* Euthanasia.com, http://www.euthanasia.com/hung.html (site visited July 4, 2003) (discussing the rejection of a challenge to laws banning assisted suicide by Hungary's highest court).

Chapter 4: Arguments from Fairness and Equal Protection

1. *See, e.g., Cruzan,* 497 U.S. 261; *Superintendent of Belchertown State Sch. v. Saikewicz,* 370 N.E.2d 417 (Mass. 1977); *In re Conroy,* 486 A.2d 1209 (N.J. 1985).

2. *See Cruzan,* 497 U.S. at 270–71; Alan Meisel, *The Right to Die* § 9.7 (1988) & 181–87 (Supp. 1992).

3. *Cruzan,* 497 U.S. at 273.

4. *In re Quinlan,* 355 A.2d 647 (N.J. 1976).

5. *See, e.g.,* Otlowski, *Voluntary Euthanasia* 54–55, 191–92; ch. 4.6, *infra.*

6. *See Quill,* 80 F.3d at 729.

7. *Cruzan,* 497 U.S. at 296 (Scalia, J., concurring).

8. *See Bland,* [1993] A.C. at 881 (opinion of Lord Browne-Wilkinson).

9. *Id.* at 865.

10. *Id.* at 881.

11. *Id.* at 866.

12. *Id.* at 887, 898.

13. *See* U.K. Dept. of Health, *Harold Shipman's Clinical Practice 1974–1998: A Clinical Audit Commissioned by the Chief Medical Officer* (2000) (hereinafter U.K. Dept. of Health, *Harold Shipman's Clinical Practice 1974–1998*) (finding that Shipman, convicted of murdering 15 of his patients, had 297 "excess deaths" compared to other similarly situated physicians).

14. 755 Ill. Comp. Stat., 35/9(f) (emphasis added). For many other analogous examples, *see* ch. 3.9, *supra.*

15. *Quill,* 521 U.S. at 798, 801.

16. "There is perhaps nothing in the entire field of law which has called forth more disagreement, or upon which the opinions are in such a welter of confusion," as causation doctrine. W. Page Keeton (ed.), *Prosser and Keeton on the Law of Torts* 263 (5th ed., 1984) (hereinafter *Prosser and Keeton*).

17. The example is taken from *id.* at 264 & n.6.

18. *See* Deborah Sharp, *Web-Wired Courtroom Lets World Attend Fla. Trial,* Aug. 17, 1999, USA Today, at 3A.

19. *Quill,* 80 F.3d at 729.

20. Epstein, *Mortal Peril* 285.

21. *Id.* at 292.

22. *Quill,* 521 U.S. at 801.

23. *Id.* at 802 (internal quotation marks omitted).

24. *See* 4 *New Catholic Encyclopedia,* Double Effect, Principle of, 1021 (1967).

25. Timothy Quill *et al., The Rule of Double Effect—A Critique of Its Role in End-of-Life Decision Making,* 337 New Eng. J. Med. 1768 (1997) (hereinafter Quill, *The Rule of Double Effect*).

26. *See* ch. 3.3, *supra.*

27. *See* Jeremy Bentham, *Principles of Morals and Legislation* ch. 8. After parsing out intended from unintended consequences and admitting that the "goodness and badness of a man's intentions" is "of no small importance," Bentham (characteristically) argued that a preferable way of determining whether an action is good or bad depends on whether its results bring "pain or pleasure: or on account of its effects." *Id.* We shall take up Benthamite consequentialist arguments for assisted suicide in chapters 7 and 8.

28. Oliver Wendell Holmes, Jr., *The Common Law* 3 (1881) (hereinafter Holmes, *Common Law*).

29. *Cf.* John Finnis, *Intention and Side-Effects, in Liability and Responsibility: Essays in Law and Morals* 61–63 (R. G. Frey and Christopher W. Morris eds., 1991) (hereinafter Finnis, *Intention and Side-Effects*).

30. The underlying link between double effect, individualism, and free will I have sought to identify has been voiced by Charles Fried along these lines:

> It is natural that the most stringent moral judgment should relate to intentional acts. . . . Morality is about the good and the right way of our being in the world *as human beings.* We relate to the world as human beings as we pursue our purposes in the world, as we act intentionally. . . . This primacy of intention explains why in law and morals a sharp line is drawn between the result, [which is intended,] . . . and the concomitant[] [result], [which is not intended.]

Charles Fried, *Right and Wrong* 27 (1978). *See also, e.g.*, Alan Donagan, *The Theory of Morality* 157–64 (1977); John Finnis, *Allocating Risks and Suffering: Some Hidden Traps*, 38 Cleve. St. L. Rev. 193 (1990).

31. *Morrisette v. United States*, 342 U.S. 246, 250 (1952) (Jackson, J.).

32. *Id.* at 251–52. In a case illustrating this point, the U.S. Supreme Court has held that it violates the Eighth Amendment to preclude a felony murder defendant facing potential execution from presenting evidence to the jury that he did not intend the death as a mitigating factor that might help him avoid the ultimate punishment: "[T]his is not to question, of course, that those who engage in serious criminal conduct which poses a substantial risk of violence, as did the present petitioners, deserve serious punishment regardless of whether or not they possess a purpose to take life. And the fact that death results, even unintentionally, from a criminal venture need not and frequently is not regarded by society as irrelevant to the appropriate degree of punishment. But society has made a judgment, which has deep roots in the history of the criminal law, distinguishing at least for purpose of the imposition of the death penalty between the culpability of those who acted with and those who acted without a purpose to destroy human life." *Lockett v. Ohio*, 438 U.S. 586, 626 (1978) (opinion of White, J.).

33. Roscoe Pound, Introduction to Francis Sayre, *Cases on Criminal Law* xxxvi–vii (1927).

34. Glanville Williams, *Oblique Intention* [1987] C.L.J. 417, 425. *See also* Glanville Williams, *Textbook of the Criminal Law* 84–85 (2d ed. 1983) (hereinafter Williams, *Criminal Law*).

35. *See* Williams, *Criminal Law* 85.

36. Andrew Ashworth, *Principles of Criminal Law* 149 (1991) (hereinafter Ashworth, *Criminal Law*).

37. H.L.A. Hart, *Punishment and Responsibility* 119–20 (1968). *See also* A. P. Simester & Winnie Chan, *Intention Thus Far* [1997] Crim. L. R. 704, 715 (arguing that the deaths caused by Williams's hypothetical terrorist are "so intimately bound up with the villain's intended actions as to be inseparable, and it would be wrong to call them mere side effects").

38. *See* Holmes, *Common Law* ch. 1.

39. This example is drawn from M. Cathleen Kaveny, *Inferring Intention from Foresight*, 120 L. Q. Rev. 81, 86 (hereinafter Kavney, *Inferring Intention*).

40. David Orentlicher, *The Legalization of Physician Assisted Suicide: A Very Modest Revolution*, 38 B.C. L. Rev. 443, 456 (1997) (hereinafter Orentlicher, *Legalization*). *See also* Brendan Thompson, *Final Exit: Should the Double Effect Rule Regarding the Legality of Euthanasia in the United Kingdom Be Laid to Rest?*, 33 Vand. J. Transnat'l L. 1035, 1057 (2000) (hereinafter Thompson, *Double Effect*).

41. Thompson, *Double Effect*, 33 Vand. J. Transnat'l L. at 1057 (footnotes omitted).

42. *See* Model Penal Code § 2.02 cmt. 2 (collecting citations to state statutes).

43. *Id.* § 2.02(2)(a)(i).

44. *Id.* § 2.02(2)(b)(ii).

45. *Id.* § 2.02 cmt. 2.

46. 1 National Commission on Reform of Federal Law Working Papers 124 (1971).

47. LaFave & Scott, *Criminal Law* 216.

48. *Id.*

49. *Id.* at 218.

50. For examples where the distinction matters in federal (let alone state) criminal law, *see, e.g., Haupt v. United States,* 330 U.S. 631 (1947); *Dennis v. United States,* 341 U.S. 494 (1951) (treason); *Hartzel v. United States,* 322 U.S. 680 (1944) (espionage); 18 U.S.C. § 81 (arson requires "willful[]" and "malicious[]" conduct); *id.* § 113 (assault: "(a) . . . with intent to commit murder or rape . . . (b) with intent to commit any felony, except murder or rape"); *id.* § 201 (bribery and graft "with intent to influence"); *id.* § 373 (solicitation of another to commit a crime of violence "with intent" that the other person commit such a crime); *id.* § 471 (counterfeiting and forgery "with intent to defraud"); *id.* § 521 ("intend[ing] to promote or further the felonious activities of the criminal street gang"); *id.* § 594 (intimidation of voters "for the purpose of"); *id.* § 1072 ("willfully" concealing escaped prisoners); *id.* § 2101 ("intent" to aid and abet riots).

51. *Restatement (Second) of Torts* § 8A (1965) (emphasis added).

52. Model Penal Code § 2.02(b)(ii).

53. *See Prosser and Keeton* 33–34.

54. *See id.*

55. *See* Model Penal Code § 2.02 cmt. 2.

56. Sir John Smith & Brian Hogan, *Criminal Law* 53–54 (8th ed., 1996) (hereinafter Smith & Hogan, *Criminal Law*). For similar views by other English criminal textbook writers, *see, e.g.,* Ashworth, *Criminal Law* 149–53; Williams, *Criminal Law* 84–87. *But see* Alan R. White, *Grounds of Liability: An Introduction to the Philosophy of the Law* 82–92 (1985) (arguing for respecting intent/foresight distinction in English criminal law).

57. *In Director of Public Prosecutions v. Smith,* [1961] A.C. 290, the Lords effectively turned "intent to inflict grievous bodily harm" into an objective "reasonable person test." There, the Lords held that the defendant committed murder when he drove off with a policeman clinging to his car not because he wished to do the officer harm, but because the death would have been foreseeable by reasonable person in his position. *Smith's* equation of intent not with what the defendant intended or foresaw, but with what a "reasonable person" would have foreseen (a result Holmes might have applauded) was met with "widespread and severe criticism." *Regina v. Woollin,* [1999] 1 A.C. 82. In 1967, Parliament reversed *Smith's* "reasonable person" test, *see* The Criminal Justice Act, 1967, § 8, but, since then, the law surrounding the mens rea element for murder has been "in a state of disarray" and a source of much dispute. *Regina v. Hyam,* [1975] A.C. 55. *See also Regina v. Moloney,* [1985] A.C. 905; *Regina v. Nedrick,* [1986] 1 W.L.R. 1025; *Regina v. Hancock,* [1986] A.C. 455.

58. *Woollin,* [1999] 1 A.C. at 96.

59. The conventional view that intent may be inferred from foresight is the focus of a provocative challenge by M. Cathleen Kaveny. *See* Kavney, *Inferring Intention,* 120 L. Q. Rev. at 86.

60. *Woollin,* [1999] 1 A.C. at 96 (emphasis added).

61. 481 U.S. 137 (1987).

62. 458 U.S. 782 (1982).

63. 481 U.S. at 143 (internal quotation marks omitted).

64. *Id.* at 144 (internal quotation marks omitted).

65. *Id.* at 150.

66. *Id.* at 151–52.

67. *See id.* at 154–58 (discussing, *inter alia, Lockett,* 438 U.S. at 625–26; *see* n.32, *supra*). While the Court's holding clearly distinguishes between intent and at least some species of foreseeability, in dicta the Court arguably created some needless confusion. Quoting the passage from LaFave and Scott's treatise discussed above, the Court noted that "[t]raditionally one intends certain consequences when he desires that his acts cause those consequences or knows that those consequences are substantially certain to result." 481 U.S. at 150 (internal quotation marks omitted). But, in its dicta, the Court would have been better to acknowledge the next sentence from LaFave and Scott, cited above, explaining that "the modern view . . . is that it is better to draw a distinction between intent (or purpose) on the one hand and knowledge on the other."

68. *See generally Federal Sentencing Law and Practice* §§ 3A.1.3, 3A1.4, 3D1.1 (Thomas W. Hutchison *et al.* eds., 2003) (discussing sentencing enhancements for any crime involving a terrorist plot, multiple counts, or the physical restraint of a victim).

69. *See* ch. 3, *supra.*

70. Edmund Wingate, *Justice Revived; Being the Whole Office of a Country JP Briefly, and Yet More Methodically and Fully Than Ever Yet Extant* 61, 88 (1661).

71. Blackstone, *Commentaries* 189.

72. *See* Coke, *Third Institute* 54.

73. 1 Hale, *Pleas* 411.

74. *See id.* at 412.

75. Model Penal Code § 210.5 cmt. 1, at 91–92.

76. *See also* ch. 3, *supra* (citing cases and statutes defining euthanasia as a species of murder—*i.e.,* intentional homicide).

77. *See Compassion in Dying,* 79 F.3d at 858 (Klienfeld, J., dissenting). Chief Justice Rehnquist adopted Judge Klienfeld's analogy. *See Quill,* 521 U.S. at 802.

78. *See* appendix A, *infra.*

79. Wis. Stat. Ann. § 940.12 (emphasis added).

80. Tex. Penal Code § 22.08(a) (emphasis added).

81. Cal. Penal Code § 401.

82. Va. Code Ann. § 8.01-622.1.

83. Model Penal Code § 2.06 cmt. 6(c). *See also id.* § 2.06(3)(a); *Federal Criminal Jury Instructions* § 10.01A[3] & cmt. at I-394 to I-395 (Josephine R. Potuto *et al.* eds., 1993).

84. Model Penal Code § 2.06 cmt. 6(c).

85. *United States v. Falcone,* 109 F.2d 579, 581 (2d Cir.), *aff'd without passing on the issue,* 311 U.S. 205 (1940); *United States v. Peoni,* 100 F.2d 401 (2d Cir. 1938) (Hand, J.).

86. Model Penal Code § 2.06 cmt. 6(c).

87. Ashworth, *Criminal Law* 377.

88. English law, again, does not entirely follow the American approach; though there is a "conflict of authority," many English courts would find secondary liability when the accomplice *knows* of the principal's intended course of action. *See id.* at 377–78; Smith & Hogan, *Criminal Law* 135.

89. *See* Model Penal Code § 210.5 cmt. 2, at 102.

90. While intent is the traditional and vastly more predominant mens rea rule for aiding and abetting crimes like assisted suicide, states are, of course, free to legislate different rules, and a few, such as Maryland and Iowa, have done so, enacting statutes banning the *knowing* assistance of suicide. *See* appendix A, *infra.* The traditional intent require-

ment associated with aiding and abetting liability applies, moreover, only to prosecutions for *secondary* liability; the state is free to try to secure a conviction on the basis of *primary* liability. Cases of euthanasia, where the assister *intentionally* acts as the causal agent of death, are treated, as explored in chapter 3, as a form of murder. But primary liability can also be secured on lesser showings of mens rea—laws exist in almost every jurisdiction treating *reckless* or *negligent* homicide as lesser offenses. To win, of course, the prosecutor must convince the jury not only of the requisite mental element, but also that the doctor did not just assist the death (as in cases of assisted suicide) but actually was its cause. This also poses a significant hurdle and safeguard against "drag-net" prosecutions. But while such cases are infrequent and (deliberately) hard to prove, neither are they unheard of. *See, e.g., People v. Duffy*, 185 A.D.2d 371, 586 N.Y.S.2d 150 (1992); *State v. Bauer*, 471 N.W.2d 363 (Minn. Ct. App. 1991); *People v. Cleaves*, 229 Cal. App. 3d 367, 280 Cal. Rptr. 146 (1991); *Hinson v. State*, 18 Ark. App. 14, 709 S.W.2d 106 (1986); *Chanslor v. State*, 697 S.W.2d 393 (Tex. App. 1985); *People v. Campbell*, 124 Mich. App. 333, 335 N.W.2d 27 (1983); *State v. Marti*, 290 N.W.2d 570 (Iowa 1980); *Commonwealth v. Schwartzentruver*, 389 A.2d 181 (Pa. Super. Ct. 1978); *Persampieri v. Commonwealth*, 343 Mass. 19, 175 N.E.2d 387 (1961).

91. American Med. Ass'n, Council on Ethical and Judicial Affairs, *Decisions Near the End of Life*, 267 Journ. of the Amer. Med. Ass'n. 2229, 2230, 2233 (1992) (hereinafter AMA, *Decisions Near the End of Life*).

92. Motion for Leave To File Brief as *Amicus Curiae* and Brief of the American Medical Association, the California Medical Association, and the Society of Critical Care Medicine as *Amicus Curiae* in Support of Petitioners, *Washington v. Glucksberg*, No. 96–110, at 15 (U.S. filed Aug. 19, 1996) (emphasis added) (hereinafter AMA, *Amicus Brief*). *See also Brief of the American Hospital Association as Amicus Curiae* in Support of Petitioners, *State of Washington v. Glucksberg*, No. 96–110.

93. *House of Lords Report* HL Paper, 21-I of 1993–1994 Session, vol. 1, ¶¶ 242, 243.

94. Of course, any person remains privileged under current law to interfere with a suicide attempt; thus, a doctor convinced that the patient seeking to discontinue care intends to die *could* intercede, but, even so, the legal privilege to intercede imposes no duty on the physician to act. While states can go beyond the traditional understanding of assisted suicide and enact laws proscribing more than *intentional* acts designed to assist a suicide, very few have done so. *See* note 90, *supra*.

95. *See* ch. 4.4, *supra*.

96. Thompson, *Double Effect*, 33 Vand. J. Transnat'l L. at 1057–58.

97. *See Kevorkian*, 527 N.W.2d at 733–34.

98. *Id.*

99. Griffiths, *et al.*, *Euthanasia and Law* 164–65 (emphasis added).

100. *See, e.g.*, Helga Kuhse, *The Sanctity of Life Doctrine in Medicine* 97 (1987) (hereinafter Kuhse, *Sanctity of Life Doctrine*); Finnis, *Intention and Side-Effects* 55–61.

101. *See* Kuhse, *Sanctity of Life Doctrine* 94.

102. *See, e.g.*, Phillipa Foot, *The Problem of Abortion and the Doctrine of Double Effect*, in *Killing and Letting Die* 156–65 (Bonnie Steinbock ed., 1980).

103. Griffiths, *et al.*, *Euthanasia and Law* 166.

104. *See* ch. 4.4, *supra*. Incidentally, Griffiths is also incorrect in suggesting that motives are irrelevant to secular law—at least in America. By way of example, consider recent "hate crimes" legislation: these laws, by definition, focus on criminal acts *motivated*

by distaste for particular minority groups, and establishing the defendant's motive is an essential element of the government's proof. *See, e.g., Apprendi v. New Jersey,* 530 U.S. 466 (2000).

105. *Quill,* 521 U.S. at 802 (emphasis added).

106. *The Jonestown Massacre* (Karl Eden ed., 1993). Of course, it became clear from subsequent investigation that many who died with Jones and in similar tragedies did not intend to die as either a means or an end but were coerced or deceived—*i.e.,* straightforwardly murdered.

107. *Glucksberg,* 521 U.S. at 750–51.

108. *Id.*

109. Quill, *The Rule of Double Effect,* 337 New Eng. J. Med. 1768.

110. Griffiths *et al., Euthanasia and Law* 166.

111. *See* note 85, *supra.*

112. Griffiths *et al., Euthanasia and Law* 271.

113. *Id.* at 297 n.65.

CHAPTER 5: *CASEY* AND *CRUZAN*

1. *See* 521 U.S. at 723–27.

2. Henry Hart, *Foreword: The Time Chart of the Justices,* 73 Harv. L. Rev. 84, 99 (1959).

3. Ronald Dworkin, *Taking Rights Seriously* 126 (1977).

4. Charles Curtis, *Lions under the Throne* (1947).

5. *Glucksberg,* 521 U.S. at 769.

6. *Casey,* 505 U.S. at 851.

7. As Justice Scalia has asked:

> [I]t is obvious to anyone applying "reasoned judgment" that the same adjectives can be applied to many forms of conduct that this Court . . . has held are *not* entitled to constitutional protection. . . . It is not reasoned judgment that supports the Court's decision; only personal predilection. . . . [W]hen a strict interpretation of the Constitution . . . is abandoned . . . we are under the government of individual men, who for the time being have power to declare what the Constitution is, according to their own views of what it ought to mean.

Id. at 984 (Scalia, J., dissenting) (internal quotation marks omitted).

8. *See, e.g., Adamson v. California,* 332 U.S. 46, 68 (1947) (Black, J., dissenting); *Griswold v. Connecticut,* 381 U.S. 479, 507 (1965) (Black, J., dissenting); *Stovall v. Denno,* 388 U.S. 293, 305 (1967) (Black, J., dissenting); *In re Winship,* 397 U.S. 358, 376 (1970).

9. *See* 491 U.S. 122 (denying asserted nontextual due process right only because of lack of historical evidence suggesting its importance).

10. *See Casey,* 505 U.S. at 984 (Scalia, J., dissenting).

11. Much light on this bit of backstage Court history has been shed by the release of Justice Blackmun's papers five years after his death. Justice Blackmun kept (and retained) punctilious notes of the Court's private conferences, and his papers filled some 1,500 boxes, including a treasure trove of information about the Court's deliberations in *Casey.*

12. *TXO Production Corp. v. Alliance Resources Corp.,* 509 U.S. 443, 470 (1993). *See also*

Albright v. Oliver, 510 U.S. 266, 275 (1994); *United States v. Carlton*, 512 U.S. 26, 39 (1994) (Scalia, J., concurring in the judgment) ("If I thought that 'substantive due process' were a constitutional right rather than an oxymoron. . . .").

13. *See, e.g., TXO*, 509 U.S. at 470; *Carlton*, 512 U.S. at 39.

14. *Moore*, 431 U.S. at 546 (White, J., dissenting).

15. 302 U.S. 319, 325 (1937).

16. *See* 410 U.S. at 129–41 (detailing ancient, common law, and contemporary legal provisions against abortion).

17. *Id.* at 152–56.

18. 79 F.3d at 805.

19. 388 U.S. 1.

20. 505 U.S. at 852.

21. *Id.*

22. *See* generally *Compassion in Dying*, 79 F.3d at 813 (citations omitted).

23. *See* 505 U.S. at 854–58.

24. *Lawrence*, 539 U.S. at 574.

25. 491 U.S. at 127 n.6.

26. 505 U.S. at 847.

27. *See* ch. 3.1, *supra*.

28. *See id.*

29. *Compassion in Dying v. Washington*, 85 F.3d 1440, 1444 (9th Cir. 1996) (dissenting from denial of rehearing *en banc* by the full court).

30. *See* 505 U.S. at 852. Justice Scalia raised much the same question in *Lawrence*, contending that "State laws against bigamy, same-sex marriage, adult incest, prostitution, masturbation, adultery, fornication, bestiality, and obscenity" are all at risk if we take seriously what Justice Scalia derided as *Casey*'s "famed sweet-mystery-of-life passage." 539 U.S. 588, 590. As Justice Scalia put it, *Casey*'s autonomy language either "'casts some doubt' upon either the totality of our jurisprudence or else (presumably the right answer) nothing at all." *Id.* at 588 (Scalia, J., dissenting).

31. *See* 410 U.S. at 158 (1973) (emphasizing that the fetus is not a protected "person" under the Fourteenth Amendment). *But see Thornburgh v. American College of Obstetricians & Gynecologists*, 476 U.S. 747, 791–92 (1986) (White, J., dissenting) (arguing that the right to terminate a pregnancy differs from the right to use contraceptives because the former involves the death of a person while the latter does not).

32. *See* ch. 7 for a more detailed discussion about the unwanted consequences that might be associated with legalization.

33. *Roe*, 410 U.S. at 158.

34. 79 F.3d at 816.

35. *Id.* at 801 (citing *Roe*).

36. *Cruzan*, 497 U.S. at 278 (internal quotation marks omitted).

37. *Id.*

38. *Id.* at 279.

39. *Id.*

40. The Court held, specifically, that Missouri had a legitimate interest in ensuring that any decision to refuse life-sustaining care is a personal one made by the patient, not by surrogates, in order to ensure against cases of abuse and mistake: "It cannot be disputed that the Due Process Clause protects an interest in life as well as an interest in re-

fusing life-sustaining medical treatment. Not all incompetent patients will have loved ones available to serve as surrogate decisionmakers. And even where family members are present, there will, of course, be some unfortunate situations in which family members will not act to protect a patient. A State is entitled to guard against potential abuses in such situations." *Cruzan*, 497 U.S. at 281 (internal quotation marks omitted). The Court also held that a "State may properly decline to make judgments about the 'quality' of life that a particular individual may enjoy, and simply assert an unqualified interest in the preservation of human life to be weighed against the constitutionally protected interests of the individual." *Id.*

Chapter 6: Autonomy Theory's Implications for the Debate over Assisted Suicide and Euthanasia

1. *See* ch. 1 notes 18–20, *supra.*

2. I do not seek to provide a map to the ever growing debate over autonomy in moral theory. My purpose is solely to outline the autonomy debate in general terms in order to assess its application to the assisted suicide debate, seeking to keep a potentially vast topic within manageable, yet useful bounds.

3. Joseph Raz, *The Morality of Freedom* 372–73 (1988).

4. *Id.* at 374.

5. *Id.* at 373.

6. John Rawls, *A Theory of Justice* 11 (1989).

7. Raz, *The Morality of Freedom* 207.

8. *See, e.g.,* H.L.A. Hart, *Law, Liberty, and Morality* 30–43 (1963); Bruce Ackerman, *Social Justice in the Liberal State* 386–89 (1980); Loren Lomasky, *Persons, Rights, and the Moral Community* 231–54 (1987); Jeremy Waldron, *Autonomy and Perfectionism in Raz's Morality of Freedom*, 62 So. Cal. L. Rev. 1097, 1127–30 (1989); Ronald Dworkin, *Foundations of Liberal Equality*, in *The Tanner Lectures on Human Values* 60–70 (Grethe B. Petersen ed., 1990).

9. David A. J. Richards, *Toleration and the Constitution* 252 (1989) (hereinafter Richards, *Toleration*).

10. David A. J. Richards, *Kantian Ethics and the Harm Principle: A Reply to John Finnis*, 87 Colum. L. Rev. 433, at 464 (1987). Note Richards' use of the word "define" and other language that anticipates *Casey's* autonomy discussion.

11. Ronald Dworkin, *A Matter of Principle* 205–6 (1985). In the end, however, Rawls does sanction at least one deviation from strict neutrality. His theory presupposes individuals of equal means and ability pursuing their notions of the good; but, of course, people do not start off life on equal terms materially. Rawls would, thus, permit (pursuant to his difference principle) the state to deviate from equal distribution of primary goods to enable the worst-off sufficient means to pursue their own conceptions of the good. *See* Rawls, *A Theory of Justice* 76.

12. Raz, *The Morality of Freedom* 381.

13. *Id.* at 395.

14. *Id.* at 412.

15. *Id.* at 126.

16. John Stuart Mill, *On Liberty* 9 (E. Rappaport ed., 1978).

17. Richards, *Toleration* 239.

18. Raz, *The Morality of Freedom* 414.

19. *See, e.g.*, Robert George, *Making Men Moral* 140 n.24 (1993). "Rawls says that 'justice as fairness requires us to show that modes of conduct interfere with the basic liberties of others or else violate some obligation or natural duty before they can be restricted.' Inasmuch as, for Rawls, 'obligations' are obligations of fairness and 'natural duties' are owed to others, it seems reasonable to conclude that Rawls himself understands his theory to imply a version of the harm principle which would, at minimum, exclude moral paternalism." *Id.* (internal citations omitted).

Other notable exponents of the harm principle include Joel Feinberg and Robert Nozick. *See, e.g.*, Joel Feinberg, *The Moral Limits of the Criminal Law: Harm to Others* (1984); Joel Feinberg, *Offense to Others* (1985); Joel Feinberg, *Harm to Self* (1986); Joel Feinberg, *Harmless Wrongdoing* (1987); Robert Nozick, *Anarchy, State, and Utopia* ix (hereinafter Nozick, *Anarchy*) (1974) (advocating the harm principle and contending that the state violates individuals' rights if it uses its "coercive apparatus . . . to prohibit activities for their *own* good or protection"). Whether Nozick is an antiperfectionist, however, is not altogether clear. *See* Nozick, *Anarchy* 48–51.

20. Raz, *The Morality of Freedom* 418–19.

21. *See id.* at 418.

22. George, *Making Men Moral* 173–75.

23. *Id.* at 177.

24. *Id.* at 215.

25. *Id.* at 185.

26. Declaration of Independence ¶ 2 ("We hold these truths to be self-evident, that all men are created equal, that they are endowed by their Creator with certain unalienable Rights, that among these are Life, Liberty and the pursuit of Happiness.").

27. George, *Making Men Moral* 185–86.

28. *Id.* at 188.

29. *Id.*

30. *Cruzan*, 497 U.S. at 300 (Scalia, J., concurring).

31. *Id.* at 215.

32. *Id.* at 34.

33. *See, e.g.*, Feinberg, *Harm to Self* 18–19 (dueling); *id.* at 75–79 (slavery contracts); Mill, *On Liberty* ch. 5, ¶ 11 (slavery contracts).

34. Feinberg, *Harm to Self* at 79.

35. *Id.*

36. *Id.*

37. *See* chs. 1, 3.8, *supra*.

38. *See* Letter from the World Federation of Right-to-Die Societies, quoted in *House of Lords Report* HL Paper, 21-I of 1993–1994 Session, vol. 3, at 182.

39. *See Compassion in Dying*, 49 F.3d at 590; ch. 7.2, *infra* (discussing how "terminal" patients lived for months and years after their diagnosis).

40. Robert Sedler, *Constitutional Challenges to Bans on "Assisted Suicide": The View from Without and Within*, 21 Hastings Const. L. Quar. 777, 794 (1994) (emphasis added).

41. Oral testimony of Ronald Dworkin before the Select Committee on Medical Ethics of the House of Lords, quoted in *House of Lords Report* HL Paper, 21-I of 1993–1994 Session, vol. 1, at 23, 28.

42. David A. J. Richards, *Sex, Drugs, Death, and the Law* 248–49 (1982) (hereinafter Richards, *Sex, Drugs*).

43. *See also* Brock, *Life and Death* 206 (1993) ("[i]f self-determination is a fundamental value, then the great variability among people on this question [of when assisted suicide might be justified] makes it especially important that individuals control the manner, circumstances, and timing of their dying and death").

44. Gerald Dworkin, *Paternalism*, reprinted in *Morality and the Law* 124 (Robert Baird and Stuart Rosenbaum eds., 1988).

45. *Id.*

46. Richards, *Sex, Drugs* 226.

47. Otlowski, *Voluntary Euthanasia* 203–6.

48. *Id.*

49. *Id.* at 204.

50. Feinberg, *Harm to Self* 354.

51. Sherry F. Colb, *A Controversy over the Netherlands' New Euthanasia Legislation*, Findlaw.com (Jan. 17, 2001).

52. *Id.* (emphasis added).

53. *See* ch. 3.8, *supra*.

54. *See* Walter Land and Thomas Gutmann, *Ethics in Living Organ Transplantation*, in 6 Langebeck's Archives of Surgery 394, 515 (1999), *available at* http://trans.klinikum.uni-muenchen.de/ (site visited Jan. 25, 2005).

55. *See Mass Suicide Involved Sedatives, Vodka and Careful Planning*, CNN, March 27, 1997, at http://www.cnn.com/US/9703/27/suicide/index.html (site visited Jan. 26, 2005).

56. *See* Laurie Goodstein, *Followers Surrendered All but Illusion of Free Will*, Washington Post, Mar. 30, 1997, at A1.

57. *See* Karl Vick, *Silent Apocalypse of a Ugandan Cult; Outward Serenity Hid Preparations for a Suicidal Inferno That Killed More than 300*, Washington Post, Mar. 20, 2000, at A1.

58. Alan Hall, *German Net Cannibal: Had Londoner on Menu*, The Times (July 24, 2003) (emphasis added).

59. *See* Manslaughter Verdict for Cannibal, BBC News (Jan. 30, 2004), available at http://news.bbc.co.uk/2/hi/europe/3443293.stm. After much media attention to the case and some criticisms of the result, the German courts announced a retrial on the ground the first trial may have been too lenient. The new trial is ongoing as this book goes to press.

60. *See* Anthony Faiola, *Internet Suicides Plaguing Japan*, Wash. Post, Aug. 24, 2003, A1.

61. Associated Press, *Judge Blocks Band's Suicide Show*, Oct. 2, 2003, *available at* http://www.usatoday.com/life/music/news/2003-10-02-suicide-concert_x.htm (site visited Jan. 25, 2004).

62. *See* Alisa Ulferts, *Bill Would Ban Suicide Done for Entertainment*, St. Petersburg Times, Oct. 29, 2003, *available at* http://www.sptimes.com/2003/10/29/State/Bill_would ban_suicid.shtml (site visited Jan. 25, 2005); Joni James and Carrie Johnson, *New Law Bans Staging Suicide*, St. Petersburg Times, May 12, 2004, *available at* http://www.sptimes.com/2004/05/12/State/New_law_bans_staging.shtml (site visited Jan. 25, 2005).

CHAPTER 7: LEGALIZATION AND THE LAW OF UNINTENDED
CONSEQUENCES

1. This point is not lost even on those who most strongly support legalization of euthanasia. *See, e.g.,* Otlowski, *Voluntary Euthanasia* 190 (eschewing utilitarian-based arguments for legalization while endorsing autonomy-based arguments).

2. See ch. 2.4, supra.

3. Belgium's law has been in force for only a short period, as of this writing. *See* Reuters, *Belgium Approves Euthanasia Bill*, May 16, 2002, *at* http://www.chninternational.com/belgium_approves bill_on_euthana.htm (site visited Oct. 3, 2005). The Australian law was in place only for a matter of months. *See* Rights of the Terminally Ill Act, 1995. And, little has been published about Switzerland's experience.

4. *See, e.g.,* Samia A. Hurst & Alex Mauron, *Assisted Suicide and Euthanasia in Switzerland: Allowing a Role for Non-Physicians*, Feb. 1, 2003, *at* http://bmj.bmjjournals.com/cgi/content/full/ 326/7383/271 (site visited Oct. 3, 2005). At least some of the published evidence from the brief Australian experiment does not offer reason for much confidence that assisted suicide was practiced there with tremendous care. *See generally* Kissane, *Deadly Days in Darwin* 192.

5. Margaret Pabst Battin, *Should We Copy the Dutch? The Netherlands' Practice of Voluntary Euthanasia as a Model for the United States, in* Euthanasia: The Good of the Patient, the Good of Society 95, 102 (Robert I. Misbin ed., 1992).

6. *See* Jocelyn Downie, *The Contested Lessons of Euthanasia in the Netherlands*, 8 Health L.J. 119, 128 (2000)(hereinafter Downie, *The Contested Lessons of Euthanasia*) (claiming that the notion that euthanasia is widespread "is simply not supported by the data").

7. Epstein, *Mortal Peril*, at 322.

8. Posner, *Aging and Old Age* 242 & n.23 (footnote omitted).

9. Otlowski, *Voluntary Euthanasia* xiii. *See also* Cantor, *On Kamisar*, 102 Mich. L. Rev. at 1828 (to same effect).

10. See Herbert Hendin, *The Dutch Experience, in The Case Against Assisted Suicide: For the Right to End-of-Life Care* 97, 99 (Kathleen Foley and Herbert Hendin eds., 2002).

11. See Griffiths *et al., Euthanasia and Law* 51–52.

12. See *id.* at 53.

13. *See id.* at 58–59; Hendin, *The Dutch Experience* 99. For detailed, if sometimes conflicting, accounts of all Dutch cases and experience prior to 1984's seminal Dutch Supreme Court decision, *see* Gomez, *Regulating Death*; Griffiths *et al., Euthanasia and Law*; Hendin, *The Dutch Experience* 38.

14. *See* Griffiths *et al., Euthanasia and Law*, app. 2, at 323–24. A translation of the Dutch *Schoonheim* case is provided in *id.* app. 2, at 322–28.

15. See *id.* app. 2, at 324 In the previous year, the patient had signed a living will in which she manifested her wish to have euthanasia be performed if she suffered from a condition "in which no recovery to a tolerable and dignified condition of life was to be expected." *Id.* app. 2, at 323.

16. *See id.* app. 2, at 322–23.

17. *See id.,* app. 2, at 326–28. Article 293 of the Dutch Criminal Code forbade an individual from taking the life of another even after the latter's "express and earnest request"; Article 294 made it unlawful to "intentionally incite[] another to commit suicide,

assist[ ] in the suicide of another, or procure[ ] for that other person the means to commit suicide." *Id.* app. 1, at 308 (translating Dutch statutes).

18. *Id.*, app. 2, at 326–27.

19. *See* Lagerway, *Guidelines for Euthanasia*, 3 issues L. & Med. 429. Under the guidelines, a request for assistance in dying had to be voluntary, well-considered, and persistent, and the patient had to be experiencing unacceptable suffering; the physician was also required to consult a colleague. *Id.* at 431–33.

20. *See* Executive Summary, *Physician-Assisted Suicide and Euthanasia in the Netherlands: A Report to the House Judiciary Subcommittee on the Constitution*, 14 issues L. & Med. 301, 313 (1998) ("[The Guidelines] made clear that physicians could practice euthanasia under the Guidelines and not fear prosecution.").

21. Griffiths *et al.*, *Euthanasia and Law*, app. 2, at 329–38. A translation of the Dutch *Chabot* case is provided in *id.*

22. See *id.* app. 2, at 329–30.

23. See *id.* app. 2, at 330.

24. *See id.*

25. *See id.*

26. *Id.* app. 2, at 331 & n.23.

27. *See id.* app. 2, at 331 & n.24.

28. *See id.* app. 2, at 332.

29. *Id.*

30. *Id.*

31. *See id.* app. 2, at 329.

32. *See id.* app. 2, at 329–30.

33. *Id.* app. 2, at 334–35.

34. *See id.* app. 2, at 337–38.

35. *Id.* at 153.

36. See *House of Lords Report* HL paper, 21-I of 1993–1994 Session at 65.

37. Termination of Life on Request and Assisted Suicide (Review Procedures) Act, Stb. 2001, nr. 137, ch. 2, art. 2, § 1 (Neth.), *available at* http://www.nvve.nl/english (hereinafter "2001 Dutch Act") (translating the Dutch law; site visited Oct. 3, 2005).

38. *Id.* ch. 2, art. 2, § 1(b).

39. *See id.* ch. 2, art. 2.

40. *Id.* ch. 2, art. 2, § 4.

41. 41.*Id.* ch. 2, art. 2, § 3.

42. Academisch Ziekenhuis Groningen, Protocol waarborgt zorgvuldigheid bij levenseinde kind (Oct. 29, 2004), *available at* http://www.azg.nl/azg/nl/nieuws/ persberichten/43604. An English translation of the hospital's press release is available at Target="_Blank", Groningen Protocol: The Press Release of the University Hospital Groningen, English Translation, A Protocol to Guarantee Carefulness When Actively Ending a Child's Life, *at* http://blogger.xs4all.nl/wdegroot/articles/16952.aspx (site visited Dec. 20, 2004).

43. *See id.*

44. *See* Paul J. van der Maas *et al.*, *Euthanasia, Physician-Assisted Suicide, and Other Medical Practices Involving the End of Life in the Netherlands, 1990–1995*, 335 New Eng. J. Med. 1699 (1996) (hereinafter van der Maas *et al.*, *Euthanasia 1996*).

45. *See* Bregje D. Onwuteaka-Philipsen *et al.*, *Euthanasia and Other End-of-Life De-*

cisions in the Netherlands in 1990, 1995, and 2001, 362 *Lancet* 395 (2003) (hereinafter Onwuteaka-Philipsen *et al., Euthanasia 2001*).

46. *See id.* at 395; van der Maas *et al., Euthanasia 1996,* 335 New Eng. J. Med. at 1699.

47. *See* Onwuteaka-Philipsen *et al., Euthanasia 2001,* 362 *Lancet* at 395–96; van der Maas *et al., Euthanasia 1996,* 335 New Eng. J. Med. at 1699–1700.

48. Onwuteaka-Philipsen *et al., Euthanasia 2001,* at 396; van der Maas *et al., Euthanasia 1996,* 335 New Eng. J. Med. at 1700.

49. The Netherlands has a total population of approximately sixteen million. World Health Org., Netherlands, *at* http://www.who.int/countries/nld/en (site visited Dec. 20, 2004).

50. *See* WHO Statistical Information System, World Health Org., Table 1: Numbers of Registered Deaths, Netherlands—1999, *at* http://www3.who.int/whosis/mort/table1_process.cfm (site visited Dec. 20, 2004).

51. Onwuteaka-Philipsen *et al., Euthanasia 2001,* 362 *Lancet* at 396 & tbl. 1.

52. *See id.*

53. *See id.* There is a similar divergence in the data for physician-assisted suicide. *Id.* The physician interview results show that the incidence of assisted suicide rose from 0.3% of all deaths in 1990 to 0.4% in 1995, and then dropped to 0.1% in 2001. *Id.* Meanwhile, the death certificate data suggest that the incidence of assisted suicide remained constant in all three years at 0.2% of all deaths. *Id.*

54. Johanna H. Groenewoud *et al., Clinical Problems with the Performance of Euthanasia and Physician-Assisted Suicide in the Netherlands,* 342 New Eng. J. Med. 551 (2000).

55. *See id.* at 555 tbl.5.

56. *See* Onwuteaka-Philipsen *et al., Euthanasia 2001,* 362 *Lancet* at 396 & tbl.1. While these data seem to suggest that nonconsensual killings decreased slightly, the Surveys' authors have been cautious to reach such a conclusion, explaining that "chance fluctuation cannot be ruled out as an explanation" for the change between 1990 and 1995, adding that their "1990 interview study did not permit sufficiently reliable estimates of this variable." van der Maas *et al., Euthanasia 1996,* 335 New Eng. J. Med at 1704.

57. Downie, *The Contested Lessons of Euthanasia* 132. *See also* Cantor, *On Kamisar,* 102 Mich. L. Rev. at 1828.

58. *See* Margaret Pabst Battin, *A Dozen Caveats Concerning the Discussion of Euthanasia in the Netherlands,* in *The Least Worst Death: Essays in Bioethics on the End of Life* 130, 137 (1994) (hereinafter *The Least Worst Death*).

59. *See id.*

60. *Id.*

61. *See* N.Y. State Task Force, *When Death Is Sought* 133–34 (1994).

62. *Id.*

63. *See* Onwuteaka-Philipsen *et al., Euthanasia 2001,* 362 *Lancet* at 395.

64. *See id.*

65. *See* notes 44 and 45, *supra,* and accompanying text.

66. *See* Onwuteaka-Philipsen *et al., Euthanasia 2001,* 362 *Lancet* at 395.

67. Keown, *EEPP* 95–96.

68. *Id.*

69. *See id.* at 93, 95–96.

70. *See id.*

71. *See* WHO Statistical Information System, World Health Org., Table 1: Numbers of Registered Deaths, United States of America— 1999, *at* http://www3.who.int/whosis/ mort/ table1_process.cfm (site visited Dec. 20, 2004).

72. *See* Onwuteaka-Philipsen *et al.*, *Euthanasia 2001*, 362 *Lancet* at 396 & tbl.1 (using statistics from the death certificate study).

73. Keown, *FFPP* 105 (footnotes omitted); *see also* John Keown, *Further Reflections on Euthanasia in the Netherlands in the Light of the Remmelink Report and the Van Der Maas Survey*, in *Euthanasia, Clinical Practice and the Law* 219, 230 (Luke Gormally ed., 1994) (hereinafter Keown, *Further Reflections*) (discussing the 1990 Survey results); R. L. Marquet *et al.*, *Twenty Five Years of Requests for Euthanasia and Physician Assisted Suicide* in *Dutch General Practice: Trend Analysis*, 327 Brit. Med. J. 201 (2003).

74. R. L. Marquet *et al.*, *Twenty Five Years of Requests* at 201.

75. *See id.*

76. *See* John Keown, *The Law and Practice of Euthanasia in the Netherlands*, 108 L. Q. Rev. 51, 65 (1992).

77. Karin L. Dorrepaal *et al.*, *Pain Experience and Pain Management among Hospitalized Cancer Patients: A Clinical Study*, 63 Cancer 593, 598 (1989).

78. Keown, *EEPP* 111.

79. Keown, *Further Reflections* 229 (quoting the government's report).

80. *Id.*

81. Onwuteaka-Philipsen *et al.*, *Euthanasia 2001*, 362 *Lancet* at 395–96. Such an age-based study was not performed in 1990.

82. The materials reported in Onwuteaka-Philipsen *et al.*, *Euthanasia 2001*, 362 *Lancet* at 395, are less specific than those found in prior surveys. For example, they do not disaggregate 2001 data for persons between birth and 49, and between 50 and 64, as the 1995 Survey did.

83. *Id.* at 396–97.

84. Keown, *EEPP* 113.

85. Gerrit van der Wal *et al.*, *Evaluation of the Notification Procedures for Physician-Assisted Death in the Netherlands*, 335 New Eng. J. Med. 1706, 1708 (1996) (hereinafter van der Wal *et al.*, *Notification Procedure*).

86. Reporting data is not included in Onwuteaka-Philipsen *et al.*, *Euthanasia 2001*, but it is summarized in Tony Sheldon, *Only Half of Dutch Doctors Report Euthanasia, Study Says*, 326 Brit. Med. J. 1164 (2003). *See also* World Federation of Right to Die Societies, *Netherlands: Euthanasia Reports Decline by 15 Percent over 4 Years* (Apr. 29, 2003) (noting that "it is suspected the actual 'mercy killing' figure is double the amount of recorded cases" and that "many doctors still do not trust the commissions and get annoyed and worried when the commission seeks additional information about specific cases," and quoting Reina de Valk, chairperson for the national body encompassing the various regional reporting commissions, that "'[t]ime is needed to win the confidence of many doctors'"), *at* http://www.worldrtd.net/news/world/?id=534 (site visited Nov. 6, 2005).

87. van der Wal *et al.*, *Notification Procedure*, New Eng. J. Med. at 1708.

88. Keown, *EEPP* at 113.

89. Griffiths *et al.*, *Euthanasia and Law* 268.

90. *Id.* at 245–46.

91. *Id.* at 282.

92. *See generally id.* at 267–98.

93. *See id.* at 286–87.

94. *Id.* (emphasis added).

95. *See* U.K. Dep't of Health, Harold Shipman's Clinical Practice 1974–1998 at 1–2 (finding that Shipman, who was convicted of murdering fifteen of his patients, had 297 "excess" deaths compared to other similarly situated physicians), *available at* http://www.dh.gov.uk/assetRoot/04/06/50/46/04065046.pdf (site visited Oct. 5, 2005); *see also* James M. Thunder, *Quiet Killings in Medical Facilities: Detection and Prevention*, 18 issues L. & Med. 211, 213 (2003) (noting that, over the last twenty-five years, at least 18 American health workers suspected of being responsible for approximately 455 "mercy killings" inside medical facilities have been charged with attempted murder, murder or manslaughter, and that 12 have been convicted).

96. Griffiths *et al.*, *Euthanasia and Law* 286–87.

97. *Compare id.* 292, *with id.* 257.

98. Epstein, *Mortal Peril* 326–27.

99. Otlowski, *Voluntary Euthanasia* xx.

100. Or. Rev. Stat. § 127.805(1).

101. *Id.* § 127.800(3).

102. *Id.* § 127.800(12).

103. *Id.* § 127.805(1). One of the witnesses cannot be related to the patient, stand to benefit under the patient's estate, or be connected to the medical facility where the patient is being treated. *Id.* § 127.810(2). Nor can the attending physician serve as a witness. *Id.* § 127.810(3). If the patient is a resident in a long-term care facility, one of the witnesses must be an individual designated by the facility that meets qualifications imposed by Oregon's Department of Human Services. *Id.* § 127.810(4).

104. *Id.* § 127.815(a), (d).

105. *Id.* § 127.825.

106. See *id.* § 127.815(l).

107. *Id.* § 127.850.

108. *See id.* § 127.855(1).

109. *Id.* § 127.855.

110. *Id.* § 127.865(1)(a).

111. Keown, *EEPP* 171.

112. Melinda A. Lee *et al.*, *Legalizing Assisted Suicide—Views of Physicians in Oregon*, 334 New Eng. J. Med. 310, 334 (1996) (hereinafter Lee, *Legalizing Assisted Suicide*).

113. Office of Disease Prevention and Epidemiology, Or. Dep't of Human Servs., Fifth Annual Report on Oregon's Death with Dignity Act 21 tbl. 3 (2003), *available at* http://www.ohd.hr.state.or. us/chs/pas/year5/02pasrpt.pdf (hereinafter "Fifth Annual Report") (site visited Oct. 5, 2005).

114. *See* Keown, *EEPP* 171.

115. Office of Disease Prevention and Epidemiology, Or. Dep't of Human Servs., Fourth Annual Report on Oregon's Death with Dignity Act 9–10 (2002), *available at* http://www.ohd.hr.state.or.us/chs/pas/ year4/01pasrpt.pdf (hereinafter Fourth Annual Report) (site visited Oct. 5, 2005); *see also* Katrina Hedberg *et al.*, *Legalized Physician-Assisted Suicide in Oregon, 2001*, 346 New Eng. J. Med. 450, 451 (2002).

116. *See* Eli Robins, *The Final Months: A Study of the Lives of 134 Persons Who Committed Suicide* 10–12 (1981); Stengel, *Suicide and Attempted Suicide* 51–53 (1964); Bar-

raclough *et al.*, *A Hundred Cases of Suicide*, 125 Brit. J. Psychiatry 355; Conwell, *Rational Suicide and the Right to Die*, 325 New Eng. J. Med. 1100; Thomas Grisso and Paul S. Applebaum, *The MacArthur Treatment Competence Study: III. Abilities of Patients to Consent to Psychiatric and Medical Treatments*, 19 Law & Hum. Behav. 149 (1995); Hendin, *Physician Assisted Suicide*, 150 Am. J. of Psychiatry 143; Shneidman, *Rational Suicide and Psychiatric Disorders*, 326 New Eng. J. Med. 889 (1992).

117. *See* Lee, *Legalizing Assisted Suicide*, 334 New Eng. J. Med., at 312–13.

118. Steven D. Passik *et al.*, *Oncologists' Recognition of Depression in Their Patients with Cancer*, 16 J. Clinical Oncology 1594, 1597 (1998).

119. Fifth Annual Report at 20 tbl. 3.

120. Fourth Annual Report at 8. Other "health-care providers" (presumably nurses, but this is not clear from the Oregon report) were present in 52% of 2001 cases, *see id.* at 10, and 78% percent of cases in 2002, *see* Fifth Annual Report at 10.

121. Fifth Annual Report at 13, 21 tbl. 3 (describing that complications include coughing, vomiting, living for hours or days after consuming lethal medication, and seizures).

122. Ezekiel J. Emanuel *et al.*, *The Practice of Euthanasia and Physician-Assisted Suicide in the United States: Adherence to Proposed Safeguards and Effects on Physicians*, 280 Journ. of the Amer. Med. Ass'n 507, 509 (1998).

123. *See* ch. 7.1 notes 55–56, *supra*, and accompanying text.

124. Fifth Annual Report at 4.

125. *Id.* at 13.

126. *Id.* at 21 tbl. 3.

127. *Id.*

128. Oregon, First Year's Experience at 2.

129. *Id.* at 9; *see also* Fifth Annual Report at 14 ("[O]ur numbers . . . do not include patients and physicians who may act outside the law.").

130. Kathleen Foley and Herbert Hendin, *The Oregon Experiment*, in *The Case against Assisted Suicide* 144, 159 (hereinafter Foley and Hendin, *The Oregon Experiment*).

131. *See id.*

132. Fifth Annual Report at 4.

133. N. Gregory Hamilton, *Oregon's Culture of Silence*, in *The Case against Assisted Suicide* 175, 180–81; *see also* Foley and Hendin, *The Oregon Experiment* 144–45.

134. Hamilton, *Oregon's Culture of Silence* 180–81 (footnote omitted); *see also* Foley and Hendin, *The Oregon Experiment* 145.

135. *See* ch. 7.1 notes 64–67, *supra*, and accompanying text.

136. *See* Fifth Annual Report at 11.

137. There were 44 prescriptions for lethal doses of medication in 2001, compared to 39 in 2000, 33 in 1999, and 24 in 1998. Fifth Annual Report at 4.

138. *See id.*

139. *See* ch. 7.2 note 117, *supra*, and accompanying text.

140. *See* Second Year's Experience at tbl. 2; Three Years of Legalized Physician-Assisted Suicide at 19 tbl. 3; Fourth Annual Report at 16 tbl. 3; Fifth Annual Report at 20 tbl. 3.

141. 146.Linda Ganzini *et al.*, *Attitudes of Oregon Psychiatrists toward Physician-Assisted Suicide*, 153 Am. J. of Psychiatry 1469, 1474 (1996) (hereinafter Ganzini *et al.*, *Attitudes*).

142. AMA, *Decision Near the End of Life*, 267 JAMA at 2232.

143. *Id.*

144. Fifth Annual Report at 21 tbl. 3.

145. Ganzini *et al.*, *Attitudes*, 153 Am. J. of Psychiatry at 1473.

146. *See* ch. 7.1 notes 77–80, *supra*, and accompanying text.

147. Linda Ganzini *et al.*, *Physicians' Experiences with the Oregon Death with Dignity Act*, 342 New Eng. J. Med. 557, 559–60 (2000).

148. *See* Foley and Hendin, *The Oregon Experiment* 146–50.

149. *See id.* at 156–58.

150. *See id.* at 146.

151. *See id.*

152. *See id.*

153. *See id.*

154. *See id.*

155. *See id.* at 147.

156. *See id.*

157. *See id.*

158. *Id.* at 149.

159. Peter Reagan, *Helen*, 353 *Lancet* 1265, 1266 (1999).

160. *See* Foley and Hendin, *The Oregon Experiment* 169.

161. *See id.* at 156.

162. *See id.*

163. *Id.*

164. *See id.*

165. *See id.*

166. *Id.*

167. *See id.*

168. *Id.* at 157.

169. *Id.*

170. *See id.*

171. *See House of Lords Report* HL Paper, 21-I of 1993–1994 Session at 66.

172. *See* U.S. Census Bureau, Statistical Abstract of the United States: 2001, at 27 (121st ed. 2001).

173. *See* Joseph P. Shapiro and David Bowermaster, *Death on Trial: The Case of Dr. Kevorkian Obscures Critical Issues—and Dangers*, U.S. News & World Rep., Apr. 25, 1994, at 31, 39.

174. *See Ohioans Divided on Doctor Assisted Suicide Issue*, UPI, June 28, 1993 (on file with author).

175. *See* Charles S. Cleeland *et al.*, *Pain and Its Treatment in Outpatients with Metastatic Cancer*, 330 New Eng. J. Med. 592, 595 (1994).

176. *See id.*

177. *See* Richard D. Moore *et al.*, *Racial Differences in the Use of Drug Therapy for HIV Disease in an Urban Community*, 330 New Eng. J. Med. 763, 763 (1994).

178. Patricia A. King and Leslie E. Wolf, *Lessons for Physician-Assisted Suicide from the African-American Experience*, in *Physician Assisted Suicide: Expanding the Debate* 91, 101 (Margaret P. Battin *et al.* eds., 1998).

179. *See id.*

180. *See id.*

181. BA Comm'n on Legal Problems of the Elderly, *ABA Memorandum in Opposition to Resolution No. 8 on Voluntary Aid in Dying*, 8 issues L. & Med. 117, 120 (1992) (emphasis omitted). "The lack of access to or the financial burdens of health care hardly permit voluntary choice for many. What may be voluntary in Beverly Hills is not likely to be voluntary in Watts. Our national health care problem should be our priority—not endorsement of euthanasia." *Id.* at 118.

182. *See* Brief of Am. Med. Ass'n, Am. Nurses Ass'n & Am. Psychiatric Ass'n *et al.* as Amici Curiae in Support of Petitioners, *Glucksberg* (No. 96–110), *available at* 1996 WL 656263; Brief Amicus Curiae of Am. Hosp. Ass'n in Support of Petitioners, *Glucksberg* (No. 96-110) & *Quill* (No. 96-1858), *available at* 1996 WL 656278; Can. Med. Ass'n, CMA Policy, Euthanasia and Assisted Suicide (1998), *available at* http://www.cma.ca/index.cfm/ci_id/3214/la_id/1.htm (site visited Oct. 24, 2005); Med. Ethics Dep't, Brit. Med. Ass'n, Euthanasia & Physician Assisted Suicide: Do the Moral Arguments Differ? (Apr. 1998), *available at* http://www.bma.org.uk/ap.nsf/Content/Euthanasia+and+physician+assisted+suicide:+Do+the+moral+arguments+differ%3F; World Med. Ass'n, Policy, World Medical Association Statement on Physician-Assisted Suicide (Sept. 1992), *available at* http://www.wma.net/e/policy/p13.htm.

183. N.Y. State Task Force on Life & the Law at vii–ix.

184. *Id.* at 125.

185. *Id.* at 96.

186. *Id.* at 141.

187. *See* Mich. Comm'n on Death & Dying, Final Report of the Michigan Commission on Death and Dying (1994).

188. *See id.* at 5–7.

189. *Id.* at 6.

190. *House of Lords Report* HL Paper, 21-I of 1993–1994 Session at 49. During the brief experiment with legalization in the Northern Territory of Australia, a consultant was commissioned by the government to explain its goals and operation to Aboriginal communities. *See* John Finnis, *Euthanasia, Morality, and Law, Comments at the Fritz B. Burns Lecture* (Nov. 22, 1996), in 31 Loyola of Los Angeles L. Rev. 1123, 1144 n.75 (1998). Despite his initial support for the law, the deep fear Aboriginal communities expressed about the law's implications for them led the consultant to advise the Northern Territory legislature to repeal the statute. *See id.* (referring to unpublished reports on file with John Finnis).

191. *See, e.g.,* Otlowski, *Voluntary Euthanasia* 452 ("A central feature of the Dutch health care system is the comprehensive scheme of national health insurance. . . . This is to be contrasted with the situation in some countries, such as the USA. . . . Since the Netherlands has a health care system available to every citizen, there are not the same financial pressure on patients, as there may be in some countries, for the performance of active voluntary euthanasia.").

192. *House of Lords Report* HL Paper, 21-I of 1993–1994 Session at 67.

193. Ada Jacox *et al.*, *New Clinical-Practice Guidelines for the Management of Pain in Patients with Cancer*, 330 New Eng. J. Med. 651, 651 (1994).

194. Griffiths *et al.*, *Euthanasia and Law* 304 n.5.

195. *See id.* at 31 (describing the Dutch health-care system).

196. Foley and Hendin, *The Oregon Experiment* 156.

197. *See* Wesley J. Smith, *Doctors of Death: Kaiser Solicits Its Doctors to Kill*, Nat'l

Rev. Online (Aug. 19, 2002), *at* http://www.nationalreview.com/comment/comment-smith081902.asp (site visited Oct. 24, 2005).

198. *Id.*

199. *Id.*

200. Otlowski, *Voluntary Euthanasia* 248.

201. *Id.* (emphasis added).

202. *See* ch. 3.8, *supra.*

203. *See id. See also, e.g.*, Griffiths *et al.*, *Euthanasia and Law* 285–92; Kamm, *Physician-Assisted Suicide* 28, 35–36 (stating that a doctor has a "duty to relieve physical suffering" and provide a requested legal dose as well as kill); Mann, *Meanings of Death* 11, 21–22.

204. *See* ch. 7.1 *supra.*

205. *See* chs. 3, 10.2, 10.3. *infra.*

206. Otlowski, *Voluntary Euthanasia* 224.

207. *See id.* at 482–83.

208. *Id.*

209. Cantor, *On Kamisar*, 102 Mich. L. Rev. at 1825.

210. Gina Kolata, *Court Ruling Limits Rights of Patients: Care Deemed Futile May Be Withheld*, N.Y. Times, Apr. 22, 1995, § 1, at 6.

211. *See id.*

212. *See id.*

213. *See id.*

214. *Id.*

215. Mann, *Meanings of Death* 21.

216. *Id.* at 21–22.

217. *See* Nat Hentoff, *A Duty to Die?*, Washington Post, May 31, 1997, at A19.

218. Mann, *Meanings of Death* 22.

219. *Id.*

220. *Id.* at 23.

221. The unintended consequences of legalization would surely include, as well, the fact that it would leave some set of persons who remain morally and religiously opposed to assisted suicide and euthanasia in a position similar to the one in which abolitionists found themselves in antebellum America or contemporary abortion and capital punishment opponents find themselves today—in distress at even passive participation in a regime that facilitates what they believe to be wrong. The social division and unrest associated with such discontent is yet one more "cost" that would have to be figured into any utilitarian calculus hoping to encompass comprehensively the assisted suicide debate.

222. Griffiths *et al.*, *Euthanasia and Law* 26 (emphasis omitted).

223. John Griffiths, *The Slippery Slope: Are the Dutch Sliding Down or Are They Clambering Up?*, in *Asking to Die* 93, 100 (1998) (hereinafter Griffiths, *Slippery Slope*); *see also* Griffiths *et al.*, *Euthanasia and Law* 27 (arguing to the same effect).

224. *See* N. Gregory Mankiw, *Principles of Economics* 68 (2d ed. 2001). Theoretically, some goods may violate the law of demand ("Giffen goods," so named for economist Robert Giffen); their demand curves slope upward because of an exceptionally large negative income effect which dominates the substitution effect. *Id.* at 479. Thus, some suggest that potatoes were in fact a Giffen good during the Irish potato famine of the nine-

teenth century. Potatoes were such a large part of people's diet that when the price of potatoes rose, it had a large income effect. People responded to their reduced living standard by cutting back on the luxury of meat and buying more of the staple food of potatoes. *Id.* Whether any Giffen good has ever been discovered, however, remains a matter of substantial dispute among economists, and, in any event, Griffiths does not invoke the Giffen good theory in his argument for an assisted suicide exception to the law of demand.

225. *See* Griffiths *et al.*, *Euthanasia and Law* 27 & n.23; Griffiths, *Slippery Slope* 100 & nn.6–8; *see also* Brief of Amicus Curiae Bioethicists Supporting Respondents, *Quill* (No. 95-1858) & *Glucksberg* (No. 96-110).

226. *See* van der Maas *et al.*, *Euthanasia 1996*, 335 New Eng. J. Med. at 1702 tbl. 2.

227. *Id.* at 1705. In Washington state, a survey found that 12% of physicians had received requests for physician-assisted suicide and 4% had received a request for euthanasia in the prior year; 24% of these requests were granted. *Id.*

228. *See, e.g.*, Quill, *The Ambiguity of Clinical Intentions*, 329 New Eng. J. Med. at 1039–40; Timothy E. Quill, *Death and Dignity: A Case of Individualized Decision Making*, 324 New Eng. J. Med. 691 (1991); Quill, *The Rule of Double Effect*, 337 New Eng. J. Med. 1768.

229. *See* Diane E. Meier *et al.*, *A National Survey of Physician-Assisted Suicide and Euthanasia in the United States*, 338 New Eng. J. Med. 1193, 1193 (1998).

230. Daniel Q. Haney, *Six Percent of Doctors Say They Have Assisted Patient Suicides*, Washington Post, Apr. 23, 1998, at A9 (referring to a survey performed by Diane E. Meier of the Mount Sinai School of Medicine and quoting Dr. Ezekiel Emanuel of the National Institutes of Health who has estimated that 3% to 13% of all physicians have "hastened" the death of a patient); *see also* Keown, *EEPP* 62 (noting the results of that study); Dick L. Willems *et al.*, *Attitudes and Practices Concerning the End of Life: A Comparison between Physicians from the United States and from the Netherlands*, 160 Archives Internal Med. 63, 66 (2000) (reporting the results of a study comparing Dutch and Oregonian doctors, and concluding that far fewer American doctors receive requests for euthanasia and physician-assisted suicide, as well as intentionally assist patients in dying).

231. van der Maas *et al.*, *Euthanasia 1996*, 335 New Eng. J. Med. at 1705.

232. Paul van der Maas and Linda L. Emmanuel, *Factual Findings*, in *Regulating How We Die: The Ethical, Medical, and Legal Issues Surrounding Physician-Assisted Suicide* 151, 159 (Linda L. Emmanuel, ed., 1998); *see also* Keown, *EEPP* 61–62 (discussing British and American evidence that suggests that the practice of euthanasia and assisted suicide is uncommon).

233. Brief of the Am. Geriatrics Soc'y as Amicus Curiae Urging Reversal of the Judgments Below, *Glucksberg*, 1996 WL 656290, at *10 (No. 96-110).

234. Helga Kuhse, *From Intention to Consent: Learning from Experience with Euthanasia*, in *Physician Assisted Suicide: Expanding the Debate* 252, 263 (hereinafter Kuhse, *From Intention to Consent*).

235. *Id.*

236. *See* Kuhse *et al.*, *End of Life Decisions in Australian Medical Practice*, 166 Med. J. Australia 191, 194–95 (1997); Kuhse, *From Intention to Consent* 263.

237. *See* Kuhse, *From Intention to Consent* 263–66.

238. *See* ch. 7.2 note 80, *supra*, and accompanying text.

239. *See* ch. 7.2 notes 90–95, *supra,* and accompanying text.

240. *See* Kuhse *et al., Australian Medical Practice.*

241. *See* http://www.vesv.org.au/docs/worldfed.htm.

242. *See generally, e.g.,* Singer, *Practical Ethics* 169–76, 181–91.

243. *See infra* chs. 3.8 and 9.1.

244. *See* Kuhse *et al., Australian Medical Practice* 191–92.

245. *See id.* at 191.

246. *See* tbl. 7.1, *supra.*

247. *See* Kuhse, *Australian Medical Practice* 195. The Kuhse-Singer study was poorly designed to identify true cases of passive euthanasia. Participants were asked whether they had withheld or withdrawn treatment with the "explicit intention of not prolonging life or of hastening death." *Id.* at 194; *see also* Kuhse, *From Intention to Consent* 262. But this question obviously risks conflating different things; physician-assisted suicide and euthanasia, as we have discussed, involve actions where an intent to end life is present. An intention "not to prolong life" is unclear and not necessarily the same thing at all, arguably embracing decisions where no intent to end life is present at all, but simply an intent to avoid burdensome or futile care. *See* Keown, *EEPP* 18–30; Neil M. Gorsuch, *The Right to Assisted Suicide and Euthanasia,* 23 Harv. J. Law & Pub. Policy (2000) at 652–53.

248. Kuhse, *Australian Medical Practice* 195.

249. *See id.* at 194 tbl. 3 (reporting that in 62 of 289 surveys regarding omissions of care, doctors simply did not report their discussions, if any, with patients).

250. *See* van der Maas *et al., Euthanasia 1996,* 335 New Eng. J. Med. at 1704 tbl. 4.

251. *See* Kuhse, *Australian Medical Practice,* at 191.

252. *See id.* at 194 tbl. 3.

253. *See* van der Maas *et al., Euthanasia 1996,* 335 New Eng. J. Med. at 1701 tbl. 1.

254. *See id.* at 1704 tbl. 4.

255. Kuhse and Singer suggest that nonvoluntary active euthanasia is also more pervasive in Australia than in the Netherlands—representing fully 3.5% of all deaths, compared with 0.8% and 0.7% of deaths in the Netherlands in 1990 and 1995, respectively. Kuhse, *Australian Medical Practice* 196 tbl. 5. This, if reliable, could be a significant finding, although the authors do not draw much attention to the fact that Australian doctors are apparently more likely to have some discussion with their patients before killing them: 65% of Australian doctors who killed without "explicit" consent reported that the patient either expressed a wish for the procedure or at least discussed the action, compared with 52% of similarly situated Dutch doctors. *See id.* at 194 tbl. 3; van der Maas *et al., Euthanasia 1996,* 335 New Eng. J. Med. at 1704 tbl. 4.

256. Robert Manne, Opinion, *Research and Ye Shall Find,* Bioethics Res. Notes, Mar. 1997, at 1, 1–2 (hereinafter Manne, *Opinion*); *see also* Kuhse, *Australian Medical Practice* 196 tbl. 5.

257. van der Maas *et al., Euthanasia 1996,* 335 New Eng. J. Med. at 1701 tbl. 1.

258. Manne, *Opinion* at 1–2 (emphasis added). Further calling into question Kuhse's and Singer's results, a Belgian study also showed that all medical decisions concerning the end of life (MDEL) accounted for 39.3% of deaths, a figure in line with findings in the Netherlands, and only a fraction of the findings Kuhse and Singer reported in Australia. *See* Luc Deliens *et al., End-of-Life Decisions in Medical Practice in Flanders, Belgium: A Nationwide Survey,* 356 Lancet 1806, 1808 tbl. 1 (2000). The Belgian study did

suggest that patients actively killed without consent represented 3.2% of all deaths, approximating the result found in Australia, *id.* at 1810 tbl. 5, although the Belgium study estimates that in 38% of these cases some discussion had been held or a wish had been stated, *id.* at 1809 tbl. 4.

259. Memorandum from Sheldon Bradshaw, assistant attorney general, U.S. Department of Justice, and Robert J. Delahunty, special counsel, U.S. Department of Justice, to the attorney general, U.S. Department of Justice, *Whether Physician-Assisted Suicide Serves a "Legitimate Medical Purpose" Under the Drug Enforcement Administration's Regulations Implementing the Controlled Substances Act* (June 27, 2003), in 17 Issues L. & Med. 269 (2002) (original pagination omitted).

260. *See* Keown, *EEPP* 63.

261. *See* ch. 7.2, notes 129–30, *supra.*

262. *See* tbl. 7.3, *supra,* and accompanying text.

263. Griffiths *et al., Euthanasia and Law* 245–46; *see also* Keown, *EEPP* 63.

264. *See* Williams, *The Sanctity of Life.*

265. *See* Yale Kamisar, *Some Non-Religious Views against Proposed Mercy Killing Legislation,* 42 Minn. L. Rev. 969 (1958).

266. John Finnis, *Natural Law and Natural Rights* 115 (1980) (hereinafter Finnis, *Natural Law). See generally* Raz, *The Morality of Freedom* 321–68 (1986).

267. Margaret Pabst Battin, *Euthanasia: The Fundamental Issues,* in *The Least Worst Death* 101, 119 (emphasis added).

268. *Id.* (footnote omitted).

269. *Id.*

270. *See id.*

271. *See id.*

272. *See id.*

273. Joel Feinberg, *An Unpromising Approach to the "Right to Die",* in Freedom and Fulfillment: Philosophical Essays 260, 273–74 (1992).

274. Williams, *The Sanctity of Life* 283.

275. *See* Williams, *Textbook of Criminal Law* 37 (rejecting the notion that punishment is justified on the theory that society's intent is not to harm offenders through incarceration but to prevent crime (with punishment being an unintended side effect), and arguing that punishment is justified by "utilitarian opinion" under the theory that any harm done to offenders is outweighed by the benefit of preventing graver evils from occurring to future victims).

276. Rodriguez v. Attorney Gen. of Canada & Attorney Gen. of B.C., [1993] 3 S.C.R. 519, 522 (Can.).

277. *House of Lords Report* HL Paper, 21-I of 1993–1994 Session at 49.

278. 521 U.S. at 785 (Souter, J., concurring).

CHAPTER 8: TWO TEST CASES

1. *See* Posner, *Aging and Old Age* 243–53.

2. *See id.*

3. *Id.* at 247–48.

4. *Id.* at 237.

5. *See* ch. 7 note 116, *supra*, and accompanying text.

6. *See* World Health Org., Suicide Rates (Per 100,000), by Gender and Age, USA, 1950–2000, *at* http://www.who.int/mental_health/media/en/374.pdf (site visited Dec. 20, 2004).

7. Posner, *Aging and Old Age* 250–51 (footnote omitted).

8. *Id.* at 251.

9. *See, e.g., Moultrie v. Martin*, 690 F.2d 1078, 1083 n.7 (4th Cir. 1982) ("Statisticians usually use 95% or 99% confidence levels."); *FTC v. Swedish Match*, 131 F. Supp. 2d 151, 160–61 (D.D.C. 2000) (rejecting use of an 85% confidence level); *Procter & Gamble Co. v. Chesebrough-Pond's Inc.*, 588 F. Supp. 1082, 1088 & n.19 (S.D.N.Y. 1984) (stating that a 95% confidence level is sufficient to be considered statistically significant).

10. *See* Posner, *Aging and Old Age* 250 n.34 ("Data on assisted-suicide laws are from Julia Pugliese, 'Don't Ask—Don't Tell: The Secret Practice of Physician-Assisted Suicide,' 44 *Hastings Law Journal* 1291, 1295 n.20 (1993).").

11. Julia Pugliese, Note, *Don't Ask—Don't Tell* 44 Hastings L.J. 1291, 1295 n.20 (1993).

12. States that, although not mentioned in Julia Pugliese's note, do have statutes banning assisted suicide include Georgia, Offering to Assist in Commission of Suicide, Criminal Penalties, Ga. Code Ann. § 16-5-5 (Lexis 2003); Illinois, Inducement to Commit Suicide, 720 Ill. Comp. Stat. Ann. 5/12-31 (West 2002); Iowa, Assisting Suicide, Iowa Code Ann. § 707A.2 (West 2003); Kentucky, Causing a Suicide—Assisting in a Suicide, Ky. Rev. Stat. Ann. § 216.302 (Michie 1999); Louisiana, Criminal Assistance to Suicide, La. Rev. Stat. Ann. § 14:32.12 (West 1997); Maryland, Assisting Another to Commit or Attempt Suicide, Md. Code Ann., Crim. Law § 3-102 (Michie 2002); North Dakota, Assisting the Commission of Suicide—Causing Death by Suicide—Penalties, N.D. Cent. Code § 12.1-16-04 (Michie 1997); Rhode Island, Prevention of Assisted Suicide, R.I. Gen. Laws Ann. § 11-60-03 (Lexis 2002); South Carolina, Assisted Suicide; Penalties; Injunctive Relief, S.C. Code Ann. § 16-3-1090 (West 2003); and Tennessee, Assisted Suicide, Tenn. Code Ann. § 39-13-216 (Lexis 2003). *See also* appendix A, *infra*. Still other states not on Pugliese's list condemn assisted suicide as a matter of common law. *See, e.g., Kevorkian*, 527 N.W.2d at 716 (permitting prosecution of Kevorkian under common law before Michigan enacted a statute banning assisted suicide).

13. Posner, *Aging and Old Age* 252–53.

14. *See id.* at 252–53; *cf. Daubert v. Merrell Dow Pharms., Inc.*, 509 U.S. 579, 592–95 (1993).

15. *See* ch. 7.4, *supra*.

16. *See* Posner, *Aging and Old Age* 252 n.39.

17. *See* appendix B, *infra* for data and calculations underlying figure 8.2.

18. *See id.*

19. *See* appendix B, *infra*, for data and calculations underlying figures 8.3 and 8.4.

20. *See* World Health Org., Suicide Rates (per 100,000), by Gender, Netherlands, 1950–2000, *at* http://www.who.int/mental_health/media/en/338.pdf (site visited Dec. 20, 2004) (hereinafter Netherlands Suicide Rates).

21. *See id.*

22. *See* discussion ch. 7.4, *supra*.

23. Posner, *Aging and Old Age* 249–50.

24. *See* Netherlands Suicide Rates (stating that suicides per 100,000 deaths in the Netherlands were 10.1 in 1980, 11.3 in 1985, 9.7 in 1990, 9.8 in 1995, and 9.4 in 2000).

25. *See* ch. 7.1, note 50, *supra*.

26. *See* tbl. 7.1, *supra*. The Dutch also record thousands of cases where patients are intentionally killed by omission without their consent, including some 8,750, or 6.78% of all deaths, in 1990 (again, 1995 data was not published). *See* ch. 7.2, notes 68–70, *supra*, and accompanying text.

27. Posner, *Aging and Old Age* 249–50.

28. *See id.*

29. *See, e.g.*, Richard D. McBride and Fred S. Zufryden, *An Integer Programming Approach to the Optimal Product Line Selection Problem*, 7 Marketing Sci. 126 (1988); Kamalini Ramdas and Mohanbir S. Sawhney, *A Cross-Functional Approach to Evaluating Multiple Line Extensions for Assembled Products*, 47 Mgmt. Sci. 22 (2001).

30. Posner seeks to supplement his empirical case for legalization by positing that terminally ill persons would find comfort in knowing that they could choose to die on demand even if they never use the option. *See* Posner, *Aging and Old Age* 239. Living would become more bearable, the argument runs, knowing that death is easily available. *See id.* at 239–40. But Posner makes no attempt to quantify how many people would find an unrealized option to obtain assisted suicide to be valuable, how valuable they would find it, or how the psychic benefit of a never-used option compares against the harms that may attend the regularized practice of assisted suicide—both actual (for example, people killed without their consent as a result of accident or abuse) as well as psychic (for example, people who are frightened that they might be killed without consent even if they are never so killed).

31. *See id.* at 244.

32. *See id.* at 245 n.27.

33. *See id.*

34. *Id.*

35. *See id.* at 243–44.

36. *See id.* at 244.

37. *Id.*

38. *Id.*

39. *Id.*

40. Mill, *On Liberty* 9.

41. Posner, *Aging and Old Age* 244 (emphasis added).

42. *Id.* at 237 (emphasis added).

43. *Id.* at 238.

44. *Id.* at 257.

45. *Id.*

46. *Id.*

47. Epstein, *Mortal Peril* 305.

48. *Id.*

49. *Id.* at 304.

50. *Id.* at 304–5.

51. *Id.* at 305 (emphasis added).

CHAPTER 9: AN ARGUMENT AGAINST LEGALIZATION

1. By way of example, Otlowski devotes two paragraphs of her book to arguments along these lines, and then only in the context of religious commands, ignoring strong secular grounds for prohibiting intentional killing. *See* Otlowski, *Voluntary Euthanasia* 214–15.

2. *See, e.g.,* Joseph Boyle, *Sanctity of Life and Suicide: Tensions and Developments within Common Morality* 221, in *Suicide and Euthanasia* (Baruch Brody, ed., 1989) (hereinafter Boyle, *Sanctity of Life and Suicide*); Aquinas, *ST* part 2 of the Second Part, Q. 64, a. 2–6 (arguing that a murderer loses his human dignity by engaging in criminal activity); John Finnis, Joseph Boyle and Germain Grisez, *Nuclear Deterrence, Morality and Realism* (1988). One of the authors of *Nuclear Deterrence* once thought that capital punishment is consistent with this norm, though he subsequently changed his view: *see* John Finnis, *Aquinas* 282, 293 (1998). Nor do I seek here to engage the abortion debate. Abortion would be ruled out by the inviolability-of-life principle I intend to set forth *if,* but only *if,* a fetus is considered a human life. The Supreme Court in *Roe,* however, unequivocally held that a fetus is not a "person" for purposes of constitutional law. *See* ch. 5.2, *supra.*

3. *See* George, *Making Men Moral* 12–14.

4. *See* ch. 3.1, *supra*; Aristotle, *Ethics* § 1107a9–17.

5. *See* ch. 3.2, *supra.*

6. *See, e.g.,* John Finnis, *Moral Absolutes: Tradition, Revision and Truth* 1–30 (1991); Finnis, *Natural Law* chs. 3–5; Robert George, *Recent Criticisms of Natural Law Theory,* 55 U. Chi. L. Rev. 1371 (1988) (hereinafter George, *Recent Criticisms*).

7. To say that a good is self-evident is not, of course, to say that everyone will recognize it as such. In our Declaration of Independence, we hold the rights to life, liberty, and the pursuit of happiness to be self-evident; not every society has (or does). *See* George, *Recent Criticisms,* 55 U. Chi. L. Rev. at 1410–12.

8. Finnis, *Natural Law* 86.

9. Declaration of Independence ¶ 2.

10. *House of Lords Report* HL Paper, 21-I of 1993–1994 Session ¶ 237.

11. 14 Q.B.D. 271 (1884).

12. *Id.*

13. *Id.*

14. 26 F. Cas. 360, 1 Wall Jr. 1 (C.C.E.D. Pa. 1842). Sentencing defendants in cases like *Dudley* and *Holmes* may, of course, pose a different and difficult task, and courts have recognized the need for some leniency. In *Dudley,* the Court imposed a death sentence that was later commuted by the Crown to six months' imprisonment. Holmes was initially sentenced to six months' imprisonment, though the punishment was later remitted.

Benjamin Cardozo later vigorously defended the result in *Holmes*: "Where two or more are overtaken by common disaster, there is no right on the part of one to save the lives of some by the [intentional] killing of another. There is no rule of human jettison." Benjamin Cardozo, *Life and Literature* 113 (1930). And states have codified *Holmes*'s teaching. *See, e.g.,* Wis. Stat. Ann. tit. 45, § 939 ("Pressure of natural physical forces which causes the actor reasonably to believe that his act is the only means of preventing imminent public disaster, or imminent death or great bodily harm to himself or another and which causes him so to act, is a defense to the prosecution for any crime based on that act except that if the prosecution is for murder the degree of the crime is reduced to manslaughter."); Ky. Rev. Stat. Ann. ch. 500, § 500.410; Mo. Ann. Stat. tit. 38, § 563.026.

15. Posner, *Aging and Old Age* 241.

16. Dworkin, *Life's Dominion* 69.

17. *Id.* at 93.

18. *Id.* at 230.

19. *See* ch. 3.8; ch. 6.5; ch. 7.1, ch. 8.2, *supra*.

20. Posner, *Aging and Old Age* 256–57.

21. *Id.* at 257.

22. Epstein, *Mortal Peril* 323.

23. Linacre Centre Submission, reprinted in *Euthanasia, Clinical Practice and the Law* 124 (Luke Gormally ed., 1994).

24. *See Morrisette*, 342 U.S. at 250; ch. 4.3, *supra*.

25. The moral and legal significance of the intent-foresight distinction is discussed and defended in chapter 4.

26. *See* ch. 4.5, *supra*.

27. *See* ch. 4.5, *supra*.

28. *Falcone*, 109 F.2d at 581. *See also* ch. 4, *supra*. Thus, while Timothy Quill has criticized intent as a difficult standard to establish in individual cases, it is a difficult standard to establish *by design*, and a standard that helped Quill himself avoid prosecution for his role in providing sleeping aids to a patient who used them to kill herself. *See* chs. 1 and 4.6, *supra*.

29. Keown, *EEPP* 235.

30. Raz, *The Morality of Freedom* 418–19; *see also* ch. 6.3, *supra*.

31. *See* George, *Making Men Moral* 185–86.

32. While the primary risk associated with a wrongful slavery contract is unwanted enslavement, the risk of a wrongful act of assisted suicide is an unwanted death.

33. *See* Model Penal Code § 3.04.

34. *See, e.g.*, Model Penal Code § 2.04; *State v. Kelly*, 478 A.2d 364 (N.J. 1984); *Commonwealth v. Ross*, 416 A.2d 1092 (Pa. 1979).

35. *See* ch. 3.4, *supra*.

36. *See, e.g.*, Model Penal Code § 3.04(2)(b)(i) & (ii).

37. *See* ch. 7.2, *supra*.

38. *See* ch. 9.1, *supra*.

39. *See* Model Penal Code, § 3.02, cmt. 3.

40. *Id.*

41. *See also* ch. 10.2, *infra* (discussing invocation of necessity doctrine by Lord Justice Brooke in a recent case before the English Court of Appeal).

42. Model Penal Code, § 3.04.

43. *See id.* § 3.11(1) & cmt. 1.

44. *Id.*

45. Sanford Kadish has queried whether the first mate's decision in *Holmes* to throw overboard excess passengers, like the moutaineer's decision to cut the rope, could have been argued as a case of self-defense. Sanford Kadish, *et al.*, *Criminal Law and Its Processes*

921 n.32 (5th ed. 1989). And perhaps it could have been: whereas the intent to kill (at least as a means) is manifest and undeniable in *Dudley*, the first mate in *Holmes* did not kill his passengers but apparently ordered them overboard. Accordingly, it is possible that he may not have wanted to see them dead but hoped to see them survive in the water until a rescue ship arrived. Of course, as with any claim of self-defense, a detailed appreciation of the facts is necessary. For example, did the first mate wait until the last possible second (like the mountaineer) before ordering his passengers overboard? Did he provide them whatever assistance was available to make their survival more likely? Ultimately, for our purposes, however, whether *Holmes* might have been argued as a case of self-defense does nothing to advance (and even further undercuts) the case for necessity doctrine in the law of intentional homicide.

46. Singer, *Practical Ethics* ii; Singer, *Rethinking Life and Death* rear cover.

47. Singer, *Practical Ethics* 170.

48. *Id.*

49. *Id.* at 171.

50. *Id.* at 94.

51. *Id.* at 171. For analogous views, *see, e.g.,* Jeffrey Reiman, *Abortion and the Ways We Value Human Life* (1999) (hereinafter Reiman, *Abortion*).

52. *Id.*

53. *Id.* at 182.

54. *See* ch. 7.1, *supra.*

55. *See* ch. 6.1, *supra.*

56. Singer, *Practical Ethics* 173 (emphasis added).

57. *Id. See also* Reiman, *Abortion.*

58. Singer, *Practical Ethics* 173.

59. *Id.* at 187.

60. *Id.* at 188.

61. Perhaps somewhat surprisingly, given his views, Singer includes a substantial afterword in *Practical Ethics* expressing shock at having been identified by some Germans, while on a speaking tour in their country, with the eugenics ideology of National Socialism. *Id.* at 337–59. *See also* Nat Hentoff, *Doctor Death: A Newborn Is Not a Person*, Village Voice (Feb. 23–29, 2000) (comparing Singer's position that it is acceptable to kill innocent persons intentionally with Nazi ideology).

62. *Id.* at 173.

63. *Id.* at 89.

64. Dworkin, *Life's Dominion* 195.

65. Singer, *Practical Ethics* 117.

66. *Id.* at 89–90.

67. *Id.* at 88.

68. *Id.* at 110–11.

69. *Id.* at 117.

70. *Id.* at 119.

71. Singer quotes an anti-infanticide activist, Nuala Scarisbrick, as having described his position as meaning that "[an] unwanted [infant] is . . . guilty of a capital offense." Singer responds candidly that "Nuala Scarisbrick was not so far off the mark." Singer, *Rethinking Life and Death* 128–29.

72. *See* ch. 9.2, *supra.*

73. Singer's *actions*, as opposed to his *writings*, appear to support the traditional "species-based" understanding of personhood. It has been reported that Singer hired, at considerable expense, health-care workers to provide comfort and dignity for his mother, who suffered from Alzheimer's disease and is no longer able to remember or recognize others and who, thus, may not qualify as a "person" to him. Peter Berkowitz, *The Utilitarian Horrors of Peter Singer: Other People's Mothers*, The New Republic (Jan. 10, 2000).

74. 891 F. Supp. 1429.

75. Of course, the lack of a rational fit between Oregon's asserted purposes and its statutory regime would be even more intolerable under a strict scrutiny or intermediate level review.

76. 107 F.3d 1382.

77. *Lee v. Oregon*, 891 F. Supp. 1429, 1434 (D. Or. 1995), *overruled on other grounds*, 107 F.3d 1382 (9th Cir. 1997).

78. *E.g., J.E.B. v. Alabama*, 511 U.S. 127 (1994); *Mississippi University for Women*, 458 U.S., 718, 724 (1982); *Stanton v. Stanton*, 421 U.S. 7, 13 (1975); *Harris v. Forklift Systems*, 510 U.S. 17 (1993).

79. *E.g., Craig v. Boren*, 429 U.S. 190 (1976).

80. *See also* ch. 9.1, *supra*.

81. *See, e.g., Lawrence*, 539 U.S. at 580–81 (O'Connor, J., concurring in the judgment) (arguing that antisodomy laws based on belief that homosexuality is "devia[nt]" should be struck down on equal protection grounds); *Romer v. Evans*, 517 U.S. 620 (1996) (disallowing state statute seeking to deny benefits to homosexuals); *Department of Agriculture v. Moreno*, 413 U.S. 528 (1973) (striking down food stamp law that precluded households containing an individual unrelated to any other members of the household from receiving food stamps on the ground that it discriminated against "hippies"); *Eisenstadt*, 405 U.S. 438 (overturning legal distinction in access to contraceptives between married and unmarried persons); *Cleburne v. Cleburne Living Center*, 473 U.S. 432, 440 (1982) (rejecting law that required homes for the mentally disabled to obtain a special use permit when other residences, like fraternities and apartment buildings, did not have to obtain such a permit).

82. *Compassion in Dying*, 49 F.3d at 590.

83. *Lee*, 891 F. Supp. at 1434.

84. Or. Rev. Stat. § 426.231, *et seq*. While an ordinary physician may hold mentally ill persons who are dangerous to themselves for a period of twelve hours, any further detention must be preceded by an examination from a qualified mental health expert. *Id.*

85. 891 F. Supp. at 1436.

86. *Id.*

87. *Id.* at 1437.

88. *See, e.g.*, ch. 7.2, *supra* (discussing the case of Ms. Cheney and her daughter).

89. *Id.*

CHAPTER 10: TOWARD A CONSISTENT END-OF-LIFE ETHIC

1. *See* ch. 4.1, *supra*.

2. 331 F.2d 1000 (D.C. Cir. 1964).

3. *Id.* at 1009.

4. 362 So. 2d 160 (Fla. App. 1978).

5. *Id.* at 162.

6. *Id.* at 161, 162–63. Likewise, in *Eichner v. Dillon*, 426 N.Y.S.2d 517 (1980) the New York Court of Appeals recognized the right to withdraw a life-sustaining respirator but also specifically added that, on the facts before it, the withdrawal of the respirator involved no "*intent to die.*" *Id.* at 544 (emphasis added).

7. 529 A.2d 404 (N.J. 1987).

8. 529 A.2d at 410–11.

9. *Id.*

10. 529 A.2d at 411. Other cases have involved similar patients and have been resolved with similar reasoning. *See, e.g., Bartling v. Superior Court*, 209 Cal. Rptr. 220 (Ct. App. 1984); *Tune v. Walter Reed Army Medical Hosp.*, 602 F. Supp. 1452 (D.D.C. 1985).

11. 529 A.2d at 412.

12. 225 Cal. Rptr. 297 (Ct. App. 1986).

13. C. Everett Koop and Edward R. Grant, *The Small Beginnings of Euthanasia: Examining the Erosion in Legal Prohibitions against Mercy-Killing*, 2 Notre Dame J.L. Ethics & Pub. Pol'y 585, 629 (1986).

14. *Id. See also* Michael R. Flick, *The Due Process of Dying*, 79 Cal. L. Rev. 1121, 1128 (1991) (physician arguing that Bouvia's demand to die was the product of mental illness).

15. 225 Cal. Rptr. at 305 (quoting trial court).

16. *Id.* at 306.

17. In the end, after her two-year wrangle in court, Bouvia changed her mind and opted to continue her feeding tube. *See* Nat Hentoff, *Elizabeth Bouvia and the ACLU: I Used to Go to the ACLU for Help, Now They're Killing Us*, Village Voice, July 30, 1996, at 10.

18. *Bouvia*, 225 Cal. Rptr. at 1146.

19. *Id.*

20. *Id.* at 1146, 1147.

21. 801 P.2d 617 (Nev. 1990).

22. *Id.* at 620.

23. *Id.* at 624.

24. After the petition was granted by the lower court, Bergstedt had the ventilator removed and was dead by the time the case made its way to the state Supreme Court, which chose to hear the case anyway.

25. 801 P.2d at 625, 627.

26. *Id.* at 626.

27. *Id.* at 634.

28. *Id.* at 635.

29. *Id.* at 633 n.4 (internal quotations marks omitted).

30. *Id.* at 626.

31. *Id.*

32. [1993] Fam. 95.

33. *Id.* at 112.

34. *Id.*

35. *Id.*

36. *Id.* at 113. In addition to her limited capacity, the court added that the mother's influence appeared to have overborne T's own will and suggested that courts faced with similar cases should, in the future, examine whether the patient is "very tired, in pain or depressed," such that he or she "will be much less able to resist having his will overborne" and also examine "the relationship of the 'persuader' to the patient. . . . [because] [t]he influence of parents on their children . . . can be, but is by no means necessarily, much stronger than would be the case in other relationships." *Id.* at 113–114.

37. [2002] 1 FLR 1090.

38. *Id.* at 1114.

39. *Id.*

40. *Id.* at 1115.

41. *See* ch. 3, *supra.*

42. This is *not* to say that persons in the shoes of Bouvia or Bergstedt—nonterminal patients dependent on medical intervention—cannot refuse care that will foreseeably result in their deaths; it is only to say that the facts in those cases seem to suggest Bouvia and Bergstedt did, in fact, intend to kill themselves.

43. *See also* Meisel, *The Right to Die* § 3.2, at 45 (collecting cases). Indeed, battery doctrine traditionally has included an exception permitting volunteers to intercede to prevent an act of suicide. *See* ch. 3, *supra.*

44. *See* ch. 4.2, *supra.*

45. Ill. Comp. Stat., ch. 755, § 35/9(f) (emphasis added). For many other analogous examples, *see* ch. 3, *supra.*

46. *See* ch. 4.5, *supra.*

47. To be sure, the requirement of proof regarding the assister's intention sets a high bar before the government may enmesh itself in private affairs, and prosecutions are purposefully rare. As we saw in chapter 4, some, such as John Griffiths, reject focusing on intention and therefore see no distinction between refusals of care and assisted suicide. Precisely because of this absence of any distinction, Griffiths seeks to impose a comprehensive state-run "regulatory regime" that would treat refusals of care, provisions of palliative care, assisted suicide, and even nonvoluntary euthanasia as an undifferentiated mass—presumably imposing the same consultation requirements, waiting periods, and reporting requirements that are currently required for assisted suicide and euthanasia in jurisdictions where they are lawful. Such global state intervention is not logically dictated, however, for those who recognize an intent-based distinction between various of these practices—and Griffiths himself acknowledges that many doctors he interviewed were "critical" of his comprehensive regulatory proposal precisely because they sense assisted suicide cases to be different and meriting different treatment from the run of cases involving the refusal of treatment precisely because the former cases necessarily involve the intentional taking of life and the latter cases do not. *See* Griffiths, *Euthanasia & Law* 297 n.65.

48. *In re Infant Doe*, No. GU8204–004A (Monroe County Cir. Ct. Apr. 12, 1982) (unpublished declaratory judgment) at 1.

49. "Virtually all individuals with Down's syndrome have some degree of developmental retardation. The range of IQ scores has been wide, but most individuals are trainable by adulthood. Social skills usually are closer to the normal range than performance

abilities. . . . The degree of mental retardation is quite variable, but most children learn to walk and develop some communication skills; there is a steady progress of development, at a slower pace than usual . . . [and c]hildren reared at home have higher IQs than those reared in institutions." A. Rudolph, *Pediatrics* 244 (17th ed. 1983).

50. *See* R. Behrman and V. Vaughan, *Nelson Textbook of Pediatrics* 893–94 (12th ed. 1983).

51. *In re Infant Doe*, declaratory judgment at 1–3.

52. *Id.*

53. *Id.*

54. *No Decisions Yet on Possible Prosecution*, Bloomington Sunday Herald-Times, at 1, col. 3 (Apr. 10, 1983).

55. *In re Phillip B.*, 92 Cal. App. 3d 796, 156 Cal. Rptr. 48 (1979), *cert. denied*, 445 U.S. 949 (1980).

56. *Id.* at 801, 156 Cal. Rptr. at 51.

57. *Id.* at 802, 156 Cal. Rptr. at 51.

58. *Id.* at 803, 156 Cal. Rptr. at 52.

59. *Id.*

60. *Id.*

61. *See* Griffiths, *Euthanasia and Law* 200.

62. Specifically, the judge remarked that, "[i]n nearly every case [involving a Down's syndrome child] if the parents want the child the doctor will give them every encouragement to have it and keep it. But if not[,] the likelihood of the child ever being taken into another family, either by adoption or fostering, is very remote and the most likely course is that it will be placed in some form of institution. So it is not just a simple question of saying: it is a mongol child; it will have to be put down. It is a case, say the defence, in putting this case before you, of where the most careful and agonising consideration has to be given as to what should be done in the best interests of the child." *Quoted in* Luke Gormally, *Note: Regina v. Arthur, in Euthanasia, Clinical Practice and the Law* 104–7 (Luke Gormally ed., 1994)(hereinafter Gormally, *Note*).

63. For details and views on the unreported Pearson case, *see* Gormally, *Note*; Helga Kuhse, *A Modern Myth. That Letting Die Is Not the Intentional Causation of Death: Some Reflections on the Trial and Acquittal of Dr. Leonard Arthur*, 1 Journal of Applied Philosophy 21–38 (1984).

64. *See generally* John Keown, *Restoring Moral and Intellectual Shape to the Law After Bland*, 113 L.Q. Rev. 481 (1997).

65. The Department of Health and Human Services also promulgated new regulations under Section 504 of the Rehabilitation Act of 1973 forbidding discrimination by parents against handicapped newborns. When the federal government requested a hospital's records to see if there was a violation of its rule, however, a legal challenge ensued and the U.S. Supreme Court eventually overturned the department's rules, holding that Congress's intent in banning discrimination based on handicap under Section 504 was to focus upon discrimination by federally funded doctors and agencies; such a law was too thin a reed on which to rest the promulgation of regulations directed at parents, especially when the states, not the federal government, have traditionally overseen and regulated the parent-child relationship. *See Bowen v. American Hosp. Ass'n*, 476 U.S. 610 (1986).

66. Specifically, the state must formulate a plan to ensure "prompt notification by in-

dividuals designated by and within appropriate health-care facilities of cases of suspected medical neglect (including instances of withholding of medically indicated treatment from disabled infants with life-threatening conditions); and . . . authority, under State law, for the State child protective services system to pursue any legal remedies, including the authority to initiate legal proceedings in a court of competent jurisdiction." 42 U.S.C. § 5106a(b)(2)(B).

67. *Id.* § 5106(g).

68. *Id.*

69. *Id.*

70. Singer, *Rethinking Life and Death* 113 (1994).

71. *Id.* at 112.

72. *See* Ind. Code Ann. § 31-34-1-9.

73. Ariz. Rev. Stat. Ann § 36–2281(A) & (B) (emphasis added).

74. *Id.* § 36-2284(D). Drawing the line between ordinary cases where parental decisions are given wide latitude and life-and-death decisions where they are reasonably subject to greater scrutiny, the Arizona statute adds that "[t]his section shall not be construed to prevent an infant's parent, parents or guardian from refusing to give consent to medical treatment or surgical care which is not medically necessary, including care or treatment which either: 1. Is not necessary to save the life of the infant. 2. Has a potential risk to the infant's life or health that outweighs the potential benefit to the infant of the treatment or care. 3. Is futile treatment or treatment that will do no more than temporarily prolong the act of dying when death is imminent." *Id.* § 36-2284(C). The statute adds a further layer of deference to doctors by providing that "[i]n determining whether any of the possible medical treatments will be medically necessary for an infant, reasonable medical judgments in selecting among alternative courses of treatment shall be respected." *Id.* § 36-2281(D).

75. *See In re A*, [2001] Fam. 147.

76. For a detailed description of the twins' medical condition and the facts of the case, *see id.* at 156–71.

77. Contrast this with another English decision—*Bland*—where the Lords failed to acknowledge that omissions of care *can* amount to a violation of a duty of care (and murder). *See* ch. 4.1, *supra*; ch. 10.2, *infra*.

78. *In re A*, [2001] Fam. at 178 (internal quotation marks omitted).

79. *Id.* at 194 (internal quotation marks omitted).

80. *Id.* at 195 (internal quotation marks omitted).

81. *See, e.g., id.* at 198–99 (opinion of Lord Justice Ward).

82. *Id.* at 199.

83. *Id.*

84. *Id.* at 216–17.

85. *Id.* at 203–4.

86. *Id.* at 255.

87. *Id.* at 229.

88. *Id.* at 236.

89. *Id.* at 239.

90. *See* A. P. Simester and G. R. Sullivan, *Criminal Law Theory and Doctrine* (2002).

91. 1990 Survey, Translated in Keown, *Further Reflections* 229.

92. *See* ch. 9.3, *supra*.

93. *Holmes*, too, seemed to involve a case of intentional killing, though some have suggested otherwise and raised the possibility that the defendants actions there could have been (though they were not) defended under the self-defense rubric without any need to resort to necessity at all. *See* ch. 9.3, *supra*. In either event, *Holmes* would not be inconsistent with the narrow necessity rule we are considering.

94. *See* European Convention art. 2(1) (emphasis added).

95. *In re A*, [2001] Fam. at 256 (emphasis added).

96. *Id.* at 238 (emphasis added).

97. Living wills and other advance directives are typically subject to statutory directives against judicial interpretations that might condone euthanasia. *See*, e.g., Ill. Comp. Stat., ch. 755, § 35/9(f). For many other analogous examples, *see* ch. 3, *supra*.

98. 497 N.E. 2d 626, 647 (Mass. 1986) (internal quotation marks omitted).

99. *Id.* at 632.

100. *Id.* at 633.

101. *Id.* at 634–35. The court also mentioned the state's interest in protecting innocent third parties, such as dependents, but none was present in this case. The court stated that the state had a further interest in maintaining the ethical integrity of the medical profession, but this question largely folds into the question whether removing the G-tube constitutes an assault on the preservation of life or an act of suicide. If the act is not one of suicide, then there is no reason to suppose it would be necessarily antithetical to medical ethics.

102. *See* chs. 7.7 and 8.1, *supra* (discussing the consequentialist's incommensurability problem).

103. *Brophy*, 497 N.E.2d at 635–36.

104. *See* ch. 8, *supra*.

105. *See* ch. 4.1, *supra*.

106. *Brophy*, 497 N.E. 2d at 633.

107. 370 N.E. 2d 417 (Mass. 1977).

108. *Id.* at 420.

109. *Id.* at 419, 421.

110. *Id.* at 425.

111. *Id.* at 425–26.

112. Of course, a guardian's duty to a ward extends beyond avoiding intentional killings and encompasses a duty to undertake a careful and proportionate decision even where death is an unwanted side effect. The guardian in this case seemed to have exercised just such care.

113. [1993] A.C. 789.

114. Keown, *EEPP* 218.

115. *Bland*, [1993] A.C. at 865. *See also* ch. 4.2, *supra* (discussing the act-omission distinction drawn by the Lords in *Bland*).

116. *See* John Keown, *Euthanasia in The Netherlands: Sliding Down the Slippery Slope?* in *Euthanasia Examined: Ethical, Clinical, and Legal Perspectives* 270–71 (John Keown, ed., 1995) (emphasis added).

117. *See Bland*, [1993] A.C. at 809–14, 817–18.

118. *Id.* at 870 (Lord Goff).

119. *Id.* at 869, 899.

120. *See, e.g., Conroy,* 486 A.2d at 1234–35; Meisel, *Right to Die* § 4.6, at 82–87 (collecting cases and providing overview of problems associated with efforts to distinguish "ordinary" from "extraordinary" treatment).

121. *See* Keown, *EEPP* 239 *et seq.*; John Finnis, *Bland: Crossing the Rubicon?,* 109 L. Q. Rev. 329, 335 (1993).

122. *Conroy,* 486 A.2d at 1235 (internal quotation marks omitted).

123. *Bland,* [1993] A.C. at 830.

124. *Id.* at 804.

125. Keown, *EEPP* 230.

126. [1993] A.C. at 814–15.

127. Keown, *EEPP* 232.

128. 28 P.2d 151 (Cal. 2001).

129. *Id.* at 156.

130. *Id.* (internal quotation marks omitted).

131. *Id.* at 161 (internal quotation marks omitted).

132. *Id.* at 162 (internal quotation marks omitted).

133. *Id.* at 162–63 (internal quotation marks and citations omitted).

134. *Id.* at 161.

135. *Id.* at 169.

136. *Id.*

137. *Id.* at 174.

138. *Id.*

139. *Id.* at 153.

140. *Id.* at 156

141. *Id.* at 175.

142. Ill. Comp. Stat., ch. 755, § 35/9(f).

EPILOGUE

1. ___ U.S. __, 126 S. Ct. 904 (2006).

2. *Id.* at 924, 914.

3. *Id.*

4. *Id.* at 925.

5. The Court's statutory interpretation in *Gonzales* might be said to be consistent with and illustrative of Justice Breyer's interpretive theory of "active liberty," discussed in his 2004 Tanner Lectures at Harvard and recently published in book form. *See* Stephen Breyer, *Active Liberty: Interpreting Our Democratic Constitution* (2005). "My thesis is that courts should take greater account of the Constitution's democratic nature when they interpret constitutional and statutory texts. That thesis encompasses well-known arguments for judicial modesty: The judge, compared to the legislator, lacks relevant expertise. The people must develop the political experience and they must obtain the moral education and stimulus that comes from correcting their own errors. Judges, too, must display that doubt, caution, and prudence, that not being too sure of oneself, that Judge Learned Hand described as the spirit of liberty. . . . [I]ncreased emphasis upon that objective by judges when they interpret a legal text will yield better law—law that helps a

community of individuals democratically find practical solutions to contemporary social problems." *Id.* at 5, 6 (internal quotation marks and ellipses omitted).

6. That said, the Court did describe the Oregon statutory regime in a manner that is open to being interpreted as endorsing how the law was drafted. To take just one example, the Court described the Oregon law as requiring attending physicians to "ensure a patient's choice is informed, and refer patients to counseling if they might be suffering from a psychological disorder or depression causing impaired judgment." *Id.* at 4. Such a description may very well reflect the aspirations of the Oregon regime, but it does not seem to be an entirely accurate description of that regime in practice. For example, as we saw in chapter 7, many Oregon physicians admit they aren't good at recognizing depression and other mental ailments; prescribing physicians do not have the sort of long-term relationships with their patients needed in many cases to diagnose depression; doctors under Oregon's regime are not required to ensure the patient's choice to die is informed and rational at the time patients actually choose to ingest the lethal medication; and prescribing doctors refer patients to psychiatric specialists to look for evidence of depression or other mental disorders only in a very (and increasingly) small subset of cases.

7. *See, e.g.,* John Keown, *The Mackay Report on the Assisted Dying for the Terminally Ill Bill: An Unbalanced Basis for Debate* (forthcoming from the Care Not Killing Alliance); Care Not Killing website, *available at* http://www.carenotkilling.org.uk (site visited March 28, 2006).

8. *See* International Task Force on Euthanasia and Assisted Suicide, Update 2006, vol. 20, no. 1, *available at* http://www.internationaltaskforce.org/iua35.htm (site visited March 28, 2006).

9. *Id.*

10. Oregon Department of Human Services, *Eighth Annual Report on Oregon's Death With Dignity Act* (March 9, 2006), *available at* http://www.oregon.gov/DHS/ph/pas/ (site visited March 28, 2006).

11. After growing rapidly from 1999 through 2002, the number of prescriptions written has remained in the sixties over the last three years; whether some, all, or none of this slackening in demand has been due to the overhang of uncertainty associated with the Ashcroft Directive and the ensuing litigation that only recently culminated in the *Gonzales* decision remains to be seen.

12. As noted in chapter 7, Oregon first sought to study how many of these doctors are connected to assisted suicide advocacy groups but then curiously reversed course and chose to leave that question unaddressed.

13. White persons accounted for 97% of assisted suicides in Oregon through 2005 but 87% of that state's population. *See* U.S. Census Bureau, State & County QuickFacts, *available at* http://quickfacts.census.gov/qfd/states/41000.html (site visited March 28, 2006).

14. Clive Seale, *National Survey of End-of-Life Decisions Made by UK Medical Practitioners,* 20 Palliative Medicine 3 (2006).

15. The study also found that Belgium and the Netherlands and Switzerland, where assisted suicide and euthanasia are more tolerated, have combined rates of assisted suicide and euthanasia (voluntary and nonvoluntary) far higher than those of certain other Euopean countries where the practices are less tolerated: Netherlands (5.12% of all deaths), Belgium (2.26%), Switzerland (1.53%) versus Italy (0.11%) and the U.K. (0.36%). *Id.* at 7.

16. *Id.* at 6.

17. The 0.90% figure includes only acts of *affirmative* nonvoluntary euthanasia. As discussed in chapter 7, one can make a good argument that, counting acts of omissions or withdrawals of care performed without patient consent, the rate of nonvoluntary euthanasia is much higher in the Netherlands. In any event, the rates of killing without consent seem to be much higher in European countries that have tended to express a permissive attitude toward assisted suicide than those that have adopted a stricter approach: Belgium (2.26%), Netherlands (0.90% or more), Switzerland (0.61%) versus Italy (0.11%) or the U.K. (0.36%). *Id.*

18. The study also revealed an additional methodological flaw in the Singer-Kuhse study discussed in chapter 7, noting that the exceptionally high percentage of deaths in Australia it found caused by medical decisions concerning the end of life, or MDELs, may be attributable to the fact that Singer-Kuhse study rested on deaths nominated by the surveyed doctors for study rather than on a perhaps more objective survey of death certificates. "The effect of this is to artificially inflate the proportion of deaths receiving [MDELs], a point not appreciated by the Australian investigators." *Id.* at 6.

19. *Id.* at 6, 8.

20. *Id.* at 8.

21. *See, e.g., Dutch Consider Legalizing Infanticide,* Newsmax.com (March 27, 2006), *available at* http://www.newsmax.com/archives/ic/2006/3/27/115852.shtml (site visited March 28, 2006).

22. Eduard Verhagen and Pieter Sauer, *The Groningen Protocol—Euthanasia in Severely Ill Newborns,* 352 New England Journal of Medicine 959, 960 (2005).

23. *Id.* at 960.

24. Marije L. van der Lee, *et al., Euthanasia and Depression: A Prospective Cohort Study Among Terminally Ill Cancer Patients,* 23 Journal of Clinical Oncology 6607 (2005).

25. "Our clinical impression was that such requests were well-considered decisions, thoroughly discussed with healthcare workers and family. We thought the patients requesting euthanasia were more accepting of their impending deaths and were therefore expected to find them to be less depressed. To our surprise, we found that a depressed mood was associated with more requests." *Id.* at 6611.

26. *Id.*

27. "In order to assess whether the prevalence of depressed mood increased with shorter life expectancy, which could have been an alternative explanation for our findings, we examined the association between depressed mood and survival among those patients dying without euthanasia. . . . There was no association between mood and survival." *Id.* at 6610.

28. Writing in response to the Dutch study, Ezekiel Emanuel of the National Institutes of Health, has provocatively suggested that "the fact that depression may be a natural reaction to a desperate situation does not mean it should not be treated. . . . That people are depressed because of their impending death should warrant, rather than preclude, . . . treatment. . . . The oncology system has responded admirably to making pain, making it a fifth vital sign; dispelling prejudice, ignorance, and false claims about its treatment; encouraging more aggressive use of opioids and other pain medications; and developing pain services. We need to be equally proactive about routinely screening for and treating depression and other psychological disorders among cancer patients. Depression could be a sixth vital sign." Ezekiel J. Emanuel, *Depression, Euthanasia, and Improving End-of-Life Care,* 23 Journal of Clinical Oncology 6456, 6457 (2005).

Bibliography

CASES

A, In re, [2001] 2 W.L.R. 480, [2001] Fam. 147.
Adamson v. California, 332 U.S. 45 (1947).
Airedale N.H.S. Trust v. Bland, [1993] A.C. 789.
Albright v. Oliver, 510 U.S. 266, 275 (1994).
Applications of the President and Directors of Georgetown College, 331 F.2d 1000 (D.C. Cir. 1964).
Apprendi v. New Jersey, 530 U.S. 466 (2000).
Auer v. Robbins, 519 U.S. 452 (1997).
Aven v. State, 277 S.W. 1080 (Tex. Crim. App. 1925).
B, In re, [2002] 1 FLR 1090.
Bartling v. Superior Court, 163 Cal. App. 3d 186 (Cal. 2d App. Div. 1984).
Blackburn v. State, 23 Ohio St. 146 (Ohio 1872).
Bouvia v. Superior Court (Glenchur), 225 Cal. Rptr. 297 (Cal. App. 2d 1986).
Bowen v. American Hospital Association, 476 U.S. 610 (1986).
Bowers v. Hardwick, 478 U.S. 186 (1986).
Brophy v. Northeast Sinai Hospital, Inc., 497 N.E.2d 626 (Mass. 1986).
Buck v. Bell, Superintendent of the Virginia Colony for Epileptics and Feeble Minded, 274 U.S. 200 (1927).
Burnett v. People, 68 N.E. 505 (1903).
Chanslor v. State, 697 S.W.2d 393 (Tex. App. 1985).
Colyer, In re, 660 P.2d 738 (Wash. 1983).
Commonwealth v. Bowen, 13 Mass. 356 (1816).
Commonwealth v. Hicks, 82 S.W. 265 (1904).
Commonwealth v. Mink, 123 Mass. 422 (1877).
Commonwealth v. Ross, 416 A.2d 1092 (Pa. 1979).
Commonwealth v. Schwartzentruver, 389 A.2d 181 (Pa. Super. Ct. 1978).
Compassion in Dying v. Washington, 85 F.3d 1440 (9th Cir. 1996).
Compassion in Dying v. Washington, 79 F.3d 790 (9th Cir. 1995), *vacated en banc*, 79 F.3d 790 (9th Cir. 1995).
Compassion in Dying v. Washington, 850 F. Supp. 1454 (W.D. Wash. 1994).
Conroy, In re, 486 A.2d 1209 (N.J. 1985).
Craig v. Boren, 429 U.S. 190 (1976).
Cruzan v. Director, Missouri Department of Health, 497 U.S. 261 (1990).
Daniels v. Williams, 474 U.S. 327 (1986).

Daubert v. Merrell Dow Pharm. Co., Inc., 509 U.S. 579 (1993).

Dennis v. United States, 341 U.S. 494 (1947).

Director of Public Prosecutions v. Smith, [1961] A.C. 290.

Dred Scott v. Sandford, 19 How. 393 (1857).

Eichner v. Dillon, 426 N.Y.S.2d 517 (1980).

Eisenstadt v. Baird, 405 U.S. 438 (1972).

Emmund v. Florida, 458 U.S. 782 (1982).

Farrell, In re, 108 N.J. 335, 529 A.2d 404 (N.J. 1987).

FDIC v. Meyer, 510 U.S. 471 (1994).

Gonzales v. Oregon, ___ U.S. __, 126 S. Ct. 904 (2006).

Grace v. State, 69 S.W. 529 (Tex. Crim. App. 1902).

Griswold v. Connecticut, 381 U.S. 479 (1965).

Harris v. Forklift Systems, 510 U.S. 17 (1993).

Hartzel v. United States, 322 U.S. 680 (1944).

Haupt v. United States, 330 U.S. 631 (1947).

Hinson v. State, 18 Ark. App. 14, 709 S.W.2d 106 (Ark. App. 1986).

Infant Doe, In re, No. GU 8204-004A (Monroe County Cir. Ct. Ind. April 12, 1982).

J.E.B. v. Alabama, 511 U.S. 127 (1994).

Katzenbach v. Morgan, 384 U.S. 641, 657 (1966).

Lawrence v. Texas, 123 S. Ct. 2472 (2003).

Lee v. Oregon, 891 F. Supp. 1429 (D. Or. 1995), overruled, 107 F.3d 1382 (9th Cir. 1997).

Lochner v. New York, 198 U.S. 45 (1905).

Lockett v. Ohio, 438 U.S. 586 (1978).

Loving v. Virginia, 388 U.S. 1 (1967).

McKay v. Bergstedt, 801 P.2d 617 (1990).

Marbury v. Madison, 5 U.S. 137 (1803).

Martin v. Commonwealth, 84 Va. 1009, 37 S.E.2d 43 (1946).

Meyer v. Nebraska, 262 U.S. 390 (1923).

Mississippi University for Women, 458 U.S., 718, 724 (1982).

M'Naughten's Case, House of Lords, 10 Cl. & F. 200, 8 Eng. Rep. 718 (1843).

Michael H. v. Gerald D., 491 U.S. 110 (1989).

Moore v. East Cleveland, 413 U.S. 494 (1977).

Morissette v. United States, 342 U.S. 246 (1952).

Oregon v. Ashcroft, 192 F. Supp. 2d 1077 (D. Ore. 2002).

People v. Campbell, 124 Mich. App. 333, 335 N.W.2d 27 (Mich. App. 1983).

People v. Cleaves, 229 Cal. App. 3d 367, 280 Cal. Rptr. 146 (Cal. App. 1991).

People v. Duffy, 185 A.D.2d 371, 586 N.Y.S.2d 150 (N.Y. App. Div. 1992).

People v. Roberts, 178 N.W. 690 (1920).

Persampieri v. Commonwealth, 343 Mass. 19, 175 N.E.2d 387 (Mass. 1961).

Phillip B., In re, 92 Cal. App. 3d 796, 156 Cal. Rptr. 48 (1979), *cert denied*, 445 U.S. 949 (1980).

Planned Parenthood v. Casey, 505 U.S. 833 (1992).

Pretty v. United Kingdom, [2002] 2 FCR 97 (European Court of Human Rights, Fourth Section Apr. 29, 2002).

Quill v. Koppell, 870 F. Supp. 78 (S.D.N.Y. 1994).

Quill v. Vacco, 80 F.3d 716 (2d Cir. 1996).

Quinlan, In re, 355 A.2d 647 (N.J. 1976).

Regina v. Dudley and Stephens, 14 Q.B.D. 271 (1884).

Regina v. Gaylor, D. & B. 228, 169 Eng. Rep. 1011
C.C.R. 1857).

Regina v. Hyam, [1975] A.C. 55.

Regina v. Ledington, [1839] 9 Car. & P. 7992.

Regina v. Moloney, [1985] A.C. 905.

Regina v. Nedrick, [1986] 1 W.L.R. 1025.

Regina (Pretty) v. Director of Public Prosecutions, [2001] 1 AC 800.

Regina v. Woollin, [1999] A.C. 82.

Rex v. Croft, [1944] K.B. 296 (C.C.A.).

Rex v. Russell, [1832] 1 Moody C.C. 35692.

Rodriguez v. British Columbia (Attorney General), [1993] 3 S.C.R. 519.

Satz v. Perlmutter, 362 So.2d 160 (Fla. App. 1978).

Skidmore v. Swift & Co., 323 U.S. 134 (1944).

Snyder v. Massachusetts, 291 U.S. 97 (1934).

Stanton v. Stanton, 421 U.S. 7, 13 (1975).

Staples v. United States, 511 U.S. 600 (1994).

State v. Bauer, 471 N.W.2d 363 (Minn. App. 1991)

State v. Cobb, 229 Kan. 522, 625 P.2d 1133 (1981).

State v. Fuller, 203 Neb. 233, 278 N.W.2d 756 (1979).

State v. Kelly, 478 A.2d 364 (N.J. 1984).

State v. Marti, 290 N.W.2d 570 (Iowa 1980).

State of Michigan v. Kevorkian, 447 Mich. 436, 527 N.W.2d 714 (1994).

Stoval v. Denno, 388 U.S. 293 (1967).

Strauder v. West Virginia, 100 U.S. 303 (1879).

Superintendent of Belchertown State School v. Saikewicz, 370 N.E.2d 417 (Mass. 1977).

T, In re, [1993] Fam. 95.

Thomas Jefferson Univ. Hos. v. Shalala, 512 U.S. 504 (1994).

Thornburgh v. American College of Obstetricians & Gynecologists, 476 U.S. 747 (1986).

Tison v. Arizona, 481 U.S. 1437 (1987).

Tune v. Walter Reed Army Medical Hospital, 602 F. Supp. 1452 (D.D.C. 1985).

Turner v. State, 119 Tenn. 663, 108 S.W.2d 1139 (1908).

Twining v. New Jersey, 211 U.S. 78 (1908).

TXO Production Corp. v. Alliance Resources Corp., 509 U.S. 443, 470 (1993).

United States v. Holmes, 26 F. Cas. 360, 1 Wall Jr. 1 (C.C.E.D. Pa. 1842).

United States v. Carlton, 512 U.S. 26, 39 (1994).

United States v. Falcone, 109 F.2d 579 (2d Cir. 1940).

United States v. Mead Corp., 533 U.S. 218 (2001).

United States v. Oakland Cannibas Buyers' Cooperative, 532 U.S. 483 (2001).

United States v. Peoni, 100 F.2d 401 (2d Cir. 1938).

United States v. Salerno, 481 U.S. 739 (1987).

United States v. X-Citement Video, Inc., 513 U.S. 64 (1994).

Vacco v. Quill, 521 U.S. 793 (1997).

Washington v. Glucksberg, 521 U.S. 702 (1997).

Wendland v. Wendland, 28 P.2d 151 (Cal. App. 2001).

Whitney v. California, 274 U.S. 357 (1927).
Winship, In re, 397 U.S. 358 (1970).
Wisconsin v. Yoder, 406 U.S. 205 (1972).
Yick Wo v. Hopkins, 118 U.S. 356 (1886).

STATUTES AND CONSTITUTIONAL PROVISIONS

U.S. Const. amend. V
U.S. Const. amend XIV
18 U.S.C. § 81
18 U.S.C. § 113
18 U.S.C. § 201
18 U.S.C. § 373
18 U.S.C. § 471
18 U.S.C. § 521
18 U.S.C. § 594
18 U.S.C. § 1072
18 U.S.C. §2101
42 U.S.C. § 5106
42 U.S.C. § 14401, *et seq.*
42 U.S.C. § 14402(b)(1)(2), (4)
21 C.F.R. Part 1306
Del. Const. of 1792, art. 1 § 15
N.H. Const. pt. 2, art. 89 (1783)
Md. Const. of 1776, decl. of rts. § 24
N.C. Const. of 1778
N.J. Const. of 1776, art. 17
Ala. Code § 22-8A-10 (1990)
Alaska Stat. Ann. § 18.12.080(a), (f) (1996)
Ariz. Rev. Stat. Ann. § 36-3210 (Supp. 1996)
Ark. Code Ann. (1991 and Supp. 1995)
    § 20-13-905(a), (f)
    § 20-17-210(a), (g)
Cal. Heath & Safety Code Ann. §§ 7191.5(a), (g) (West Supp. 1997)
Cal. Penal Code § 401
Cal. Prob. Code Ann. § 4723 (West Supp. 1997)
Cal. Welf. & Inst. Code § 5250 (West 1984)
Colo. Rev. Stat. (1987 and Supp. 1996)
    § 15-14-504(4)
    § 15-18-112(1)
    § 15-18.5-101(3)
    § 15-18.6-108
Conn. Gen. Stat. § 19a-575 (Supp. 1996)
D.C. Code Ann. (1995 and Supp. 1996)
    § 6-2430
    § 21-2212

Del. Code Ann., Tit. 16, § 512 (Supp. 1996)
Fla. Stat. § 765.309(1), (2) (Supp. 1997)
Ga. Code Ann. (1996)
   §31-32-11(b)
   § 31-36-2(b)
Haw. Rev. Stat. § 327D-13 (1996)
Idaho Code § 39-152 (Supp. 1996)
Ill. Comp. Stat., ch. 755 (1992)
   § 35/9(f)
   § 40/5
   § 40/50
   § 45/2-1
Ind. Code (1994 and Supp. 1996)
   § 16-36-1-13
   § 16-36-4-19
   § 30-5-5-17
Iowa Code (1989 and West Supp. 1997)
   §§ 144A.11.1–144A.11.6
   § 144B.12.2
   §707A.2
Kan. Stat. Ann. § 65-28, 109 (1985)
Ky. Rev. Stat. Ann. § 311.638 (Baldwin Supp. 1992)
Ky. Rev. Stat. Ann. ch. 500 § 500.410
La. Rev. Stat. Ann. 40, § 1299.58.10(A), (B) (West 1992)
Md. Ann. Code § 5-611(c) (1994)
Md. Ann. Code § 27-416 (1994)
Mass. Gen. Laws 201D, § 12 (Supp. 1997)
Me. Rev. Stat. Ann. Tit. 18-A, § 5-813(b), (c) (West Supp. 1996)
Mich. Comp. Laws Ann. § 700.496(20) (West 1995)
Minn. Stat. (Supp. 1997)
   § 145B.14
   § 145C.14
Miss. Code Ann. (Supp. 1997)
   § 41-41-117(2)
   § 41-41-119(1)
Mo. Ann. Stat. tit. 38, § 563.026
Mo. Rev. Stat. (1992)
   § 459.015.3
   § 459.055(5)
   § 563.026
Mont. Code Ann. (1995)
   § 50-9-205(1), (7)
   § 50-10-104(1), (6)
Model Penal Code § 2.02
   § 2.04
   § 2.06
   § 3.02

§ 3.04
§ 4.01
§ 210.5
Neb. Rev. Stat. (1995)
§ 20-412(1), (7)
§ 30-3401(3)
N.J. Stat. Ann. (West 1996)
§ 26:2H-54(d), (e)
§ 26:2H-77
N.M. Stat. Ann. § 24-7A-13(B)(1), (C) (Supp. 1995)
N.Y. Mental Hyg. Law § 9.41 (McKinney Supp. 1983–84)
N.Y. Pub. Health Law §§ 2960–2994 (McKinney 1994)
N.Y. Penal Code§ 125.15(3)
§ 125.20(2)
§ 125.25(1)(a)
Nev. Rev. Stat. § 449.670(2) (1996)
N.C. Gen. Stat. (1993)
§ 90-320(b)
§ 90-321(f)
N.D. Cent. Code (1991)
§ 23-06.4-01
§ 23-06.5-01
N.H. Rev. Stat. Ann. (1996)
§ 137-H:10
§ 137-H:13
§ 137-J:1
Ohio Cent. Code Ann. 2133.12(A), (D) (Supp. 1996)
Oregon Rev. Stat.
§ 127.805, et seq.
§ 426.231
Okla. Stat. Ann. Tit. 63 (1996)
§ 3101.2 (C)
§ 3101.12(A),(G)
Pa. Cons. Stat. § 5402(b) (Supp. 1996)
R.I. Gen. Laws (1996)
§ 23-4.10-9(a), (f)
§ 23-4.11-10(a), (f)
S.C. Code Ann. (Supp. 1996)
§ 44-77-130
§ 44-78-50(A), (C)
§ 62-5-504(O)
S.D. Codified Laws (1994)
§ 34-12D-14
§ 34-12D-20
Tenn. Code Ann. (Supp. 1996)
§ 32-11-110(a)
§ 39-13-216

Tex. Health & Safety Code Ann. (1992)
  § 672.017
  § 672.020
  § 672.021
Tex. Penal Code § 22.08 (1999)
Utah Code Ann. (1993)
  § 75-2-1116
  § 75-2-1118
V.I. Code Ann., Tit. 19, § 198(a), (g) (1995)
Va. Code Ann. (1994)
  § 8.01-622.1
  § 54.1-2990
Vt. Stat. Ann. Tit. 18 § 5260 (1987)
W. Va. Code (1995)
  § 16-30-10
  § 16-30A-16(a)
  § 16-30B-2(b)
  § 16-30B-13
  § 16-30C-14
Wash. Rev. Code § 9A.36.060(1) (1994)
Wash. Rev. Code (Supp. 1997)
  § 70,122.070 (1)
  § 70.122.100
Wis. Stat. (Supp. 1996)
  § 154.11 (1) (6)
  § 154.25(7)
  § 155.70(7)
  § 939
  § 940
Wyo. Stat. (1994 Supp. 1996)
  § 3-5-211
  § 35-22-109
  § 35-22-208
The Criminal Justice Act, 1967 § 8
Suicide Act, 1961, Ch. 60.
Rights of the Terminally Ill Act 1995 (N. Terr. Austl.) §§ 2–4.

Books, Articles, and Miscellany

Ackerman, Bruce, *Social Justice in the Liberal State* (1980).
Addison, G. C., *Law of Torts* (3d ed., 1870).
Alexander, Leo, *Medical Science under Dictatorship*, 241 New Eng. J. Med. 39–47 (1949).
American Bar Association, Commission on Legal Problems of the Elderly, *Memorandum in Opposition to Resolution No. 8 on Voluntary Aid in Dying*, 8 issues in L. & Med. 117 (1992)

American Hospital Association, Brief of Amicus Curiae, *State of Washington v. Glucksberg*, No. 96-1110 (U.S. Supreme Court).

American Medical Association, Council on Ethical and Judicial Affairs, *Decisions Near the End of Life*, 267 Journ. of the Amer. Med. Ass'n 2230 (1992).

American Medical Association et al., Brief of Amicus Curiae in Support of Petition for Certiorari, *State of Washington v. Glucksberg*, No. 96-1110 (U.S. Supreme Court).

Anderson, Sherwood, *Dinner in Thessaly*, 95 The Forum 40–41 (1936).

Anonymous, *It's Over Debbie*, 259 Journ. of the Amer. Med. Ass'n 272 (1988).

Aquinas, Thomas, *Summa Theologiae* (trans. Fathers of the English Dominican Prov.; Daniel Sullivan, rev. 1952).

Aristotle, *Nicomachean Ethics* (J.A.K. Thomson trans., 1953).

Ashworth, Andrew, *Principles of Criminal Law* (1991).

Augustine, *The City of God* (R. W. Dyson ed., 1998).

Baird, Robert, and Rosenbaum, Stuart (eds.), *Morality and the Law* (1988).

Barraclough, Brian, et al., *A Hundred Cases of Suicide: Clinical Aspects*, 125 Brit. J. Psychiatry 355 (1974).

Barry, Robert, *The Development of the Roman Catholic Teachings on Suicide*, 9 Notre Dame J.L. Ethics & Pub. Pol'y 449 (1995).

Battin, Margaret, *The Least Worst Death: Essays in Bioethics on the End of Life* (1994).

———, *Should We Copy the Dutch? The Netherlands' Practice of Voluntary Euthanasia as a Model for the United States*, in *Euthanasia: The Good of the Patient, The Good of the Society* 95 (Robert I. Bisbin, ed., 1992).

Battin, Margaret, et al. (eds.), *Physician Assisted Suicide: Expanding the Debate* (1998).

Behrman, R., and Vaughan, V., *Nelson Textbook of Pediatrics* (1983).

Bentham, Jeremy, *Principles of Morals and Legislation* (1907).

Berkowitz, Peter, *The Utilitarian Horrors of Peter Singer: Other People's Mothers*, The New Republic (Jan. 10, 2000).

Biskupic, Joan, *Unanimous Decision Points to Tradition of Valuing Life*, Washington Post, at A1 (June 27, 1997).

Blackstone, William, *Commentaries on the Laws of England* (1769).

Bloch, Kate E., *The Role of Law in Suicide Prevention: Beyond Civil Commitment—A Bystander Duty to Report Suicide Threats*, 9 Stan. L. Rev. 929 (1987).

Bork, Robert H., *The Tempting of America: The Political Seduction of the Law* (1989).

Boyle, Joseph, *Sanctity of Life and Suicide: Tensions and Developments within Common Morality*, in *Suicide and Euthanasia* (Baruch Brody ed., 1989).

Boyle, J. P. (ed.), *The Papers of Thomas Jefferson* (1952).

Bracton, *On the Laws and Customs of England* (Samuel E. Thorne, ed., 1968).

Brewer, E. Cobham, *The Dictionary of Phrase and Fable* (1894).

Breyer, Stephen, *Active Liberty: Interpreting Our Democratic Constitution* (2005).

Brock, Dan, *Life and Death: Philosophical Essays in Biomedical Ethics* (1993).

———, *Voluntary Active Euthanasia*, Hastings Center Report 22, no. 2 (1992).

Cain, Charles (comp.), *Key Events in the History of Michigan's Debate over Abortion and Assisted Suicide*, The Detroit News, at A8 (Mar. 2, 1997).

Calabresi, Guido, *A Common Law for the Age of Statutes* (1982).

Callahan, Daniel, *The Troubled Dream of Life: Living with Mortality* (1993).

Cantor, Norman, *On Kamisar, Killing and the Future of Physician-Assisted Death* 102 Mich. L. Rev. 1793, 1825 (2004).

Cardozo, Benjamin, *Life and Literature* (1930).

Cicero, *De Finibus III* (Rackham trans., 1914).

———, *De Senectute* (J. Allen & J. Greenough trans. & eds., 1866).

Cleeland, Charles S., et al., *Pain and Its Treatment in Outpatients with Metastatic Cancer*, 330 New Eng. J. Medicine 592 (1994).

CNN.com/WORLD, *Dutch Law Stokes Death Debate*, http://www6.cnn.com/2001/WORLD/europe/04/11/euthanasia.debate/ (site visited Sept. 10, 2001).

Coke, Edward, *Third Institute* (1644).

Colb, Sherry F., *A Controversy over the Netherlands' New Euthanasia Legislation*, Findlaw.com (Jan. 17, 2001).

Comment, 30 Yale L.J. 408 (1921).

Conwell, Y., and Caine, E. *Rational Suicide and the Right to Die: Reality and Myth*, 325 New Eng. J. Med. 1100 (1991).

Council of Europe's Recommendation 1418 (1999).

Curtis, Charles, *Lions under the Throne* (1947).

Cushing, J. (ed.), *The Earliest Acts and Laws of the Colony of Rhode Island and the Providence Plantations, 1647–1719* (1977).

———, *The Earliest Printed Laws of Pennsylvania, 1681–1713* (1978).

———, *The Earliest Printed Laws of South Carolina, 1692–1734* (1978).

Darwin, Charles, *Descent of Man and Selection in Relation to Sex* (2d ed. 1882).

Death in a Consumer Society (Editor's Choice), 326 Brit. Med. J. (Feb. 1, 2003).

Declaration of Independence of the United States of America.

Deliens, Luc, et al., *End-of-Life Decisions in Medical Practice in Flanders, Belgium: A Nationwide Survey*, 356 Lancet 1806 (2000).

Department of Health, *Harold Shipman's Clinical Practice 1974–1998: A Clinical Audit Commissioned by the Chief Medical Officer* (2000).

Doctor-Assisted Suicide—A Guide to Web Sites and the Literature http://web.lwc.edu/administrative/library/suic.htm. (site visited Sept. 15, 1999).

Dolbee, Sandi, *Right to Die Measure Rejected by State Voters*, San Diego Union-Tribune (Nov. 4, 1992).

Donagan, Alan, *The Theory of Morality* (1977).

Dorrepaal, Karin L., et al., *Pain Experience and Pain Management among Hospitalized Cancer Patients: A Clinical Study*, 63 Cancer 593 (1989).

Dowbiggin, Ian, *A Merciful End: The Euthanasia Movement in America* (2003).

Downie, Jocelyn, *The Contested Lessons of Euthanasia in the Netherlands*, 8 Health L.J. 119 (2000).

Drug Enforcement Agency, California Marijuana Information, http://www.usdoj.gov/dea/ongoing/calimarijuana.html (site visited Aug. 16, 2003).

Dworkin, Ronald, *Assisted Suicide: The Philosophers' Brief*, 44 New York Review of Books 41 (March 27, 1997).

———, *Euthanasia, Morality, and Law*, 31 Loyola of Los Angeles L. Rev. 1147 (1998).

———, *Foundations of Liberal Equality*, in *The Tanner Lectures on Human Values* (Grethe Peterson ed., 1990).

———, *Life's Dominion: An Argument about Abortion and Euthanasia* (1993).

———, *A Matter of Principle* (1985).

———, *Taking Rights Seriously* (1977).

Eden, Karl (ed.), *The Jonestown Massacre* (1993).

Elks, Martin A., *"The Lethal Chamber": Further Evidence for the Euthanasia Option*, 31 Mental Retardation 201–7 (1993).

Ely, John Hart, *Democracy and Distrust* (1981).

Emmanuel, E. J., *Depression, Euthanasia, and Improving End-of-Life Care*, 23 Journal of Clinical Oncology 6456, 6457 (2005).

Emmanuel, E. J., et al., *The Practice of Euthanasia and Physician-Assisted Suicide in the United States: Adherence to Proposed Safeguards and Effects on Physicians*, 220 Journ. of the Amer. Med. Ass'n 507 (1998).

Emmanuel, Linda L. (ed.), *Regulating How We Die: the Ethical, Medical, and Legal Issues Surrounding Physician-Assisted Suicide* (1997).

Epstein, Richard, *Mortal Peril: Our Inalienable Right to Health Care?* (1999).

Euthanasia.com http://www.euthanasia.com/belgiumlaw.html (site visited July 4, 2003).

Feinberg, Joel, *Freedom and Fulfillment* (1995).

———, *Harm to Self* (1986).

———, *Harmless Wrongdoings* (1987).

———, *The Moral Limits of the Criminal Law: Harm to Others* (1984).

———, *Offense to Others* (1985).

———, *An Unpromising Approach to the "Right to Die,"* in Freedom and Fulfillment: Philosophical Essays (1992).

Feldbrugge, F.J.M., *Good and Bad Samaritans: A Comparative Study*, 14 Am. J. Comp. Law 630 (1967).

Finnis, John, *Allocating Risks and Suffering: Some Hidden Traps*, 38 Cleve. St. L. Rev. 193 (1990).

———, *Aquinas* (1998).

———, *Bland: Crossing the Rubicon?*, 109 L. Q. Rev. 329 (1993).

———, *Euthanasia, Morality, and Law*, 31 Loyola of Los Angeles L. Rev. 1123 (1998).

———, *Intention and Side-Effects*, in *Liability and Responsibility: Essays in Law and Morals* (R. G. Frey and Christopher W. Morris eds., 1991).

———, *Moral Absolutes: Tradition, Revision and Truth* (1991).

———, *Natural Law and Legal Reasoning*, 38 Cleve. St. L. Rev. 1 (1990).

———, *Natural Law and Natural Rights* (1980).

Finnis, John, et al., *Nuclear Deterrence, Morality and Realism* (1988).

Flick, Michael R. *The Due Process of Dying*, 79 Cal. L. Rev. 1121 (1991).

Foley, Kathleen, and Hendin, Herbert (eds.) *The Case against Assisted Suicide: For the Right to End-of-Life Care* (2002).

Foley, Kathleen, and Hendin, Herbert, *The Oregon Experiment*, in *The Case against Assisted Suicide: For the Right to End-of-Life Care* (Kathleen Foley and Herbert Hendin eds., 2002).

Foot, Phillipa, *The Problem of Abortion and the Doctrine of Double Effect*, in *Killing and Letting Die* (Bonnie Steinbeck ed., 1980).

Fried, Charles, *Right and Wrong* (1978).

Ganzini, L., et al., *Attitudes of Oregon Psychiatrists toward Physician-Assisted Suicide* 153 Am. J. of Psychiatry 1469 (1996).

———, *Physicians' Experiences with the Oregon Death With Dignity Act*, 342 New Eng. J. Med. 557 (2000).

Geer, Russell (trans.), *Letters, Principal Doctrines, and Vatican Sayings* (1997).

George, Robert, *Making Men Moral* (1993).

———, *Recent Criticisms of Natural Law Theory*, 55 U. Chi. L. Rev. 1371 (1988).

———, *Self Evident Practical Principles and Rationally Motivated Action: A Reply to Michael Perry*, 64 Tulane L. Rev. 997 (1990).

Gittleman, David K., *Euthanasia and Assisted Suicide*, 92 Southern Med. J. 370 (Apr. 1999).

Gomez, Carlos, *Regulating Death: Euthanasia and the Case of the Netherlands* (1991).

Gormally, Luke, *Note: Regina v. Arthur*, in *Euthanasia, Clinical Practice and the Law* (Luke Gormally ed., 1994)

Gormally, Luke (ed.) *Euthanasia, Clinical Practice and the Law* (1994).

Gorsuch, Neil M., *The Right to Assisted Suicide and Euthanasia*, 23 Harv. J. Law & Pub. Policy 599 (2000).

———, *The Legalization of Assisted Suicide and The Law of Unintended Consequences*, 2004 Wisc. L Rev. 1347 (2004).

Grant, Madison, *The Passing of the Great Race* (1916).

Green, P. E., and Krieger, A. M., *Models and Heuristics for Product Line Selection*, 4 Marketing Science 1 (1985).

Griffiths, John, *Assisted Suicide in the Netherlands: The Chabot Case*, 58 Mod. L. Rev. 232 (1995).

———, *Recent Developments in the Netherlands Concerning Euthanasia and Other Medical Behavior That Shortens Life*, 1 Med. Law. Int. 347 (1994).

———, *The Regulation of Euthanasia and Related Medical Procedures That Shorten Life in the Netherlands*, 1 Med. Law. Int. 137 (1994).

———, *The Slippery Slope: Are the Dutch Sliding Down or Are They Clambering Up?*, in *Asking to Die: Inside the Dutch Debate about Euthanasia* (David C. Thomasma et al. eds., 1998).

Griffiths, John, et al., *Euthanasia and Law in the Netherlands* (1998),

Grisez, Germain, *Toward a Consistent Natural Law Ethics of Killing*, 15 Am. J. of Jurisprudence 64 (1970).

Grisso, T., and Appelbaum, P. S., *The MacArthur Treatment Competency Study: III. Abilities of Patients to Consent to Psychiatric and Medical Treatments*, 19 Law & Hum. Behav. 149 (1995).

Groenewoud, J. H., et al., *Clinical Problems with the Performance of Euthanasia and Physician-Assisted Suicide in the Netherlands* 342 New Eng. J. Med. 551 (2000).

Gross, R. H., et al., *Early Management and Decision-Making for the Treatment of Myelomeningocele*, 72 Pediatrics 450 (1983).

Hale, Matthew, *Pleas of the Crown* (Phila. 1847).

Hamilton, N. Gregory *Oregon's Culture of Silence*, in *The Case against Assisted Suicide: For the Right to End-of-Life Care* (Kathleen Foley and Herbert Hendin eds., 2002).

Haney, Daniel Q., *Six Percent Of Physicians in Survey Say They Have Assisted Patient Suicides*, Washington Post., at A9 (April 23, 1998).

Hart, H.L.A., *Law, Liberty, and Morality* (1963).

———, *Punishment and Responsibility* (1968).

Hart, Henry, *Foreword: The Time Chart of the Justices*, 73 Harv. L. Rev. 84 (1959).

Hedberg, Katrina, et al., *Legalized Physician-Assisted Suicide in Oregon, 2001*, 346 New Eng. J. Med (2002).

Heinz, Spencer, *Assisted Suicide: Advocates Weigh In*, Oregonian, Dec. 9, 1994.

Hemlock Society, *Final Exit* (1991).

———, *Physician Assistance in Dying: Legislation by State* http://www.hemlock.org//common/states_12.html (site visited Sept. 15, 1999).

Hendin, Herbert, *The Dutch Experience*, in *The Case against Assisted Suicide: For the Right to End-of-Life Care* (Kathleen Foley and Herbert Hendin eds., 2002).

Hendin, Herbert, and Klerman, Gerald, *Physician-Assisted Suicide: The Dangers of Legalization*, 150 Am. J. of Psychiatry 143 (1993).

Hentoff, Nat, *Doctor Death: A Newborn Is Not a Person*, Village Voice (Feb. 23–29, 2000).

———, *A Duty to Die?*, Washington Post at A19 (May 31, 1997).

———, *Elizabeth Bouvia and the ACLU: I Used to Go to the ACLU for Help, Now They're Killing Us*, Village Voice (July 30, 1996).

Holmes, Jr., Oliver Wendell, *The Common Law* (1881).

Hooton, Earnest, *The Future Quality of the American People*, 154 The Churchman 11–12 (1940).

Huber, Peter W., *Galileo's Revenge: Junk Science in the Courtroom* (1991).

Humphry, Derek, *Law Reform*, 20 Ohio N.U. L. Rev. 729 (1993).

Humphry, Derek, and Clement, Mary, *Freedom to Die: People Politics and the Right to Die Movement* (2000).

Hutchison, Thomas W., et al. (eds.), *Federal Sentencing Law and Practice* (2003).

International Task Force on Euthanasia and Assisted Suicide, Update 2006, vol. 20, no. 1, http://www.internationaltaskforce.org/iua35.htm (site visited March 28, 2006).

Jacox, Ada, et al., *New Clinical-Practice Guidelines for the Management of Pain in Patients with Cancer*, 330 New Eng. J. Med. 651 (1994).

James, Bernard, *Lawrence, Bollinger*, The National L. J., S8 (Aug. 4, 2003).

Kadish, Sanford, et al., *Criminal Law and Its Processes* (5th ed. 1989).

Kamisar, Yale, *Some Non-Religious Views against Proposed Mercy-Killing Legislation*, 42 Minn. L. Rev. 969 (1958).

Kamm, Frances, *Physician-Assisted Suicide, Euthanasia, and Intending Death* in *Physician Assisted Suicide: Expanding the Debate* 28 (Margaret P. Battin et al. eds., 1998).

Kant, Immanuel, *Fundamental Principles of the Metaphysics of Morals* (Thomas Kingsmill Abbott trans., 1949).

Kaveny, M. Cathleen, *Inferring Intention from Foresight*, 120 L. Q. Rev. 81 (January 2004).

Keeton, W. Page (ed.), *Prosser and Keeton on the Law of Torts* (5th ed. 1984).

Kennedy, F., *The Problem of Social Control of the Congenital Defective*, 99 Am. J. of Psychiatry 13 (1942).

Keown, Damien, *Buddhism and Bioethics* (1995).

Keown, John, *Euthanasia, Ethics and Public Policy: An Argument against Legalisation* (2002).

———, *Euthanasia in the Netherlands: Sliding Down the Slippery Slope?* in *Euthanasia Examined: Ethical, Clinical, and Legal Perspectives* (John Keown ed., 1995).

———, *Further Reflections on Euthanasia in the Netherlands in the Light of the Remmelink Report and the Van Der Maas Survey*, in *Euthanasia, Clinical Practice and the Law* (Luke Gormally ed., 1994).

———, *The Law and Practice of Euthanasia in the Netherlands*, 108 L. Q. Rev. 51 (1992).

———, *The Mackay Report on the Assisted Dying for the Terminally Ill Bill: An Unbalanced Basis for Debate* (forthcoming from the Care Not Killing Alliance).

————, *Restoring Moral and Intellectual Shape to the Law After* Bland, 113 L. Q. Rev. 481 (1997).

————, *Some Reflections on Euthanasia in the Netherlands*, in *Euthanasia, Clinical Practice and the Law* (Luke Gormally ed., 1994).

———— (ed.), *Euthanasia Examined: Ethical, Clinical, and Legal Perspectives* (1995).

Kimsma, Gerrit, and van Leeuwen, Evert, *Euthanasia and Assisted Suicide in the Netherlands and the USA: Comparing Practices, Justifications and Key Concepts in Bioethics and Law*, in *Asking to Die: Inside the Dutch Debate about Euthanasia* (David C. Thomasma ed., 1998).

King, Patricia, and Wolf, Leslie, *Lessons for Physician-Assisted Suicide from the African-American Experience*, in *Physician Assisted Suicide: Expanding the Debate* (Margaret Battin et al. eds., 1998).

Kissane, David, *Deadly Days in Darwin*, in *The Case against Assisted Suicide: For the Right to End-of-Life Care* (Kathleen Foley and Herbert Hendin eds., 2002).

Knox, Richard A. *Study Finds ICU Doctors Withholding Treatment*, Boston Globe (Feb. 18, 1995).

Kolata, Gina, *Court Ruling Limits Rights of Patients*, N.Y. Times, sec. 1 at 6 (April 22, 1995).

Koop, C. Everett, and Grant, Edward R., *The Small Beginnings of Euthanasia: Examining the Erosion in Legal Prohibitions against Mercy-Killing*, 2 Notre Dame J.L. Ethics & Pub. Pol'y 585 (1986).

Krakauer, John, *Into Thin Air* (1997).

Kuepper, Stephen Louis, *Euthanasia in America, 1890–1960: The Controversy, the Movement, and the Law*, Ph.D. diss., Rutgers University, 1981.

Kuhse, Helga, *From Intention to Consent: Learning from Experience with Euthanasia*, in *Physician Assisted Suicide: Expanding the Debate* (Margaret Battin et al. eds., 1998).

————, *A Modern Myth. That Letting Die Is Not the Intentional Causation of Death: Some Reflections on the Trial and Acquittal of Dr. Leonard Arthur*, 1 J. of Applied Philosophy 21 (1984).

————, *The Sanctity of Life Doctrine in Medicine* (1987).

Kuhse, Helga, et al., *End of Life Decisions in Australian Medical Practice*, 166 Med. J. Australia 191, 194–95 (1997).

LaFave, Wayne, and Scott, Austin, *Criminal Law* (1986).

Lagerwey, Walter (trans.), *Guidelines for Euthanasia*, 3 issues in L. & Med. 429 (1988).

Land, Walter, and Gutmann, Thomas, *Ethics in Living Organ Transplantation*, in 6 Langbeck's Archives of Surgery 394, 515 (1999), available at http://trans.klinikum.uni-muenchen.de/.

Landes, William, and Posner, Richard, *Salvors, Finders, Good Samaritans and Other Rescuers: An Economic Study of Law and Altruism*, 7 J. Leg. Stud. 83 (1978).

Lee, Melinda A., et al., *Legalizing Assisted Suicide—Views of Physicians in Oregon*, 334 New. Eng. J. Med. 310 (1996).

Lennox, William G., *Should They Live? Certain Economic Aspects of Medicine*, 7 The American Scholar, 454–66 (1938).

Linacre Centre Submission to the House of Lords, reprinted in *Euthanasia, Clinical Practice and the Law* (Luke Gormally ed., 1994).

Lomasky, Loren, *Persons, Rights, and the Moral Community* (1987).

McCall, William, Associated Press, *Oregon Backed on Assisted Suicide*, Yahoo!News http://dailynews.yahoo.com/h/ap/20011121/us/assisted_suicide_courts.html (site visited Nov. 29, 2001).

McBride, R. D., and Zufryden, S. F., *An Integer Programming Approach to the Optimal Product Line Selection Problem*, Marketing Science 126 (1988).

MacDonald Michael, and Murphy, Terence, *Sleepless Souls: Suicide in Early Modern England* (1990).

McKim, D., *Heredity and Human Progress* (1900).

Mair, A. W., *Suicide*, in *Encylopedia of Religion and Ethics* (J. Hastings ed., 1992).

Mankiw, N. Greggory, *Principles of Economics* (2d. ed. 2001).

Mann, Patricia, *Meanings of Death* in *Physician Assisted Suicide: Expanding the Debate* (Margaret Battin et al. eds., 1998).

Manne, Robert, *Research and Ye Shall Find, Bioethics Research Notes* 9(1) (Southern Cross Bioethics Institute, March 1997).

Marker, Rita, *Deadly Compassion: The Death of Ann Humphry and the Case against Euthanasia* (1993).

Marquet, R. L., et al., *Twenty-five Years of Requests for Euthanasia and Physician Assisted Suicide*, in *Dutch Practice: Trend Analysis*, 327 Brit. Med. J. (2003).

Marzuk, P. M., et al., *Increase in Suicide by Asphyxiation in New York City after the Publication of Final Exit*, 329 New Eng. J. Med. 1508 (1993).

Mathews, Jay, *Term Limits, Assisted Suicide, Abortion Rights Losing in Washington*, Washington Post, sec. 1 (Nov. 6, 1992).

Marzen, Thomas, et al., *Suicide: A Constitutional Right?*, 24 Duquesne L. Rev. 1 (1985).

Meier, Diane E., et al., *A National Survey of Physician-Assisted Suicide and Euthanasia in the United States*, 338 New Eng. J. Med. 1193 (1998).

Meisel, Alan, *The Right to Die* (1989 & 1992 Supp.).

Meskill, William, *Is Suicide Murder?* 3 Colum. L. Rev. 379 (1903).

Michigan Commission on Death & Dying, *Final Report* (1994).

Mill, John Stuart, *On Liberty* (E. Rappaport ed., 1978).

Moore, Richard D., et al., *Racial Differences in the Use of Drug Therapy for HIV Disease in an Urban Community*, 330 New Eng. J. Med. 763 (1994).

Murphy, Brian, *Kevorkian Silent, Starts Prison Term*, Detroit Free Press http://www.freep.com/news/xtra2/qkevo14.htm (Apr. 14, 1999).

National Commission on Reform of Federal Law Working Papers (1971).

National Conference of Catholic Bishops Committee for Pro-Life Activities, *Nutrition and Hydration: Moral and Pastoral Reflections*, 15 J. Contemp. H. L. Pol'y 455 (1999).

NBC News, *Doctor-Assisted Suicide, State by State* http://www.msnbc.com/modules/statebystate/state.asp?state=Michigan&ST=MI&2w=no#marker (site visited Sept. 15, 1999).

New York State Task Force on Life and the Law, *When Death Is Sought: Assisted Suicide and Euthanasia in the Medical Context* (1994).

Note, *Antinuclear Demonstrations and the Necessity Defense*, 5 Vt. L. Rev. 103 (1980).

Note, *Necessity as a Defense to a Criminal Trespass in an Abortion Clinic*, 48 Crim. L. Rev. 509 (1979).

Note, *The Right to Die and Physician-Assisted Suicide*, 105 Harv. L. Rev. 2030 (1991).

Nozick, Robert, *Anarchy, State, and Utopia* (1974).

Ohioans Divided on Doctor Assisted Suicide Issue, UPI, June 28, 1993.

Onwuteaka-Philipsen, Bregje D., et al., *Euthanasia and Other End-of-Life Decisions in the Netherlands in 1990, 1995, and 2001*, 362 Lancet 395 (2003).

Oregon Department of Human Services, *Eighth Annual Report on Oregon's Death With Dignity Act* (2006).

———, *Fifth Annual Report on Oregon's Death With Dignity Act* (2003).

Oregon Health Department, *Fourth Annual Report on Oregon's Death with Dignity Act* (2002).

———, *Oregon's Death with Dignity Act: The First Year's Experience* (1998).

Orentlicher, David, *The Legalization of Physician Assisted Suicide: A Very Modest Revolution* (1997).

Otlowski, Margaret, *Voluntary Euthanasia and the Common Law* (2000).

Parachini, Allan, *Bringing Euthanasia to the Ballot Box*, L.A. Times (April 10, 1987).

Passik, S. D., et al., *Oncologists' Recognition of Depression in Their Patients with Cancer*, 16 J. Clinical Oncology 1594–1600 (1998).

Plato, *Laws* (David Gallup ed., 1999).

———, *Phaedo* (Benjamin Jowett ed., 2000).

———, *The Republic* (Allan Bloom ed., 1991).

Pollock, Frederick, and Maitland, Frederic, *The History of English Law before the Time of Edward I* (2d ed. 1952).

Posner, Richard, *Aging and Old Age* (1995).

Potuto, Josephine R., et al. (eds.), *Federal Criminal Jury Instructions* (1993).

Pound, Roscoe, Introduction to Sayre, *Cases on Criminal Law* (1927).

Public Agenda Online http://www.publicagenda.org/issues/news.cfm?issue_type= right2die#MPPOASAE (site visited Jan. 15, 2001)

Pugliese, Julia, *Don't Ask—Don't Tell: The Secret Practice of Physician-Assisted Suicide*, 44 Hastings L.J. 1291 (1993).

Quill, Timothy, *The Ambiguity of Clinical Intentions*, 329 New Eng. J. Medicine 1039 (1993).

———, *Death with Dignity*, 324 New Eng. J. Med. 691 (1991).

Quill, Timothy, et al., *Care of the Hopelessly Ill: Proposed Clinical Criteria for Physician Assisted Suicide*, 327 New Eng. J. Med. 1380, 1381 (1992).

Quill, Timothy, et al., *The Rule of Double Effect—A Critique of Its Role in End-of-Life Decision Making*, 337 New Eng. J. Medicine 1768 (1997).

Ramdas, Kamalini, and Sawhney. Mohanbir S., *A Cross-Functional Approach to Evaluating Multiple Line Extensions for Assembled Products*, 47 Mgmt. Sci. vol. 1 (2001).

Randolph, A., *Pediatrics* (1983).

Rawls, John, *A Theory of Justice* (1989).

Raz, Joseph, *The Morality of Freedom* (1988).

Reagan, Peter, *Helen*, 353 Lancet 1265 (1999).

Recent Decisions, 7 Va. L. Rev. 147 (1920).

Reiman, Jeffrey, *Abortion and the Ways We Value Human Life* (1999).

Report of the Select Committee on Medical Ethics, House of Lords, HL Paper 21-I, Session 1993–1994.

Richards, David A. J., *Kantian Ethics and the Harm Principle: A Reply to John Finnis*, 87 Colum. L. Rev. 433 (1987).

———, *Sex, Drugs, Death, and the Law* (1982).

———, *Toleration and the Constitution* (1989).

The Right to Kill, Time Magazine, at 53 (Nov. 18, 1935).

Robins, Eli, *The Final Months* (1981).

Scalia, Antonin, *The Rule of Law as a Law of Rules*, 56 U. Chi. L. Rev. 1175 (1989).

Schneidman, E. S., *Rational Suicide and Psychiatric Disorders*, 326 New Eng. J. Med. 889 (1992).

Scott, Arthur P., *Criminal Law in Colonial Virginia* (1930).

Scott, S. (trans.), *The Civil Law* (1932).

Seale, Clive, *National Survey of End-of-Life Decisions Made by UK Medical Practitioners*, 20 Palliative Medicine 3 (2006).

Sedler, Robert A., *Constitutional Challenges to Bans on "Assisted Suicide": The View from Without and Within*, 21 Hastings Const. L. Quar. 777 (1994).

Select Library of Nicene and Post-Nicene Fathers of the Church, various dates and trans. (Eerdmans rpt., 1976–79).

Shapiro, Joseph P., and Bowermaster, David, *Death on Trial: The Case of Dr. Kevorkian Obscures Critical Issues—and Dangers*, U.S. News & World Rep. 31 (Apr. 25, 1994).

Sharp, Deborah, *Web-Wired Courtroom Lets World Attend Fla. Trial*, USA Today (Aug. 17, 1999).

Sheldon, Tony, *Only Half of Dutch Doctors Report Euthanasia, Study Says*, 326 Brit. Med. J. (2003).

Simester, A. P., and Sullivan, G. R., *Criminal Law Theory and Doctrine* (2000 and 2002 Update).

Simester, A. P., and Chan, W., *Intention Thus Far* [1997] Crim. L. Rev. 704.

Singer, Peter, *Practical Ethics* (1993).

———, *Rethinking Life and Death* (1994).

Smith, Sir John, and Hogan, Brian, *Criminal Law* (8th ed. 1996).

Smith, J. C., *Justification and Excuse in the Criminal Law* (1989).

Smith, Wesley J., *Doc Knows Best: It'll Be Too Late for You If He's Wrong*, Guest Comment, National Review Online (Jan. 6, 2003).

Spencer, Herbert, *A System of Synthetic Philosophy* (1860).

Stengel, Erwin, *Suicide and Attempted Suicide* (1964).

Swift, Zephaniah, *A System of the Laws of the State of Connecticut* (1796).

Thomasma, David C., *Asking to Die: Inside the Dutch Debate about Euthanasia* 35 (1998).

Thompson, Brendan, *Final Exit: Should the Double Effect Rule Regarding the Legality of Euthanasia in the United Kingdom Be Laid to Rest?*, 33 Vand. J. Transnat'l L. 1035 (2000).

Thunder, James, *Quiet Killings in Medical Facilities: Detection & Prevention*, 18 issues in L. & Med. 211 (2003).

van der Lee, Marije L., et al., *Euthanasia and Depression: A Prospective Cohort Study Among Terminally Ill Cancer Patients*, 23 Journal of Clinical Oncology 6607 (2005).

van der Maas, Paul, et al., *Euthanasia, Physician-Assisted Suicide, and Other Medical Practices Involving the End of Life in the Netherlands, 1990–1995*, 335 New Eng. J. Med. 1699 (1996).

van der Maas, Paul, and Emmanuel, Linda L., *Factual Findings*, in *Regulating How We Die: The Ethical, Medical, and Legal Issues Surrounding Physician-Assisted Suicide* (Linda L. Emmanuel ed., 1998).

van der Wal, Gerrit, et al., *Evaluation of the Notification Procedures for Physician-Assisted Suicide in the Netherlands*, 335 New Eng. J. Med. 1706 (1996).

Verhagen, Eduard, and Sauer, Pieter, *The Groningen Protocol—Euthanasia in Severely Ill Newborns*, 352 New Eng. J. Med. 959, 960 (2005).

Waldron, Jeremy, *Autonomy and Perfectionism in Raz's Morality of Freedom*, 62 So. Cal. L. Rev. 1097 (1989).

Warrick, Pamela, *Suicide's Partner*, L.A. Times, Part E, col. 2 (Dec. 6, 1992)

Weinreb, Lloyd, *The Case for a Duty to Rescue*, 90 Yale L.J. 247 (1980).

Wharton, Francis, *Criminal Law* (1874).

Whether Physician-Assisted Suicide Serves a "Legitimate Medical Purpose" Under the Drug Enforcement Administration's Regulations Implementing the Controlled Substances Act, 17 issues L. & Med. 269 (2002).

White, Alan R., *Grounds of Liability: An Introduction to the Philosophy of the Law* (1985).

Whitmore, William H. (ed.), *The Colonial Laws of Massachusetts of 1672* (1887).

Wilkerson, Isabel, *Prosecutors Seek to Ban Doctor's Suicide Device*, N.Y. Times, sec. 1, at 6, col. 5 (Jan. 5, 1991).

Willems, Dick L., et al., *Attitudes and Practices Concerning the End of Life: A Comparison between Physicians from the United States and from the Netherlands,* 160 Archives Internal Med. 63 (2000).

Williams, Glanville, *Euthanasia and Abortion* 38 Colo. L. Rev. 178–201 (1966).

———, *Oblique Intention* [1987] C.L.J. 417, 425.

———, *The Sanctity of Life and the Criminal Law* (1958).

———, *Textbook of the Criminal Law* (2d ed. 1983).

William and Mary Quart., 16 (August 26, 1661).

Wingate, Edmund, *Justice Revived; Being the Whole Office of a Country JP Briefly, and Yet More Methodically and Fully Than Ever Yet Extant* (1661).

Wolbarst, Abraham, *The Right to Die* 94 The Forum 330–32 (1935).

Wolfrom, Richard, *The Criminal Aspect of Suicide*, 39 Dick. L. Rev. 47 (1934–35).

Woodman, Sue, *Last Rights: The Struggle over the Right to Die* (1998).

York, Byron, *Doctors of Death: Kaiser Solicits Its Doctors to Kill,* Guest Comment, National Review Online (Aug. 19, 2002).

Index